SUPER MEALS
FROM
SUPERMARKETS

JOE FAMULARO

■ ■ ■ ■

Learn to use your supermarket
to do everything you hoped it could—
and more—
with unusual combinations of food,
absolute time-saving techniques
and recipes you will cook forever

■ ■ ■ ■

All good wishes
Joe Famularo

BARRON'S
New York

All inquiries should be addressed to:
Barron's Educational Series, Inc.
250 Wireless Boulevard
Hauppauge, New York 11788

International Standard Book No. 0-8120-4511-4

Library of Congress Catalog Card No. 90-33368

Library of Congress Cataloging-in-Publication Data

Famularo, Joseph J.
    Super Meals from Supermarkets : learn to use your supermarket to
do everything you hoped it could and more with unusual combinations of
food, absolute time saving techniques, and recipes you will cook forever
/ Joe Famularo.
        p.   cm.
    ISBN 0-8120-4511-4
    1. Cookery.   2. Convenience foods.   I. Title.
TX652.F35   1990
641.5—dc20   90-33368
                                                     CIP

PRINTED IN THE UNITED STATES OF AMERICA
012   8800   10 9 8 7 6 5 4 3 2 1

Design by Milton Glaser, Inc.
Illustrations by Chi-ming Kan

CONTENTS

ACKNOWLEDGMENTS

Wheeling a supermarket cart across the country, filling it to the brim and cooking everything from apples to zucchini was no small task. It was made easier for me because of the help I received from (1) food companies who shared their knowledge and recipe suggestions, (2) supermarket personnel, and (3) family and friends who voiced opinions, contributed ideas and offered encouragement and inspiration.

My thanks to American Stores Co., Irvine, CA; Campbell Soup Co., Camden, NJ; Christie Brown and Co., Toronto, Ontario; CPC International, Englewood Cliffs, NJ; Del Monte USA/Nabisco, East Hanover, NJ; Farms of Texas Co., Alvin, TX; Empire Foods, Mifflintown, PA; Friendship Dairies, Inc., Friendship, NY; George A. Hormel and Co., Austin, MN; Golden Blossom Honey, Doylestown, PA; The Gorton Group, Gloucester, MA; Kikkoman Foods, Inc., Walworth, WI; Lundberg Family Farms, Richvale, CA; Martha White Foods, Nashville, TN; Nutrasweet Co., Deerfield, IL; Pet, Inc., St. Louis, MO; Quaker Oats Co., Chicago, IL; Sun Diamond Growers, Stockton, CA; and Van Camp Seafood Inc., San Diego, CA.

My special thanks also to Kevin Crosse and Bernadette Brooks at Albertsons, Johnny Ortiz at Kuane's Food Store and Mario Chavez at Skaggs Alpha Beta, all in Santa Fe, NM; to Joe Smith, Al Simek, Bill Tito and Sheila Doria at Grand Union in Pawling, NY; to Susan Weekly at Faustos, Mary Nunez at Winn Dixie and Andy Catarino at Pantry Pride, all in Key West, FL; and to Joe Thompson, Fish Department Manager, Joe Dies, Front End Manager, and David Devers, Co-Manager at A & P Food Bazaar in New York City.

My sincere thanks to Miriam Barnes, Marion Cleveland, Sandy Dennis, Betty and John Hettinger, Lillian Lopez, Lydia Moss, Georgiana and Armando Orsini, Ginny and Bill Scarpa, Marguerite and Tom Whitney—especially to Bernie Kinzer, my sisters Mary Tassiello and Louise Imperiale, and my mother Angela, who was able to see this work completed.

Joe Famularo
Key West, Florida

INTRODUCTION

More than ever, Americans are demanding about food. We want it to taste like gourmet fare, yet we want it to be ready in a flash. We want it all—delicious, healthy and easy.

To meet this cross-country challenge, supermarkets have changed. They have been redesigned and now offer in one place all the food specialties available to the American consumer—who now has a bigger selection, better choices and some of the best food bargains in the world. For the supermarkets, it is good business. In 1987, more than 171 billion dollars were spent in them. Consumers, on average, go to supermarkets 2 1/2 times a week. They demand quality, taste and convenience. The food is all there, but does everyone know what to do with it? What do we do with Knorr chicken, beef and, yes, fish cubes? Is Campbell's potato soup the ultimate or can it be combined into a better, different soup? How does one use the many cheeses available? Does one ignore the fresh pasta counter? What about fresh tuna, fresh monkfish? Open a can of tuna or salmon—is there anything one can do with them to make them tastier and the family happier? This is what this book is all about: how we can get super meals from supermarkets.

I'm the first to admit that I dislike waiting in supermarket checkout lines and I can rarely go through the so-called express lanes with my full basket of goodies. But I try to think positively and conclude that supermarkets and their suppliers do keep me in mind. Just look at their inventive and timesaving practices. Take the fresh salad bars, for example. If I'm in a hurry, I may plan a salad and do it from scratch for a lunch or light supper. If I'm *really* in a hurry I can use the supermarket salad bar as a source for ready-to-use food: cut-up tomatoes, sliced mushrooms, chopped scallions, sliced zucchini and pickles, trimmed cauliflower and broccoli florets, cheese cut into cubes, sliced celery stalks—all ready to use however I like. The new pasta corners have fresh pastas just for the asking. Anything wrong with dried pasta? No, in fact it is excellent, but fresh pasta cooks faster; and the tortellini are already made, the manicotti filled.

There's time to be saved at the cheese counters, too; they combine cream cheese with horseradish, cheddar with nuts, other cheeses with herbs. The fishmonger has done some timesaving chores also: he has shelled shrimp and cooked it, and he has lobster, crab and surimi ready to go into salads, soups and main courses. The deli people barbecue our chickens and ribs, make our potato salad and cole slaw. My supermarket has its own bakery, and the whole-grain breads are especially good. But making my own bread is not as difficult as it once was anyway, what with all the bread, muffin and cake mixes.

The greengrocer has every imaginable vegetable and herb, and I enjoy finding something new to try. How easy to buy fresh herbs, use what I need and freeze the rest for later use. How simple to buy fresh parsley at a bargain price, remove the stems, wash and dry it, bag and freeze it—what a timesaver.

In the early days, one thought of a supermarket as a place where shelves were lined with canned goods only—no longer a valid image. My supermarket, typical of many across the country, has special new sections:

Today's Catch—Fresh From the Sea
Garden-fresh Vegetables and Orchard-ripe Fruit
The Butcher Block—Prime Meats and Fine Fowl
Grains and Health Foods
Sweet Shoppes—Freshly Dipt Candies
Cheese Corners and International Cheese Boards
Fresh Pasta—Cut to Your Size
Salad Bars—Save Time
    and even FRESH FLOWERS for tonight's dinner table!

As carts are pushed through supermarket aisles, fruits and vegetables are piled high in glistening mounds, pristine boxes and glossy cans make geometric shelf designs, turkey breasts and chicken thighs sit plumply in temperature-controlled cases and fish shimmer on crystalline beds of shaved ice. A still-life of American wholesomeness.

Yet behind this picture are millions of concerned consumers, sometimes reaching states of paranoia, arguing about apples peppered with pesticides or meat infused with drugs. How safe is American food? The answer from most of the experts is, very safe. The country's food is, in fact, the safest in its history and among the safest in the world. The actual dangers to human health appear small. We have no real reason to be fearful of sitting down to supper but we have every reason to demand improvements in our food. To make good food better, the government needs to tighten its regulatory standards and tighten up and widen its inspection and enforcement programs.

In a world where devoted cookie devourers spend hours pointing up the differences in shape, form and taste between an Oreo and a Hydrox, it might be considered folly for a manufacturer to fiddle with an accepted and fast-selling American phenomenon. Yet this is exactly what is happening today. The Sunshine Company has changed the palm oil shortening in its cookies to soybean and cottonseed. Sunshine hasn't just altered its cookie formula; it's moving on to do the same with other products. Their labels now read, "America's only nationally marketed cholesterol-free, tropical oil–free, creme-filled chocolate sandwich cookie." They, like others, believe that they have to go in this direction to safeguard the market share of their established products against consumer backlash, and to increase revenues by creating products wanted by the general public.

Of course, some companies make changes in their products simply to ride the bandwagon. Oat bran is being added to almost everything including doughnuts, but in amounts that have nothing to do with lowering cholesterol levels. Yet the down-with-cholesterol movement is one of the strongest to face the food industry, which in the past has battled the salt, sodium and MSG wars. The list of companies responding to this latest consumer concern is impressive, including such giants as Keebler, General Mills, Nabisco, Kellogg, General Foods, Procter and Gamble, Pepperidge Farms, and Sunshine Biscuits. Some companies go beyond product formula changes. Keebler, for one, has hired Dr. Kenneth H. Cooper, the fitness expert who authored the bestselling *Controlling Cholesterol,* for special promotional events. And there are new companies and new products. Alpine Lace makes fine low-fat, low-sodium, low-cholesterol cheese. It has been reported that sales went from less than a million dollars in 1984 to almost 75 million in 1988.

Best Foods of CPC International, Inc., recently introduced a cholesterol-free mayonnaise with no egg yolks. Their president's hope is that this product will "put the mayonnaise back in a lot of sandwiches" (can you believe that mayonnaise is a $650-million-a-year business?). Others say, however, that consumers are fickle, and though they seem concerned about cholesterol levels, they tend not to act as rationally about it as their concern suggests. They prove their point by discussing the Edsels of the food business. In the early '80s, Borden brought out a low-fat potato chip, but with disappointing sales, the product was withdrawn. Is the public at fault? Perhaps so, for many members of the food world believe that the public perceives anything labeled as a health food to be something that tastes like boiled shoeleather. After all, they claim that the person who eats rich chocolate cookies is not that interested in cholesterol anyway, because if he were he'd be eating spinach. In spite of cynics both in and out of the food industry, there is a definite step forward to make products healthier. Let's hope it continues.

Recently one of the major olive oil companies made pound cake with olive oil instead of butter and gave free samples to shoppers in many supermarkets. Sound crazy? Not at all. Olive oil is cholesterol-free—and next to butter it is a saint.

Light oil was conceived in the U.S., not in Italy. The truth of the matter is that there is almost no difference between the "light" and the "heavy" oils. Each has about 40 calories per teaspoon and the same fat level. Actually it's difficult to improve on regular olive oil, at least from a health point of view. The milder or light brands are merely blends of oils with a lighter color and milder taste. It's interesting to note that the results of the olive oil in cake demonstrations showed that shoppers who tasted the cake thought it was good, and they actually bought cakes made with oil in the supermarket's bakery department.

I remember as a child going to the local "supermarket"—actually it was the A & P store around the corner, not too different from most other local grocery stores. There was a father/manager and sometimes a son/assistant and that was about the extent of the staff. My, what has happened since those early years. Brand-new ingredients, reformulated products, updated terminology, hi-tech preparation methods and timesaving appliances—this last item alone is responsible for a myriad of changes.

As I looked through recipes I've been accumulating for years, I realized how dated they were and how badly they needed modernization. As I develop new recipes, I feel I can't stick with the old techniques and must become modern in that area, too.

I learned and developed my cooking skills in various ways—from my family, by doing and experimenting, and from cookbooks, magazines and newspaper articles. Reading recipes is a passion with me, almost like journeying to foreign lands and tasting the exotic flavors. For many years, cooking has occupied many, many hours of my time. Without exaggeration, on occasion I have spent three full days preparing a special meal. One day a couple of years ago, all my guests raved about a supermoist chocolate brownie–type cake I had served (see recipe on page

235), and everyone wanted the recipe knowing that it would take hours to accomplish. I was shocked that not one of these sophisticated "foodies" suggested or even hinted at the shortcut method I had used. One guest was the owner of a well-known restaurant whose pastry chef has two full-fledged assistants, and everything there is made from scratch. Well, to make a long story short, I revealed that I had used a cake mix I'd bought a few hours prior to the meal and that I embellished it. One could have cut the silence instead of the cake, but the next day several called for the recipe.

Since that time a new consciousness has developed in me—the constant question of how in the dickens I was going to give four or five hours to preparing a single dish from scratch every time I had someone for dinner. (Just run out of homemade chicken, beef or fish stock and you'll know what I mean.) In these many years of serious cooking, no one has ever asked, "Is your chicken stock homemade?" If they asked me today, the simple answer would be no.

Here's what I've tried to do in this book:

1. Replace many "from scratch" procedures with timesaving packets (soup and recipe mixes, for example), frozen foods and so on.

2. Drop ingredients not easily obtainable today and add many new items.

3. Eliminate or reduce fats and salt to be more in line with today's recommended eating styles.

4. Write recipes I hope are easier than ever to understand and follow.

5. Reduce the number of cooking steps (for example, sifting flour wherever possible) and the number of ingredients (substituting self-rising flour for all-purpose when practical).

6. Although I am unable to depend on a microwave for every cooking need, there is no question about its value to me. Therefore, for most recipes I've included the microwave procedure in addition to the traditional. Not always to save time—cooking rice in my microwave takes a little longer than the stovetop method, but I prefer to microwave it.

Finally, in their zeal to talk health, many food marketers and some manufacturers have lost sight of the fact that Americans won't eat food if they don't like the way it tastes. A can of beans by itself or a package of frozen corn may taste bland. But on the very next supermarket shelf is another can or jar of something which, when added to the beans or corn, will upscale the taste of it. After all, aren't we all seeking no-sweat exercises and tasty, low-calorie, nutritious foods? Isn't this the American dream of having one's cake and eating it too? The purpose of this book is not only to emphasize the importance of healthy food but to emphasize the importance of taste to the millions of Americans who supermarket shop.

GUIDELINES FOR BETTER SHOPPING AND EATING

*T*here are three essential nutrients that give us energy: protein, carbohydrate and dietary fat. Of the three, the one receiving the most attention these days is fat. We need fat in our diet; it helps form cell membranes, it provides the necessary fatty acids our bodies can't make, and it carries the fat-soluble vitamins (A, D, E and K). Everyone admits that fat increases the enjoyment of eating, adds to the flavors of food and actually helps satisfy our appetites. If a meal has some fat, we don't get hungry again too quickly.

The problem with fat is that we eat too much of it. The Dietary Guidelines for Americans issued by U.S. health officials recommend that we get no more than one third of our daily calories from fat. The American Heart Association is tougher. They recommend no more than 30 percent—that we should limit our intake of cholesterol to 100 milligrams per 1,000 calories, with a daily maximum of 300 milligrams.

We all know that the average American consumes more than that. About 40 to 45 per cent of our daily calories come from fat and we take in more than 600 milligrams of cholesterol each day.

TYPES OF FAT

*S*aturated fats—i.e., those in meat and dairy products—are usually of animal origin and are solid at room temperature. "Saturated" is a chemical term referring to the amount of hydrogen present. All fats have some, but saturated fat is, indeed, saturated with it.

Unsaturated fats—e.g., such vegetable oils as corn, soybean and safflower—are of vegetable origin and are liquid at room temperature. Though most vegetable oils are quite unsaturated, there are exceptions—namely palm and coconut oil, both of which are highly saturated. There are two kinds of unsaturated fat: monounsaturated and polyunsaturated, of which the latter is "more unsaturated."

Cholesterol is a fatty substance found only in foods of animal, not plant, origin. Cholesterol has been associated with hardening of the arteries, in which plaque accumulates on the insides of artery walls and interferes with the flow of blood. Interruption of blood flow to the heart results in a heart attack; interruption to the brain results in a stroke.

Our bodies manufacture fat from any source of calories, not just from foods containing dietary fat. Both body and dietary fats have some good in them: they help supply energy; they cushion bones and vital organs, protecting them from injury; and they insulate the body against extremes of cold and heat.

The experts agree that the rule must be: *cut back on fat, saturated fat and cholesterol.* To decrease fat in your diet, you do *not* have to surrender favorite foods altogether. Don't eliminate all fat from your diet; remember that it is essential to human health. But one should select lower-fat alternatives (skim versus whole milk and so on), and eat smaller portions of high-fat foods less often (once a week versus five times). Whichever way you look at it, the solution to the fat question is in moderation: eat only a moderate amount of all kinds of fat and the risk of heart disease (and diabetes) will be decreased and blood pressure will be lowered.

CHECKLIST FOR FAT REDUCTION

READ PACKAGE LABELS

Most canned and packaged foods print the number of calories and grams of fat in each serving. Develop a habit of studying these and let calorie/fat content determine the balance in your menu plan.

IT'S A MATTER OF CHOICE

Choose low-fat or skim milk products. Eliminate organ meats and egg yolks. Choose leaner meats, poultry and fish (and even then remove most of the fat).

Use more dried beans and peas (good protein and low fat). Choose whole-grain breads and cereals and eat more vegetables and fruit.

IT'S A MATTER OF TRIMMING

Cut away visible fats from meat and remove most visible skin from poultry. Remove fats from casseroles, soups, stews and food cooked in skillets. Grill, broil and poach foods more often.

IT'S A MATTER OF PLANNING

If one meal is high in fat, the next should be low. Plan low-fat foods as main courses instead of side dishes: include low-fat soups, salads, beans and rice. Plan for more high-fiber plant food meals (use lentils and beans in salads, oatmeal in meat loaves, fruit in stuffings).

GUIDELINES FOR COOKING

The best way to reduce saturated fat when you cook is to bake, broil, barbecue, microwave or steam foods. If you must fry, (1) use as little cooking oil as possible; (2) use monounsaturated and polyunsaturated oils (most foods are a mixture of saturated and unsaturated fat, both mono- and polyunsaturated. Monounsaturated oils, such as olive oil, have no effect on blood cholesterol, whereas polyunsaturated, such as canola or safflower, tend to lower cholesterol); (3) when browning meat, use a combination of margarine and oil such as canola (rapeseed, the least saturated of all), safflower or corn oil (the next best for polyunsaturates) or olive oil (a good monounsaturate, especially good because a little of it goes a long way in flavoring food); (4) don't use lard or butter as they undo the benefits of having trimmed the meat or fowl. Microwaving is a good way to cook because less oil is required. Steaming foods is one of the best methods because it retains vitamins and, as a rule, no fat is needed to enhance the flavor (use herbs instead). If stewing or using a slow cooker, allow fat to solidify by cooling and then remove it. Don't cook meat in its own juices; use racks whenever possible.

OTHER TIPS:

1. Store oils in tightly closed containers and keep them in dark, cool places, or in the refrigerator.
2. Use fresh foods as much as you can.
3. Any food should be kept and stored in airtight containers.
4. Discard any food that tastes or smells odd.
5. Do *not* reuse oil once used for frying. Toss it.
6. Barbecue instead of frying foods. But remember, to avoid flareups, don't char food, remove as much fat and skin as possible from fowl and meats, and baste foods with marinades instead of butter. If using foil, punch small holes in it to release fat so meat doesn't cook in it.

EXPRESS CHECK-OUT

MICROWAVE TIPS

1 Microwaves do not brown food, so it is best to use toppings or dark batters to add color to baked items.

2 Microwaved foods are sensitive to timing. Ranges of microwave times are given to accommodate the differing cooking speeds of various microwave ovens. Always begin with the minimum time given and go beyond it if needed.

3 If your microwave has no carousel, put the baking container on an inverted saucer and rotate baking container a quarter turn several times to promote even cooking.

4 If using square dishes, especially for cakes, breads, etc., use small foil triangles to cover corners to reflect microwaves. Corners are exposed to the most energy and can cause overcooking.

5 "Standing time" is cooking time too, so don't shortcut it.

6 Fill muffin cups or cake containers only half-full. Microwaves tend to expand batters more than conventional ovens. This is why batter for 12 muffins for conventional ovens makes 18 to 24 microwaved muffins.

7 To return crystallized honey to a liquid state, microwave on HIGH (100%) for 30 to 40 seconds.

8 Microwave lemons at MEDIUM (50%) for 1 1/2 minutes; then squeeze and more juice will come forth.

9 To peel shallots, put in untied plastic bag and microwave at MEDIUM-HIGH (70%) for 1 1/2 to 2 minutes, shaking bag two or three times.

10 To clean bottom of microwave, lay a wet towel there and microwave at MEDIUM (50%) for 1 minute. Then wipe clean. Or boil water in 2-cup measure for 3 minutes; steam will help soften any crusted-on food.

SUPERMARKET CREDO

"If it isn't fresh, it isn't good" has for years been a flag-waving slogan of many foodies who have considered canned, bottled, packaged or frozen foods to be poor relatives of the "only" food—fresh food. Of course, it's difficult to argue with that and I, too, have joined the chorus—knowing all the while that there are some canned and frozen foods I couldn't live without. I have to admit that many canned and frozen foods have played an important part in my kitchen, enough so that I have come to consider them classics. They are listed in alphabetical order, not in order of importance.

ARGO (and KINGSFORD) CORNSTARCH, made by Best Foods of CPC International, Inc., is a carbohydrate occurring naturally in the corn kernel. It can be used as a thickener for smooth gravies, sauces, glazes, soups, stews and casseroles, as well as pie and cake fillings. Very few lemon meringue pies are made without it, but it is excellent in place of flour when sautéing or frying foods.

BIRDS EYE FROZEN GREEN PEAS are as versatile as any vegetable can be. You can use as few or as many as you wish and keep the rest frozen. With pasta, in salads, soups, pot pies and as a garnish, their uses are exhausting.

BORDEN'S AMERICAN CHEESE SINGLES, as American as apple pie and delicious on top of one, too. Each slice is wrapped in plastic. Easy to store, melt, grill and eat just as is. See grilled cheese.

BORDEN'S SWEETENED CONDENSED MILK, a real oldie, famous as far back as Civil War days when unshaven cooks chanted "No teats to pull, no hay to pitch; you just punch a hole in the son of a bitch." It's in every supermarket today for Key Lime Pie and many other desserts that couldn't be made without it.

BROADCAST CORNED BEEF HASH, famous for many years, needs little or no identification. As a rule it is garnished with a poached egg, but these days the egg isn't really necessary. Heat it in a greased nonstick skillet over low heat so it develops a crisp crust.

CHICKEN OF THE SEA TUNA from the Van Camp Seafood Co. in St. Louis, Missouri, still carries the blonde mermaid with wand. As a food, it is ready in a minute, can be given many treatments and is simply a handy item to have on the shelf at all times. Packed in spring water or oil in various sizes.

CAMPBELL'S CREAM OF TOMATO AND CREAM OF POTATO by the Campbell Soup Company, founded in 1869 in Camden, New Jersey (still the site of one of its production facilities and its corporate headquarters) and many years later immortalized by Andy Warhol. I find both these soups have as many uses as Cream of Mushroom. They combine well with other soups and other foods.

DEL MONTE TOMATO SAUCE is one of many of the company's products. But I find this is a staple because of its versatility in soups, stews and casseroles, and with beans, rice, vegetables and pasta.

DINTY MOORE BEEF STEW by Hormel. Of course it's canned but it tastes good and it has big hunks of beef. Enjoy it right out of the can, heated, or create a new recipe.

DOXSEE CLAM JUICE. Using it is considerably less trouble than making fish stock from scratch. Make fresh fish stock when necessary, but bottled clam juice is often a satisfactory substitute—especially in chowders, soups and casseroles.

GOLDEN BLOSSOM HONEY is a blend of premium honeys (white clover, sage buckwheat and orange). It is the oldest brand of honey, its label hasn't changed in 60 years, and it is sold along the eastern states from the Canadian border to Florida, in Puerto Rico and the Virgin Islands.

GOYA ARTICHOKES (quartered and marinated). Just open the jar lid and a tasty appetizer is at hand. Keep at room temperature unless the jar has been opened. Add red pepper flakes and serve on toast pieces or Ritz crackers, add to salads and pasta dishes.

GULDEN'S MUSTARD. The craze for Dijon-type mustard doesn't seem to abate—and I'm one of its admirers—but plain old American Gulden's is still a delight on sandwiches, meats and in salad dressing.

HEINZ TOMATO KETCHUP. Too many people use this only on French fries and with hamburgers—delicious. But it has many other uses as well—a tablespoon in mayonnaise, in barbecue sauces, in sweet and sour sauces.

HELLMANN'S (and BEST FOODS) MAYONNAISE. As a native New Yorker, I appreciate the fact that Richard Hellmann operated a small deli on Columbus Avenue in Manhattan. He introduced mayonnaise in 1903 (talk about a classic) and the world has not been the same. (By the way, it's Hellmann's on the East Coast and Best Foods on the West). It is low in cholesterol (5 milligrams per serving) and low in sodium (80 milligrams per serving). A no-cholesterol type is now available. I especially like the wide-mouthed jars, too.

HORMEL HOT CHILI WITH BEANS, developed in 1930, is now the world's largest-selling brand of chili. Along with the beef are red Idaho beans, ripe tomatoes and spices. Just heat and serve.

HILLSHIRE FARM SMOKED SAUSAGE is a handy item to refrigerate and use in small quantities as needed. I often add small pieces of it to scrambled eggs, baked beans, steamed broccoli or any greens. A little goes a long way.

KNORR CHICKEN BOUILLON CUBES are one of many products in a unique range of fine foods for the preparation of entrees, soups, side dishes and appetizers. I use them more than any other of the Knorr products, as

chicken broth is essential to many dishes.

KNORR HOLLANDAISE SAUCE. I use this to save time. See page, where it is used as a base for gorgonzola sauce on pasta.

KNOX GELATIN is a household word. It is indispensable, and a box of it lasts a long time in the pantry in spite of its constant use.

MONARI FEDERZONI BALSAMIC VINEGAR —until recently not available in most supermarkets. It is more expensive than ordinary white, red or cider vinegars, but it has taken hold of the American imagination as something to adorn salad greens and as a marinade ingredient. The newest classic food item.

PALM OIL

Palm oil is in the process of being eliminated from all of our products. Several of our product lines have already been successfully reformulated, and within the next year all reformulations will have been accomplished. The ingredient listings on the packages of many Gorton's products will continue to indicate the possible presence of palm oil even though the oils have been discontinued. This is because of existing package inventory as well as the normal flow of finished product through distribution channels.

Gorton's of Gloucester
Gloucester, Massachusetts

NESTLÉ SEMISWEET CHOCOLATE MORSELS are probably in everyone's pantry. I keep several packages and use them by the half-cup or full cup whenever I need chocolate. They are easier to melt in the top of a double boiler than broken-up bulk chocolate.

PROGRESSO CANNELLINI BEANS are perhaps not as popular as pork and beans but are considerably more versatile. Two of the best combinations are to simply add olive oil and garlic to the beans (sauté garlic in oil, then add the beans and heat through) or to mix them with some cooked greens (escarole, spinach, or celery) and add some chicken broth.

PROGRESSO PLUM TOMATOES. For most of us, it is next to impossible to find really ripe tomatoes all year long. I use these red-ripe plum tomatoes instead. Put them through a food mill to rid them of seeds, or chop by hand. A classic, without question.

QUAKER OATS— starting the day with hot oatmeal is only the beginning. All day long, add them to cookies, bread, muffins and meat loaves.

RO-TEL TOMATOES AND GREEN CHILIES— from the lower Rio Grande Valley in Texas, this flavorful mixture is a combination of chili peppers, cilantro and spices. Add it to stews, casseroles and chili or simply combine with cannellini beans, heat and serve.

RONZONI THIN SPAGHETTI #9— regular spaghetti is #8. It's difficult to explain why the thinner one is better, but it is.

SKIPPY SUPER CHUNK PEANUT BUTTER. Peanut butter made its debut in 1932 and this particular brand contains over 90 percent roasted peanuts. High in protein: 2 tablespoons contain 9 grams (10 per cent of the U.S. recommended daily allowance) with no cholesterol. Peanut butter is also a good source of polyunsaturates, magnesium, niacin and phosphorus.

WISHBONE CREAMY ITALIAN DRESSING. Actually lower in calories and sodium than many homemade salad dressings, this is a handy item for it can be used in place of mayonnaise (try it on eggs or in tuna salad, or in deviled eggs). It is an excellent dip for raw vegetables and I brush it on chicken before broiling it.

THREE'S A CROWD

Lucky Stores, Inc., a wholly owned subsidiary of American Stores Company (Jewel Food Stores, Acme Markets, Star Market and Jewel Sav-on), operates 347 stores throughout California and in southern Nevada. The company has an interesting policy called "Three's A Crowd," a program that calls for additional checkstands to open each time there are three customers waiting in line, and E-Z checkout, which permits customers to pay for their groceries with a bank ATM card. Lucky continues to add bakeries, delicatessens, floral departments, service fish (fresh fish served to order), salad bars and pharmacies to new and remodeled stores. New concepts have been successfully tested at selected stores, including Chinese kitchens, where chefs prepare entrees for takeout, and "smokehouse sausage" shops, where more than 90 smoked items are produced regularly.

EXPRESS CHECK-OUT

FROZEN FOODS

1 Tape store label on meat package rewrapped for freezing. Cut, weight, cost and date will be available for future reference.

2 Thaw frozen bread in a brown bag in 325°F oven for 5 minutes if no microwave is available.

3 Frozen sourdough rolls can be grated for breadcrumbs.

4 Cheddar, Swiss and some other cheeses freeze well. Take advantage of sales on these items and freeze.

5 Freeze egg whites in plastic bags; to thaw, put bag in warm water.

6 Don't overcook frozen food; many foods soften when defrosted and reheated.

7 Most foods should be thawed slowly. Before reheating, thaw in refrigerator. Casseroles may take as long as 1 1/2 days in refrigerator or about 1/3 that time at room temperature.

8 Flavors fade when food is frozen for too long. Think of storing most foods in the freezer at 0°F (−18°C) for no longer than three months.

We have some salad bars and some fresh pasta counters. On a long-range basis we acknowledge a steady skewing toward healthier eating habits and are thus expanding seafood, poultry and fresh produce to meet this challenge of change. Formulations in our bakeries have eliminated the palm and coconut oils, and we've put quite a bit more emphasis on low-sodium and low-fat foods, as well as increasing our ingredient disclosure information on food labels. And in the southeast part of the state (Dade and Broward counties) we have carefully but steadily increased our selections of

Hispanic foods and increased our bilingual capabilities in advertising, store signage and personnel.
R. William Schroter, V.P.
PUBLIX Supermarkets, Inc.
Lakeland, Florida

DATES ON PACKAGES

Recent surveys show that many consumers are still confused about the meaning of a date on a package. The date *always* means the day by which the product must be sold. It does *not* mean the day by which it should be eaten.

Artificially preserved dairy products can be dated up to seven weeks in advance. This means they have a longer shelf life than those products with no preservatives. But whichever way one looks at it, the ones with the shorter pull dates are on the shelf a shorter time and are therefore fresher. Look for products with no preservative chemicals or additions and *always check for dates.*

SUPERMARKET SAVVY

READING LABELS AND CLAIMS

The government requires that all but about 300 grocery products list their ingredients in descending order by weight. Although this is a step in the right direction, one still might not know how much of a particular type of ingredient is used. For example, some products show several oils or sugars; they are listed individually but if lumped together they might constitute the primary ingredient. In addition to ingredients, about half of all packaged foods show nutritional information. If a product makes a claim about nutrition, it must show it. It must also be shown if the product has added nutrients or if it's for a special dietary use.

Although most people these days are interested in knowing about fat, cholesterol, sodium and additives, such information is not required by the government. When you see it, it is put there voluntarily by the manufacturer. Efforts are being made to update labels but they still basically deal with protein, vitamins and minerals—subjects that were of more interest 15 or 20 years ago. Sodium content has only recently

been required by the Food and Drug Administration. There is no requirement to state how much of the fat in a product is saturated and unsaturated, which of course would be a lot more helpful and meaningful. Although calories are shown, we don't know the percentage coming from fat, so the fat content is not in true perspective. Fiber, surely on everyone's mind today, is not a label requirement. Nor is cholesterol unless the product is claiming something special.

Be aware of these considerations:

1. If the word "natural" is used on a package, it has little meaning for it is not regulated. But when applied to meat and fowl, it means that there has been a minimum of processing and that the product is free of artificial ingredients, so here it has some meaning.

2. "Partially hydrogenated soybean and/or coconut oil . . ." Soybean oil is polyunsaturated; coconut is saturated. Which oil was used? The label is not required to spell this out.

3. Check the portion size. For example, on a stuffing mix, the

breakdown is for a 1/2-cup serving. Some people, in fact most, will eat more, so calories and nutrients have to be adjusted upward. If comparing the calorie contents of two packages, be sure serving sizes are equal or the comparison is off.

4. "No cholesterol" markings can be misleading, for only animal products contain cholesterol. Yet if a particular product contains palm or coconut oil, that means highly saturated fat—which are believed to raise blood cholesterol levels.

5. "Enriched" and "fortified": "enriched" means that some of the nutrients lost in processing have been replaced. In "fortified" products, nutrients have been added that were not there in the first place, as in most cereals.

6. "Low calorie" and "reduced calorie": if "low," the government requirement means less than 40 calories per serving; if "reduced," food must have at least 1/3 less calories than the foods they mimic—e.g., some ersatz cheeses.

7. "Sugarless" or "sugar-free" does not pertain to artificial sweeteners. Foods containing sucrose or any other sugar, such as glucose, fructose, corn syrup or honey, may legally be labeled sugar-free. But a food can be labeled sugar-free and still contain calories from sugar alcohols, such as sorbitol, xylitol and mannitol.

8. "Sodium-free" means fewer than 5 milligrams per serving; "very low sodium" means no more than 35; "low sodium" means up to 140 milligrams per serving. "Reduced sodium" means at least 75 percent less sodium than in the regular product.

It's not easy to read labelese, but it is important to learn.

WINES AND SPIRITS

Some supermarkets have fully stocked wine and spirits sections. If yours doesn't, it is still important to comment on this subject because wines and spirits play a role in fine cooking. Countries with great cuisines produce their own wines; those that do not have fairly unsophisticated food.

Cooking with wine and spirits can transform an ordinary dish into a masterpiece, and quite frankly, can also ruin it. Cooking "with alcohol" may not be the way to say it, for it's really more a matter of cooking the alcohol away. Ordinary wine has an alcohol content of 10 to 13 percent (a result of natural fermentation); when placed over heat, the alcohol evaporates and the liquid left has to be fully cooked if it is to be edible. Supermarkets offer "cooking wines" but I believe there is no such thing—either a wine is fit to drink or it isn't, and if it isn't, don't cook with it. The taste of a bad wine is merely intensified by cooking. It is not necessary to cook with great wines (their special vintage character will be lost over heat), but it is important to use wine with a full body and a specific flavor. For example, in Italy most people cook with local wines and often the local wine itself has been the basis and reason for the creation of a specific regional dish.

Wine is often used as a marinade ingredient. Years ago it was used to

preserve meat and fowl; only recently has it been used to create flavor. But still, wine will tenderize the poorest cut of meat or the oldest chicken. Since the quality of meat and fowl has greatly improved over the years, today wine is used to gain flavor.

Fortified wines, especially Marsala, Madeira and Port, are especially flavorful in cooking. But don't cook these wines as long as you would most table wines, for they'll lose their bouquet. A Madeira sauce will give life to canned hams and a tablespoon of good Madeira will transform most ordinary vegetable purees to food-of-the-gods status. Port is especially good with fruit and cheese. Marsala is hardly cooked in *zabaglione;* it is in veal marsala, yet its flavor seems to hold up.

When I see recipes calling for champagne as an ingredient, I use a good dry white wine except for a fresh fruit dessert. Champagne isn't meant to be cooked; it loses its effervescence as soon as heat is applied.

Although beer is effervescent like champagne, it can be used in cooking; it's a lot tougher and sturdier and will hold up to heat. Like wine, it tenderizes meat (there's nothing quite as tasty as slow-cooked beef and onions with beer). It's especially good in batters, too.

Distilled spirits have many uses in cooking. One of the best has to do with the process of deglazing a skillet. As meat and fowl brown, dark specks of intense flavor collect on the bottom of the pan. Adding some bourbon or cognac, gin or Calvados will dissolve the crust in the skillet as the alcohol burns away and a glaze is formed, which is added to the main dish for lots more flavor. Rum or bourbon does wonders to my supermarket pie on page 246.

Sweet liqueurs work well in desserts; as a rule, only a few tablespoons are needed to flavor a particular recipe. It doesn't matter if the alcohol is not totally cooked away.

To sum up, I'd say that Americans know how to drink wine, whiskies and liqueurs; I do wish more of us would learn to "cook it away" in the kitchen.

FARM-FRESH DAIRY FOOD

Dairy counters offer the humblest of ingredients, yet these foods often provide the most delicious meals. Eggs, milk, cottage cheese and sour cream are still low-cost foods, and they have remained pure—at least they seem so when compared to all of today's food trends, with their chic ingredients and stylish concoctions. What could be more hearty (and simple) than poached eggs on ranch-style potatoes, or more tasty (and simple) than a salad of low-fat cottage cheese with ranch dressing and fresh strawberries.

Because of heavy turnover, most of us assume the eggs we buy in our supermarkets are fresh. They probably are, but if we wanted to put this to a test, we could check their buoyancy. A fresh, newly laid egg is relatively heavy and if put in a glass of water it will sink to the bottom and lie flat. An older egg will stand upright (air pockets in eggs expand with age and make them more buoyant). Freshness can also be judged once the egg is broken; the fresher egg has a sturdier, more rounded and compact yolk, and the white is thick and cuddles the yolk. An older egg is the opposite: its yolk is flatter and more spread out, and the white's consistency is thin. The yolk is also off to one side instead of in the center. I store eggs in their cartons in the least cool part of the refrigerator. Their pores make them prone to picking up other food odors; I don't know why refrigerator manufacturers created open bins for eggs.

To cook most egg dishes, use gentle heat to keep the whites creamy and the yolks moist. If the heat is high, the whites will become rubbery and the yolks will dry out.

Clarified butter is not, to my knowledge, sold in supermarkets, so you have to make it. Melt butter and skim off the white froth from the top. The clear yellow liquid is the clarified butter, which must be spooned or poured off carefully, leaving the lacy curds in the bottom of the pan to be discarded.

Crème fraîche is available in some supermarkets. It's delicious on desserts and fruits and in some sauces. It can be made by adding 2 tablespoons buttermilk or sour cream to 1 cup heavy cream and shaking vigorously. Let the mixture stand at room temperature, covered, until thickened, a minimum of 8 hours or overnight. It will keep in the refrigerator for about a week.

In this section, eggs are presented in various ways—sometimes with other dairy products, sometimes with vegetables, meat or fish. Yogurt, sour cream, and cottage cheese are made into dips and spreads. Cottage cheese is used as a main ingredient in quiche and also in a delicious salad with strawberries.

EXPRESS CHECK-OUT

DAIRY

1 Butter may be frozen. Wrap carefully to prevent absorption of other flavors and it will keep for months.

2 One-half cup plain yogurt combined with the juice of 1/2 lemon and 1 teaspoon chopped fresh dill makes a quick and easy fish sauce, especially with cold poached fish.

3 A combination of oil and butter is better for sautéing than either alone. Use in a ratio of 1 tablespoon oil to 2 tablespoons butter. The oil permits the butter to reach a higher temperature without burning.

4 To set whites more easily when poaching eggs, add some salt or a teaspoon of vinegar to water.

5 To separate eggs easily, break egg into small funnel; white will go through and yolk stays in funnel.

6 When cooking eggs sunnyside up, baste eggs with whatever fat is being used. Always cover pan to set egg whites and to keep yolks soft.

7 When boiling eggs, bring water to boil first, then reduce heat to simmer. Lower eggs into water and time them from that moment. To soft-boil a large egg, time 4 minutes; a small egg, 3 minutes.

8 To make garlic butter, use 6 tablespoons unsalted butter, 1 teaspoon salt, 1/2 teaspoon ground pepper and 2 tablespoons minced fresh garlic. Mix thoroughly and keep in refrigerator until ready to use.

9 When cooking with sour cream, don't let it come to a boil; it will break and curdle. Always stir it in carefully.

10 Use eggs at room temperature for most recipes. They beat better and have greater volume. When separating, don't get yolk into whites and vice versa; if you do, volume won't be as great. Separated yolks and whites may be frozen.

POACHED EGGS ON RANCH-STYLE POTATOES

■ *Serves 4* ■

*T*his is hearty enough to serve for brunch or lunch. Fried eggs may be substituted for poached eggs, but poached are more eye-appealing and seem better suited for this particular dish. Here's a great way to use the many varieties of frozen potatoes.

1   *package (20 ounces) frozen potatoes (thick fries, shoestrings, hash browns)*
1   *tablespoon olive or vegetable oil*
1   *garlic clove, minced*
2   *tablespoons finely chopped green chilies*
1   *can (8 ounces) tomato sauce or stewed tomatoes*
1/4   *teaspoon chili powder*
1   *teaspoon finely chopped fresh oregano or 1/4 teaspoon dried*
8   *eggs, poached*

1 Cook potatoes according to package directions.

2 Meanwhile, heat oil and sauté garlic and chilies just until garlic begins to turn color. Add tomato sauce or stewed tomatoes, chili powder and oregano. Bring to a boil, lower heat and simmer about 5 minutes.

3 Divide potatoes among warm plates and place 2 poached eggs on top. Spoon several tablespoons of sauce over eggs and potatoes without covering completely; some sauce should be on the side of the plate. Serve immediately.

MICROWAVE: (1) Cook potatoes as directed on package. (2) In a dish, combine oil, garlic and chilies and cook on HIGH (100%) 1 1/2 minutes. Add tomato sauce or stewed tomatoes, cover with plastic and cook on HIGH 5 minutes. (3) To poach 4 eggs at a time, pour 2 tablespoons water and 1/4 teaspoon white vinegar into each of four 6-ounce custard cups. Cook on HIGH (100%) 1 to 1 1/2 minutes until water boils. Break 1 egg into each cup, prick yolk lightly with toothpick, cover loosely with plastic and cook on MEDIUM-HIGH (70%) 1 1/2 to 2 1/2 minutes or until done to desired firmness.

SUPERMARKET SAVVY

BUTTERMILK

Soured or fermented milk was used in ancient societies, and even today cultured buttermilk is probably the most popular fermented beverage in this country. It is also used in baking and salad dressings, and many manufacturers produce a low-fat variety. Look for the kind that tastes deliciously rich, yet has less than half the fat of regular milk and less calories. It should be made with active cultures and with NO additives, NO preservatives, NO artificial flavorings and not a single grain of added salt.

EGGS AND CREAM IN RAMEKINS

■ *Serves 4* ■

*T*his is an especially good way to cook eggs if there are to be more than four servings, because the eggs all cook at the same time so you avoid using two skillets and "waiting turns." Serve with warm toast, bread or muffins. The presentation is special and the ramekins are well worth the investment, for there are many things that can be cooked in them.

4 *tablespoons butter or margarine*
4 *eggs, room temperature*
4 *tablespoons heavy cream*
salt and paprika

1 Preheat oven to 325°F (170°C). Place 1 tablespoon butter or margarine in each of 4 ramekins and arrange on a baking tray. Place in oven just until butter is melted. Remove from oven.

2 Break a whole egg into each ramekin. Add a tablespoon of cream and a sprinkle of salt and paprika. Bake until eggs are set, about 10 minutes. Serve in ramekins.

MICROWAVE: (1) Divide butter or margarine among microwave-safe cups and cook on HIGH (100%) for 1 minute. (2) Break an egg into each cup, prick yolk lightly with toothpick, and add cream, salt and paprika. Cover loosely with plastic wrap. Cook 1 1/2 to 2 1/2 minutes on MEDIUM-HIGH (70%) until eggs set.

FANCIER EGGS AND CREAM IN RAMEKINS: Put pinches of your favorite herbs (tarragon, basil, thyme) in bottoms of ramekins just before adding eggs. In addition to cream and paprika, sprinkle with Parmesan cheese; omit salt.

EGG TOAST, PARISIAN STYLE

■ *Serves 2 or 3* ■

*E*veryone likes French toast. Here is a special version of it. Serve with honey, jellies, jams and butter.

2 *eggs, lightly beaten*
1/4 *cup milk*
1/4 *cup honey*
pinch of salt
6 *slices firm bread, crusts removed*

Combine eggs, milk, honey and salt in a shallow dish and mix well. Dip bread in mixture and brown on both sides in a buttered skillet or on a greased griddle.

POACHED EGGS WITH SALSA VERDE

■ *Serves 4* ■

Salsa verde has personality. It can be bought in plastic containers, cans or bottles, or you can make it (see page 261). This is a great dish for breakfast any day, and is especially good for Sunday breakfast, brunch or lunch.

4   *flour tortillas, 6 to 8 inches in diameter*
1   *cup salsa verde, heated*
8   *eggs, freshly poached and trimmed*
2   *cups grated Monterey Jack cheese*
1/4   *cup finely chopped cilantro*

1 Heat tortillas over medium to high heat in dry skillet about 15 seconds per side. Place one on each of 4 warm plates.

2 Spoon 3 tablespoons heated sauce on each tortilla and arrange 2 eggs on top. Divide cheese over eggs and run under broiler for a minute or so to melt cheese. Spoon additional sauce over cheese and sprinkle with cilantro. Serve right away.

MICROWAVE: (1) To poach eggs, add 2 tablespoons water and 1/4 teaspoon vinegar to four 6-ounce custard cups. Cook on HIGH (100%) 1 to 1 1/2 minutes until water boils. Break 1 egg into each cup, prick yolk once with toothpick, cover loosely with plastic and cook on MEDIUM-HIGH (70%) 1 1/2 to 2 1/2 minutes. (2) Microwave 4 more eggs as in step 1 and continue with recipe as above.

POACHED EGGS WITH HAM, TURKEY AND HOLLANDAISE

■ *Serves 4* ■

This is a version of eggs benedict, but it's easier to make with the packaged hollandaise sauce mix and the deli-sliced ham and turkey.

1   *packet (0.9 ounce) Hollandaise Sauce mix*
4   *slices homestyle white bread, toasted and kept warm*
4   *slices thinly sliced ham*
4   *slices thinly sliced turkey or chicken*
8   *eggs*
1/4   *cup finely chopped fresh parsley or finely sliced scallions*

1 Make hollandaise sauce according to package directions. Keep warm in top of double boiler.

2 Arrange a slice each of ham and turkey on each slice of toasted bread. Cover with foil and keep warm in a low oven.

3 Poach eggs and trim edges. Place a toast slice with ham and turkey on a warm individual plate and top with 2 poached eggs. Add several spoonfuls of hollandaise to each; top with parsley or scallions. Serve right away.

MICROWAVE: (1) To poach eggs, add 2 tablespoons water and 1/4 teaspoon vinegar to four 6-ounce custard cups. Cook on HIGH (100%) 1 to 1 1/2 minutes until water boils. Break 1 egg into each cup, prick yolk lightly with toothpick, cover loosely with plastic and cook on MEDIUM-HIGH (70%) 1 1/2 to 2 1/2 minutes. (2) Microwave 4 more eggs as in step 1. (3) Continue with step 2 above. Assemble toast, ham, turkey, eggs and hollandaise and place two (or all 4 if you can) in a glass pie plate. Microwave on MEDIUM-HIGH (70%) 4 to 5 minutes until heated through. If not using carousel, turn 3 or 4 times during cooking.

SMOKED SALMON OMELET

■ *Serves 1* ■

Use a nonstick skillet about 8 inches in diameter. To make it easier to handle the omelet, don't overload it with filling; 2 or 3 tablespoons is enough.

1   *tablespoon butter*
2   *eggs, room temperature*
salt and pepper
1   *thin slice smoked salmon*
2   *tablespoons cottage cheese*
additional butter

1 Melt 1 tablespoon butter in the skillet but do not let it brown.

2 Quickly beat the eggs with the salt and pepper in a small bowl and add to the skillet when butter is hot. Let eggs set—count to 5 or 6—and then push the edges of the eggs an inch or so to the center to let uncooked egg run over to edge of pan. When egg is set (less than 30 seconds), tilt the pan to move egg more to one side. Add the salmon slice and cheese and fold over half of the egg. Cook a little longer—count to 10—and turn the omelet onto a warm plate. Adjust it to the center of the plate with a fork, or do it by hand. Scoop up a little butter on a fork and run it over the top of the omelet to give it a gleam.

MICROWAVE: To serve 2 to 4, increase eggs to 4; add 1/4 cup milk and 1/4 teaspoon baking powder. Double the amount of salmon but cut it into small pieces.
(1) Place butter in a 9-inch pie plate and microwave at HIGH (100%) 30 to 45 seconds. (2) Separate eggs. Add milk, baking powder, salmon, salt and pepper to yolks and beat well. Whip egg whites until stiff but not dry. Fold yolk mixture into whites and transfer to prepared pie plate. (3) Microwave at MEDIUM (50%) until center is set, 4 to 6 minutes. If not using carousel, turn plate twice during cooking.

SHIRRED EGGS WITH RICOTTA CHEESE AND ORANGE ZEST

■ *Serves 4* ■

An elegant, easy preparation for a special breakfast, lunch or first course of dinner. Serve with toasted or grilled whole-grain bread slices.

butter for ramekins
8   tablespoons heavy cream
2   teaspoons grated or finely chopped orange zest (see Note)
8   tablespoons ricotta cheese
4   eggs, room temperature
1   tablespoon finely chopped fresh tarragon or 1 teaspoon dried salt and pepper to taste

1 Preheat oven to 350°F (180°C). Liberally butter 4 ramekins and arrange on a baking tray. Mix cream with orange zest; spoon 1 tablespoon of mixture into each ramekin. Add 2 tablespoons ricotta, making a slight indentation in center of each to hold the egg.

2 Break an egg into each ramekin. Add another tablespoon of cream mixture to each. Sprinkle with tarragon, salt and pepper. Bake in oven for 10 minutes or until eggs are set.

NOTE: Some supermarket spice shelves have dried grated orange peel in spice jars. Use this only if you can't find a fresh orange.

MICROWAVE: (1) Combine half of cream with zest and ricotta in 4 microwave-safe custard cups. Break an egg into each. Add remaining cream. Sprinkle with tarragon, salt and pepper. Cover loosely with plastic wrap. Cook at MEDIUM-HIGH (70%) 3 to 4 minutes or until eggs are set.

GINNY SCARPA'S FRENCH TOAST

■ *Serves 6* ■

This is so good that I serve it for breakfast, for brunch and as a dessert after soup or salad at lunch. It's great as an afternoon snack with coffee, tea or a glass of milk.

8   ounces cream cheese, softened and divided into 6 pieces
2   packages (12 slices) frozen French toast, plain or cinnamon
powdered sugar
fruit jams, jellies and/or fresh fruit

1 Preheat oven to 450°F (230°C). Spread 1 portion of cream cheese on each of 6 slices of toast (frozen is fine). Cover with a second slice. Bake until heated through, about 6 to 8 minutes.

2 Remove from oven and trim off crusts if you wish (see note). Cut each sandwich in half diagonally. Sprinkle toast with powdered sugar and garnish each triangle with jam, jelly and/or fruit.

MICROWAVE: Assemble sandwiches. Cook 3 at a time on HIGH (100%) 4 minutes. Complete recipe as above.
Note: You'll find it easier to trim crusts if you cool the French toast slightly. But I like it piping hot.

COTTAGE CHEESE AND SPINACH QUICHE

■ *Serves 6* ■

*O*ne cup of cooked small broccoli florets can be used in place of the spinach. With the convenience of cottage cheese and ready-made pie shells, this represents little kitchen work for a pleasant result. The quiche makes an ideal lunch; serve it with a crisp green salad with vinaigrette.

16   ounces cottage cheese
2/3   cup grated Gruyère or swiss cheese
  1   cup fresh spinach julienne, uncooked
  2   eggs, beaten
  1   medium onion, finely chopped
several pinches nutmeg
salt and pepper
  1   baked 10-inch pie shell
1/2   cup seasoned breadcrumbs

1 Preheat oven to 350°F (180°C). In a large bowl, combine cheeses, spinach, eggs, onion, nutmeg, salt and pepper and mix well. Transfer to pie shell. Sprinkle breadcrumbs over top, covering entire surface.

2 Bake about 40 minutes or until quiche is set. Allow to rest for a few minutes before cutting and serving.

MICROWAVE: (1) Place prepared crust in microwave-safe pie plate and prick with fork. Cook on HIGH (100%) 4 minutes. (2) Fill pie shell as above, reserving crumbs. Cook on MEDIUM (50%) 18 minutes. Add crumbs to top and run under broiler for a minute to brown lightly. Let stand 5 minutes before serving.

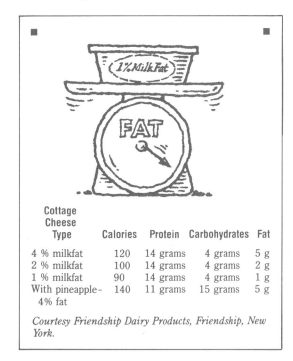

Cottage Cheese Type	Calories	Protein	Carbohydrates	Fat
4 % milkfat	120	14 grams	4 grams	5 g
2 % milkfat	100	14 grams	4 grams	2 g
1 % milkfat	90	14 grams	4 grams	1 g
With pineapple– 4% fat	140	11 grams	15 grams	5 g

Courtesy Friendship Dairy Products, Friendship, New York.

GOURMET BORSCHT WITH SOUR CREAM

■ *Serves 4* ■

There is nothing wrong with a jar of store-bought borscht, but it can become more of a gourmet item by adding a little more.

1   *quart prepared borscht*
2   *medium-size boiled potatoes, quartered, or 2/3 cup mashed potatoes*
3/4 *cup sour cream*
2   *tablespoons grated onion or 1/4 teaspoon onion powder*
salt

Combine all ingredients in food processor or blender and process until smooth. Chill and serve ice cold.

SOUR CREAM AND TUNA DIP

■ *Makes 2 cups* ■

An easy appetizer for a large crowd, this will keep refrigerated for several days. Serve with corn or other chips, crackers or crisp, raw vegetables.

2   *cups sour cream*
1   *can (7 ounces) tuna drained*
1   *envelope (1.3 ounces) onion soup mix*
juice of 1/2 lemon
1/2 *teaspoon dried dillweed*
additional dried dillweed for garnish

Combine all ingredients in a bowl and mix well by hand. Transfer to a serving bowl, sprinkle a little more dillweed on top.

SOUR CREAM

The custardlike consistency and tangy flavor of sour cream are produced by the addition of a culture to fresh sweet cream, which is then pasteurized and homogenized. Sour cream is used, not just as a garnish, but also as an essential ingredient in many recipes. My grandmother used sour cream in baking and I remember her saying that her cakes and breads were lighter and stayed fresher because of it.

SUPERMARKET SAVVY

CURDS AND CALORIES

There can be a fair amount of confusion about buying cottage cheese because of the many types available, which include low-fat; with fruit, chives or vegetables; 4 percent milkfat; 2 percent fat; even 1 percent fat. On top of this there is large-curd, small-curd and California-style cottage cheese, as well as soft-curd, smooth-curd and pot-style. No wonder the confusion.

Governmental standards are primarily concerned with milkfat content, and the rule is this: to be labeled "cottage cheese," the minimum milkfat is 4 percent. Less than 4 percent requires the manufacturer to show the product as low-fat cottage cheese, and this must be followed by the amount of fat as a percentage—usually either 1 or 2 percent.

The milkfat level determines the number of calories; be aware, too, that fruit will more than likely add to the calorie count. As for curd size or type of cheese, that is just a manufacturer's way of making his product sound different. The size of curd has nothing to do with the calorie count; larger curds are firmer cheeses and smaller curds are smoother.

ONION AND GARLIC CHEESE

■ *Makes about 1 cup* ■

*T*his is a low-calorie cheese spread that is easy to make ahead. Spread it on pieces of celery or on cucumber slices.

8   *ounces farmer cheese*
2   *garlic cloves, minced*
2   *scallions, white and green parts, thinly sliced*
2   *tablespoons skim milk*
salt and white pepper

Break up cheese in a bowl. Sprinkle in remaining ingredients and mix with fork until thoroughly blended. Chill to develop flavor, but remove from refrigerator 10 to 15 minutes before serving.

VARIATION: Substitute 1 teaspoon caraway seed and 1/2 teaspoon dried dillweed for garlic and scallions.

NOVA SCOTIA LOX WITH CHEESE AND ONIONS

■ *Makes about 1 cup* ■

The lox, cheese and onions combine here to make a great flavor. For fancy situations, fill small tomatoes and serve as hors d'oeuvre; but for most of the time, spread on small squares of pumpernickel, rye or bread crisps such as toasted bagel pieces.

    8   ounces farmer cheese
    1   slice (about 1 ounce) Nova Scotia lox,
        minced
  1/4   cup grated onion
    2   tablespoons fresh lemon juice
white or black pepper

Break up cheese in a bowl. Add lox to cheese with remaining ingredients. Mix well with a fork and chill. Remove from refrigerator about 20 minutes before serving for best flavor.

VARIATION: Substitute skim milk for lemon juice. Spread on bread slices and add one small caper to the center of each.

COTTAGE CHEESE

Cottage cheese is made with fresh whole milk that is skimmed, pasteurized and cooked in vats, where the milk is solidified through the addition of a culture. Once it has set as a soft custard, the curd is cut into millions of squares with stainless steel wires, then allowed to rest and expel whey. Then it is cooked again. The goal is to separate the curd from the whey through agitation, then to drain off the whey. The resultant curd is then washed with fresh water and it receives an application of a cream dressing. Low-fat cottage cheeses receive a leaner cream dressing, which of course means fewer calories. Cottage cheese has been called the perfect food, for it is low in calories but high in proteins, vitamins and minerals (though unfortunately the washing process rinses away most of the calcium in the milk).

Farmer cheese is similar to cottage cheese but drier. Farmer cheeses come in bars or loaves, usually 8 ounces but up to 3 pounds in weight.

HONEY BUTTER SPREAD

■ Makes about 1/2 cup ■

This is especially delicious on coarse whole-grain and oatmeal breads. It is also excellent on hot biscuits, rolls and corn bread.

1/2 cup (1 stick) butter, room temperature
1/4 cup honey

Combine butter and honey and mix well. Serve in a bowl, or butter each bread slice or biscuit and heat at 375°F (190°C) for a few minutes until bread is warm and butter is melted.

YOGURT AND AVOCADO DIP

■ Serves 4 to 6 ■

This is a make-ahead appetizer that gets better as it sits in the refrigerator for several hours, or even overnight.

1 cup plain yogurt
1 ripe avocado, peeled, seeded and chopped
3 scallions, chopped
juice of 1 small lemon
pinches of dried herbs, such as oregano and tarragon
salt and pepper

1 Combine all ingredients in processor bowl and blend until smooth. Taste and adjust flavor with more lemon juice or seasonings.

2 Serve with toast or crackers.

YOGURT

During biblical times in the Middle East, yogurt was made from goat's, mare's or yak's milk. Today, under strict factory controls, it is made from cow's milk, and it is one of the most popular items on supermarket shelves. Yogurt is low in calories but high in protein, calcium and other important nutrients. Although it is available plain, it is marketed with many fruit flavors, which is one of the reasons for its popularity. A versatile product, it can be used in salad dressings, sauces, soups and main dishes.

BROWN BREAD ONION AND CHEESE SANDWICHES WITH RAISINS

■ *Serves 4* ■

An easy way to give flavor to cottage cheese. Enjoy this with a green salad.

12 ounces low-fat cottage cheese
1/2 package (1.2 ounces) onion soup mix
8 slices brown bread
1 cup raisins

1 Combine cheese and onion in processor and blend well. Spread 4 slices of bread thickly with mixture.

2 Sprinkle 1/4 cup raisins over each slice. Cover with second slice of bread and cut in halves or thirds.

SUPERMARKET SAVVY

■ ■

BUTTER BUDS

I never thought I'd find a substitute for butter but I have—the natural butter-flavor granules called Butter Buds. A 1/2-ounce (14.2 g) packet is equal in flavor to 1 stick of butter. The 1/2-ounce packet holds 8 level teaspoons, which are mixed with 1/2 cup (4 ounces) of hot tap water; this makes 4 ounces of liquid butter flavor that can be poured over baked potatoes, asparagus, corn on the cob, peas and other vegetables, and used with fish, pasta, rice and pancakes. Even in the dry state, Butter Buds can be sprinkled on steaks, roasts and hot vegetables. I use it often in casseroles, sauces and soup because 4 ounces of liquid Butter Buds has 48 calories (4 ounces of butter or margarine has 800) and it has 99 percent less cholesterol than butter.

FLOURS, MUFFIN MIXES, CEREALS AND GRAINS

Along with the food revolution in this country there has been a significant increase of national interest in wholesome eating. More and more of us are cracking down on weight problems and, unfortunately, some have begun new eating regimens after receiving disturbing medical reports. So it's easy to understand the interest in bran, high fiber and other healthful foods.

Many food processors have reformulated their products to appeal to customers who now concentrate on exercise and healthier food. Their questionable additives having been reduced or dropped, such foods are moving to center stage. Nowhere is this change more noticeable than in breads and cereals. There is an appealing abundance of interesting, tasteful and wholesome ingredients for breadmaking today.

Dietary fiber, the kind found naturally in such foods as bran cereals, wholewheat bread, vegetables and fruits, is considered essential to good health. Researchers at the University of Kentucky College of Medicine in Lexington say that adding a commercially available natural therapeutic fiber to one's diet can reduce artery-clogging blood cholesterol. Not all food fibers are equal in their healthful properties, but many health organizations say the most effective diet for chronic disease prevention is liberal in complex carbohydrates and fiber and limited in fat. So enjoy your bran muffins, but go easy on the butter.

EXPRESS CHECK-OUT

FLOURS/CEREALS

1 YEAST FACTS: (a) Too much heat will kill it; liquid should not be over 105°F (40°C). (b) Once dough is mixed, fermentation can be retarded by covering and refrigerating for up to 24 hours.

2 Fresh yeast may be stored in freezer. First cut it into small pieces—i.e., a piece large enough for one loaf or batch of bread—and wrap tightly in plastic or freezer wrap. Add to water not over 95°F (35°C). Granulated yeast can go into water up to 115°F (46°C).

3 Quick bread texture should be pebbly, that is, coarser and more crumbly than cake. The trick is not to overbeat batter; simply mix wet and dry ingredients just until no flour streaks show.

4 Baking powder will lose its strength in time. Buy a small can and toss it after four or five months if not used up. Expiration dates on cans do not seem realistic.

5 Day-old muffins may be refreshed by quickly dipping them in cold milk or water and reheating in the oven.

6 To make Melba toast, cut a frozen loaf of unsliced white bread into 1/8-inch-thick slices. Trim crusts, lay slices on a baking sheet in a single layer and bake in a preheated 225°F (110°C) oven 45 minutes or until pale gold and crisp. Store in airtight container.

7 Put honey container in hot water to thin for pouring over French toast, waffles, muffins and so on, or thin out in the microwave.

8 Add grated lemon zest and 2 tablespoons wheat germ to pancake mix for a more interesting pancake.

9 Make homemade vanilla extract by splitting 5 vanilla beans and adding to a pint of cognac or vodka. Seal tightly and let stand for 2 weeks. All supermarkets carry pure vanilla extract; don't use artificial.

CHURCH BAZAAR DATE NUT LOAVES

■ *Makes 5 to 6 small loaves* ■

*E*veryone hurries to pile goodies on church bazaar tables. Here's one loaf that becomes five. Wrap each in clear cellophane, tie with a pretty bow and they'll sell fast. Two 8 1/2-ounce packages of mix make 6 small loaves. To chop dates more easily in food processor, oil blade and add 1/4 cup of the muffin mix.

2 eggs or egg substitutes
2/3 cup milk
2 packages (7 ounces each) muffin mix, or 2 packages (8 1/2 ounces each) corn muffin mix
1 cup chopped pitted dates
1 cup chopped pecans

1 Preheat oven to 350°F (180°C). Grease 5 tiny loaf pans (4 1/2 x 2 1/2 x 1 1/2 inches); set aside.

2 Beat eggs in a mixing bowl. Add milk and muffin mix and blend in dates and pecans just until evenly moistened; do not overmix. Divide batter among the prepared pans.

3 Bake for 30 minutes or until a pick inserted in center comes out clean. Cool on racks.

FONTINA CHEESE BREAD WITH BACON AND OLIVES

■ *Makes 1 loaf* ■

2 1/2 cups all purpose flour
3 tablespoons sugar
2 teaspoons baking powder
1/2 teaspoon baking soda
1 teaspoon salt
1 teaspoon dry mustard
1/4 cup margarine, room temperature
1 cup shredded Fontina cheese
1 egg
1 cup buttermilk
6 slices bacon, cooked crisp and crumbled
1 cup pitted olives, coarsely chopped

1 Preheat oven to 375°F (190°C). Grease 8 1/2 x 4-inch loaf pan. In one bowl, combine flour, sugar, baking powder and soda, salt and mustard. Cut in margarine with a fork until mixture resembles coarse meal. Stir in cheese.

2 In another bowl, beat egg and buttermilk until well blended. Add to flour mixture and stir only until no flour streaks show. Stir in bacon and olives.

3 Pour batter into prepared pan and bake until pick inserted in center comes out clean, 30 to 40 minutes. Cool on rack.

MANGO BREAD WITH COCONUT

■ *Makes 1 loaf* ■

1   cup sugar
1/4   cup vegetable oil
2   eggs, beaten
1   cup pureed mango
2   cups Bisquick or other biscuit mix
1/2   cup grated coconut

1 Preheat oven to 350°F (180°C). Grease 9 x 5-inch loaf pan and line with waxed paper. Cream sugar with oil. Add eggs, mango and bread mix and blend well. Stir in coconut.

2 Pour batter into prepared pan and bake until pick inserted in center comes out clean, 50 to 60 minutes. Let cool before removing from pan.

OAT BREAD WITH APRICOTS AND WALNUTS

■ *Makes 1 loaf* ■

2   cups Bisquick or other buttermilk baking mix
1   cup instant rolled oats
2/3   cup sugar
1   teaspoon baking powder
generous pinch of salt
3/4   cup chopped dried apricots
2/3   cup chopped walnuts
2   eggs, beaten
3/4   cup milk

1 Preheat oven to 350°F (180°C). Grease a 9 x 5-inch loaf pan. Combine baking mix, oats, sugar, baking powder and salt in a large bowl.

2 Pour batter into prepared pan. Bake until pick inserted in center comes out clean, about 1 hour. Let stand in pan about 10 minutes, then invert loaf onto rack to cool before slicing.

SUPERMARKET SAVVY

WHAT IS SOLUBLE FIBER?

Dietary fiber comes in two types: soluble and insoluble. Foods may contain both types but some foods are better sources of one type than the other. Oats, for example, are an excellent source of cholesterol-reducing soluble fiber. Whole wheat products are a primary source of insoluble fiber, which helps prevent constipation. Both types of fiber are important to a healthy diet, but generally only soluble fiber helps reduce cholesterol.

POTATO TARRAGON BISCUITS

■ *Makes 16 2 3/4-inch biscuits* ■

*I*nstant mashed potatoes work here as long as you follow package directions. Use 1 cup.

1   cup buttermilk
2   tablespoons butter or margarine, melted
1   tablespoon honey
1/2 teaspoon baking soda
2   cups all purpose flour
1   tablespoon brown sugar
2   teaspoons baking powder
1   tablespoon finely chopped fresh tarragon
     or 1 teaspoon dried
1   cup mashed potatoes

1 Preheat oven to 400°F (200°C). Generously grease baking sheet. Combine buttermilk, butter, honey and baking soda in a small bowl.

2 In a larger bowl, combine flour, brown sugar, baking powder and tarragon and mix well. Mix in potatoes and buttermilk mixture.

3 Roll dough out 1/2 inch thick and cut out biscuits. Arrange on prepared baking sheet. Bake until golden brown, about 15 minutes. Serve hot.

WILD RICE BREAD WITH PECANS

■ *Makes 1 loaf* ■

*M*ake a loaf of this delicious bread and toast it for breakfast. At lunch or dinner, it will be a conversation piece if you serve it with cheese as part of the salad course.

1/2   cup butter or margarine
1/4   cup honey
2   large eggs
1   cup cooked wild rice
2/3   cup chopped pecans
1 1/4 cups wholewheat flour
1 1/2 teaspoons baking powder
1   teaspoon salt
1/2   teaspoon ground cloves
3/4   cup milk

1 Preheat oven to 350°F (180°C). Generously grease 8 × 4 1/2-inch loaf pan. Cream butter and honey in a large bowl until light and smooth. Beat in eggs one at a time. Fold in rice and pecans.

2 In another bowl, combine flour, baking powder, salt and cloves. Stir into egg mixture a little at a time, alternating with milk. Pour into prepared pan.

3 Bake until a pick inserted in center comes out clean, about 50 minutes. Let cool for about 10 minutes, then turn out on a rack to cool before slicing.

SUPERMARKET CALZONE

■ *Serves 6* ■

The dough is made with buttermilk baking mix and milk.

1   *pound pork sausage*
1   *can (15 ounces) tomato or spaghetti sauce*
2   *garlic cloves, minced, or 1/2 teaspoon garlic powder*
1/2 *teaspoon each dried basil and oregano*
2 1/2 *cups buttermilk baking mix, such as Bisquick*
2/3 *cup milk*
2   *cups (8 ounces) shredded or grated mozzarella cheese*

1 Preheat oven to 350°F (180°C). Sauté sausage meat until browned in a large skillet. Add tomato sauce, garlic and herbs and heat thoroughly.

2 Combine buttermilk baking mix and milk in a bowl. Cut dough in half. Press one half into 8-inch square baking dish. Spoon sausage mixture over dough and sprinkle with 1 cup mozzarella.

3 Roll remaining dough into 8-inch square and place atop mozzarella. Sprinkle with remaining cheese. Bake 30 minutes. After 20 minutes of baking, move to lower third of oven.

GOAT CHEESE PIZZA WITH SALAMI SLIVERS

■ *Serves 4* ■

Use prepared pizza dough, found in tubes on refrigerated supermarket shelves, and this is a snap. Salami and olives are available at most deli counters. If you can't find goat cheese, substitute crumbled feta or shredded mozzarella.

1   *tube (10 ounces) pizza dough, refrigerated*
8   *ounces goat cheese, crumbled*
4   *ounces sliced salami, cut into 1/4-inch slivers*
1/2 *cup black Moroccan, Sicilian or Greek olives, pitted and coarsely chopped*
3   *tablespoons olive oil*
1   *tablespoon dried oregano*

1 Preheat oven to 425°F (220°C). Unroll packaged dough and cut into 4 rectangles. Place on large baking sheet or jelly roll pan and pat to 1/8-inch thickness.

2 Sprinkle cheese over dough, leaving a narrow margin at edges so cheese won't melt over. Add salami and olives; sprinkle with oil and oregano.

3 Bake 10 to 12 minutes until edges brown. Serve hot.

PEPPERONI PIZZA WITH SCALLIONS

■ *Serves 10* ■

Here's a good way to use pepperoni. Cut the slices into small pieces and sprinkle over dough.

1   pizza crust to fit 15 x 10-inch jelly roll pan
1   jar (15 1/2 ounces) spaghetti sauce
1   tablespoon Italian seasoning
4   ounces pepperoni, sliced and cut into small pieces
2   cups (8 ounces) shredded mozzarella cheese
1   cup thinly sliced scallions
1/4   cup grated Parmesan cheese

1 Preheat oven to 425°F (220°C). Fit crust into jelly roll pan. Combine spaghetti sauce and seasoning and spread over dough with rubber spatula. Sprinkle evenly with pepperoni, mozzarella, scallions and Parmesan.

2 Bake for 20 minutes or until crust is golden. Serve hot.

BAKED SOUTHERN CHEESE GRITS

■ *Serves 6* ■

If you haven't eaten grits, you don't know what you're missing. They are a versatile and sophisticated dish if prepared properly and served in an interesting way. Grits are good with egg dishes, but try them also in place of potatoes with chicken, beef, ham and all cuts of pork and lamb. Since they're easy to cook and will hold in the oven, they are ideal with grilled meats.

6   cups chicken broth or water plus 2 chicken bouillon cubes
1 1/2   cups quick-cooking grits
1/4   cup butter
3   eggs
1/3   cup milk
1   cup shredded cheddar cheese

1 Preheat oven to 425°F (220°C).

2 Bring broth to boil in a large saucepan with bouillon cubes. Slowly stir in grits and cook about 5 minutes or until thickened. Add butter.

3 Beat eggs with milk in a small bowl. Briskly stir into grits. Add cheese and stir again. Transfer mixture to a large ovenproof dish and bake 45 minutes. Serve hot.

MICROWAVE: (1) Combine broth and grits in a 10-cup microwave-safe dish and cook uncovered on HIGH (100%) 15 minutes. (2) Remove from oven and stir in remaining ingredients. Cover and cook on HIGH 2 minutes. Let stand 5 minutes before serving.

CORN BREAD, TEX-MEX STYLE

■ *Makes one 8-inch square pan* ■

For a spicy corn bread use 2 tablespoons finely chopped jalapeño peppers in place of the green chilies.

1	*egg*
1	*can (8 1/2 ounces) cream-style corn*
2	*tablespoons vegetable oil*
1/2	*cup milk*
1	*teaspoon sugar*
1	*cup self-rising cornmeal mix*
2	*tablespoons finely chopped green chilies*
1 1/4	*cups (about 5 ounces) grated sharp cheddar cheese.*

1 Preheat oven to 450 °F (230°C). Grease 8-inch square pan.

2 Beat egg in a large bowl. Add ingredients in order listed, blending after each addition. Pour mixture into prepared pan and bake 20 to 25 minutes or until golden.

MICROWAVE: Pour batter into 9-inch round baking dish. Place in oven on inverted saucer. Cook on MEDIUM-HIGH (70%) 5 minutes. If not on carousel, turn dish 3 times.

SUPERMARKET SAVVY

CORNMEAL

Dried white or yellow corn that has been ground is known simply as plain cornmeal. Government standards require that it be enriched with iron and the B vitamins; this is done after grinding.

When salt and baking powder are added to the cornmeal (manufacturers figure their own appropriate amounts), it becomes self-rising cornmeal. Some manufacturers add flour also, to make self-rising cornmeal mix. The cornmeal itself provides the nutlike flavor and crunch; salt adds some flavor and the baking powder or soda is the leavening that makes the cornbread rise.

Only a few other ingredients are required to make good corn bread: to create tenderness, fat is added; liquid (water, buttermilk or milk) holds the dough together; and if eggs are added, the bread texture becomes lighter and less crumbly. Lastly, some sugar accents the nutty flavor and will provide a more golden crust.

COUNTRY STYLE CORN BREAD

■ *Makes one 9-inch skillet* ■

*I*n the South the better cooks always grease and preheat their black iron pans. The batter will sizzle when poured into it; it makes a crustier corn bread. If you don't use a skillet, use a 9-inch square pan, a mold for 16 corn sticks or a pan for 12 regular muffins. Whatever is used, heat it before adding the batter.

      2   cups self-rising cornmeal mix
  1 3/4   cups buttermilk
    1/4   cup vegetable oil or melted shortening

1 Preheat oven to 450°F (230°C). Grease skillet or other pan and place in oven.

2 Combine cornmeal mix, buttermilk and oil in a large bowl. Mix well and pour into baking pan. If using a muffin or corn stick pan, do not fill more than 2/3 full.

3 Bake 20 to 25 minutes for a skillet or square pan, 15 to 18 minutes for muffins or corn sticks.

SOUTHERN CORN BREAD

■ *Makes one 9-inch skillet* ■

*T*he Indians introduced cornmeal to the early English settlers and it has become a key item in American cuisine. Instead of a skillet bread, you can make a 9-inch square bread, 16 corn sticks or 12 regular muffins.

      1   large egg
  1 1/3   cups milk or 1 3/4 cups buttermilk
    1/4   cup vegetable oil or melted shortening
      2   cups self-rising cornmeal mix

1 Preheat oven to 450°F (230°C). Grease skillet or other baking pan and place in the oven.

2 Beat egg in a large bowl. Add milk, then oil and flour and mix well. Pour batter into skillet or other pan; if using a muffin or corn stick mold, do not fill more than 2/3 full.

3 Bake 20 to 25 minutes for a skillet or pan, 15 to 18 minutes for muffins or corn sticks.

MICROWAVE: Pour batter into 9-inch round baking dish. Place in oven on inverted saucer. Cook on MEDIUM-HIGH (70%) 5 minutes. If not on carousel, turn dish 3 times.

CHEDDAR CHEESE CORN MUFFINS

■ *Serves 6* ■

This will make 6 to 8 regular muffins or 12 to 14 small ones, 8 to 10 corn sticks, or one iron skillet bread 6 inches in diameter. Double the recipe, if you wish—they will go fast.

1   package (6 ounces) buttermilk cornbread
    mix
2/3   cup water
1   egg, beaten
2   ounces shredded cheddar cheese

1 Preheat oven to 450°F (230°C). Grease baking pan with bacon grease, butter, margarine or vegetable oil and place in the oven until pan is hot.

2 Combine mix, water and egg and whisk until well blended. Remove pan from oven and pour in batter. Sprinkle with cheese. Bake for 15 or 20 minutes or until golden. Let rest for a few minutes before removing from pan.

MICROWAVE: Spoon batter into 18 to 24 paper-muffin cups, filling each half full. (Small microwave-safe ramekins may be used with paper cups inside.) Cook 6 muffins on HIGH (100%) 2 to 3 minutes or until a pick comes out clean. Rearrange muffins 1 or 2 times during baking if not on carousel. Repeat with remaining muffins.

POLENTA

■ *Serves 6* ■

Top this with sautéed mushrooms and/or sausage pieces.

3 1/2   cups water
1   cup cornmeal
1   tablespoon olive oil
1/2   teaspoon salt
2   tablespoons butter or margarine,
    optional
1/4   cup grated Parmesan cheese
1/4   cup chopped fresh basil or 1 tablespoon
    dried
1   jar (15 1/2 ounces) spaghetti sauce,
    heated

Bring water to boil. Stir in cornmeal, oil and salt and simmer 20 to 25 minutes or until creamy, stirring most of the time. Remove from heat and stir with wire whisk, adding butter if you wish. Spoon onto individual heated plates. Top with a few tablespoons sauce, leaving some polenta showing. Sprinkle with cheese and basil and serve.

MICROWAVE: (1) Combine water, cornmeal, olive oil and salt in 3-quart microwave-safe dish. Cover and cook on HIGH (100%) 5 minutes. Stir and cook 5 minutes longer. Add butter and stir with wire whisk. (2) Check spaghetti sauce jar to see if it is microwavable; if not, transfer sauce to bowl, cover and cook on HIGH 3 minutes.

ZOE'S CLASSIC BLUEBERRY MUFFINS

■ *Makes 12* ■

Fresh or frozen blueberries may be used. If frozen, be sure to thaw and drain well. If using all purpose flour, sift with 1 tablespoon baking powder and 3/4 teaspoon salt.

2   cups sifted self-rising flour
3   tablespoons sugar
1   cup milk
1   egg
3   tablespoons vegetable oil
1   cup blueberries

1 Preheat oven to 425°F (210°C). Grease 12 muffin cups.

2 Mix flour and sugar in bowl. Mix milk, egg and oil in another bowl.

3 Add egg mixture to flour and stir just until evenly moistened; do not over-mix. Fill muffin cups 2/3 full. Bake 20 minutes or until browned.

NO-CHOLESTEROL, NO-EGG RAISIN BRAN MUFFINS

■ *Makes 12* ■

The secret ingredients are the applesauce and honey in addition to the raisin bran.

1 1/2   cups raisin bran cereal
1   cup wholewheat flour
1   tablespoon baking powder
1   teaspoon cinnamon
pinch of salt
1/2   cup applesauce
1/3   cup skim milk
3   tablespoons honey
3   tablespoons vegetable oil

1 Preheat oven to 400°F (200°C). Place cereal in large bowl. Sift flour, baking powder, cinnamon and salt into cereal.

2 In another bowl, combine applesauce, milk, honey and oil. Stir into cereal mixture. Arrange paper cups in muffin pans and fill 3/4 full with batter. Bake until brown, about 25 minutes.

MICROWAVE: Spoon batter into 18 to 24 paper-muffin cups, filling each half full. (Small microwave-safe ramekins may be used with paper cups inside.) Cook 6 muffins on HIGH (100%) 2 to 3 minutes or until a pick comes out clean. Rearrange muffins 1 or 2 times during baking if not on carousel. Repeat with remaining muffins.

CHOCOLATE VANILLA WHOLE-GRAIN MUFFINS

■ *Makes 12 large or 24 small muffins* ■

Cereal manufacturers are producing whole-grain cereals because of consumer demand, and they're making them without adding preservatives, salt and sugar. Not much sugar is added to this recipe—1/4 cup sugar means 1 teaspoon in each large muffin and only 1/2 teaspoon in the small ones. Of course there is the chocolate, but this is a small price to pay for an otherwise healthy and delicious muffin.

2	cups whole-grain cereal, such as bran flakes
1 1/4	cups milk
3	tablespoons vegetable oil
1	teaspoon vanilla
1	egg, beaten
1 1/4	cups all purpose flour
1/4	cup sugar
1/3	cup sweet ground chocolate or cocoa powder
1	tablespoon baking powder
48	small semisweet chocolate chips

1 Preheat oven to 400°F (200°C). Generously grease muffin pans. Stir together cereal, milk, vegetable oil and vanilla in a bowl. Let stand for about 5 minutes. Fold in egg.

2 Sift flour, sugar, chocolate and baking powder into another bowl.

3 Add flour mixture to cereal, stirring only to combine; do not overmix.

4 Half-fill prepared muffin cups. Add 2 chips to small muffins and 4 to large, then add more batter to fill pans. Bake for about 20 minutes or until pick inserted in center comes out clean.

MICROWAVE: Spoon batter into 18 to 24 paper-muffin cups, filling each half full. (Small microwave-safe ramekins may be used with paper cups inside.) Cook 6 muffins on HIGH (100%) 2 to 3 minutes or until a pick comes out clean. Rearrange muffins 1 or 2 times during baking if not on carousel. Repeat with remaining muffins.

■   ■

SWEET VANILLA DIET SPREAD

makes 1/3 cup

Have no conscience about using this spread. It is about as low in calories as any "butter" spread can get. Use it on muffins, bread, toast and pancakes.

1/3	cup reduced-calorie margarine
5	packets sugar substitute, such as EQUAL
1/2	teaspoon vanilla

Mix ingredients until well combined. Store in refrigerator.

GINGER MUFFINS

■ *Makes 12* ■

*T*hese are delicious served warm with butter, jelly, jam or ripe peaches. In some ways, candied ginger is easier to work with than fresh or powdered; here is one way. These brown nicely if baked traditionally; if microwaved, they will be delicious but white.

3/4 cup sugar
 3 tablespoons minced candied ginger
 2 cups all purpose flour
 1 tablespoon baking powder
 1 cup milk
 2 eggs, beaten
1/2 cup heavy cream
 6 tablespoons butter, melted

1 Preheat oven to 400°F (200°C). Grease muffin tins.

2 Process sugar and ginger together in food processor to pulverize ginger (don't overdo; little pieces of ginger will add texture). Combine with flour and baking powder in a bowl.

3 In another bowl, combine milk, eggs, cream and butter and mix well. Add to ginger mixture and stir just until evenly moistened; do not overmix.

4 Fill each muffin cup 2/3 full. Bake 20 to 25 minutes or until pick inserted in center comes out clean. Serve warm.

MICROWAVE: Spoon batter into 18 to 24 paper-muffin cups, filling each half full. (Small microwave-safe ramekins may be used with paper cups inside.) Cook 6 muffins on HIGH (100%) 2 to 3 minutes or until a pick comes out clean. Rearrange muffins 1 or 2 times during baking if not on carousel. Repeat with remaining muffins.

SOUR CREAM MUFFINS

■ *Makes 12* ■

 2 eggs
1/4 cup sugar
 1 cup sour cream
 2 cups buttermilk baking mix, such as Bisquick
 1 teaspoon grated lemon zest
1/2 teaspoon nutmeg
2/3 cup golden raisins

1 Preheat oven to 375°F (190°C). Grease muffin tin. Beat eggs and sugar well and blend in sour cream. Add baking mix, lemon zest and nutmeg and stir only until evenly moistened. Fold in raisins.

2 Distribute batter among prepared muffin cups and bake 15 minutes or until browned and a pick inserted in center comes out clean.

MICROWAVE: Spoon batter into 18 to 24 paper-muffin cups, filling each half full. (Small microwave-safe ramekins may be used with paper cups inside.) Cook 6 muffins on HIGH (100%) 2 to 3 minutes or until a pick comes out clean. Rearrange muffins 1 or 2 times during baking if not on carousel. Repeat with remaining muffins.

OATMEAL MUFFINS WITH PEACHES

■ *Makes 12* ■

This is a health muffin, completely free of cholesterol.

1 1/2   *cups quick-cooking or regular rolled oats*
1 1/4   *cups all purpose flour*
1/2   *cup dark brown sugar, packed*
1   *teaspoon nutmeg*
1   *teaspoon baking powder*
3/4   *teaspoon baking soda*
1   *egg white*
1   *cup pureed fresh or canned peaches (do not puree completely smooth)*
1/2   *cup skim milk*
1/2   *cup vegetable oil*
Optional topping:
2   *tablespoons margarine, melted*
1   *tablespoon brown sugar, packed*
1/2   *teaspoon nutmeg*

1 Preheat oven to 400°F (200°C). In one bowl, combine oats, flour, brown sugar, nutmeg, baking powder and soda and mix well.

2 Beat egg white until frothy in another bowl. Add peaches, milk and oil and mix well. Fold into oat mixture and stir only until evenly moistened.

3 Line muffin tins with 12 paper cups and fill with batter. If you wish, mix topping ingredients and sprinkle over muffins. Bake for 20 minutes or until pick inserted in center comes out clean.

MICROWAVE: Spoon batter into 18 to 24 paper-muffin cups, filling each half full. (Small microwave-safe ramekins may be used with paper cups inside.) Cook 6 muffins on HIGH (100%) 2 to 3 minutes or until a pick comes out clean. Rearrange muffins 1 or 2 times during baking if not on carousel. Repeat with remaining muffins.

PARSLEY AND PARMESAN CHEESE MUFFINS

■ *Makes 12* ■

Cheddar cheese in muffins seems to be popular, but try these with parsley and Parmesan.

2   *cups self-rising flour*
1   *cup (4 ounces) grated Parmesan cheese*
1/2   *cup finely chopped parsley*
1   *teaspoon dry mustard*
1/2   *teaspoon chili powder*
1   *egg*

1   *cup milk*
1/4   *cup vegetable oil*

1 Preheat oven to 425°F (220°C). Combine flour, cheese, parsley, mustard and chili powder in a bowl.

2 Beat egg in another bowl. Add milk and oil and blend well. Add to flour mixture quickly and stir briefly; do not overmix. Grease muffin cups and fill 2/3 full with batter.

3 Bake until golden, about 20 minutes.

MICROWAVE: Spoon batter into 18 to 24 paper-muffin cups, filling each half full. (Small microwave-safe ramekins may be used with paper cups inside.) Cook 6 muffins on HIGH (100%) 2 to 3 minutes or until a pick comes out clean. Rearrange muffins 1 or 2 times during baking if not on carousel. Repeat with remaining muffins.

WHOLEWHEAT AND WALNUT MUFFINS

■ *Makes 12* ■

1	cup wholewheat flour
1	cup all purpose flour
1/3	cup brown sugar, packed
1	cup coarsely chopped walnuts
1	tablespoon baking powder
1	teaspoon salt, optional
1	large egg
1	cup whole or skim milk
1/4	cup vegetable oil

1 Preheat oven to 400°F (200°). Generously grease shiny aluminum muffin tin. Combine flours, brown sugar, walnuts, baking powder and salt in a large bowl.

2 Beat egg in another bowl. Add milk and oil and blend well. Pour quickly into dry ingredients and stir just until evenly moistened.

3 Pour batter into prepared muffin cups, filling each 2/3 full. Bake until golden, about 15 minutes.

MICROWAVE: Spoon batter into 18 to 24 paper-muffin cups, filling each half full. (Small microwave-safe ramekins may be used with paper cups inside.) Cook 6 muffins on HIGH (100%) 2 to 3 minutes or until a pick comes out clean. Rearrange muffins 1 or 2 times during baking if not on carousel. Repeat with remaining muffins.

SUPERMARKET SAVVY

MUFFINS

There seems to be a muffin craze sweeping the country. Market shelves are overflowing with a myriad of muffin mixes. There is no mystery about making muffins, but keep these points in mind:
1. First mix all dry ingredients together in one bowl.
2. Blend the liquid ingredients in another bowl.
3. Mix the liquid with the dry ingredients; don't overmix. Remember that the batter should be lumpy.
4. Brown the muffins in shiny aluminum pans, each cup 2/3 full of batter.
5. Reheat muffins either in the microwave in plastic wrap for a few seconds or in a 400°F (200°C) regular oven in foil for about 15 minutes.

ZUCCHINI WALNUT MUFFINS

■ *Makes 12* ■

Zucchini made its mark in bread and here it makes its debut in muffins. Use small (6-inch) zucchini if possible; with larger ones, seeds must be removed before grating. Vegetable oil is used instead of butter or margarine and the added attractions are chives and walnuts. A really comforting muffin.

   2   cups all purpose flour
   1   tablespoon baking soda
   1   teaspoon salt
1/2   teaspoon baking powder
   3   eggs, room temperature
   1   cup sugar
   1   cup vegetable oil
   2   cups grated zucchini
1/4   cup finely chopped chives or 1 tablespoon dried
   1   cup chopped walnuts

1 Preheat oven to 375°F (190°C). Grease muffin tins. Sift flour, baking soda, salt and baking powder.

2 Combine eggs and sugar and beat until thick and smooth. Add oil and beat again until smooth. Add zucchini, chives, walnuts and flour mixture and stir just until evenly moistened.

3 Fill each muffin cup 2/3 full with batter. Bake for 20 to 25 minutes or until pick inserted in center comes out clean. Let muffins rest 10 minutes before turning out.

MICROWAVE: Spoon batter into 18 to 24 paper-muffin cups, filling each half full. (Small microwave-safe ramekins may be used with paper cups inside.) Cook 6 muffins on HIGH (100%) 2 to 3 minutes or until a pick comes out clean. Rearrange muffins 1 or 2 times during baking if not on carousel. Repeat with remaining muffins.

SOPHIE JEAN'S OATMEAL COOKIES

■ *Makes about 5 dozen* ■

I like plain oatmeal cookies but some people like to add nuts, coconut flakes, raisins, and, of course, chocolate chips.

   1   cup brown sugar, firmly packed
1/2   cup sugar
   1   egg
3/4   cup vegetable oil
1/4   cup water
   1   teaspoon vanilla
   3   cups uncooked rolled oats
   1   cup all purpose flour
1/2   teaspoon baking soda
Pinch of salt

1 Preheat oven to 350°F (180°C). Combine first 6 ingredients and blend well. Add remaining ingredients and blend well.

2 Drop dough by rounded full teaspoonfuls on greased cookie sheets and bake 12 minutes or until golden.

"6 BOY" OATMEAL

■ *Serves 6* ■

Here's a way to spiff up oatmeal for a Sunday, holiday or special occasion. Use pretty bowls and vary items as you wish—for example, use currants in place of raisins, pineapple chunks in place of apple and so on. The name is a takeoff on the traditional way of serving curry—with each condiment separately presented by a servant boy.

4   *cups water*
salt
2   *cups quick-cooking rolled oats*
1/2   *cup each chopped dates, raisins, coconut flakes, sliced bananas, chopped nuts and chopped apple (do not prepare banana and apple until ready to serve)*
milk and sugar

1 Bring water to boil with salt. Stir in oats and cook 1 minute, stirring several times. Remove from heat and cover.

2 Arrange dates, etc., in 6 small bowls and set in center of table. Place a small spoon in each bowl.

3 Serve oatmeal in bowls and let each person spoon whatever he or she wishes over oatmeal, adding milk and sugar if desired.

MICROWAVE: (1) Use individual 2-cup microwave-safe bowls, containing 2/3 cup water, pinch of salt and 1/3 cup oats in each. (2) Cook on HIGH (100%) 1 1/2 to 2 minutes or until thickened. Mix before serving. Serve with condiments as above, plus milk and sugar.

OATMEAL WITH STEWED PRUNES AND CREAM

■ *Serves 4* ■

This is one of my favorite breakfast dishes. Use milk on weekdays, cream on Sundays.

2 2/3   *cups water*
pinch of salt
1 1/2   *cups quick-cooking rolled oats*
16   *canned pitted prunes in syrup*
8   *tablespoons prune juice from jar*
1/2   *cup heavy cream or half-and-half*

1 Bring water to boil with salt. Stir in oats and cook 1 minute, stirring several times. Remove from heat and cover.

2 Distribute oatmeal among 4 bowls. Top each with 4 prunes. Pour 2 tablespoons prune juice over prunes and top with 2 tablespoons cream.

MICROWAVE: To cook oats, see above. Add prunes, juice and cream as above.

OATMEAL CHOCOHOLIC

■ *Serves 2* ■

Chocolate finds its way into everything; why not oatmeal? It is not necessary to add sugar. You'll be surprised at the delicious combination.

1 1/3   cups water
pinch of salt
   2/3   cup quick-cooking rolled oats
1 to 2   tablespoons semisweet chocolate chips
milk

1 Bring water to boil with salt. Stir in oats and cook 1 minute, stirring several times. Remove from heat.

2 Add chocolate chips, cover and let stand about 1 minute. Serve with milk.

MICROWAVE: To cook oats, see page 31. Add chocolate before serving as above.

CHOCOLATE WAFFLES WITH ORANGE FLAVOR

■ *Serves 2* ■

A wonderful combination of flavors.

    2   eggs, separated
  1/2   cup (1 stick) unsalted butter or
        margarine, melted
  3/4   cup sugar
    3   ounces unsweetened chocolate, melted
1 1/2   cups all purpose flour
    1   tablespoon instant espresso
    2   teaspoons baking powder
pinch of salt
  1/2   cup milk
  1/2   cup heavy cream
  1/2   teaspoon orange extract

1 Preheat waffle iron. Combine yolks, butter, sugar and chocolate in bowl. Mix until smooth.

2 Combine flour, coffee, baking powder and salt in another bowl. Sift into first bowl, add milk and mix well. Beat egg whites until stiff and fold into mixture.

3 Cook batter in hot waffle iron, repeating until all batter is used.

4 Whip cream until soft peaks form. Fold in orange extract. Serve waffles hot with orange flavored cream.

CANNED AND PACKAGED SOUPS, DRIED BEANS AND OTHER LEGUMES

Dried legumes, perhaps except for flageolets and fava beans, are available on supermarket shelves all year long. They are one of the best buys, and are hard to beat for nutritional value. Almost all legumes (beans, lentils and peas) are high in calcium, thiamine, potassium, iron and vitamins A and C. When they are combined with grains such as corn, rice or wheat, they provide complete protein—probably the reason that they are sometimes called "poor man's meat."

Legumes have been cultivated for centuries. They are a mainstay in Europe and the Middle East, where they are a basic food, served both hot and cold. Today this staple has reached new gastronomic heights as an "in-food," appearing in lentil salads, stewed black-eyed peas, and exotic purees of every variety of bean and pea. In Mexico and in South and Central America (not to mention Texas and other southern states), the black bean, or the red, pink, pinto or kidney bean is part of practically every meal. An exciting combination I enjoyed recently was in Key West, Florida, at Louie's Backyard: lightly sautéed grouper fillet atop stewed black beans with crisped plantain shavings on the side.

Be sure to wash and pick over dried legumes and remove foreign matter, if you find any—nothing serious but worth a minute or two to sort and rinse. Many recipes call for soaking overnight; that's OK, but there is a quicker procedure: combine 1 pound legumes with 8 cups water, bring to boil and boil 2 minutes. Cover, remove from heat and let stand 1 hour. Then use as called for in recipe. It is surely amazing and comforting to know there's so much goodness in a small plastic bag of legumes, and for so little money.

EXPRESS CHECK-OUT

SOUPS

1 If soup is too salty, put in a peeled raw potato and cook 5 minutes. Remove potato and soup is less salty.

2 Thicken soups as you wish by adding instant potato flakes; add gradually and stir to test for thickness.

3 Coffee filters can be used to strain clear soups.

4 Do not add salt to water when cooking beans, as skins will toughen during cooking.

5 In hot summer months, consider using quick method of soaking beans (see above), as they are more likely to ferment if soaked overnight.

6 Cook dried chickpeas (garbanzos or ceci) like dried beans. But consider canned chickpeas as a timesaver. Canned chickpeas make a good puree to go with grilled meats, game and poultry; or add your favorite salad dressing to canned, drained chickpeas for a quick, uncooked side dish.

7 Two soup ideas: (1) To canned lentil soup, add 1 cup cooked Swiss chard pieces and 2 tablespoons fresh lemon juice; (2) Add 1/2 teaspoon dried sage to canned tomato soup.

8 Instead of flour, cornstarch or arrowroot to thicken soups, consider adding a cooked vegetable puree—carrot, leek, potato and so on, depending on type of soup.

CARROT SOUP WITH GINGER, CURRY AND MINT

■ *Serves 4* ■

One of the most delicious soups in this book. Garnish with chopped fresh mint, scallion or parsley.

2 tablespoons butter
2 teaspoons curry powder
6 carrots, peeled and cut into thin slices (about 3 cups)
2 white boiling potatoes, peeled and cubed
1 onion, coarsely chopped
3/4-inch piece fresh ginger, peeled and minced
3 tablespoons finely chopped fresh mint or 1 teaspoon dried
1 garlic clove, minced
5 cups chicken broth
1/4 teaspoon white pepper or to taste
1/4 cup light cream, optional

1 Melt butter in a large saucepan with cover. Add curry powder and cook 1 minute, stirring constantly.

2 Add all remaining ingredients except cream and bring to boil. Lower heat, cover and simmer for 20 to 25 minutes or until carrots are very tender.

3 In blender or processor, process mixture in batches until smooth. Return to pan in which it was cooked. Add cream if you wish. Reheat just to boiling point and serve in warmed individual bowls or a warm soup tureen.

MICROWAVE: (1) Melt butter with curry powder in large, deep container and cook on HIGH (100%) 1 minute. Add all remaining ingredients except cream and cook on HIGH 15 minutes, stirring twice. Process as in step 3, above. (2) Remove from microwave and blend in cream. Garnish with chopped fresh mint, scallion or parsley.

SUPERMARKET SAVVY

NUTRITION NOTES

For those individuals who eat little or no meat, a knowledge of nutrition is important to be sure protein intake is adequate. A warning to those who depend on eggs and cheese for protein: you may be eating too much fat and increasing your cholesterol level. Consider more skim milk products and restrict egg yolks to two or three a week. Better still, to get the more complete protein found in animal-based foods, learn to combine beans or peas with grains (see lentils and rice, page 50, and lima beans with barley, page 39). In any case, eat as much dark green leafy vegetables as you can at each meal; their vitamin B12 and calcium are important to everyone.

CHILLED CARROT AND LEEK SOUP

■ *Serves 4* ■

It's easy to puree vegetables; simply cook in as little water as possible until tender, then drain and puree in blender or food processor. In this recipe, you can substitute the same amount of pureed broccoli, spinach or carrots.

1 1/2   *cups water*
  1   *cup carrot puree*
  1   *package (2.4 ounces) leek soup and recipe mix*
  2   *cups half-and-half or milk*
  2   *tablespoons finely chopped fresh dill or 1 teaspoon dried dillweed*

1 Combine water, puree, and soup mix in a saucepan and stir well. Bring to boil, then lower heat and cook 2 minutes.

2 Add half-and-half and dill and cook 2 minutes longer; do not boil. Transfer to nonaluminum bowl, cover and chill several hours.

MICROWAVE: (1) Combine water, puree and soup mix in a 2-quart dish and stir well. Cover with plastic and cook on HIGH (100%) 4 to 6 minutes. Let stand for 3 minutes, remove plastic and stir in half and half and dill. Transfer to a large container, cover and chill several hours.

CHICKEN CANNELLINI SOUP

■ *Serves 4 to 6* ■

Chicken broth with real chicken pieces, dotted with fresh vegetables and topped with Parmesan cheese, can hardly be better. This is a winner.

  3   *tablespoons unsalted butter or margarine*
  2   *carrots, very thinly sliced*
  2   *celery stalks, strings removed, very thinly sliced*
  2   *small onions, very thinly sliced*
  1   *garlic clove, minced*
  8   *cups chicken broth*
  2   *boneless chicken breast halves, skin and fat removed, cut into strips*
  1   *can (19 ounces) cannellini beans, drained*
1/2   *to 1 cup grated Parmesan cheese*
1/4   *cup chopped fresh parsley*

1 Melt butter in large saucepan and sauté carrots 5 minutes. Add celery and onions and cook 5 minutes longer. Add garlic and sauté 1 minute.

2 Add chicken broth, chicken pieces and beans and heat through. Serve in individual bowls with a sprinkle of cheese and parsley; pass remaining cheese separately.

MICROWAVE: (1) Combine butter, carrots, celery and onions in 3-quart bowl and cook, covered, on HIGH (100%) 4 minutes. (2) Add garlic, stock, chicken and beans and cook, covered, on HIGH 6 minutes. Serve as above.

VELVET CLAM CHOWDER WITH SHERRY

■ *Party for 12* ■

Some supermarkets feature restaurant- or foodservice-size cans. In addition to being good buys, they are ideal for parties or large kitchen get-togethers. (If this size can of clam chowder is not available, combine smaller cans to make 6 cups.) This party soup takes little time to prepare and all ingredients are readily available. If, by chance, fennel is not to your liking, use fresh or dried dill. Or simply chop some chives or scallions and sprinkle over the soup.

1   can (51 ounces or 3 pounds, 3 ounces)
    New England clam chowder
1   bottle (8 ounces) clam juice
3   cups milk
2   cups heavy cream or half-and-half
2   cans (6 1/2 ounces each) chopped clams
1/4 cup sherry
1/4 cup finely chopped fresh fennel greens or
    1/2 teaspoon fennel seed.

Combine all ingredients in large saucepan and stir well. Bring just to boiling point, then lower heat and simmer about 15 minutes to cook away the raw taste of the sherry. Serve in large warm tureen or in individual warm soup bowls.

MICROWAVE: (1) Combine chowder and clam juice in large, deep container and cook on HIGH (100%) 10 minutes, stirring 2 or 3 times. (2) Blend in milk, cream, chopped clams and sherry and cook on MEDIUM-HIGH (70%) 6 minutes.

SUPERMARKET SAVVY

BABY FOODS SOUP

Nutritious baby foods can be used to make extra-fast soups. As a rule, jars of baby food have no salt added, nor modified starches, artificial colors, flavors or preservatives. There are many to choose from. For example, a tasty light cream of carrot soup can be made with 2 cups water, 2 chicken bouillon cubes (to make 2 cups broth, or use 1 larger cube which makes 2 cups), 2 jars (6 ounces each) baby food carrots and 1/3 cup half and half. Dissolve bouillon in water, add carrots and heat to boiling point. Add half and half and heat through. This will serve 3 to 4. Experiment with other vegetables, too.

GOLDEN CORN AND CLAM CHOWDER

■ *Serves 6* ■

Begin with an ordinary can of clam chowder and enhance it with more clam juice and clams, enrich it with some cream, dazzle it with corn, and the end result is a most flavorful dish of chowder.

2 cans (15 ounces each) condensed New England clam chowder or 3 cans (10 3/4 ounces each)
1 can (16 ounces) whole kernel corn, drained
2 cups milk
1 cup heavy cream or half and half
1 bottle (8 ounces) clam juice
1 can (6 1/2 ounces) chopped clams
3 tablespoons dry sherry
1/2 cup finely chopped scallions
paprika

Combine all ingredients except scallions and paprika in large saucepan and stir well. Bring just to boil, then lower heat and simmer about 15 minutes to cook away raw taste of sherry. Transfer chowder to large warm tureen or warm individual soup bowls. Garnish with chopped scallions and a sprinkle of paprika.

MICROWAVE: (1) Combine canned clam chowder, corn, milk and clam juice in large, deep container. Cook on HIGH (100%) 10 minutes, stirring twice. (2) Blend in cream, chopped clams and sherry and cook on MEDIUM-HIGH (70%) 6 minutes. Garnish with scallions and paprika.

SPLIT PEA AND BROWN RICE SOUP WITH CURRY

■ *Serves 8* ■

A delicious combination of high-protein, low-fat foods that make a filling, flavorful soup.

2 cups dried split peas
7 cups chicken broth or water (see Note)
1 large onion, coarsely chopped
2 large potatoes, peeled and cut into 1/2-inch cubes
2 large carrots, peeled and cut into 1/2-inch cubes
salt and pepper

2 tablespoons butter or margarine
1 tablespoon curry powder
1 cup cooked brown rice

1 Place split peas in large strainer and rinse under cool water, tossing several times. Remove any debris.

2 Combine peas, 6 cups broth or water, onion, potatoes, carrots, salt and pepper in heavy saucepan with cover. Bring to boil, then lower heat, cover and cook 1 1/2 to 2 hours or until peas are cooked.

3 While mixture is coming to boil, melt butter in small skillet. Add curry powder and blend well. Cook 1 minute, being sure not to blacken butter. With rubber spatula, transfer curry mixture to soup pot.

4 When soup is cooked, puree in batches in food processor. Return to soup pot, reheat and add more broth or water to obtain desired consistency. Add cooked rice. If still too thick, thin with more chicken broth or water.

Note: Use canned chicken broth or bouillon made from cubes.

MICROWAVE: (1) Combine all ingredients except rice in large, deep container (at least 3 quarts). Cover and cook on HIGH (100%) 10 minutes. (2) Reduce power to MEDIUM (50%) and cook 90 minutes, stirring 3 times. (3) Remove from oven. Puree in batches. Add rice. If too thick, thin with more broth or water.

LIMA BEAN SOUP WITH BARLEY, TOMATOES AND FRESH LEMON

■ *Serves 6 to 8* ■

I used to walk past shelf after shelf of dried legumes, but not anymore. They take time to soak, but if you do it overnight, you'll find you can cook enough to freeze for another whole meal.

2 cups dried small lima beans, soaked and drained
2 quarts water
1/2 cup barley
2 cups chopped canned plum tomatoes
2 garlic cloves, minced
2 medium onions, cut into 1/4-inch slices
4 carrots, cut into 1/4-inch slices
4 celery stalks, cut into 1/4-inch slices
salt and pepper
2 parsley sprigs, coarsely chopped
4 whole cloves
1 bay leaf, cut into 3 pieces
1 lemon, cut into 8 wedges, seeds removed

1 In a heavy saucepan with tight-fitting cover, combine all ingredients except parsley, cloves, bay leaf and lemon. Bring to boil, then lower heat, cover and simmer until beans and carrots are fully cooked, about 30 minutes.

2 As soon as saucepan is placed on burner, cut a 6-inch square of cheesecloth and place parsley, cloves and bay leaf pieces in center; tie opposite ends to form a bag. Add to soup at beginning of cooking and remove it at end.

3 Serve soup in with lemon wedges.

VARIATION: Eliminate barley. Ten minutes before end of cooking, add 1 package (10 ounces) frozen corn.

ZESTY GREEN PEA SOUP

■ *Serves 4* ■

Here's another way to mix canned soups for a tasty result. This can stand on its own for a lunch dish. Serve it with a sliced tomato vinaigrette salad and a hot biscuit, or with one of the tasty corn breads in this book.

1   can (10 3/4 ounces) split pea soup with
     ham and bacon
1   can (10 3/4 ounces) beef broth or bouillon
2   cans water (use one of the cans above)
1   can (8 1/2 ounces) young peas

1 Combine the undiluted soups and water in a saucepan and bring to boil, stirring often. Simmer 5 minutes or until blended and hot.

2 Add peas and heat through.

MICROWAVE: (1) Combine and blend pea soup, beef broth and water in 2-quart container. Cook on high (100%) 6 minutes. (2) Add peas and cook on high 2 minutes.

CREAM OF SCALLION SOUP WITH WATERCRESS SWIRL

■ *Serves 6* ■

1/2   cup (1 stick) unsalted butter or margarine
  4   cups sliced scallions, white and green
       parts
1/4   cup all purpose flour
  3   cups chicken broth, heated
  3   cups milk, heated
salt and pepper
  2   bunches watercress, 2 inches of stems cut
       off
  3   tablespoons milk, half-and-half or heavy
       cream

1 Melt butter in large saucepan, add scallions and cook slowly, covered, until limp, about 15 minutes; do not brown.

2 Sprinkle flour over scallions, mix well and cook 5 minutes longer. Add warmed broth and milk a little at a time, stirring. Simmer 15 minutes. Puree in batches in food processor. Season with salt and pepper.

3 Meanwhile, blanch watercress about 1 minute and squeeze dry. Puree with 3 tablespoons milk, half-and-half or heavy cream. Pour soup into individual bowls and swirl in spoonfuls of pureed watercress. Serve right away.

MICROWAVE: (1) Combine butter and scallions in 3-quart bowl. Cover and cook on HIGH (100%) 5 minutes. (2) Stir in flour, broth and milk. Cover and cook on HIGH 5 minutes. Let stand 5 minutes. Puree in food processor. Season with salt and pepper. (3) In another bowl, combine watercress with 1/2 cup water, cover and cook on HIGH 2 minutes. Puree with milk or cream and proceed as above.

POTATO SOUP WITH TOMATO AND TARRAGON

■ *Serves 4* ■

Serve this soup with Parmesan toast points. To make them, toast bread slices (if using French or Italian bread, grill or broil the slices). Spread lightly with butter and sprinkle with grated Parmesan cheese. Run under broiler.

1   can (10 3/4 ounces) condensed cream of
    potato soup
1   can (10 3/4 ounces) condensed tomato
    soup
1   can (10 3/4 ounces) chicken broth
1 1/4   cups skim or whole milk
1   tablespoon finely chopped fresh tarragon
    or 1/2 teaspoon dried
1   tablespoon butter, optional

1 Combine undiluted potato and tomato soups in saucepan. Add stock and milk and bring slowly to boiling point. Lower heat and simmer 3 to 4 minutes. Turn off heat.

2 Stir in tarragon. For a richer soup, add butter and allow to melt before serving.

MICROWAVE: (1) Combine all ingredients except butter in large, deep container. Blend with wire whisk. Cook on HIGH (100%) 5 minutes, then on MEDIUM-HIGH (70%) 5 minutes. Remove from oven, add butter if you wish, stir to melt and serve hot.

CREAM OF PUMPKIN SOUP

■ *Serves 4 to 6* ■

1   can (16 ounces) pumpkin puree
3   cups chicken broth
1   medium potato, coarsely chopped and
    parboiled
1   medium onion, coarsely chopped and
    parboiled
1   cup half-and-half
salt
pinch each of nutmeg and white pepper

1 Combine pumpkin, chicken broth, potato and onion in large saucepan and bring to boil. Lower heat and simmer, covered, about 15 minutes; be sure potato is cooked. Puree in food processor in batches and return to pan in which soup was cooked.

2 Add half-and-half, salt, nutmeg and pepper and bring just to boiling point. Serve hot.

MICROWAVE: (1) Combine potato and onion in 3-quart dish with 1/4 cup water. Cover and cook on HIGH (100%) 6 minutes. Drain. (2) Add pumpkin and chicken broth. Cover and cook on HIGH 6 minutes. Puree in processor and return to dish. Add half-and-half, salt, nutmeg and pepper. Cover and cook on MEDIUM-HIGH (70%) 4 minutes.

SUPERMARKET SAVVY

PUMPKINS

Pumpkins are low in calories and a good source of Vitamin A. If you have space, grow them in your garden and make your own puree. A 5-pound pumpkin will yield at least 4 cups puree, which will freeze for almost a year. They grow on long vines that produce two or three pumpkins. Many seed catalogues feature hybrids with amusing names like Jack-O-Lantern, Small Sugar and Funny Face, but the best for cooking are Spookies and Cheyenne Bush (they're smaller and their flesh is not so fibrous). Supermarkets sell whole pumpkins in season; if you want to make your own puree without growing them, here's how to do it.

Pumpkin Puree

makes about 4 cups

1 *firm, bright orange pumpkin, about 5 pounds, without cracks or blemishes*

1. Cut pumpkin in half. Remove and discard seeds (or reserve for toasting) and fibers. Slice and remove skin, then cut into 1-inch pieces.
2. Steam over boiling water for about 15 minutes or until chunks are tender; pierce with a knife or fork to test for doneness. Process in batches until pureed.

To Toast Pumpkin Seeds

2 *tablespoons vegetable oil*
1 *cup pumpkin seeds, washed and dried well*
1 *teaspoon ground cumin, optional*
salt

1. Oil your hands and rub seeds between them. Continue until all seeds are lightly rubbed. Place oiled seeds in large, flat baking pan and shake to distribute evenly.
2. Preheat oven to 400°F (200°C). Bake seeds 10 minutes. Sprinkle with cumin and salt, mix well and bake 5 more minutes or until seeds are toasted.

CHILLED CUCUMBER SOUP WITH SOUR CREAM

■ *Serves 4* ■

2 *large cucumbers, peeled and quartered lengthwise*
3 *cups chicken broth*
1/2 *cup dry white wine*
1 *tablespoon finely chopped fresh dill or 1 teaspoon dried dillweed*

1/4 *cup cold water*
2 *tablespoons cornstarch*
2/3 *cup sour cream*
salt and white pepper
chopped chives or scallions

1 Cut out seedy parts of cucumber. Chop cucumber coarsely and combine with about 1 cup broth in food processor. Blend until coarsely pureed. Transfer to saucepan and add remaining broth, wine and dill. Bring to boil, then lower heat and simmer 15 minutes, uncovered.

2 Combine water and cornstarch and pour into soup mixture. Simmer 5 minutes, stirring constantly. Refrigerate soup at least 2 hours.

3 To serve, stir in sour cream and season with salt and pepper. Serve in individual soup bowls, large cups or oversize glasses. Garnish with chopped chives or scallions.

MICROWAVE: (1) Combine ingredients as in step 1 above. Cover and cook on HIGH (100%) 8 minutes. Let stand 3 minutes. (2) Combine cornstarch and water and add to cucumber mixture. Stir well. Cover and cook on HIGH (100%) 2 minutes. (3) Refrigerate until well chilled. Stir in sour cream before serving.

SKIM MILK SWEET POTATO SOUP

■ *Serves 4* ■

Canned sweet potatoes work well here, but if you prefer, use an equivalent amount of fresh ones. In either case, this is an exotic and delicious soup. It keeps in the refrigerator for several days and may be frozen.

1   *quart skim milk*
2   *scallions, white and green parts, coarsely chopped*
2   *chicken bouillon cubes*
3   *tablespoons cornstarch*
1   *teaspoon curry powder*
1/2   *teaspoon allspice*
1   *can (16 ounces) sweet potatoes, drained*
2   *tablespoons sugar, optional*
2   *tablespoons fresh lemon juice*

1 Combine 1 cup milk, scallions, bouillon cubes, cornstarch, curry powder and allspice in food processor and blend well using on/off turns. Transfer to large saucepan.

2 Add remaining milk and cook mixture over medium heat until thick. Meanwhile, puree sweet potatoes in processor and add to milk mixture with sugar. Bring to boil, stirring frequently. Add lemon juice, stir again and serve hot.

MICROWAVE: (1) Follow step 1 above but transfer to large, deep container. Add remaining milk and cook on HIGH (100%) 6 minutes, stirring twice. (2) Puree sweet potatoes in food processor, and add to soup with sugar. Cook on MEDIUM-HIGH (70%) 5 minutes. Stir in lemon juice and serve.

TOMATO BISQUE WITH TARRAGON

■ *Serves 4* ■

There is nothing more beautiful and better tasting than a really red-ripe tomato, but when they are not around, canned plum tomatoes work well in this soup.

1   can (35 ounces) plum tomatoes
2   tablespoons butter or margarine
1   cup coarsely chopped onions
2   garlic cloves, coarsely chopped
1   cup water
1   large chicken bouillon cube
2   tablespoons chopped fresh tarragon or 1/2
    teaspoon dried
salt and pepper
1/2 cup mayonnaise

1 Put tomatoes and liquid through food mill to strain out seeds. Set aside.

2 Melt butter in saucepan and sauté onions just until they begin to change color. Add garlic and sauté 30 seconds longer.

3 Add tomatoes, water, bouillon cubes, tarragon, salt and pepper and bring to boil. Lower heat and simmer 10 minutes. Puree in food processor until smooth. Fold in mayonnaise and serve hot, or chill in refrigerator overnight and serve cold.

MICROWAVE: (1) Complete step 1 as above. (2) Combine butter and onions in 2-quart dish and cook on HIGH (100%) 2 minutes. (3) Add all remaining ingredients except mayonnaise. Cover with plastic and cook on HIGH (100%) 8 minutes. Let stand 3 minutes. Puree in food processor and fold in mayonnaise.

■   ■

CANNED TOMATO SOUP

Here are some ideas:

1. *To 1 can (10-1/2 ounces) condensed tomato soup, add an equal amount of fresh milk, 1 teaspoon curry, and a pinch of salt. Bring to the boil point, but do not boil. This serves 3. Into each serving, add 1 slice American cheese, cut into 1/2-inch cubes.*

2. *To 1 can (10-1/2 ounces) condensed tomato soup, add 1 can (10-1/2 ounces) condensed bean soup, 2-1/2 cups chicken stock or water. In a skillet, fry 1 slice bacon until crisp; remove bacon and set aside. In fat, saute 1/2 cup thinly sliced onions. When lightly browned, add to soup. Crumble bacon into soup and add a pinch of red pepper flakes. Serve hot.*

TANGY TOMATO CHOWDER WITH NOODLES

■ Serves 4 ■

Soupmaking at its easiest because most of the work has been done by can, packet, cube and so on.

1   can (16 ounces) Mexican- or
    Italian-style stewed tomatoes
1 1/2   cups water
1   chicken bouillon cube
1   packet (1.3 ounces) chicken noodle soup
    mix
1   teaspoon finely chopped fresh tarragon
    or 1/2 teaspoon dried
1/2   cup grated Parmesan or Romano cheese

1 Drain tomatoes, reserving liquid, and chop. Combine liquid with water and bouillon cube in saucepan and bring to boil.

2 Add soup mix, tarragon and chopped tomatoes and bring to boil. Lower heat and simmer 10 minutes. Serve hot, passing cheese separately.

MICROWAVE: (1) Combine liquid from stewed tomatoes, water and bouillon cube in 2-quart dish and cook on HIGH (100%) 4 minutes or until boiling. Stir in soup mix, tarragon and tomatoes and cook on HIGH (100%) 8 to 10 minutes. If not using carousel, stir 2 or 3 times.

TOMATO SOUP WITH LEMON

■ Serves 4 ■

Canned soups line many supermarket shelves, and they are usually good by themselves. One joy, however, is to combine them to create different textures and tastes. This one couldn't be simpler.

1   can (10 3/4 ounces) condensed tomato
    soup
1   can (10 3/4 ounces) chicken broth
1 1/2   cups water
1/2   teaspoon grated lemon zest
juice of 1 lemon
1   teaspoon finely chopped fresh tarragon
    or 1/2 teaspoon dried
1   tablespoon butter

1 Combine tomato soup, chicken broth, water, lemon zest and juice in saucepan and whisk over medium heat until well combined. Bring to boil, lower heat and simmer 5 minutes, stirring frequently.

2 Add tarragon and butter and stir until butter is melted. Serve hot.

MICROWAVE: (1) Blend tomato soup, chicken broth, water, lemon zest and juice in large, deep container and cook on HIGH (100%) 6 minutes. Stir in tarragon and butter.

CHILLED TOMATO SOUP WITH TEQUILA

▪ Serves 4 ▪

Although this recipe calls for tequila, you have two options: use vodka instead, or use neither and just enjoy the chilled tomato soup, which is loaded with flavor.

　4　cups canned plum tomatoes with liquid or
　　　ripe fresh tomatoes, blanched and cored
　1　package (1.9 ounces) French onion soup
　　　and recipe mix
　1　cup water
1/3　cup fresh celery leaves
juice of 1 small lemon
　2　tablespoons Worcestershire sauce
dash of hot pepper sauce
1/2　cup tequila

1 Put tomatoes with liquid through food mill to strain out seeds.

2 Combine all ingredients and process in batches in food processor or blender. Transfer soup to large bowl or nonaluminum pan, cover and refrigerate at least 1 hour.

3 Stir well before serving. For a super touch, serve in oversize wineglasses or double old-fashioned glasses.

CREAM OF TURNIP SOUP

▪ Serves 4 ▪

This is an interesting soup, especially for those not usually fond of turnips.

1 1/2　pounds white turnips, pared and sliced
　　　　(about 5 cups)
　　4　cups chicken broth
　　2　tablespoons chopped onion
　　1　tablespoon unsalted butter or margarine
　　2　cups milk, heated
salt and pepper
sugar, optional
　　1　tablespoon shredded carrot

1 Steam turnips in 2 cups chicken broth 10 to 15 minutes, replenishing broth as it cooks off to maintain 2 cups liquid.

2 In small skillet, sauté onion in butter until translucent. Puree onion with turnips, 2 cups broth and milk in food proc-

essor in batches. If too thick, thin with more broth. Season with salt and pepper. Taste soup; if it is bitter, add a little sugar to sweeten it.

3 Transfer hot soup to warm soup bowls, garnishing with shredded carrot.

MICROWAVE: (1) Peel and dice turnips and place in deep bowl. Add 1/2 cup chicken broth, cover and cook on HIGH (100%) 7 minutes. (2) Add remaining ingredients, cover and cook on HIGH 4 minutes. Puree and serve as above.

LIGHT VEGETABLE SOUP AROMATIC

■ *Serves 4* ■

A beautiful, delicate soup.

6	*cups canned chicken broth*
1	*lime*
1	*small, whole chili pepper, washed*
1	*lemon grass stalk, cut into 1-inch pieces, or 1 teaspoon dried*
12	*snow peas, strings removed, cut diagonally into 1/4-inch-wide julienne*
1/2	*small yellow crookneck squash, pulp removed, shredded*
2	*large red radishes, shredded*
1	*scallion, thinly sliced*

salt and pepper

1 Combine broth, grated lime zest (reserve pulp), chili and lemon grass in saucepan and bring to boil. Lower heat, cover and simmer 10 minutes.

2 Strain into another nonaluminum saucepan. Add juice from lime and return to boil. Add vegetables and cook 2 minutes. Check seasoning, adding salt and pepper as needed; do not add salt without tasting. Serve hot.

MICROWAVE: (1) Combine broth, grated lime zest, chili and lemon grass in deep container and cook on HIGH (100%) 4 minutes. (2) Strain into another container. Add lime juice and vegetables, cover and cook on HIGH 2 minutes. Add salt and pepper as needed; do not add salt without tasting.

SUPERMARKET SAVVY

LEMON GRASS

It's not unusual to find lemon grass in Bangkok, Singapore and Hong Kong and to enjoy it in many Oriental and Thai dishes. It is also easily found in the Chinatowns on the East and West coasts. What surprised me recently was to find this lemony, fragrant grass in my supermarket. When making a bouquet garni, tie one stalk of it with parsley, bay leaves and thyme for use in stews and sauces. It is delightful in light soups. Lemon grass leaves are used only to flavor foods; they are not edible. But if the inner section of the stalk is peeled and sliced thinly, it is good in salads and rice dishes (use 2 or 3 peeled stalks). It can also add a significant touch to marinades, and by all means, use it when grilling foods: put several tender inner stalks in chicken or fish cavities, or place some stalks in the wire baskets used to grill whole fish. A neat trick is to cut the grass into small pieces and put them in a teaball, which you can hang on the inner edge of the saucepan to lend fragrance to whatever is cooking.

VICHYSSOISE À LA SUPERMARCHÈ

■ *Serves 4* ■

A really good soup—in fact, one of the best in the book.

4 *cups water*
1 *pound white boiling potatoes, peeled and coarsely cut, or 1 can (16 ounces) peeled potatoes, cut up*
2 *cups chopped fresh leeks or onions*
3 *large or 6 small bouillon cubes*
   white pepper
1/2 *cup mayonnaise*
chopped chives, optional garnish

1 Combine all ingredients except mayonnaise in a large saucepan and bring to boil. Lower heat and simmer 15 minutes or until potatoes are tender.

2 Puree in food processor in batches until smooth. Return to saucepan and fold in mayonnaise. Serve hot. Or transfer to bowl, chill thoroughly and serve ice cold, garnished with chopped chives.

MICROWAVE: (1) Combine all ingredients except mayonnaise in large, deep container. Cover with plastic and cook on HIGH (100%) 10 minutes, stirring halfway through cooking. Let stand 3 minutes. Remove cover and fold in mayonnaise. Serve as above.

BAKED BEANS SUPREME

■ *Serves 6* ■

Cans and jars of baked beans can be enhanced, and here is one of the better ways to do it. Great for an outdoor picnic or kitchen party—double or triple recipe if needed.

2 *cans (16 ounces each) baked beans*
1/4 *cup maple syrup*
2 *tablespoons ketchup*
1/2 *teaspoon A-1 Steak sauce*
1/2 *teaspoon Worcestershire sauce*
4 *thin bacon slices, cut into 1/2-inch pieces*

Preheat oven to 350°F (180°C). Combine all ingredients except bacon in a baking dish. Sprinkle with bacon pieces. Bake uncovered about 30 minutes; if bacon has not browned, run under broiler.

MICROWAVE: (1) Combine all ingredients except bacon in microwave-safe dish, cover with plastic and cook on HIGH (100%) 8 minutes. Remove cover, sprinkle with bacon and cook on HIGH 3 minutes or until bacon is crisp.

BAKED BEANS TERIYAKI

■ Serves 12 ■

Baked beans are everyone's favorite. Here is a buffet or kitchen party idea—or make the whole recipe to last all week. Refrigerate and heat a little at a time in the microwave or in a small saucepan on top of the stove.

2   cans (1 pound, 12 ounces each) baked beans
1/3   cup teriyaki sauce
2   tablespoons spicy brown mustard

Combine all ingredients in large saucepan and stir well. Heat slowly, stirring occasionally, until heated through.

MICROWAVE: (1) Combine ingredients in 2-quart microwave-safe casserole. Cover and cook at MEDIUM-HIGH (70%) 8 to 12 minutes, stirring once during cooking. If not on carousel, stir 2 times. Let stand 2 minutes before serving.

SUPERMARKET SAVVY

BEANS

BLACK-EYED PEAS, also called cowpeas and yellow-eyed beans. They are often paired with rice and greens and are tasty with chicken and pork dishes.
BLACK TURTLE BEANS are used heavily in South American and Mexican soups.
BROAD BEANS, also called favas, are like limas and are associated with European dishes.
BUTTER BEANS, called limas too, are great just cooked and served with butter or margarine. They also combine well with ham and pork.
CRANBERRY BEANS are similar to pintos but have a very pink edge. They are popular in New England.
CHICKPEAS, also known as ceci beans or

garbanzos, are very versatile—used in soups and casseroles and as dips and spreads.
KIDNEY BEANS, one of the most popular, are used in many dishes. Try them cooked, cooled and served with oil/vinegar/onion dressing.
LENTILS, also very popular, were considered food for the gods in early Rome. They cook faster than other dried legumes.
PINTO BEANS, the staple of Mexican cooking, are a deep pinkish-brown. They're used in many ways.
SPLIT PEAS are yellow or green and are best known in split pea soup.
WHITE BEANS include the Great Northern, white kidney, marrow, navy and pea varieties.

GLAZED PINTO BEANS

■ *Serves 4* ■

1   small onion, chopped
4   ounces sliced bacon, cut into small pieces
1   can (29 ounces) pinto beans, drained
1/2   cup teriyaki baste and glaze sauce
2   teaspoons spicy brown mustard

1 Preheat oven to 400°F (200°C). Sauté onion and bacon in skillet until bacon is crisp. Drain fat. Add beans, teriyaki sauce and mustard and mix well.

2 Transfer to baking dish and bake 30 to 35 minutes.

MICROWAVE: (1) Combine onion and bacon in deep glass pie plate, cover and cook on HIGH (100%) 1 to 2 minutes. (2) Uncover, add remaining ingredients, recover and cook on MEDIUM-HIGH (70%) until hot and bubbling, 8 to 12 minutes. Stir once during cooking, twice if not on carousel. Let stand 2 minutes before serving.

MANY-COLORED BEAN DISH

■ *Serves 6 to 12* ■

1/2   cup each dried beans: Great Northern, red kidney, pinto and black
4   cups canned beef broth
2   tablespoons olive oil
1   large onion, coarsely chopped
3   garlic cloves, minced
1/4   cup dry sherry, Marsala or sweet vermouth
2   bell peppers (1 red, 1 yellow), cored, ribs and seeds removed, cut into 1/2-inch pieces
2   jalapeño peppers, cored, seeds removed, minced
1/2   cup chopped celery
1/2   cup chopped carrot
2   teaspoons ground cumin
freshly cooked rice
yogurt or sour cream for garnish

1 Soak beans overnight in water to cover generously, or quick-soak according to method on page 34.

2 Drain beans and place in large saucepan or soup pot. Add broth and simmer 1 1/2 hours, stirring occasionally.

3 Heat oil in skillet. Add onion, garlic and sherry, cover and simmer until onion is tender. Add peppers, celery, carrot and cumin and simmer 10 to 15 minutes or until vegetables are cooked. Add to beans and cook 4 to 5 minutes to blend flavors. Serve in warm soup bowls over hot rice. Top with a dollop of yogurt.

MICROWAVE: (1) To precook, combine beans and 2 cups water in 2-quart dish. Cover with plastic and cook on HIGH (100%) 15 minutes. Let stand 5 minutes. Remove cover, add 2 cups boiling water, recover and let stand 1 hour. Drain. (2) Add 4 cups broth to precooked beans, cover with 2 layers of plastic and cook on HIGH 35 minutes. Let stand 20 minutes. (3) In large dish, combine oil, onion, garlic, sherry, peppers, celery, carrot and cumin. Cover with plastic and cook on HIGH 5 minutes. Add vegetables to beans, stir well, recover and cook on HIGH 5 minutes.

NEW ORLEANS LENTILS WITH RED PEPPERS

■ *Serves 8* ■

Lentils and red peppers served over brown rice make a wonderful lunch dish. This may also be served as a side dish with roasted or charcoal-broiled meats and fowl—for example, grilled sausage links.

1	*cup dried lentils, rinsed and picked over*
1/4	*cup olive oil*
2	*large red bell peppers, cored, ribs and seeds removed, cut into 1/2-inch cubes*
2	*large onions, cut into 1/2-inch cubes*
1 1/2	*cups chopped canned plum tomatoes*
1	*teaspoon finely chopped fresh thyme or 1/4 teaspoon dried*

salt and pepper
pinch of red pepper flakes
4	*cups cooked brown rice*

1 Soak lentils overnight in water to cover generously, or quick-soak according to method on page 34.

2 Place drained lentils in heavy saucepan and add water to cover. Bring to boil, cover with tight lid and cook 1 hour or until tender; do not overcook.

3 Heat olive oil in large nonstick skillet and sauté peppers and onions until onions are transparent. Add tomatoes, thyme, salt, pepper and pepper flakes and simmer 5 minutes.

4 Drain lentils and add them to skillet. Cover and simmer 5 minutes longer. Serve over brown rice, or serve rice separately.

MICROWAVE: (1) Cook lentils in 2 1/2-quart dish with 4 cups water, covered with 2 layers plastic, on HIGH (100%) 35 minutes. Let stand 20 minutes. (2) In another dish, cook oil, peppers and onions on HIGH 3 minutes. Add tomatoes, thyme, salt, pepper and pepper flakes and cook 3 minutes on HIGH. (3) Add lentils, cover with plastic and cook on HIGH 4 minutes.

15-CALORIE CHILI BEAN DIP

■ *Serves 4* ■

*T*he ideal appetizer: it contains only 15 calories per tablespoon, with barely a trace of fat. And it's high in fiber.

1   *can (15 ounces) kidney beans, drained, 3 tablespoons liquid reserved*
1   *tablespoon vinegar*
1   *teaspoon chili powder*
1/4 *teaspoon ground cumin*
1   *tablespoon grated onion*
1   *tablespoon finely chopped parsley*
crisp vegetable sticks

1 Combine drained beans, liquid, vinegar, chili powder and cumin in processor or blender and process until smooth. Transfer mixture to bowl and fold in onion and parsley.

2 Refrigerate until well chilled and serve with ice-cold vegetable sticks.

GARBANZO BEAN DIP

■ *Makes 2 cups* ■

*S*coop this into a serving bowl and make a well in the center for 2 tablespoons olive oil. Garnish with chopped parsley.

1   *can (15 to 16 ounces) garbanzos, drained*
3   *tablespoons fresh lemon juice*
3   *tablespoons minced onion*
2   *large garlic cloves, minced*
1/2 *cup olive oil*
2   *tablespoons sour cream*
Salt and pepper

1 Puree garbanzos, lemon juice, onion and garlic in food processor. With machine running, pour in oil and process 10 seconds.

2 Transfer mixture to bowl. Fold in sour cream, salt and pepper. Cover and refrigerate at least 4 hours. Serve as above.

FRESH AND DRIED PASTA AND EXOTIC RICES

4

Pasta outsells all other foods of Italian origin manufactured in the U.S. today, and much of it is produced in factories owned or managed by Americans of Italian descent. In the U.S., pasta is enriched with niacin, thiamine, riboflavin and iron.

On some packages of imported factory-made pasta will be the words *pasta di pura semola di grano duro,* meaning that the product is made with the fine flour obtained from the cleaned endosperm or heart of the durum (hard) wheat grain. This is the cream of wheat and you should buy these brands. Look also for the fresh pasta section in your supermarket. You may be able to buy it by the sheet, which they will cut to size, or in plastic packages which you can empty into boiling water soon after you reach home. The quality of fresh pasta will vary, but I rarely make my own these days since I'm fond of what I get at my supermarket.

Do not run cooked pasta under hot or cold water. Drain it in a colander and shake it well to remove as much water as possible (you don't want water in the pasta to dilute your tasty sauce). If draining tubular pasta, shells, etc., shake harder to dislodge water trapped inside the pasta shapes. Return it to the pan in which it cooked, add 1 to 2 tablespoons butter or margarine, toss, add some sauce, toss again and transfer to warmed bowl or platter; add remaining sauce to top. If you're using Parmesan, add some with the butter or margarine but always serve more cheese after the pasta is presented.

EXPRESS CHECK-OUT

PASTA AND RICES

1 A colander is indispensable in cooking pasta. Get a good stainless steel one, large enough to hold 2 or more pounds of pasta. You'll find other uses for it also.

2 Grated cheeses (Parmesan, Romano, etc.), are available in supermarkets, but it is best to buy bulk pieces and grate cheese fresh as needed. Store bulk pieces wrapped tightly in plastic.

3 Canned plum tomatoes are good in many dishes, not just pasta, but they should be put through a food mill, as it removes the seeds and saves many hours of work in pureeing. Electric mixers, blenders and food processors are not good for pureeing tomatoes because they crush the seeds and integrate them into the puree—which causes bitterness.

4 If your supermarket sells fresh sheets of pasta, buy them whole and you can make your own shapes at home—*maltagliati* (oddball cuts), *quadrucci* (little squares, about 1/2 inch), *cannelloni* (rectangles 3 by 4 inches to fill as you desire), *farfalle* (butterflies cut 1 by 2 inches, pinched at the center), and of course ravioli, manicotti and lasagna.

5 Consider seafood with pasta. Look for the clam and scallop recipes in this chapter and create some of your own. As a rule, cheese is not added to pasta with fish sauces, but it's all a matter of taste.

6 Rice will triple or quadruple in bulk while cooking so use a large, heavy pan to accommodate the expansion and prevent scorching.

7 If water is hard, add one of the following while cooking to get spanking white rice: 1 tablespoon white vinegar, 1/2 teaspoon cream of tartar or 1 teaspoon fresh lemon juice.

8 To reheat leftover rice: add to boiling salted water, milk, or meat, fish or poultry stock, and cook 5 minutes. Drain and let dry slightly.

9 For perfect Carolina-type rice to serve 4, combine 1 cup long-grain rice, 1 1/2 cups water, 1 teaspoon fresh lemon juice, 1/2 teaspoon salt and 2 tablespoons butter. Bring to boil. Stir only once (repeat, only once). Lower heat; cook until water is absorbed and rice is dry, about 20 minutes.

PASTA WITH BACON, ONION AND TOMATOES

■ *Serves 4* ■

Packages of soup and recipe mixes are abundant in supermarkets. Easy to combine with water and other liquids to prepare a speedy meal, they go especially well with pastas of all kinds. Here is a good example and recipe—easy, nutritious and tasty.

> 8 *thin slices bacon, coarsely chopped*
> 1 *large onion, coarsely chopped*
> 1 1/4 *cups water*
> 1/2 *cup half-and-half*
> 1 *package (2.4 ounces) tomato with basil soup and recipe mix*
> *pinch red pepper flakes*
> *fresh or dried pasta (angel hair, spaghetti or fettuccine)*
> *1/2 to 1 cup grated Parmesan cheese*

1 Cook bacon in large skillet until crisp. Remove bacon and leave about 3 tablespoons of fat in pan. Sauté onion in bacon fat until it begins to color, about 6 to 8 minutes. Crumble cooled bacon and set aside.

2 In a bowl, combine water, half and half, soup mix and pepper flakes and mix well. Add to onions in skillet, bring to boil and cook 1 minute, stirring.

3 Cook pasta, drain (if using dried pasta, drain well; if fresh, leave moist) and add to sauce in skillet. Toss a few seconds over low heat to bring together pasta and sauce. Add crumbled bacon to top. Serve right away, passing cheese.

MICROWAVE: (1) Arrange 7 slices bacon on 3 or 4 paper towels. Cover with 2 more paper towels and cook on HIGH (100%) 6 minutes. Set bacon aside to crisp, then cool and crumble. (2) Cut 1 uncooked bacon slice into 1/2-inch pieces. Place in 3-quart bowl with onion, cover and cook on HIGH 3 minutes.

 SUPERMARKET SAVVY
■ ■ ■ ■ ■ ■ ■ ■ ■ ■ ■ ■ ■ ■ ■ ■ ■ ■

HIGH-PROTEIN PASTA

Consider the high-protein pasta now on many supermarket shelves. These are made with wholewheat, soy or Jerusalem artichoke flours fortified with natural protein and wheat gluten. Manufacturers claim considerably more protein in these products (as much as 70 percent more). They further emphasize their natural ingredients and no artificial enrichment. As a rule, no preservatives or chemicals are added to these products, nor is salt. The Jerusalem artichoke is 100-percent nonstarch; the tubers are dehydrated into an artichoke powder which retains all its natural nutrients. High-protein pastas come in all sizes and shapes, are darker in color, take a little longer to cook and may be sauced, baked or filled like homemade or fresh and regular dried pasta.

Add water, half-and-half, soup mix and pepper flakes. Cover and cook on MEDIUM HIGH (70%) 5 minutes or until boiling. (3) Cook pasta on stovetop, drain and add sauce. Serve with cheese.

SUPERMARKET PASTA AND BEANS

■ *Serves 8* ■

Here the natural proteins of pasta, beans and cheese are super for a family meal. This provides a meat-free meal if you use water instead of beef broth, but use the broth. It's almost fat-free and packed with flavor.

2 tablespoons olive oil
2 garlic cloves, minced
2 cans (16 ounces each) stewed tomatoes (see Note)
3 cups beef broth or water
1/4 cup chopped fresh parsley
1 teaspoon chopped fresh thyme or 1/2 teaspoon dried
2 cans (19 ounces each) cannellini beans, drained
12 ounces small shaped pasta, such as elbows, *radiatore* (radiators) *or farfalle* (butterflies)
1/2 cup grated Parmesan cheese

1 Heat oil in large pot and sauté garlic just until it begins to color. Add tomatoes, broth or water, parsley and thyme and cook 10 minutes. Add beans.

2 Meanwhile, cook and drain pasta. Add cooked pasta to tomato mixture and heat through. (This is a stew, not a soup. If you want a thinner consistency, add 1/2 to 1 cup or more of broth or water.)

3 Divide among warm bowls and serve, passing cheese separately.

Note: If using plain stewed tomatoes, add a sprinkle of red pepper flakes after adding beans. If using "Mexican style" or "Cajun style" tomatoes, use as is.

SUPERMARKET SAVVY

■ ■ ■ ■ ■ ■ ■ ■ ■ ■ ■ ■ ■ ■ ■ ■ ■ ■ ■ ■

PASTA AND PROTEIN

Many Americans eat more protein than they need. Meat, cheese and eggs, while high in protein, also contain saturated fat and cholesterol, which pose a risk to a healthy heart. Nonmeat protein foods, such as pasta and beans, may actually reduce the intake of fat and cholesterol.

But can a meal without meat provide the needed protein? The answer seems to be yes. Combine pasta with low-fat dairy products, or with dried peas or beans. The famous Italian dish *pasta e fagioli* (pasta and beans) is a perfect food in this sense, as it provides the proper amino acids—in other words, the needed protein.

MICROWAVE: (1) Combine oil, garlic, tomatoes, broth, and parsley in 3-quart bowl. Cover and cook on HIGH (100%) 6 minutes. Add beans, cover and cook on HIGH 6 minutes. (2) Cook pasta on stovetop, drain and add to beans. Stir well. Let stand 5 minutes before serving.

ANGEL HAIR PASTA WITH ONIONS AND RED BELL PEPPER

■ *Serves 2 to 3 as entree, 6 as first course* ■

Ahealthy, easy and very tasty appetizer or entree, and pretty to look at too.

1 tablespoon vegetable or olive oil
1 red bell pepper, cored, ribs and seeds removed, cut into 1/2-inch cubes
2 cups water
1 package (1.2 to 1.3 ounces) onion soup mix
8 ounces pasta
1/2 cup grated Parmesan cheese
1/4 cup finely chopped scallions

1 Heat oil in skillet and sauté red pepper pieces until tender.

2 Bring water to boil in saucepan and add soup mix. Simmer 8 to 10 minutes.

3 Cook pasta, drain well and return to pan in which it cooked. Add onion mixture and red peppers. Toss and cook over medium heat 2 minutes to blend flavors. Divide among warm individual plates and sprinkle with scallions. Serve right away.

BROCCOLI DI RAPE AND PASTA

■ *Serves 4* ■

4 cups coarsely chopped broccoli di rape
1/4 cup olive oil
3 garlic cloves, minced
pinch of red pepper flakes
salt and pepper
8 ounces pasta (spaghetti, vermicelli, etc.), cooked and drained
1/2 cup or more grated Parmesan cheese

1 Cut 1/2 inch or so off stems of broccoli di rape and peel away strings as you do with celery. Rinse several times. Drain and cut into 2-inch pieces. Cook in boiling salted water until tender.

2 Heat oil in large skillet and cook garlic just until it begins to change color. Add cooked broccoli to skillet with pepper flakes, salt and pepper and toss. Add cooked pasta and heat for just a minute or two while tossing. Served with grated cheese.

MICROWAVE: Cook pasta in boiling water on stovetop. (1) Prepare broccoli as in step 1 above. (2) Combine oil and garlic in a 2- or 3-quart dish, cover with plastic and cook on HIGH (100%) 3 minutes. Remove from oven and remove plastic. (3) Add broccoli and stir. Recover and cook again on HIGH 3 minutes. Remove from oven and add to cooked pasta and add pepper flakes, salt and pepper. Toss well and serve with cheese.

FARFALLE AND FENNEL SALAD

■ *Serves 4* ■

Farfalle pasta is in the shape of butterflies or bows. Here they are in an unusual coupling with fennel—which I hope you'll use fresh, if you can.

1/3 cup corn oil
1/3 cup white wine vinegar
1/3 cup water
1 package (1.4 ounces) vegetable soup and recipe mix
1/2 cup finely chopped fresh fennel or 1/2 teaspoon fennel seed
1 garlic clove, minced
1 tablespoon chopped parsley
8 ounces farfalle, cooked and drained

1 Whisk oil, vinegar and water in a bowl. Add soup mix and whisk again. Add fennel, garlic and parsley and let stand at room temperature about 30 minutes.

2 Add cooked farfalle, toss well, cover and refrigerate if not using soon. Remove from refrigerator 30 minutes before serving and stir.

PASTA WITH SUPERMARKET SAUSAGE AND MUSHROOMS

■ *Serves 4 to 6* ■

Italian-style sausage is found in most supermarkets; although it contains more fat than it should, it simply has to be cooked off and discarded. Almost any type of pasta will work here—try shapes such as wheels or corkscrews.

1 pound Italian-style sausage
3 tablespoons olive or vegetable oil
3 tablespoons butter or margarine
8 ounces mushrooms, thinly sliced
1 garlic clove, minced
1 cup frozen green peas
   salt and pepper
1 pound pasta
1 cup grated Parmesan or Romano cheese

1 Brown sausage in 1 tablespoon oil in large skillet, puncturing sausage as it cooks to help release fat. When almost brown, remove sausage and cut into 1-inch pieces. Return to skillet and finish browning for 2 to 3 minutes. Remove sausage pieces with a slotted spoon and discard all fat.

2 Melt butter in same skillet, add cooked sausage and mushrooms and cook 3 minutes, stirring frequently. Add garlic, peas, salt and pepper, cover and cook 3 minutes longer.

3 Cook pasta, drain and return to pan in which it cooked. Add half the cheese and half the sauce. Toss well and transfer to warmed bowl. Add remaining sauce and serve with remaining cheese.

TORTELLINI IN WINE-FLAVORED BROTH

■ *Serves 4* ■

The fresh pasta sold in clear containers in the supermarket is wonderfully appealing. This will serve eight as a first course. Small ravioli or other filled pasta may be used in place of tortellini.

4 1/2   cups water
1/2   cup dry white wine
1   package (1.4 ounces) vegetable soup and recipe mix
8 to 9 ounces cheese-filled tortellini
2   cups lightly packed julienned fresh spinach leaves
1/2 to 3/4 cup grated Parmesan cheese

1 Bring water and wine to boil in large saucepan and immediately add soup mix. Return to boil, lower heat and simmer, partially covered, 12 minutes.

2 Add pasta to soup and stir frequently but gently. The tortellini will rise to the top when cooked; remove one to taste for doneness. Quickly stir in spinach and serve, passing grated cheese separately.

SPAGHETTI WITH CLASSIC TOMATO AND BUTTER SAUCE

■ *Serves 3 to 4* ■

This is classic because it is simple and good. Don't expect overcooked meat with dark red tomato sauce, for this isn't it.

2   cups canned plum tomatoes with 1/2 cup juice
1/2   cup (1 stick) butter, cut into 8 pats
1   medium onion, peeled and quartered
1   medium carrot, peeled and quartered
1   teaspoon sugar, if needed
salt
8   ounces spaghetti, cooked and drained

1 Put tomatoes and juice through food mill to remove seeds and any skin that was not removed before canning. Pour into medium saucepan. Add butter, onion and carrot pieces and simmer over low heat 40 minutes, stirring frequently. Taste and add sugar if needed. Season with salt.

2 Reserve vegetables and toss sauce with cooked pasta. Add vegetables to side of pasta dish(es).

MICROWAVE: (1) Combine sauce ingredients in 2-quart dish, cover and cook on HIGH (100%) 15 minutes. (2) Cook spaghetti on stovetop and proceed as above.

THIN SPAGHETTI WITH SHRIMP AND DILL

■ *Serves 4 to 6* ■

There are two wonderful ways to prepare this simple, elegant dish. Serve both at room temperature. (1) Mix all the sauce ingredients with just-cooked pasta and serve at room temperature. (2) Combine all ingredients except shrimp, spaghetti and garnish in large, deep skillet. Bring to boil, add shrimp and cook 1 minute. Add cooked pasta and toss for 1 to 2 minutes, adding parsley and scallions.

3/4   *cup olive oil*
1/3   *cup dry white wine*
  2   *tablespoons finely chopped fresh dill or 1 teaspoon dried dillweed*
  2   *teaspoons salt*
black pepper
  1   *pound shrimp, shelled, deveined, cooked and halved lengthwise*
  8   *ounces thin spaghetti*
1/4   *cup each chopped fresh parsley and scallions*

1 Combine oil, wine, dill, salt and pepper in large bowl and mix until blended. Add shrimp and let marinate about 30 minutes.

2 Cook spaghetti, drain well and place in a large bowl or platter. Add sauce and toss well.

PASTA WITH PECANS AND GORGONZOLA

■ *Serves 4 as entree, 6 to 8 as appetizer* ■

Wonderful flavors combine here and the crunch of pecans is a treat.

  4   *tablespoons butter or margarine*
1/2   *cup pecan halves, coarsely chopped*
1/4   *cup dry white wine*
  1   *package (0.9 ounces) hollandaise sauce mix*
  1   *cup milk*
  4   *ounces Gorgonzola or blue cheese, crumbled*
  8   *ounces small pasta such as farfalle*
  2   *tablespoons chopped fresh parsley*
black pepper

1 Melt 1 tablespoon butter in a saucepan and sauté pecans until light brown. Transfer to small bowl and set aside.

2 Melt remaining butter in same saucepan. Add wine and boil 30 seconds.

3 Add packaged mix and milk to saucepan and stir well. Bring to boil, lower heat and simmer 1 minute. Remove from heat and add Gorgonzola.

4 Cook pasta and drain well. Return to pan in which it cooked. Add sauce, pecans and parsley. Toss 1 minute over medium heat and serve right away.

PENNE WITH PESTO AND DANDELION

■ *Serves 4* ■

Broccoli rape, sometimes called *rapini,* is a good substitute for the dandelion. So is arugula, which seems always available in supermarkets these days. All these greens are delicious but keep in mind that they are a bit bitter (that's what makes them good). If you use *rapini,* peel the strings on the stems and discard, as you do with celery.

8 ounces penne pasta
12 ounces fresh dandelions, rapini or arugula; if none if these is available, use 1 package (10 ounces) frozen broccoli or spinach
1/4 cup butter
1 packet (1/2 ounce) pesto sauce (for 8 ounces of pasta), prepared according to package directions
1/2 cup grated Parmesan cheese (or half-and-half Romano and Parmesan)
1 cup toasted walnuts
additional grated cheese

1 Cook pasta until al dente. Drain and keep warm.

2 Cut dandelion into 2- to 3-inch pieces. Drop into boiling water and cook about 5 minutes (the young, tender leaves won't take as long as the mature ones). Drain and return to pan in which they cooked. Add butter and toss.

3 Add pasta, pesto sauce, cheese and walnuts to greens and toss. Serve hot with more grated cheese.

SPAGHETTI WITH TOMATO, BASIL AND BACON

■ *Serves 4* ■

Soup mixes are versatile; here's a special way to use one of them.

8 thin slices bacon
1 large onion, coarsely chopped
1 garlic clove, minced
1 1/4 cups water
1/4 cup half-and-half
1 package (2.3 ounces) tomato with basil soup and recipe mix
pinch of red pepper flakes
8 ounces spaghetti, cooked and drained
1/4 cup chopped parsley or scallions

1 Cook bacon in skillet until crisp. Drain on paper towels, then crumble. Dis-card all but 3 tablespoons fat from skillet. Add onion and sauté until lightly browned, about 8 minutes. Add garlic, stir and cook 1 minute longer.

2 Combine water, half-and-half, soup mix and red pepper in bowl and mix until blended. Add to skillet. Bring to boil, lower heat and simmer 3 to 4 minutes. Pour over spaghetti and toss; add bacon and toss lightly. Garnish with parsley or scallion.

ZITI WITH RICOTTA AND A SAUTÉ OF ZUCCHINI, WALNUTS AND FRESH TOMATO

■ *Serves 8* ■

Small ziti are available in most supermarkets; however, you can use other pasta such as shells or twists. This is a simple, hearty and healthy dish. The tomato cubes should not be cooked—the idea is just to heat them through. The texture of the tomatoes should be somewhat raw and fresh.

1	pound small ziti
2	cups low-fat ricotta cheese
1/4	cup olive oil
4	zucchini (1 x 6 inches each), cut into 2-inch-long strips
2	garlic cloves, minced
1	cup coarsely chopped walnuts

pinch of red pepper flakes
salt and pepper

1	large ripe tomato, cored and cut into cubes
1/2	cup grated Parmesan cheese

1 Cook ziti to al dente stage; drain. Add ricotta and toss well to coat pasta.

2 Heat oil in large skillet. Add zucchini and cook, stirring, until lightly colored but still firm. Add garlic and walnuts and sauté 1 minute. Add pepper flakes, salt and pepper.

3 Add tomato cubes and warm through. Transfer sauce to pasta mixture. Add Parmesan, toss well and serve right away.

VERMICELLI WITH WHITE CLAM SAUCE

■ *Serves 4 to 6* ■

White sauces are available in cans but it is easy to make your own using canned clams. Carrots, scallions and red pepper flakes not only add to the taste but make a festive-looking dish.

1/4	cup olive oil
1/4	cup butter or margarine
1	carrot, peeled and finely diced
2	garlic cloves, minced
1/2	cup finely chopped scallions, including some green part

1	cup bottled clam juice
1	cup dry white wine
1/4	cup chopped fresh parsley

pinch of red pepper flakes

3	cans (7 1/2 ounces each) minced clams
1	pound vermicelli

1 Heat oil with butter in large skillet, add carrot and cook 5 minutes. Add garlic and scallions and cook just until they begin to color. Add clam juice and wine and bring to boil, then lower heat and simmer 10 minutes.

2 Add parsley, pepper flakes and canned clams with their juices and heat 3 to 4 minutes.

3 Meanwhile, cook vermicelli. Drain and toss with sauce. Adjust seasoning and serve.

MICROWAVE: (1) Heat oil with butter in 2-quart bowl on HIGH (100%) 45 seconds. Add carrot, garlic, scallions, clam juice and wine and cook uncovered on HIGH 6 minutes. Add parsley, pepper flakes and clams with juices and cook on HIGH 2 minutes. Toss with cooked pasta.

FETTUCCINE WITH CREAM OF LEEK SAUCE

■ *Serves 4* ■

*T*he sauce goes especially well with spinach fettuccine, but other types will work here also. If you use egg fettuccine, sprinkle some chives on top for a bit of color.

1	package (2.4 ounces) leek soup and recipe mix
1	cup water
1	pint half-and-half
1/4	teaspoon nutmeg
1 1/2	cups grated Parmesan cheese
8	ounces fettuccine, cooked
2	tablespoons chopped chives

black pepper

1 Combine soup mix and water in saucepan and bring to boil, stirring. Add half-and-half and nutmeg and bring almost to boil. Remove from heat, add cheese right away and stir until well blended.

2 Pour sauce over cooked fettuccine and add chives. Toss until well mixed. Divide among 4 warm plates, sprinkle liberally with black pepper and offer more cheese to be added on top.

MICROWAVE: (1) Combine soup mix, water, half-and-half and nutmeg in deep bowl, cover and cook on MEDIUM-HIGH (70%) 4 minutes. (2) Add cheese, cover and cook on MEDIUM (50%) 3 minutes. (3) Add sauce to cooked pasta, garnish with chives and sprinkle with black pepper.

ROQUEFORT AND RIGATONI

■ *Makes 2 1/2 cups sauce for 1 pound pasta* ■

Everyone associates pasta with Parmesan or Romano cheese, but some other cheeses do well also. Generally, it is best to combine stronger cheeses with heavier pasta, as in this case where Roquefort is paired with rigatoni.

2   tablespoons butter or margarine
2   tablespoons all purpose flour
2 1/2   cups milk
5   ounces Roquefort cheese, crumbled (3/4 to 1 cup)
salt and pepper
1   pound rigatoni, cooked and drained

1 Melt butter in heavy saucepan, add flour and cook over low heat, stirring, 4 to 5 minutes; do not brown.

2 Add milk about 1/2 cup at a time, cooking and stirring until smooth after each addition. When mixture has thickened, turn heat to lowest setting and simmer 30 minutes, stirring every 5 minutes or so.

3 Remove from heat and add cheese, salt and pepper. Toss with freshly cooked rigatoni and serve.

MICROWAVE: (1) Place butter in 2-quart dish and cook on HIGH (100%) 30 seconds. Stir in flour, add milk and cook on MEDIUM-HIGH (70%) until thickened, 4 to 6 minutes, stirring twice. (2) Stir in cheese and cook on MEDIUM-HIGH 1 minute longer. Stir until cheese melts to tiny lumps. Add salt and pepper and toss with cooked pasta.

SUPERMARKET SAVVY

■ ■

COOKING PASTA

To get this amount of cooked pasta:

1 cup	2 cups	4 cups	6 cups	8 cups

Use this amount of dry pasta:

2/3 c. (2 oz.)	1 1/4 c. (4 oz.)	2 1/2 c. (8 oz.)	3 3/4 c. (12 oz.)	5 c. (16 oz.)

OLD-FASHIONED WILD RICE SOUP

■ *Serves 4 to 6* ■

This is a wonderful and hearty soup; feature it as an entree or as a first course for an important dinner, such as Thanksgiving.

> 3   tablespoons unsalted butter or margarine
> 1   thick or 2 thin slices hickory-smoked bacon, cut into small pieces
> 2/3   cup wild rice, washed and drained
> 1   small onion, diced
> 1/2   cup thinly sliced celery
> 1/2   cup diced carrot
> 4 1/2   cups canned chicken broth, heated
> 1 1/2   cups heavy cream
> 1   tablespoon all purpose flour

salt and white pepper
chopped fresh parsley for garnish

1 Melt 2 tablespoons butter in a large saucepan or soup pot and sauté bacon with rice, onion, celery and carrot until vegetables are tender, 3 to 4 minutes.

2 Add broth and bring to boil, stirring frequently. Lower heat, cover and simmer 40 minutes or until rice is tender.

3 Add cream. Blend remaining butter with flour in a small dish, add to soup and stir for a minute or so until soup thickens. Add salt and pepper. Serve in warm soup bowls and add a sprinkle of fresh parsley to each.

MICROWAVE: (1) Cook wild rice according to method on this page. (2) Combine 2 tablespoons butter, bacon, onion, celery and carrot in deep dish or bowl and cook on HIGH (100%) 4 minutes. Add broth, cover and cook on HIGH 2 minutes. (3) Blend remaining butter with flour and add to mixture with cream, salt and pepper. Cook on HIGH 2 minutes. Add cooked rice, recover and cook on HIGH 1 minute.

COOKING WILD RICE

To make 1 1/2 cups cooked wild rice, place 1/2 cup uncooked wild rice in a strainer and rinse under running water. Transfer rice to a large bowl, cover with water and let stand an hour or so. Drain and rinse under cool water.

Combine rice and 2 cups water (or to enrich, use defatted chicken or beef broth) in a saucepan and bring to boil, stirring constantly. Lower heat, cover and simmer about 45 minutes or until rice is al dente. If liquid evaporates too quickly, add a little more water or broth, but this should not be necessary unless heat is too high.

MICROWAVE: Combine 1/2 cup wild rice with 1 cup water and cook on HIGH (100%) 7 minutes. Let stand 15 minutes. If cooking 2/3 cup rice, use 1 1/3 cups water, cook on HIGH 10 minutes and let stand 15 minutes. If cooking 1 cup rice, use 2 cups water, cook on HIGH 12 minutes and let stand 15 minutes.

RICE WITH OLIVES, CHIVES AND CILANTRO

■ *Serves 4 to 6* ■

Picante sauce can be quite hot, so you may want to consider medium or mild. They're all readily available.

1 1/2 *cups water*
  3/4 *cup bottled or canned picante sauce (hot, medium or mild)*
    1 *cup converted long-grain rice*
    1 *tablespoon butter or margarine pinch of salt*
  1/2 *cup sliced pitted olives*
    2 *tablespoons finely chopped cilantro*

1 Combine water and picante sauce in a saucepan and bring to boil. Add rice, butter and salt and return to boil. Lower heat, cover and simmer 20 minutes.

2 Remove from heat and uncover. Stir in olives and cilantro, cover again and let stand 5 minutes before serving.

MICROWAVE: (1) Combine water, picante sauce, rice, butter and salt in 2-quart dish. Cover and cook on HIGH (100%) 5 minutes, then on MEDIUM (50%) 20 minutes. (2) Proceed with step 2 above.

BROWNED WALNUT PILAF

■ *Serves 4 to 6* ■

White rice, long- or short-grain, cooked with browned walnuts and butter makes a delicious combination of flavors that go especially well with broiled, baked or grilled chicken.

    2 *cups canned chicken broth*
    1 *cup long-grain converted rice*
  1/4 *cup butter or margarine*
  3/4 *cup finely chopped walnuts*
generous pinch of nutmeg

1 Bring broth to boil and add rice. Return to boil, lower heat and simmer, covered, for 20 minutes or until rice is tender.

2 Heat butter slowly in a skillet until lightly browned. Add walnuts and sauté 1 minute, stirring. Remove from heat, stir in nutmeg and fold into rice.

MICROWAVE: (1) Combine broth, rice and 2 tablespoons butter in 2-quart dish. Cover and cook on HIGH (100%) 5 minutes. Reduce to MEDIUM (50%) and cook 20 minutes. Let stand 5 minutes. (2) While rice is standing, heat remaining butter or margarine in skillet on top of stove and sauté walnuts until lightly browned. Add to rice with nutmeg, stir lightly and serve.

SPICY WILD RICE

■ *Serves 4 to 6* ■

Not long ago, wild rice was available only through mail order or food specialty stores, but it is now found on the shelves of most supermarkets. It is a good bit more expensive than the more standard rices, but the end products are quite different. For a gourmet's taste treat, try this one.

1   cup wild rice
2   cups water
1   tablespoon peanut or vegetable oil
1   carrot, finely diced
1   onion, finely diced
pinch of red pepper flakes
2   tablespoons light soy sauce

1 Rinse rice in strainer under cool running water. Transfer to saucepan. Add water and bring to boil, then lower heat, cover and simmer 30 to 35 minutes or until rice is al dente; do not overcook.

2 Meanwhile, heat oil in another saucepan. Sauté carrot and onion until onion is translucent and carrot is tender. Add red pepper flakes and soy sauce and remove from heat.

3 When rice is almost done, reheat onion and carrot mixture. Add cooked rice and toss several times over high heat. Serve immediately.

MICROWAVE: (1) Combine oil, carrot and onion in large bowl and cook on HIGH (100%) 3 minutes. (2) Stir in washed rice, water and red pepper flakes. Cover and cook on HIGH 12 minutes. Let stand 15 minutes. Drain if needed. Add soy sauce, toss lightly and serve.

SHALLOTS AND RICE

■ *Serves 4 to 6* ■

I've not found frozen or canned shallots (they may exist), but it's no big deal to peel a cup of them for this tasty dish.

1   cup finely chopped shallots
2   tablespoons butter or margarine
1   tablespoon olive or vegetable oil
2   cups water
1/2   cup dry white wine
1   cup converted long-grain rice
pinch of salt
1/2   cup chopped fresh parsley
pepper

1 Sauté shallots in 1 tablespoon butter and oil until lightly browned at edges. Set aside.

2 Bring water and wine to boil in saucepan; add rice, remaining butter and salt. Return to boil, lower heat, cover tightly and simmer 20 minutes. Remove from heat.

Continued on next page

3 Add shallots, parsley and pepper. Cover and let stand about 5 minutes before serving.

MICROWAVE: (1) Place 1 tablespoon butter and oil in 2-quart shallow dish and heat on high (100%) 30 seconds. Add shallots, toss well and cook on HIGH 4 to 6 minutes or until shallots are crisp. Remove and set aside. (2) In same dish, combine water, wine, rice, remaining butter and salt. Cover and cook on HIGH 5 minutes. Reduce power to MEDIUM (50%) and cook 20 minutes. (3) Remove cover, add shallots, parsley and pepper and toss well. Cover and let stand 5 minutes before serving.

RICE CHOWDER WITH TOMATOES AND CORN

■ *Serves 6 to 8* ■

Make this in several batches and freeze it. If red, really ripe fresh tomatoes are available, use them instead of canned; skin them and cut into 1/2-inch cubes.

2	tablespoons vegetable oil
1	medium onion, coarsely chopped
2	cups water
2	cans (13 ounces each) evaporated skim milk
1	can (16 ounces) tomatoes, with liquid, chopped
1	can (7 ounces) whole kernel corn
1 1/2	cups long-grain rice
2	tablespoons chopped fresh parsley

salt and pepper

1 Heat oil in large saucepan and sauté onion until translucent.

2 Stir in all remaining ingredients and bring to boil. Lower heat, cover and simmer 15 to 20 minutes or until rice is tender.

MICROWAVE: (1) Combine oil and onion in 3-quart dish and cook on HIGH (100%) 2 minutes. (2) Add all remaining ingredients, stir well, cover and cook on HIGH 5 minutes; reduce power to MEDIUM (50%) and cook 25 minutes longer. Let stand 5 to 10 minutes or until rice is tender.

SUPERMARKET SAVVY

TEXMATI RICE

Texmati rice was developed over a number of years by cross-breeding aromatic and regular long-grain rice varieties. As far as is known, Texmati's aromatic properties come from basmati rice, a type grown in India and Pakistan.

SPECIAL RICE FOR PORK, HAM OR SAUSAGE

■ *Serves 4 to 6* ■

What might be considered a good rice dish has been turned into something unusual with the addition of brown sugar and maple syrup.

2 1/2   *cups water*
1   *cup converted long-grain rice*
1   *tablespoon butter or margarine*
pinch of salt
1/3   *cup chopped pecans*
2   *tablespoons dark brown sugar*
2   *tablespoons maple syrup*
pinch of nutmeg

1 Bring water to boil and add rice. Return to boil, lower heat, cover and simmer until rice is tender, about 15 minutes.

2 Add all remaining ingredients, toss lightly but thoroughly and serve.

MICROWAVE: (1) Combine water and rice in 2-quart bowl, cover with plastic and cook on HIGH (100%) 15 minutes. (2) Add remaining ingredients, toss lightly but well and serve.

PILAF OF BULGAR

■ *Serves 4* ■

Bulgar is precooked cracked wheat, high in fiber and protein and rich in flavor. Try using this in place of rice or potatoes.

1 2/3   *cups canned chicken broth*
1   *tablespoon butter or margarine*
1/4   *cup minced onion*
2/3   *cup bulgar*
white pepper
1/4   *cup finely chopped fresh parsley*

1 Bring broth to boil in saucepan.

2 Melt butter in skillet and sauté onion just until it begins to color. Add bulgar and sauté over high heat, stirring, for 30 seconds.

3 Stir in broth and pepper; cover. Lower heat and simmer 15 minutes or until all liquid is absorbed. Remove from heat, stir in parsley and serve.

MICROWAVE: (1) Heat butter or margarine with onion in 2-quart dish on HIGH (100%) 2 minutes. (2) Stir in bulgar and broth. Cover and cook on HIGH 5 minutes; liquid should be boiling. Reduce to MEDIUM (50%) and cook 8 to 10 minutes or until all liquid is absorbed. Stir in pepper and parsley. Let stand 5 minutes before serving.

CAROLINA PILAU RICE WITH PINE AND PISTACHIO NUTS

■ *Serves 6* ■

Here's a way to make a gourmet dish of plain white rice. Pistachios and pine nuts are in the nut sections of the supermarket. The pine nuts from China are shorter, stubbier and less expensive than those from Europe, and work just as well here.

1/4   *cup butter*
1/3   *cup pine nuts*
1/3   *cup pistachios, shelled, skins removed*
  1   *cup long-grain rice, cooked*
  2   *teaspoons powdered mace*

Melt butter in skillet and sauté nuts for 2 to 3 minutes. Add cooked rice and mace, fluff with fork and heat through.

MICROWAVE: (1) Add butter to a microwave-safe dish and cook on HIGH 45 seconds. Add nuts and cook 1 minute longer. (2) Add cooked rice (to microwave rice, see page 69) and mace, fluff with fork and cook on HIGH 30 to 60 seconds to reheat rice.

GARLICKY BROWN RICE

■ *Serves 4* ■

Brown rice may be cooked more rapidly by soaking it in water (the 2 1/2 cups below) for at least 2 hours or overnight. This will reduce cooking time to about 20 minutes.

  2   *tablespoons olive or vegetable oil*
  6   *medium onions (about 1 1/2 pounds), coarsely chopped*
  4   *large or 6 small garlic cloves, minced*
  1   *cup brown rice*
2 1/2   *cups water*

1 Heat oil in skillet and sauté onions slowly until they begin to brown, about 15 minutes. Add garlic and cook a minute or two longer.

2 Add rice and stir well, then add water. Cover and cook over very low heat until water is absorbed, about 45 minutes. Serve hot.

MICROWAVE: (1) Combine all ingredients in 2-quart dish, stir well, cover and cook on HIGH (100%) 5 minutes. (2) Reduce heat to MEDIUM (50%) and cook 30 minutes. Let stand for 5 minutes before serving.

5

THE CHEESE BOARD

There are two tales about the origin of cheese. The first has it that a Bedouin who was about to cross the desert filled his skin pouch with ewe's milk so he could refresh himself along the way. Tired from the ups and downs of the camel ride and the many hours in the hot sun, he opened the pouch, made from the dried stomach of a sheep, and instead of milk he found a watery substance around a thick white mass—what we today call whey and curds.

In essence, this story encapsulates the four essentials of cheesemaking: (1) milk, (2) a churning motion, (3) heat and (4) rennet—the product of an enzyme produced in the membrane lining of an animal's stomach. What happened to the Bedouin's milk while he was riding in the hot sun was the process of cheesemaking, known as "coagulation" or "curdling," and what the Bedouin tasted was what we call cottage cheese.

The other story has to do with a shepherd who left his lunch in a cave and forgot about it. When he returned, he saw that part of his lunch, some curd, had developed a blue veinlike mold, which he tasted and enjoyed. This represents the origin of Roquefort cheese.

Cheese was recorded very early in history; there is note of it in Mesopotamia somewhere between 3500 and 2800 B.C., and it reappears through Greek and Roman history and the Middle Ages. In 1411, Charles VI of France enacted what was probably the first law to protect a cheesemaking process, which by then had become an important industry, granting the residents of Roquefort "the monopoly of curing cheese as has been done in the caves of the Roquefort village since time immemorial." This act is still honored by French and international law. It is evident that the American taste for cheese has gone up geometrically;

evidence of this is seen in the now fabulous cheese sections of many supermarkets. I love cheese and I enjoy using it in different spreads, casseroles, quiches and tarts; with fruit, bread and, yes, brandy; in salad dressings, sandwiches, on pita and pasta. Here are many ways to use the cheeses so readily available from so many parts of the world.

EXPRESS CHECK-OUT

■ ■

CHEESE

1 The labels on packaged cheese products should note if the contents are a natural cheese or one of many substitutes—what are commonly called "process cheese products." Just know the difference. Many supermarkets have packaged cheese sections and "live cheese counters" with service as they do for pasta, meat and fish. Ask the attendants for samplings of cheese to increase your knowledge.

2 If moisture is retained in cheese, it will last longer. Therefore it is important to wrap cheese carefully when storing it in the refrigerator.

3 A good rule is to buy what you need and not try to store too much cheese. High-moisture cheeses (cottage, farmer and pot cheeses) are the quickest to deteriorate, so check dates on bottoms of containers and buy the freshest. Be sure of tight seals when storing in refrigerator.

4 Processed cheese products, stored unrefrigerated in the supermarket, may be stored unrefrigerated at home until opened. Once opened, of course, they must go into the refrigerator. Refrigerated cheese items must be refrigerated at home.

5 Natural and processed cheeses may be frozen—natural cheeses up to 8 weeks, processed cheeses up to 4 or 5 months. Be sure to wrap carefully for freezing. Ideally, it is best to freeze in 1/2-pound sizes not over 1 inch thick.

6 Thaw frozen cheese in its package in the refrigerator. Don't be upset if cheese changes color somewhat—as it thaws, natural coloring will return. Do not refreeze cheese. It simply won't work, as it loses texture and flavor.

■ ■

7 To shred cheese, use medium to large holes of cheese grater; use small holes to grate hard cheeses. Chilled cheese will shred more easily than cheese at room temperature.

8 If cheese is an ingredient in baked dishes, it is best to bake between 325°F and 375°F (170°C and 190°C). If adding shredded cheese, bring to room temperature so it will better blend into other ingredients.

9 Easy cheese-in-soup ideas: (a) Add 1/3 cup shredded Edam cheese and 1 tablespoon sherry to 10 3/4-ounce can cream of celery soup (follow directions on can), and garnish with a sprinkle of dried tarragon. (b) Add 1/4-inch cubes of provolone and bits of ham to canned pea soup (follow directions on can) and top with sprinkle of finely chopped scallions. (c) Add some shredded cheddar and a tablespoon of sherry to any seafood chowder (lobster, crab, clam, shrimp) for enrichment.

10 Garlic-and-herb-flavored Boursin, Gervais and other cheeses of this type make wonderful toppings for baked potatoes. Try adding a tablespoon of cognac, sherry or bourbon to each 2 ounces of cheese to top 2 potatoes.

SUPERMARKET SAVVY

CHEESE TYPES

GOUDA AND EDAM

These are two of the most popular of the Dutch cheeses; though they are still made in Holland, many other Dutch-style cheeses are now made in other parts of Europe, notably Scandinavia. Cow's milk is used and the curd is semisoft. Hardwood molds with cheesecloth linings are used, which explains the shape and look of these cheeses. Many of the Dutch cheeses are flavored with herbs and spices; caraway and cumin are popular. Other well-known Dutch-type cheese are Norway's Noekkelost and Kuminost, Holland's Leyden and Germany's Tilsit.

SWISS

Like the Swiss Emmentaler, these are semifirm to firm, with holes or eyes and a sweet, nutty flavor. These Swiss types are produced all over the world; the amount of curing time affects the taste of the cheese. Some of the better known are American Swiss, Austrian Alpberg, Danish Samsoe, Finnish Swiss and Lappi, Norwegian Jarlsberg.

BLUE-VEINED

The veins are made by injecting a mold that spreads throughout the cheese as it cures for varying lengths of time. It may be made with cow's or ewe's milk. The most popular are Italy's Gorgonzola, France's Roquefort, England's Stilton and Denmark's Danablu. There are others from France, such as Bleu de Bresse and Pipo' Crem', and several excellent American blues.

SOFT-RIPENING CHEESES

Mold is applied to the outside for short periods of time to ripen the cheese. The "washed-rind" types include Bel Paese (Italian), Oka (Canadian), brick (American) and Port du Salut (French). "Bloomy rind" types include Brie, Camembert, double and triple cremes, Coulommiers (all French) and Crema Dania (Danish).

HARD GRATING CHEESES

Called *grana*-type cheeses in Italy, these have been made in the Po Valley for over 700 years. There are American versions of Parmesan and Romano, but the most important of the grana group are mostly from Italy and include: grana Padano, pecorino Romano, aged Asiago, aged caciocavallo, provolone and, most importantly, Parmigiano-Reggiano (named for the region between Parma and Reggio, Italy; Italian law mandates that only cheese made in this area, where the formula has not changed for 700 years, may be called Parmigiano-Reggiano. Each year it is made only from April 1 through November 11). There is a hard grating cheese made in Switzerland called sapsago.

WHEY CHEESES

The best known is ricotta. Some people think these are not true cheeses, for they are made from the whey and are therefore byproducts. Others are Norway's Gjetost and Switzerland's sapsago, a hard grating cheese.

FRESH CHEESES

Called fresh because they are not cured. They are almost always soft, mild and white and have a short lifespan. Cottage cheese, pot cheese, farmer cheese, mozzarella, ricotta, Gervais, Petit Suisse and sometimes the brined cheese feta is included here because the curing is so slight.

STRONG-SMELLING

A very subjective grouping, to be sure, but there needs to be a place for Limburger, Liederkranz, Livarot and Muenster.

PROCESSED CHEESES

Processed cheese has essentially the same basic ingredients as "natural" cheese but with artificial additives to give the texture, taste, flavor and consistency that natural cheeses garner from bacteria and aging. Supermarket shelves can make one dizzy over the variety of processed cheeses, but basically there are five kinds: (1) pasteurized process cheese, (2) pasteurized process blended, (3) pasteurized process cheese food, (4) pasteurized process cheese spread and (5) imitation pasteurized process cheese products, all under the control of the U.S. Food and Drug Administration.

BRINE CHEESES

The best known is the Greek feta, which is pickled in brine to extend its life.

STRING CHEESES

These include the ubiquitous mozzarella and provolone. The whey is drained, the curd is dipped in hot whey and then water, and stretched and molded while it is still plastic. Scamorza and caciocavallo are growing in popularity as string cheeses and they are appearing on many supermarket shelves.

CHÈVRES

Chèvre means "goat" in French; today all goat cheeses are called chèvres. Some new farms in the U.S. are making goat cheeses, and they are becoming popular, but the more common ones are of French origin: Bucheron, Montrachet, Valençay and chevrotin.

THE BEST GRILLED CHEESE SANDWICH

■ *Makes 8 open pieces* ■

Saturday morning was housecleaning time in our home as we grew up. With two brothers and three sisters, lunch on that day (or any other) was not easy. At other meals, Mom, with her simple and effective Italian cooking, almost always pulled together satisfying and healthy food. But on housecleaning day, the responsibility for Saturday lunch was given to the youngest, my sister Louise, who loved grilled cheese sandwiches. She would layer mozzarella inside buttered crusty bread, add oregano or thyme and bake them until the cheese ran. Often she'd add a slice of tomato with chopped fresh basil and a few drops of our best olive oil. She would put sliced white American cheese over sliced bread and accent it with grated Parmesan. Each week we had a surprise. Many years later, Louise and I concocted a grilled cheese treat which we believe is special. One reason we like it is because it can be made with groceries already in the pantry or the refrigerator. Serve this sandwich with crisp cole slaw or a fresh dandelion salad.

8	*slices wholewheat or other whole-grain bread*
1/2	*cup light mayonnaise*
2	*tablespoons sour cream*
2	*tablespoons prepared horseradish*
1	*tablespoon Dijon-type mustard*
8	*thick slices American cheese (presliced and individually wrapped)*
3 to 4	*tomatoes, thinly sliced*
8	*slices bacon, halved and cooked until almost done*
	salt and pepper

1 Preheat oven to 425°F (220°C). Toast bread slices and arrange on a baking sheet.

2 In a small bowl, combine mayonnaise, sour cream, horseradish and mustard and mix well. Thickly coat each slice of toast with mixture.

3 Arrange cheese slices over bread, arrange tomato slices over cheese and crisscross 2 pieces of bacon on top. Season with salt and pepper.

4 Bake until cheese is melted, 10 to 15 minutes, then broil 4 to 6 inches from heating element 2 to 3 minutes to brown.

SUPERMARKET SAVVY

■ ■

MELTING CHEESE

If a cheese is more aged, it will melt better. Many recipes call for the addition of cheese where cooking is required; it is a good idea to keep the following cheeses in mind because of their good melting qualities. If a blue-veined cheese is to be used in cooking, be careful of the amount, as the veined cheeses become stronger as they cook.

APPENZELLER—a smooth, firm cheese, seasoned with wine and spices during curing. It is a Swiss import.

EMMENTALER—known as Switzerland Swiss cheese; has large holes and, though manufactured in large discs, it is available in supermarkets in pound blocks wrapped in plastic. It is considered the best of the Swiss cheeses.

FONTINA—the Italian import, with small holes, is considered by the experts to be the best of all the fontinas. It melts beautifully.

GRUYÈRE—from Switzerland; has smaller holes than Emmentaler. Even the varieties made outside of Switzerland melt well; Gruyère is considered one of the best cooking cheeses.

HAVARTI—a Danish cheese, often flavored with caraway seed; has tiny holes and becomes sharper with age.

RACLETTE—the cheese broiled by the Swiss for the famous dish of the same name. It's like Swiss cheese with small holes.

VELVEETA—a processed cheese; melts quickly and easily.

GRILLED BLUE CHEESE AND SAUTÉED APPLE OPEN-FACE SANDWICH

■ *Serves 2* ■

Most blue-veined cheeses are rich and creamy, and they pair well with fruit. Serve this sandwich with green beans or broccoli, dressed with an oil and fresh lemon juice.

2   *tablespoons butter or margarine*
4   *apples, cored and thinly sliced*
4   *ounces blue-veined cheese, such as Gorgonzola or Saga blue, room temperature*
4   *slices bread, toasted*

1 Melt butter in skillet, add apple slices and cook over medium heat, turning apples frequently, about 10 minutes.

2 Spread cheese on toasted bread, top with apples and run under broiler 2 to 3 minutes to melt cheese and caramelize apples. Serve right away.

BRIE AMANDINE

■ Serves 6 ■

Make as few or as many of these as needed; try the technique with rounds of cheese, such as Camembert. Serve with crackers as an appetizer or hors d'oeuvre or with the salad course. The cheese may also be served with fresh fruit.

1/2   *cup finely chopped toasted almonds*
6   *thin wedges ripe Brie, each about*
1/2 inch wide at the outer edge

1 Grind almonds in food processor, not too finely; they should have definite texture.

2 Roll brie slices in almonds and serve.

CHEESE MEASUREMENTS / BUYING AIDS

Many recipes call for cups of cheese, and this guideline may help you when purchasing cheese in bulk.

4 ounces (1/4 pound) = 1 cup shredded

1 pound cottage cheese = 2 cups

3 ounces cream cheese = 6 tablespoons

8 ounces cream cheese = 1 cup

MILK IN CHEESE

Making cheese is a fairly straightforward procedure but there are some variables—one of the most basic being the milk used, for to a large extent, that determines the quality of the product. Different areas have different kinds of vegetation and the various flavors from them will give the cheese its uniqueness. For example, there are large deposits of salt in the soil in and near Chester, an English city that produces Cheshire cheese, and these deposits impart a flavor to the milk which is transferred to the cheese and does not seem to be found anywhere else. Another variable has to do with whether the milk is raw or pasteurized. When the pasteurization process was advanced in the 1930s, milk was heated to a certain temperature and kept there to destroy disease-producing bacteria and to check fermentation-causing bacteria. Cheese made from raw milk is not as even in texture and doesn't last as long, and perhaps even the quality is not uniform, yet the raw milk cheeses are known to be more flavorful. The nutritional value for either is the same.

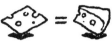

CHEESE ALTERNATIVES

■ ■

The following cheeses are popular and are almost always available in most supermarkets. There may be a time when you don't want to postpone making a particular recipe and need a substitute cheese. Here are some possibilities:

CHEDDAR: use American process, Cantal, Cheshire, Colby, Coon or Mimolette

COTTAGE CHEESE: use farmer, pot or ricotta

CREAM CHEESE: use Gervais, Neufchâtel or Petit Suisse

MOZZARELLA: Use Bel Paese, domestic Swiss, Edam, Gouda or Muenster

MUENSTER: use Bel Paese, Bonbel, brick, cream Havarti, Edam, Gouda, Monterey Jack or Port du Salut

PARMESAN: use aged Asiago, aged caciocavallo, aged kashkaval, Romano or sapsago

PROVOLONE: use caciocavallo or kashkaval

SWISS: use Alpberg, Appenzeller, Gruyère, Jarlsberg, Lappi, raclette or Samsoe

SHELL STEAKS WITH BLUE CHEESE

■ *Serves 4* ■

*I*t's difficult to improve a plain grilled, broiled or sautéed shell steak, but the last-minute addition of a Danish blue cheese topping makes an exciting dish. Before broiling the steak, trim it of excess fat.

4   thick (1 to 1 1/2 inches) shell steaks, boned and trimmed
salt and pepper
1   ounce Danish blue cheese, room temperature
2   tablespoons dry sherry
2   tablespoons finely chopped chives or scallions
1   tablespoon butter, room temperature
1/2 teaspoon bottled steak sauce

1 Check steaks to be sure they are trimmed of fat. Set out on counter and let come to room temperature. Season with salt and pepper just before cooking.

2 Combine cheese, sherry, chives, butter and steak sauce in small bowl until well blended but still textured. Broil or grill steaks to desired doneness. Spread cheese mixture over steaks and return to broiler for 1 to 2 minutes to brown top.

NOTE: The steaks may be sautéed in a skillet; if so, melt 2 tablespoons butter and add steaks. Sauté on each side. When done, remove from skillet, transfer to baking sheet, add cheese topping and broil until top browns.

CORN PUDDING WITH CHESHIRE CHEESE

■ *Serves 8 to 10* ■

This is a supermarket special. It takes little to make it and ingredients are readily available. Vermont, New York State or Wisconsin cheddar may be used in place of the Cheshire cheese.

3   *tablespoons vegetable oil*
3   *tablespoons butter or margarine*
2   *large onions, finely chopped*
1   *red bell pepper, cored, ribs and seeds removed, diced*
2   *eggs*
3   *tablespoons water*
2   *cans (17 ounces each) cream-style corn*
1   *package (1 pound) corn muffin mix*
1   *cup sour cream*
2   *cups shredded Cheshire cheese (about 8 ounces)*

1 Preheat oven to 425°F (220°C). Heat oil with butter in a skillet. Add onions and red pepper and sauté until onions are light gold.

2 Combine eggs and water in bowl and mix until smooth. Add creamed corn and muffin mix. Transfer to a well-greased 9 × 13-inch baking dish. Spread onion mixture on top of batter and spread sour cream over onions. Top with shredded cheese.

3 Bake 30 minutes. Serve right away.

MICROWAVE: (1) Combine oil, butter, onions and red pepper in dish. Cook uncovered on HIGH (100%) 3 minutes. Remove from oven and stir. (2) Combine eggs and water in bowl. Add corn and muffin mix. Transfer to 11 × 8-inch dish. Spread onion mixture on top of batter and cook on HIGH 4 minutes. (3) Spread sour cream over top and add cheddar over sour cream. Cook on HIGH 1 to 2 minutes or until cheese melts.

CHEDDAR

In the 17th century, one of the most popular of all cheeses was created in the English town of Cheddar and named after its place of origin. The colonists who came to America brought the "cheddaring" process with them and so began the manufacture of cheddar cheese in America.

Cheddar is a hard cheese with a color range from white to orange. It is made from cow's milk, either raw or pasteurized. American types include cheddar, Colby and longhorn. Monterey Jack cheese is usually included in the group.

The difference between mild, mellow and sharp cheddars is a result of aging time. A mild cheese has been cured for two to three months, a mellow one for up to six, and sharp for longer than six months. American cheddars are made in different parts of the U.S., particularly Vermont, Wisconsin and New York. The English cheeses Cheshire, double Gloucester, Leicester and Derby are also considered cheddars.

ORANGE BELL PEPPER CHEDDAR DIP

■ *Makes 1 1/2 cups* ■

Try to use something other than a green bell pepper—there's nothing wrong with them, but yellow, orange or red bells are more exciting colors for this.

1 large yellow, orange or red bell pepper
1 container (8 ounces) farmer cheese
2 ounces sharp cheddar cheese, grated
2 teaspoons spicy brown mustard
1/4 cup chopped bell pepper of another color
chili powder or paprika
thin crackers

1 Cut off top of whole pepper. Remove ribs and seeds, then cut a little off bottom so pepper stands upright.

2 Combine cheeses and mustard and fold in chopped pepper. Spoon mixture into cavity of hollowed bell pepper. Sprinkle with chili powder and serve with crackers.

BACON QUICHE WITH CHEDDAR CHEESE AND CARAWAY SEED

■ *Serves 6 to 8* ■

Cheddar, caraway and bacon combine to make an easy, tasty quiche.

1 prepared 9- or 10-inch pie shell
1 cup grated cheddar cheese (about 4 ounces)
8 slices regular or thin bacon
3 eggs, beaten
1 1/2 cups half-and-half or milk
1 teaspoon caraway seed
black pepper

1 Follow package directions to bake pie crust but bake only 5 minutes. Remove from oven; adjust oven temperature to 350°F (180°C). Sprinkle cheese into shell.

2 Cook bacon until crisp, drain on paper towels and crumble into pie shell.

3 Combine eggs, half-and-half or milk, caraway seed and pepper in a bowl and blend well. Pour into pie shell. Bake 30 to 40 minutes or until filling is set.

MICROWAVE: (1) Transfer prepared crust from foil container to microwave-safe pie dish, prick with fork and cook on HIGH (100%) 4 minutes. Add cheese. (2) Arrange bacon on roasting rack, cover with 4 paper towels and cook on HIGH until crisp, 5 to 6 minutes. Cool and crumble over cheese. (3) Mix eggs, half-and-half or milk, caraway seed and pepper in a bowl. Cook on MEDIUM (50%), stirring 3 times, 4 minutes or until slightly thickened. Pour into pie shell and cook on MEDIUM 15 minutes; if not on carousel, turn every 3 minutes. Let stand 5 minutes before serving.

CORN CHEDDAR SOUFFLÉ WITH CHIVES

■ *Serves 4* ■

Corn and cheddar have an affinity for each other and perform well in this light soufflé, which requires only two eggs. Chives add the extra touch of flavor. Since they are almost always available fresh in the supermarkets, use them that way if you can; otherwise, dried will do.

2   eggs, separated
1/2   teaspoon cream of tartar
1   cup canned whole kernel corn, drained or
    1 cup frozen, thawed
1/2   cup grated cheddar cheese
2   tablespoons finely chopped fresh chives or
    1 teaspoon dried
1   teaspoon Worcestershire sauce
salt and pepper

1 Preheat oven to 375°F (190°C). Beat egg whites until foamy. Add cream of tartar and beat until stiff.

2 Combine corn, cheese, chives, egg yolks, Worcestershire sauce, salt and pepper in a bowl and mix well. Fold in egg whites.

3 Lightly grease and flour 2-quart soufflé dish. Pour in soufflé mixture. Bake 10 minutes. Lower oven temperature to 325°F (170°C) and bake until puffed and golden, about 30 minutes longer. Serve right away.

CROCKED FARMER CHEESE

■ *Makes 1 cup* ■

The herbs and hot cherry pepper give this crock a kick. Make it a day ahead and enjoy it all the more.

8   ounces farmer cheese
1   garlic clove, minced
1   tablespoon cumin seed
1   hot cherry pepper (jarred or fresh), stemmed
    and seeds removed, finely chopped
2   teaspoons chopped fresh cilantro or oregano,
    or 1 teaspoon dried oregano

1 Combine all ingredients in food processor or blender and process until smooth. Transfer to covered crock and refrigerate to allow flavors to blend.

2 Remove from refrigerator 20 minutes before serving. Serve with thin crackers or corn chips.

SUSAN'S TWO-CHEESE AND ONION TART

■ Serves 6 to 8 ■

Cool some white wine and enjoy it with this rich and creamy tart, which combines cooked onions with two Swiss cheeses. This is hearty and delicious.

1 tablespoon Dijon-style mustard
1 prepared 10-inch deep-dish pie shell
2 tablespoons vegetable oil
1 1/4 to 1 1/2 pounds onions, thinly sliced
(about 5 cups)
1 teaspoon sugar
1 cup each loosely packed grated Swiss
Emmentaler and Swiss Gruyère cheeses
(about 4 ounces each)
2 eggs
1 cup half-and-half or milk
1/2 teaspoon nutmeg

1 Preheat oven to 400°F (200°C). Brush mustard inside bottom of pie shell and bake until lightly golden, about 10 minutes. Adjust oven temperature to 350°F (180°C).

2 Heat oil in skillet over medium-high heat. Add onions and sugar and sauté until soft and lightly golden, about 15 minutes, stirring several times. Let cool, then transfer to pie shell. Add cheese.

3 Beat eggs, half-and-half and nutmeg in a bowl. Pour over cheese, gently shaking pie plate to let egg mixture get to bottom of shell. Bake about 40 minutes or until filling is set. Cool a few minutes before slicing but serve hot.

MICROWAVE: (1) Prepare shell as above. (2) Combine oil, onions and sugar in microwave-safe dish and cook on HIGH (100%), stirring twice, 3 minutes or until onions are soft. Cool slightly and transfer to baked pie shell. (3) Cover onions with cheese. Beat eggs with half-and-half and nutmeg and pour carefully into shell. Cook on MEDIUM (50%) 16 to 25 minutes or until filling is set; if not on carousel, rotate every 3 minutes. Let stand 5 minutes before serving.

GRILLED GOAT CHEESE WITH COARSE PEPPER ON CRUSTY BREAD

■ *Serves 4* ■

*T*he simplicity of this preparation makes it elegant. Some may consider this peasant food, but it is food at its best. Serve with sliced tomatoes and a crisp green salad, both with vinaigrette dressing.

1/4   *cup olive oil*
  4   *garlic cloves, peeled and halved*
  1   *loaf Italian or French bread, halved lengthwise*
  8   *ounces goat cheese, such as Montrachet*
  2   *tablespoons finely chopped fresh thyme or 1 tablespoon dried*
coarse black pepper

1 Heat olive oil and garlic pieces in small skillet; as garlic cooks, press with a fork or wooden spoon to release more flavor.

Discard garlic as soon as pieces begin to color. Brush garlic-flavored oil on bread halves and toast under broiler. Watch bread carefully and remove it as soon as toasted. Cool just enough to handle.

2 Spread each half with goat cheese. Sprinkle with thyme, pepper and drops of remaining garlic-flavored olive oil. Return to broiler and broil until cheese begins to bubble. Cut bread halves into 4 pieces.

ELOISE CUDDEBACK'S PITA PIECES WITH PARMESAN

■ *Serves 6* ■

*O*ne of the easiest yet tastiest treats. These make wonderful tidbit appetizers with cocktails and go well with soups and salads. They tasted so good that we had to ask Eloise to make another batch.

  3   *pita breads, each about 1 1/2 ounces*
  3   *tablespoons butter or margarine*
1/2   *cup grated Parmesan cheese*

1 Preheat oven to 350°F (180°C). Cut off edge of each pita bread by removing 1/16 inch with scissors or small sharp knife. Separate halves of pita.

2 Butter each slice and arrange on baking sheet. Sprinkle with Parmesan and bake 10 minutes or until crisp and a bit brown on the edges. Remove from oven and cut each round into 6 or 8 wedges. Serve hot.

ZUCCHINI, TOMATO AND RICOTTA CASSEROLE

■ *Serves 6* ■

*T*his is tasty as is, but if you want meat in it, add 8 slices bacon, cooked and crumbled before baking, or sauté 1/2 to 1 pound link sausage until almost done, cut it into thin slices and add them before baking the casserole.

    3   tablespoons olive oil
    3   tablespoons butter or margarine
    2   large onions, chopped
    4   small zucchini (1 × 6 inches), washed,
        ends removed, sliced paper thin
    1   large garlic clove, minced
    1   can (28 ounces) plum tomatoes, well
        drained, cut in pieces
    1   tablespoon finely chopped basil or 1
        teaspoon dried
    1   cup ricotta cheese
    3/4 cup grated Parmesan or Romano cheese
    1   cup heavy cream
    2   eggs
    pinch of nutmeg

1 Heat oil and butter in 2-quart flame-proof enameled casserole. Add onions and zucchini and sauté 10 minutes, stirring frequently.

2 Preheat oven to 400°F (200°C). Add garlic to casserole and sauté 1 minutes. Remove from heat and stir in tomatoes and basil.

3 Combine ricotta, grated cheese, cream and eggs in bowl and blend well. Spread over zucchini mixture. Bake uncovered 30 minutes or until top has browned and casserole bubbles. Sprinkle with nutmeg and serve.

MICROWAVE: (1) Combine zucchini, onions and tomatoes in 2-quart dish, cover with plastic and cook on HIGH (100%) 5 minutes. Drain vegetables and leave in colander. (2) Combine oil and butter in same dish and cook on HIGH 40 seconds or until butter melts. (3) Prepare ricotta mixture, adding garlic and basil. (4) Return zucchini, onions and tomatoes to dish with butter and oil and cover with ricotta mixture. Cover with plastic and cook at MEDIUM-HIGH (70%) 15 to 20 minutes.

PORT DU SALUT CHEESE LOAF

■ *Serves 8* ■

Rolls, sticks and loaves of cheese make interesting presentations. Serve this in one piece and let the diners cut into it as an appetizer or first course.

2   cups shredded Port du Salut cheese (about 8 ounces)
3   ounces Gervais (a type of cream cheese), softened
1/4   cup dry breadcrumbs
1/4   cup toasted sesame seed
apple or cucumber slices

1 Mix cheeses and blend well. Shape into loaf about 1 1/2 inches thick.

2 Mix breadcrumbs with sesame seed and place mixture on waxed paper. Gently roll cheese loaf in crumb mixture to coat completely. Transfer to plate, cover with plastic and chill to improve flavors. Remove from refrigerator 15 minutes or so before serving with apple or cucumber slices.

SILKY ROQUEFORT QUICHE

■ *Serves 4 to 6* ■

A prepared pie shell works well here and is a real timesaver. People who like cheese will like this dish. Pie shells in the microwave are not as good as those baked traditionally, but a microwave version is offered below for those in a hurry.

3   eggs
1 1/4   cups sour cream
pinch each of pepper and nutmeg
6   ounces Roquefort cheese, finely crumbled (about 1 cup)
1   tablespoon unsalted butter, cut into small pieces
1   prepared 9-inch pie shell, baked
1/3   cup finely chopped fresh parsley

1 Preheat oven to 350°F (180°C). Beat eggs lightly in bowl. Whisk in sour cream, pepper and nutmeg; fold in cheese. Pour mixture into pie shell and dot with butter.

2 Bake until thin knife inserted in center comes out clean, about 40 minutes. Cool on wire rack 10 minutes and sprinkle entire quiche with parsley before serving.

MICROWAVE: (1) If using your own pastry recipe, prepare pastry, fit into microwave-safe pie plate and prick all over with fork. Cook on HIGH (100%) 6 minutes; if not on carousel, turn 3 times. If using prepared or frozen pie shell, transfer to microwave-safe pie plate and cook on HIGH 4 minutes. (2) Fill shell as above and cook on MEDIUM (50%) 18 minutes, then sprinkle entire quiche with parsley.

ROQUEFORT DRESSING

■ *Makes about 1 1/4 cups* ■

*S*ome people like this dressing smooth and therefore make it in a blender or food processor. I like mine with a little more texture, so I mix the ingredients by hand with a fork, or in a processor ever so briefly with quick start-and-stop movements. Use this on salads and fruit. Add a sprinkle of chopped parsley, chives or finely chopped scallions, or sprinkle with chopped walnuts, pecans or hazelnuts.

6 *ounces Roquefort cheese, room temperature, crumbled*
1/2 *cup plain yogurt or sour cream*
1/2 *cup olive oil*
3 *tablespoons white wine vinegar*
1 *tablespoon fresh lemon juice*
salt and pepper

Combine all ingredients in food processor and process using on/off turns; check consistency every other second. Or blend in bowl with fork. Store in refrigerator.

MAKE-BELIEVE RAREBIT

■ *Serves 2 to 4* ■

*F*or extra taste, serve over garlic bread.

1/4 cup hot water
1 chicken bouillon cube
3 tablespoons all purpose flour
1 1/2 cups skim milk
1/2 teaspoon dry mustard
1 teaspoon Worcestershire sauce
1 cup grated processed cheese
Salt and pepper
Fresh toast

1 Place water and bouillon cube in top of double boiler over medium heat. Stir until bouillon is dissolved. Whisk in flour and milk.

2 Add mustard, Worcestershire sauce and cheese and stir until cheese melts. Season with salt and pepper.

3 Serve over toast or grilled bread.

GORGONZOLA WITH BRANDY

■ *Makes 1 cup* ■

This is extremely simple and effective with crackers or on crisp leaves of Belgian endive, in celery hearts or as a filling for snow peas. Also excellent as a stuffing for small tomatoes, or on iced cucumber slices.

4   ounces Gorgonzola cheese, room temperature
3   ounces mascarpone or cream cheese, room
     temperature
2   tablespoons brandy or cognac
1   tablespoon milk or cream, if needed

Blend cheeses in a small bowl. Add brandy and mix again. If necessary, thin with milk or cream. Store in refrigerator but bring to room temperature before serving.

STEVE WIDUP'S PICKAPEPPA CREAM CHEESE

■ *Serves 4* ■

Pickapeppa Sauce is made in Jamaica of tomatoes, onions, sugar, cane vinegar, mangoes, raisins, tamarind, salt, pepper and spices. It can be used in many ways (in cheese dishes, on seafood, in soups, with game and roasts). Here it is simply poured over a small block of cream cheese and served as a spread for Ritz or other crisp crackers.

1   package (3 ounces) cream cheese, room
     temperature
2 to 4 tablespoons Pickapeppa sauce
Crackers

Place cream cheese in center of plate and cover with sauce. Serve with butter knife and crackers on the side.

TODAY'S CATCH—FRESH FROM THE SEA

Every natural body of water supports fish, and man has been eating fish since prehistoric times. But only recently have supermarkets introduced fresh fish sections to their public. Getting to know the supermarket fishmonger is now as important as knowing the supermarket butcher. Pollution and overfishing have already depleted the supply of freshwater and coastal fish, and today's fisherman has to go many miles from shore to catch anything (which presents problems in getting it to the customer fast and fresh). This is one reason why fish farming has become an important industry. Most mature trout you see in the markets were raised on a trout farm, probably in Idaho, which specializes in trout breeding. Catfish are bred in many southern states of the U.S.

Be careful when selecting frozen fish packages. One real problem in supermarkets is faulty refrigeration, which cause packages to thaw and refreeze. If ice is around the package edges, reject it; don't settle for ripped packages of frozen fish. Any sign of blood in a package is a sure indication of thaw and refreezing.

It's difficult to firm up cooking times for fish, but an accepted general rule is 10 minutes per inch of thickness for fresh fish and 20 per inch of thickness for frozen fish. I almost always test for doneness by using a fork to part the fish; if it is opaque and flakes (pulls apart easily so you can actually see the state of doneness), it's time to remove from heat. When grilling fish, I always insert a wooden skewer right through the body. If it meets resistance, the fish still needs cooking; if the skewer enters and pulls out easily and quickly, the fish is cooked.

EXPRESS CHECK-OUT

■ ■

FRESH FISH

1 Freeze clams for about an hour to make them easier to open with a clam knife.

2 Use long-nose pliers to pull out long bones from a salmon fillet. Locate bones by running your fingers over the fillet.

3 Frozen fish cooks better if the center is still a bit icy; this helps retain moisture.

4 To make lemon-flavored crumbs for breading fish, grind lemon zest in the food processor, then add stale or fresh bread and process with on/off turns.

5 Reject any fish that has a fishy odor; it is a sign of spoilage. A fresh fish will have a faint marine smell, mild and almost sweet.

6 Look for a moist, translucent appearance when buying fish steaks or fillets. If they are discolored at the edges and look dry, pass them by.

7 Dip fish in milk, water or melted butter before dredging in flour, cornmeal or crumbs for more crispness.

8 Good sauces for fish include aïoli (garlic mayonnaise), herbed butters (butter combined with herbs, anchovies, cooked egg, garlic and shallots) and sabayon (egg yolks and butter).

9 Use a wire basket to help turn fish on the grill without breaking it. Oil the basket first to keep fish from sticking and baste frequently through the basket.

FISH CHOWDER WITH VEGETABLES

■ *Serves 6* ■

  6 *thin slices bacon, chopped*
  1 *package (2.4 ounces) leek soup and recipe mix*
2 1/2 *cups water*
1 1/2 *cups frozen potato cubes*
 12 *ounces fresh fish fillets (sole, flounder, snapper, etc.) or 1 package (12 ounces) frozen fish fillets, cut into 1-inch chunks*
  1 *cup frozen whole kernel corn*
  1 *tablespoon finely chopped fresh tarragon or 1/2 teaspoon dried*
1 1/2 *cups half-and-half*

1 Cook bacon until crisp in large saucepan. Remove from heat and drain on paper towel, reserving 2 tablespoons fat in pan.

2 Whisk soup mix and water into bacon fat. Add potatoes and simmer until tender, about 15 minutes.

3 Add fish, corn and tarragon and simmer until fish is opaque and flaky, 4 to 5 minutes. Slowly add half-and-half and bring just to boil. Serve in large mugs or individual bowls, topped with crumbled bacon.

MICROWAVE: (1) Place bacon in 2-quart dish and cook on HIGH (100%) until crisp, 3 to 4 minutes. Add water and potatoes, cover and cook on HIGH 8 minutes. (2) Blend in leek soup mix and cook on HIGH 4 minutes. Add corn, fish, tarragon and half-and-half and cook, covered, on HIGH 3 minutes.

GROUPER WITH SHERRY AND BUTTER

■ *Serves 4* ■

  1 *tablespoon butter or margarine*
1 1/2 to 2 pounds grouper fillet, in one piece
  1 *cup dry sherry*
  1 *tablespoon finely chopped fresh dill or*
  1 *teaspoon dried dillweed*
salt and pepper

1 Spread some of butter on bottom of shallow baking pan. Lay fillet on top. Dot with remaining butter, pour sherry over fish and add dill, salt and pepper.

2 Broil until fish is flaky, 5 to 10 minutes, basting with sherry and pan juices several times. (Broiling time depends on thickness of fillet; do not overcook.) Test for doneness by inserting a fork or knife; if fish is opaque and separates easily, it's done.

MICROWAVE: (1) Place fish in large microwave-safe dish and pour sherry over. Dot with butter; sprinkle with dill, salt and pepper. Cover and cook on HIGH (100%) 9 minutes.

FISH FILLETS WITH CHILIES, TOMATOES AND OLIVES

■ *Serves 4 to 6* ■

You'll cook this often because it's very tasty and an interesting combination of flavors. An exact cooking time for the fillets is difficult to specify; it depends on their thickness. Test with a fork. As soon as the fish pulls apart easily and is opaque, it's done.

1 1/2   *pounds fish fillets (sole, flounder, catfish, snapper, etc.), rinsed and dried*
1/3   *cup teriyaki sauce*
1   *tablespoon butter or margarine*
1/2   *cup finely chopped onion or scallion*
1   *cup diced canned stewed tomatoes, drained*
1   *can (4 ounces) diced green chiles, drained*
1/4   *cup sliced black olives*
1/2   *cup water*
1   *teaspoon cornstarch*
4 to 6 *teaspoons sour cream*

1 Preheat oven to 400°F (200°C). Place fish in large, shallow dish and marinate in teriyaki sauce 15 minutes. Roll up fillets and arrange seam side down in well-greased baking dish, reserving any excess marinade.

2 Melt butter in skillet and sauté onion 3 minutes. Add tomatoes, chilies and olives and cook 3 minutes more. Add reserved marinade.

3 Stir water and cornstarch together. Blend into tomato mixture and cook until slightly thickened. Keep warm.

4 Bake fish just until it flakes and is opaque, about 7 to 10 minutes. To serve, spread sauce on warm platter or individual plates and arrange rolled fillets on top. Add a dollop of sour cream.

MICROWAVE: (1) Marinate fish as above. (2) Combine butter, onion, tomato, marinade, chilies and cornstarch in dish or bowl, cover with plastic and cook on HIGH (100%) 6 minutes or until slightly thickened. (3) Arrange fish rolls in another microwave-safe dish and cook, covered with plastic, on HIGH 6 to 8 minutes. If not on carousel, turn once during cooking.

FISH FILLETS BAKED IN WINE AND LEMON

■ *Serves 4* ■

One of the easiest ways to prepare fish in either an oven or a microwave. Use any kind of fish fillets if they are white and light.

2 *pounds fish fillets*
1 *teaspoon salt*
1/3 *cup vegetable oil*
1/4 *cup white wine*
1 *tablespoon fresh lemon juice*
1/4 *cup finely chopped fresh parsley*
lemon wedges

1 Rinse fish in cool water, drain and dry well. Sprinkle both sides with salt. Arrange in shallow container.

2 Combine oil, wine and lemon juice in small bowl and mix well. Pour over fish. Turn fish and marinate at least 30 minutes.

3 Preheat oven to 350°F (180°C). Transfer fillets to shallow baking dish and bake until opaque, brushing frequently with marinade, about 15 minutes; do not overcook. Serve garnished with parsley and lemon wedges.

MICROWAVE: (1) Marinate fish as above in shallow microwave-safe dish. Cover with plastic and cook on HIGH (100%) 8 minutes. Serve garnished with parsley and lemon.

SUPERMARKET SAVVY

■ ■

WHAT ABOUT SURIMI?

Most supermarkets carry surimi because (1) it is becoming a fixture in the U.S. diet; (2) it is a processed convenience food, cheaper than most other fish; and (3) fish is increasingly popular as a health food. Surimi is made of fish flesh, usually Alaskan pollack, minced and washed in chilled water until it becomes a thick mass. Flavorings, preservatives and stabilizers are added (e.g., sugar, salt, monosodium glutamate and starch) and the mixture is shaped into blocks, frozen and molded to mimic the real thing. Surimi is lower in fat and cholesterol than some fish but it also has less protein and is higher in sugar and salt. A typical surimi product weighing 4 ounces has 735 mg sodium—about four times what a similar amount of scallops contains, and nine times the level in flounder. Also, the manufacturing process washes out vitamins and minerals as well as omega-3 oils and fatty acids (now thought to protect people from heart disease). Yet surimi still has more protein than processed meats, eggs or yogurt.

FISH WITH CORN AND CAJUN FLAVORS

■ *Serves 4* ■

Here's a good way to use corn bread stuffing mix (just use the bread cubes without the vegetable/seasoning packet).

- 2 tablespoons butter or margarine
- 1/2 red bell pepper, cored, ribs and seeds removed, cut into 1/4-inch cubes
- 2 scallions, finely sliced
- 2 tablespoons chopped fresh parsley
- 1/2 teaspoon Cajun seasoning for fish

salt and pepper

- 1 cup corn bread stuffing mix or crumbled day old corn bread
- 3/4 cup canned, or thawed frozen corn, drained
- 1 1/2 teaspoons white wine or water
- 6 fillets of sole, flounder or other white-fleshed fish, 1/4-inch thick (about 1 1/2 pounds)
- 6 parsley leaves

1 Melt butter in skillet and sauté pepper and scallions until tender. Remove from heat and add chopped parsley, Cajun seasoning, salt, pepper, corn bread, corn and wine.

2 Preheat oven to 375°F (190°C). Rinse and dry fish pieces and lay flat in baking pan. Spread filling on wider end of each and fold smaller half over. Dot with butter and press 1 parsley leaf on top of each fillet. Bake 8 to 12 minutes or until fish is opaque.

MICROWAVE: (1) Combine butter, bell pepper, scallions, chopped parsley, Cajun seasoning, salt and pepper in 1-quart casserole. Cover and cook on HIGH (100%) 2 to 3 minutes. (2) Add corn bread, corn and wine and mix well. Spread filling on fish as in step 2 above. Cover with plastic and cook on HIGH (100%) 6 minutes or until fish is opaque. Let stand 2 minutes before serving.

LOW-FAT FISH ROLLS WITH HERBS

■ *Serves 4* ■

There's only 1 gram of fat and about 125 calories in this sure-to-please, tasty dish with an Italian accent. Use fresh or frozen fish. You may have more than four fillets; if so, simply distribute green beans accordingly.

- 1 pound flounder fillets, fresh or frozen
- 1 package (9 ounces) frozen French-style green beans
- 2 tablespoons chopped onion
- 1/2 cup boiling water
- 1 can (8 ounces) tomato sauce
- 1 teaspoon dried oregano
- 1/2 teaspoon dried basil
- 1 garlic clove, minced, or 1/8 teaspoon garlic powder
- 2 tablespoons grated Parmesan cheese

1 If fish is frozen, thaw overnight in refrigerator. Divide into fillets.

2 Preheat oven to 350°F (180°C). Add beans and onion to boiling water, cover and boil gently until beans are cooked but still crisp, about 6 to 7 minutes. Drain.

3 Distribute beans and onion among centers of fillets. Roll up, starting with narrow end. Arrange rolls in baking pan, seam side down.

4 Mix tomato sauce, oregano, basil and garlic. Pour around fish and spoon several tablespoonfuls on top, leaving some of the fish exposed. Sprinkle with Parmesan. Bake 15 minutes or until fish flakes easily and sauce is bubbling.

MICROWAVE: (1) If necessary, thaw fish. (2) Combine beans and onion in bowl with 1/4 cup water, cover and cook on HIGH (100%) 3 minutes. Drain. Fill fish as above and arrange in microwave-safe dish. (3) Combine tomato, oregano, basil and garlic. Pour into dish without covering fish completely. Sprinkle with Parmesan. Cover and cook on HIGH 7 minutes.

FISH FILLETS WITH BUTTER AND HERB SAUCE

■ *Serves 4* ■

Here's a way to liven up prepared fish fillets. The sauce adds a gourmet touch and makes the task of preparing supper easy.

1   *package (12 ounces) frozen crunchy (battered and fried) fish fillets*
1/4   *cup butter or margarine*
1/2   *small onion, minced*
1   *garlic clove, minced*
1   *tablespoon arrowroot or cornstarch*
1   *cup water*
2   *tablespoons chopped fresh parsley or 2 teaspoons dried*
1   *tablespoons chopped fresh tarragon or 1 teaspoon dried*
1   *teaspoon instant chicken bouillon or 1 chicken bouillon cube*
1   *teaspoon prepared mustard*
1   *teaspoon white wine vinegar*
pepper

1 Bake fish fillets as directed on package.

2 Melt butter or margarine in saucepan, add onion and sauté until soft. Add garlic and cook 1 minute longer. Stir arrowroot or cornstarch into water until dissolved. Add to saucepan with remaining ingredients, bring to boil and boil 1 minute. Spoon over cooked fish without covering it entirely.

MICROWAVE: (1) Microwave fish per package instructions. (2) Melt butter or margarine on HIGH (100%) 30 seconds in 1-quart bowl. Add onion and garlic and cook 1 minute longer. (3) Dissolve arrowroot or cornstarch and bouillon in water and add to bowl with remaining ingredients. Cover with plastic and cook on HIGH 3 minutes. Spoon sauce over fish without covering it entirely.

ROLLED FILLETS OF FLOUNDER WITH BROCCOLI AND CARROT FILLING

■ *Serves 4* ■

*T*his seafood recipe is for a healthier diet.

2 small broccoli stalks, fresh or frozen, cut up
2 small carrots, grated, or 1 cup frozen
    sliced carrots
1/4 teaspoon nutmeg
salt and pepper
4 flounder fillets (about 1 pound), rinsed
    and dried
2 tablespoons fresh lemon juice
1/2 cup dry white wine
paprika

1 Cook broccoli (and carrot slices if frozen) in small saucepan in ½ cup water until tender. Drain and mince in processor but do not puree. Put in small bowl (add carrot, if grated) and season with nutmeg, salt and pepper.

2 Lay fillets flat and spread broccoli mixture over each. Roll up each fillet beginning with narrow end and arrange in small skillet. Add lemon juice and wine. Sprinkle rolls with any leftover broccoli mixture plus a little more nutmeg. Cover and cook until fish flakes, 6 to 8 minutes. Sprinkle with paprika and serve right away.

MICROWAVE: (1) Cook broccoli with 2 tablespoons water on HIGH (100%) 6 minutes if fresh, 4 to 6 minutes if frozen. Combine with grated carrot, nutmeg, salt and pepper. (2) Proceed with step 2 above, except cook in microwave-safe dish on HIGH 5 to 6 minutes.

PANFRIED CATFISH FILLETS WITH PECANS AND BACON CONFETTI

■ *Serves 4* ■

*C*atfish is often cooked whole, but now the fresh fish sections offer catfish fillets too. I find them easy to handle and especially tasty.

1 to 1 1/2 pounds catfish fillets, rinsed and
        dried
juice of 1 lemon
2 eggs
3/4 cup milk
3/4 cup white or yellow cornmeal
3/4 cup all purpose flour

8 tablespoons butter or margarine
4 tablespoons vegetable oil
1/2 cup sliced scallions, white and green parts
3/4 cup pecan halves, toasted
8 slices thick bacon, cut into 1/2-inch cubes,
    cooked until crisp and drained

1 Combine fillets with all but 1 tablespoon lemon juice in a bowl and coat well. Cover and set aside.

2 Combine eggs and milk in shallow dish; combine cornmeal and flour on large plate. Dip fillets in egg mixture, then coat both sides with cornmeal mixture.

3 Heat 2 tablespoons each butter and oil in large skillet. When bubbling hot, sauté fillets on each side for a minute or two. Transfer to warm plates. When half of fillets are cooked, clean skillet and start fresh with 2 more tablespoons each butter and oil. (To speed process, use two skillets if you can.)

4 When all fillets are cooked, wipe out skillet with paper towels. Melt remaining 4 tablespoons butter, add reserved tablespoon of lemon juice and scallions and cook until butter is lightly browned. Add toasted pecans, toss and spoon over fillets. Sprinkle bacon confetti over all.

GRILLED MONKFISH ON A BED OF VEGETABLES

■ *Serves 4* ■

Monkfish, now available in most supermarket fresh fish sections, grills quickly and easily. If skewered and grilled, it is ideally set on a bed of vegetables.

*1 1/2 to 2 pounds monkfish fillets, cut into
    1 1/2-inch pieces*
1/3   cup vegetable oil
juice of 1 lemon
salt and pepper
* 4   slices bacon, room temperature*
cooked vegetables

1 Marinate monkfish pieces in vegetable oil and lemon juice for 30 minutes at room temperature or longer in the refrigerator (but bring to room temperature before grilling). Thread pieces on 4 skewers. Add salt and pepper and wrap bacon, spiral fashion, around fish.

2 When fire is ready, grill fish 4 to 5 minutes, turning every minute or so, or broil 4 inches from heat source. Bacon should be cooked.

3 Serve hot atop bed of vegetables.

GRILLED SALMON WITH GINGER GLAZE

■ *Serves 6* ■

6   *salmon fillets with skin, each about 2*
    inches wide, 5 to 6 inches long and 3/4 to
    1 inch thick at midpoint
1/4 *cup soy sauce*
1/4 *cup cream sherry*
2   *teaspoons sugar*
1   *tablespoon grated fresh ginger*
2   *garlic cloves, minced*
lemon wedges for garnish

1 Rinse and dry salmon pieces and arrange in 1 layer in glass dish.

2 Combine soy sauce, sherry and sugar in small saucepan and heat only until sugar dissolves. Add ginger and garlic and let cool. Pour over salmon, turning pieces to coat all sides. Marinate in refrigerator 2 to 3 hours or at room temperature 30 minutes.

3 Remove salmon from marinade and thread each fillet lengthwise on 2 long skewers. (Using two skewers makes it easier to turn fish.)

4 Grill fish flesh side down first, basting with marinade. Turn and grill skin side, basting again; do not overcook. Garnish with lemon wedges and serve with lemon mayonnaise sauce.

POACHED AND CHILLED SALMON STEAKS WITH PINK MAYONNAISE

■ *Serves 6* ■

An excellent way to cook fish, but don't overcook it. When chilling, be sure to cover tightly.

2   *cups water*
1   *package (1.4 ounces) vegetable soup and*
    recipe mix
1   *cup dry white wine*
2   *thin slices lime or lemon*
6   *small salmon steaks, 1 inch thick (about 2*
    pounds)
1   *cup mayonnaise*
2   *tablespoons ketchup*
1   *tablespoon fresh lime or lemon juice*
fresh or dried basil and dill (use both for
garnish)

1 In a skillet large enough to hold the salmon steaks in one layer, combine water, soup mix, wine and lime slices and bring to boil. Carefully put in salmon steaks. Liquid should cover steaks; if not, add just enough water to cover. Simmer 8 to 10 minutes or until salmon flakes easily. Transfer steaks to plate, cover and refrigerate.

2 Boil liquid in skillet over high heat until reduced to 3/4 cup; this may take 25 to 30 minutes. Strain and blend with mayonnaise, ketchup and lime juice to make a smooth, pink sauce.

3 To serve, spread some of sauce on bottom of platter. Gently peel skin from each piece of salmon, remove bones and set steaks on top of sauce. Add a sprinkle each of basil and dill. Pass remaining sauce separately.

MICROWAVE: (1) Combine water, soup mix, wine and lime slices in 2-quart microwave-safe shallow dish. Cook on HIGH (100%) 8 minutes. (2) Add salmon and cook on HIGH 4 minutes. Remove salmon, cover and refrigerate. (3) Cook salmon liquid 20 minutes to reduce to 3/4 cup. Strain and blend with mayonnaise, ketchup and lime juice. Proceed as above.

SALMON POTATO PIE WITH DILL

■ *Serves 6 to 8* ■

A gutsy dish and an alternative to the usual salmon steak. At lunchtime, serve with fresh green salad with an oil and sherry vinegar dressing.

1	*pound salmon fillet or steak*
1	*cup frozen hash brown potatoes, or 2 small potatoes cut into 1/4-inch cubes*
1/2	*cup water*
2	*eggs*
3/4	*cup mayonnaise*
2	*tablespoons all purpose flour*
1/2	*cup chopped scallions*
1	*can (4 ounces) sliced mushrooms, drained, or 3 fresh mushrooms, thinly sliced*
1/4	*cup finely chopped fresh dill or 1 tablespoon dried dillweed*
8	*ounces grated Gruyère cheese*
1	*baked 10-inch deep-dish pie shell*

1 Combine salmon and potatoes in large skillet with cover. Add water and bring to boil, then lower heat and simmer 4 minutes. Remove salmon; skin, bone and flake. Transfer to bowl with potatoes.

2 Preheat oven to 350°F (180°C). Combine eggs, mayonnaise and flour in another bowl and mix well. Add to salmon mixture with scallions, mushrooms, dill and half of cheese. Transfer to pie shell and top with remaining cheese. Bake 40 minutes. Serve hot.

MICROWAVE: (1) Combine salmon and potatoes in microwave-safe dish with 1/4 cup water, cover with plastic and cook on HIGH (100%) 2 minutes. Remove salmon; skin, bone and flake. Transfer to bowl with potatoes. (2) Proceed with step 2 above. (3) Cook pie on MEDIUM (50%) 20 minutes or until set.

SCALLOPS GRILLED WITH CREAMY ITALIAN DRESSING

■ *Serves 4* ■

If scallops aren't available, use medium to large shrimp (shelled and deveined) or 1 1/2-inch chunks of swordfish.

1 *pound fresh or frozen scallops, thawed if frozen*
1/2 *cup bottled creamy Italian salad dressing*
2 *tablespoons butter or margarine, melted*
2 *tablespoons finely chopped fresh basil or 1 teaspoon dried*

1 Marinate scallops in dressing for at least 30 minutes at room temperature,

as long as overnight in refrigerator. Remove from refrigerator 30 minutes before grilling. Drizzle with melted butter, catching excess in marinade.

2 Skewer scallops and grill or broil, basting frequently. Sprinkle with basil just before serving.

SCALLOPS IN SHRIMP BISQUE AU GRATIN

■ *Serves 6* ■

This is a version of Coquilles St. Jacques—a favorite of mine, though a time-consuming dish. To save time, I use canned shrimp or lobster bisque. Serve over a split hot biscuit, toast points or grilled Italian or French bread.

1 *tablespoon olive oil*
1 *tablespoon butter*
1 *pound bay scallops, rinsed and dried*
8 *ounces mushrooms, sliced*
1/2 *cup dry white wine*
1 *can (8 or 10 1/2 ounces) shrimp or lobster bisque, undiluted*
1 *cup grated Gruyère cheese (4 ounces)*
2 *tablespoons finely chopped dill or 1/2 teaspoon dried dillweed*

1 Heat oil and butter in skillet and sauté scallops and mushrooms until scallops are opaque. Remove with slotted spoon. Add wine to skillet, raise heat and boil until reduced and thickened. Remove from heat.

2 Heat bisque in saucepan. Add half of Gruyère, dill, scallops and white wine sauce. Transfer to one large or 6 individual gratin dishes. Top with remaining cheese. Broil 4 inches from heat source until top is golden.

MICROWAVE: (1) Combine oil and butter in 1 1/2- or 2-quart microwave-safe dish and cook on HIGH (100%) 30 seconds. Add scallops, mushrooms, wine, bisque, half of Gruyère and dill. Cook on HIGH 12 minutes. (2) Sprinkle remaining cheese over top and broil until lightly browned and bubbly.

GRILLED SEA BASS WITH SESAME AND SOY

■ *Serves 4* ■

*U*se a wire basket to grill the fish, and be sure the sea bass is really fresh.

2 whole sea bass (2 1/4 pounds each), cleaned, head and tail on, rinsed and dried
4 garlic cloves, halved
2 tablespoons white wine vinegar
1/4 cup sesame oil
1/3 cup soy sauce
6 thin slices fresh ginger, cut into thin strips
4 sprigs cilantro, cut in thirds
4 scallions, thinly sliced

1 Make 2 slashes, about 1/2 inch deep, on each side of both fish. Place in 1 or 2 glass or ceramic dishes.

2 Combine all remaining ingredients and pour over fish. Marinate 30 minutes at room temperature, turning fish after 15 minutes.

3 Prepare charcoal grill. Place each fish in hinged wire basket and set on grill when fire is ready. Cook, basting with marinade, until fish is done on both sides, about 10 minutes. (Test by inserting wooden skewer through thickest part of fish; if it meets no resistance, fish is cooked.)

HOT AND SWEET GINGER SHRIMP

■ *Serves 6* ■

*T*o clean shrimp easily, hold shrimp legs in left hand with tail away from you. Cut along back of shrimp with scissors. Open cut shell to remove vein but keep shell on. Run under cool water.

1/3 cup vegetable oil
1/4 cup light soy sauce
24 large shrimp (about 2 pounds), cleaned but with shells on, dried
4 pieces preserved ginger, minced
4 scallions, thinly sliced
2 garlic cloves, minced
1/4 cup finely chopped fresh parsley
1/2 fresh chili, finely chopped, or 1/2 teaspoon red pepper flakes

Heat oil and soy sauce in skillet large enough to hold shrimp in one layer (or in two smaller skillets). Add shrimp and cook until pink on one side. Add all remaining ingredients, turn shrimp and cook other side until pink. Toss well and serve. Entire cooking procedure should take less than 10 minutes.

MICROWAVE: (1) Combine all ingredients in large, deep microwave-safe dish. Cover and cook on HIGH (100%) 5 minutes.

HOT SAUCED SHRIMP

■ *Serves 6* ■

What fun to idle over the bottles and jars in condiment sections. The tasty, spicy ingredients for this sauce are staples and should be easy to find.

1/2 cup mayonnaise
1 tablespoon ketchup
1 teaspoon Worcestershire sauce
1/2 teaspoon hot pepper sauce
juice of 1 lemon
1 small onion, finely chopped
1 tablespoon chopped fresh parsley
2 pounds medium to large shrimp, shelled, deveined and rinsed
crab boil mix for 2 pounds shrimp
4 lemon slices
lettuce leaves for garnish

1 Combine all ingredients except shrimp, crab boil and lemon slices in bowl, mixing well. Cover and refrigerate until ready to use.

2 Boil shrimp with crab boil and lemon slices according to directions on crab boil package. Cook just until they turn pink; this will take a couple of minutes if water is boiling before shrimp are added. To serve, place shrimp on lettuce leaves and top with sauce.

MICROWAVE: (1) Prepare sauce as above. (2) Place shrimp in 3-quart microwave-safe dish. Add crab boil mix and stir to coat. Add lemon slices. Cover with plastic and cook on HIGH (100%) 7 to 8 minutes, tossing shrimp after 4 minutes to redistribute for even cooking. (3) Proceed as above.

SHRIMP, SCALLOPS AND SPAGHETTI, ITALIAN STYLE

■ *Serves 4* ■

An easy, wonderful dish. Be sure to serve with a fresh green salad, with a creamy Italian or herb dressing.

2 tablespoons butter or margarine
1 cup thinly sliced celery (2 stalks)
1 garlic clove, minced
1 jar (15 1/2 ounces) spaghetti sauce (1 3/4 cups)
1/4 cup dry white wine

8 ounces bay scallops
8 ounces medium shrimp, shelled and deveined
8 ounces spaghetti, cooked
1/4 cup chopped scallions

1 Melt butter in 2-quart saucepan and sauté celery until almost tender. Add garlic and cook 1 minute. Add sauce and wine, bring to boil, lower heat, cover and simmer 10 minutes, stirring 2 or 3 times.

2 Add scallops and shrimp and simmer until shrimp turn pink, about 5 minutes. Serve over hot spaghetti and sprinkle with scallions.

MICROWAVE: (1) Combine butter, celery and garlic in 2-quart round dish, cover and cook on HIGH (100%) 3 minutes. (2) Add sauce and wine. Recover and cook on HIGH 4 minutes. (3) Add scallops and shrimp. Recover and cook on HIGH 4 minutes. Let stand 2 minutes. Serve with cooked spaghetti and scallion garnish.

STOVETOP SHRIMP JAMBALAYA WITH SMOKED SAUSAGE

■ *Serves 4* ■

*F*or years I made jambalaya in a casserole and baked it in the oven. Here's one you can do on top of the stove in a covered skillet. Smoked sausage is available in the packaged meats section of the supermarket. Use fresh shrimp if you can; if you use frozen, thaw well before adding.

1   *tablespoon olive, corn or vegetable oil*
4   *ounces thinly sliced smoked sausage*
1   *red, yellow or green bell pepper, cored, seeded and cut into 1/2-inch cubes*
2   *garlic cloves, minced*
1   *cup long-grain rice*
1   *package (2.4 ounces) vegetable soup and recipe mix*
1   *can (16 ounces) plum tomatoes with juice, coarsely chopped*
2   *cups water*
1   *tablespoon finely chopped fresh tarragon or 1/2 teaspoon dried*
1   *pound medium shrimp, peeled, deveined, rinsed, dried and split lengthwise*

1 Heat oil in large skillet or saucepan with cover and sauté sausage and pepper 4 minutes or until they begin to brown. Add garlic and rice and stir well. Cook 4 minutes, stirring most of the time.

2 Add vegetable soup mix, tomatoes, water and tarragon and bring to boil. Lower heat and simmer 20 minutes or until rice is almost tender.

3 Stir in shrimp and cook, covered, until shrimp turn pink, about 6 minutes. Serve hot.

MICROWAVE: (1) Combine oil, pepper and garlic in 3-quart casserole. Cover and cook on HIGH (100%) 3 minutes. (2) Add all remaining ingredients. Cover and cook on HIGH 5 minutes. Reduce to MEDIUM (50%) and cook 12 minutes.

GRILLED FRESH TUNA WITH CALIFORNIA VINAIGRETTE

■ *Serves 2* ■

Don't overcook!

1/2 cup fresh orange juice
  2 tablespoons peanut oil
  1 tablespoon finely chopped or grated fresh ginger
  2 scallions, chopped
white pepper
  1 pound fresh tuna steak, about 1-inch thick
1/2 cup fresh enoki mushrooms

1 Combine all ingredients except tuna and mushrooms, mix well and set aside.

2 Place mushrooms on small sheet of foil or in small foil container and sprinkle with a few drops of oil. Place on hot grill.

3 Grill tuna at the same time, charring both sides; this should take 1 to 2 minutes per side for rare. Remove from grill and let rest a minute or so.

4 Thinly slice tuna and divide between two plates. Spoon sauce over and top with mushrooms.
  Note: If using broiler instead of grill, add mushrooms to broiler tray as soon as tuna is removed and broil 1 to 2 minutes.

SILK SNAPPER FILLETS IN LOBSTER AND TOMATO SAUCE

■ *Serves 6* ■

Silk snappers are popular in Florida but don't fret if your supermarket doesn't carry them. Use any small, white fish fillets.

 12 silk snapper fillets (about 1 1/2 pounds), rinsed and dried
  2 tablespoons butter or margarine
paprika
  1 can (8 or 10 1/2 ounces) cream of lobster soup
1/2 cup half-and-half

1/2 cup chopped ripe tomatoes, skins and seeds removed, or 1/2 cup dice canned plum tomatoes with some juice
black pepper
fresh mint leaves

1 Lightly butter rimmed baking sheet and arrange fillets on it in one layer.

Dot with butter and sprinkle with paprika. Set aside.

2 Combine lobster soup and half-and-half in saucepan and heat, stirring, until well combined. Add tomatoes and juice and cook, stirring frequently, until heated through; do not boil. Season with pepper.

3 Broil fillets about 3 minutes or until they flake. Test with fork for doneness; do not overcook.

4 Spoon 2 tablespoons sauce onto each warmed plate and place 2 fillets side-by-side on top, with 2 mint leaves between them. Serve immediately.

MICROWAVE: (1) Combine lobster soup, half-and-half, tomatoes and pepper in large microwave-safe bowl. Cover and cook on **MEDIUM-HIGH** (70%) 3 minutes (be sure bowl is deep enough to prevent boiling over). (2) Arrange fillets in 2 dishes and dot with butter and paprika. Cover with plastic and cook on HIGH 4 to 6 minutes. Proceed as above.

FISHERMAN'S STEW, PORTUGUESE STYLE

■ *Serves 6* ■

*I*f you can't get tilefish, use grouper or monkfish. If you use frozen chunks of squash or pumpkin, treat as fresh.

2   tablespoons olive or vegetable oil
1   cup chopped onion
1   garlic clove, minced
3   cups water
2   cans (16 ounces each) tomatoes, including liquid
1   tablespoon finely chopped fresh basil or 1 teaspoon dried
1   tablespoon finely chopped fresh thyme or 1 teaspoon dried
salt and red pepper flakes
1 1/2   pounds winter squash or pumpkin, fresh or frozen, cut into 1-inch pieces (about 4 cups)
2   ears corn, fresh or frozen, cut into 1-inch rounds
2   pounds tilefish fillets, cut into 1-inch pieces

1 Heat oil in large saucepan and sauté onion until soft. Add garlic and cook 1 minute. Add all remaining ingredients except fish and bring to boil. Lower heat and cook 10 minutes or until squash and corn are almost done. (If you use thawed frozen squash or pumpkin, add 5 minutes before adding fish.)

2 Add fish pieces and cook 5 minutes or until fish flakes.

MICROWAVE: (1) Combine oil and onions in large, deep microwave-safe bowl, stir and cook on HIGH 2 minutes. (2) Add all remaining ingredients except fish and cook, covered, on HIGH 5 minutes. (3) Add fish and cook, covered, on HIGH 4 minutes.

SWORDFISH STEAKS WITH BUTTER, LEMON AND CAPERS

■ *Serves 4* ■

If the steaks are large, buy two and cut in half.

4 *swordfish steaks (about 2 pounds)*
1/2 *cup water*
3 *tablespoons butter or margarine*
juice of 1 lemon
2 *tablespoons capers*
salt and pepper

1 Combine fish and water in skillet large enough to hold fish in one layer. Bring to boil, lower heat and poach fish until tender. Carefully transfer to platter or individual dishes.

2 Discard water in skillet. Add butter, lemon juice and capers to skillet, heat quickly and pour over fish. Season with salt and pepper.

MICROWAVE: (1) Place butter in microwave-safe dish large enough to hold fish in one layer and heat on HIGH (100%) 40 seconds. (2) Add fish and lemon juice and turn fish to coat both sides. Add capers, salt and pepper; cover and cook on HIGH 15 minutes.

7

BUTCHER BLOCK— PRIME MEATS AND FINE FOWL

PRIME · BUTCH · FINE

I believe that in the U.S. we can purchase the best meat and fowl in the entire world. All of us should understand the various cuts of meat and how they are used. Often the cooking method determines the cut of meat to buy—you wouldn't cook a shell steak the way you do a pot roast, for example. I find I get quite a bit of help from the butchers at the supermarket if I discuss what I plan to cook.

With beef, fillet, sirloin, top sirloin, porterhouse and Delmonico are best for grilling and broiling; for roasting there are standing rib roasts, whole fillets and boned short loins. All steaks can be sautéed but they shouldn't be as thick as those cooked on the grill. Rump, leg and shin are stewing cuts, and neck and shin do perfectly well in soups.

Pork should be white and the fat even whiter. If pork is too pink or rosy, it won't roast well. I buy loin cuts, fillet chops and ham. All of these can be eaten fresh or cured. Internal pork temperatures should reach 140°F (60°C) to destroy any trichinae present. Lamb is sheep under one year of age; it's mutton after that. We eat mainly lamb in this country. Always buy Prime or Choice.

As for poultry, most types—especially chicken and turkey—are still fairly inexpensive, and I believe their popularity is in direct relation to their versatility.

EXPRESS CHECK-OUT

MEATS AND FOWL

1 Refrigerate breaded meat or poultry for 2 hours or so before frying. Breading will adhere better.

2 When broiling or frying small sausage, skewer with wooden picks to facilitate turning.

3 When browning meats, use a combination of oil and butter (or margarine) to prevent blackening.

4 To avoid greasy, cholesterol-laden food, remove all fat and most of the skin from chicken to be used in casseroles or other one-dish meals.

5 To coat cubes of meat with flour, combine flour, seasonings and meat in plastic bag, close it and shake.

6 Don't be afraid to add a touch of curry powder or a combination of herbs to one-dish meals of meat or fowl. Add wine and broth in place of water for stews; if wine, use good-quality drinking wine.

7 Beef and lamb enjoy some strong sauces. If grilling, broiling or pan-frying a steak, combine some sour cream with bottled horseradish and serve as an accompaniment. For fancier occasions, combine 1 cup hollandaise, 1 cup whipped cream and 2 tablespoons bottled horseradish.

8 It takes a few minutes more, but marinating chicken in a little fresh lemon juice rids it of any gamey odor.

9 Shrink-wrapped meats and fowl have sell-by dates; be sure you note them. As a rule, meats at the butcher counter are no higher-priced than prepacked meats in coolers. Get to know the counter personnel to learn what is on sale and so on.

SUPERMARKET BAKE: PASTA AND BEEF WITH CHEESES

■ *Serves 4 to 6* ■

When we were kids, we always had "bakes"; our parents found this an easy way to serve many hungry mouths. This is a good family dish with plenty of protein and carbohydrates. But it should be served with greenery—a salad, broccoli or spinach cooked with lemon.

1 tablespoon olive oil
1 pound ground beef
1 package (0.9 ounce) onion-mushroom recipe soup mix (to make 2 cups)
1 can (8 ounces) tomato sauce
2 teaspoons dried basil
salt and pepper
6 ounces small shaped pasta (tubes, rotelle, shells, etc.), cooked
1/2 cup grated Parmesan or Romano cheese
1 cup shredded mozzarella cheese (4 ounces)

1 Heat oil in skillet and brown beef; Drain. Prepare 2 cups soup per packet directions and add to beef with tomato sauce, basil, salt and pepper. Cook over low heat, uncovered, about 15 minutes, stirring several times.

2 Preheat oven to 350°F (180°C). Spread half of meat mixture into 8 × 8-inch baking dish. Add pasta and sprinkle half of grated cheese over it. Spread remaining meat mixture over pasta; sprinkle mozzarella and remaining grated cheese over surface. Bake about 30 minutes or until top is nicely browned and juices are bubbling.

MICROWAVE: (1) Cook beef in oil in microwave-safe 8 × 8-inch dish on HIGH (100%) 4 to 5 minutes. Add soup, tomato sauce, basil, salt and pepper and cook on HIGH 4 minutes, stirring once. Cook on MEDIUM (50%) 10 minutes, stirring 3 times. (2) Assemble with cooked pasta as above (step 2) and cook on HIGH 3 minutes to melt cheeses.

REDSKIN CHILI

■ *Serves 6* ■

You only need six ingredients to make this easy chili dish, which can be prepared ahead and reheated.

2 pounds lean ground beef
2 medium onions, finely chopped
3 garlic cloves, finely chopped
1 can (40 1/2 ounces) red kidney beans, or an equivalent amount in smaller cans
1 can (29 ounces) tomato sauce
2 tablespoons chili powder

1 Brown beef in skillet or heavy saucepan. Drain off fat.

2 Add all remaining ingredients and simmer, stirring frequently, 40 minutes.

ANOTHER HERO (GROUND BEEF AND TOMATOES ON ROLL)

■ Serves 6 ■

We all love hamburgers but we also love heroes. Here's a simple dish with a lot of flavor. Use long hard rolls, or Italian or French bread; don't use hamburger rolls.

1 *pound lean ground beef*
1 *cup chopped onion*
1/4 *cup chopped celery*
1/4 *cup chopped red bell pepper*
1 *garlic clove, minced*
2 *tablespoons chili powder*
1 *jar (15 1/2 ounces) spaghetti sauce (about 1 3/4 cups)*
6 *long hard rolls, split, or 4-inch slices of Italian or French bread, grilled or broiled*

1 Brown beef in large skillet, stirring and breaking up meat. Drain fat.

2 Add onion, celery, red pepper, garlic and chili powder and cook 10 minutes or until vegetables are tender. Add spaghetti sauce and bring to boil. Lower heat and simmer, covered, 15 minutes.

3 Open grilled rolls and spoon meat and sauce into them. Serve hot.

MICROWAVE: (1) Combine onion, celery, red pepper, garlic and chili powder in 2-quart microwave-safe dish. Cover with plastic and cook on HIGH (100%) 4 minutes. (2) Add beef and stir to break up. Recover and cook on HIGH 5 minutes, stirring once. Spoon off fat. (3) Add spaghetti sauce, recover and cook on HIGH 4 minutes or until sauce bubbles. Proceed as above.

SUPERMARKET TAMALE PIE

■ Serves 6 ■

It's hard to believe that canned food can make something taste this good. This will become a favorite.

1 *pound ground chuck*
4 *ounces bulk pork sausage*
1 *small onion, chopped*
2 *garlic cloves, minced*
1 *can (16 ounces) stewed tomatoes, drained*
1 *package (10 ounces) frozen corn, thawed*
1 *can (8 ounces) tomato sauce*

2 *teaspoons chili powder*
salt
1 *package (8 1/2 ounces) corn muffin mix*
1 *egg*
1/3 *cup milk*
2/3 *cup shredded cheddar cheese (3 ounces)*

1 Brown beef and sausage in skillet. Stir in onion, garlic, tomatoes, corn, tomato sauce, 1 1/2 teaspoons chili powder and salt and cook, uncovered, 10 minutes. Transfer to 8-inch round or square baking dish.

2 Preheat oven to 350°F (180°C). Combine corn muffin mix, egg and milk in bowl just until blended. Spread over meat. Bake 30 minutes or until top is set. Sprinkle with cheese and reserved chili powder and bake several minutes longer to melt cheese.

MICROWAVE: (1) Combine beef, pork, onion and garlic in 8-inch round or square baking dish. Cook on HIGH (100%) 9 minutes, stir once or twice to break up meat. Drain. (2) Add tomatoes, corn, tomato sauce, 1 1/2 teaspoons chili powder and salt. Stir and cook on HIGH 6 minutes; mixture should thicken. (3) Prepare muffin mix with egg and milk and spread over beef. Cook on MEDIUM-HIGH (70%) 5 minutes, then on HIGH 6 minutes until top is set. Sprinkle with cheese and remaining chili powder. Cook on HIGH 1 to 2 minutes or until cheese melts.

RAGOUT OF BEEF WITH GREEN PEAS

■ *Serves 6* ■

A beef ragout is one of the most satisfying dishes imaginable. If red bells are not available, use any color pepper.

2	*tablespoons all purpose flour*
1 1/2	*pounds boneless beef chuck, fat trimmed, cut into 1 1/2- to 2-inch cubes*
2	*tablespoons olive oil*
1	*red bell pepper, cored, ribs and seeds removed, chopped*
1	*large onion, chopped*
2	*large carrots, cut diagonally into 1-inch slices*
1	*can (17 ounces) stewed tomatoes*
1	*can (10 3/4 ounces) condensed beef broth*
1	*can (8 ounces) tomato sauce*
2	*cups frozen green peas*

1 Place flour in plastic bag, add beef and toss to coat well. Heat oil in skillet and brown beef. Transfer to flameproof casserole. Cook pepper, onion and carrots in same skillet about 5 minutes, stirring frequently. Transfer vegetables to casserole.

2 Add stewed tomatoes, beef broth and tomato sauce, cover and simmer on top of stove 1 1/2 hours or longer until beef is tender. Stir in peas 10 minutes before end of cooking time.

MICROWAVE: (1) Combine olive oil, pepper, onions and carrots in 3-quart microwave-safe casserole and cook on HIGH (100%) 6 minutes. (2) Add all remaining ingredients except peas, cover and cook on HIGH 10 minutes, then on MEDIUM (50%) 50 to 60 minutes, stirring once or twice. If not on carousel, stir 3 or 4 times. (3) Cook frozen peas. Add to beef, then let stand 5 to 10 minutes before serving.

HAMBURGERS WITH SAUTÉED ONIONS

■ *Serves 4* ■

An extra step, sautéing chopped onions in a little butter, makes this a satisfying burger.

1   tablespoon butter or margarine
1   medium onion, finely chopped
1 1/2   pounds lean ground chuck
1   tablespoon Worcestershire sauce
1   teaspoon dried garlic flakes
salt and pepper
4   hamburger buns, toasted, grilled or broiled

1 Melt butter in skillet, add onion and sauté until soft, about 5 minutes. Remove from heat.

2 Combine beef, Worcestershire sauce, garlic, salt, pepper and cooked onion in a large bowl and mix with splayed fingers; do not overwork or pack meat. Divide in fourths and shape into 1-inch-thick patties. Grill 4 to 5 minutes per side for rare, 5 to 6 for medium or longer for well done. Serve on grilled rolls.

MICROWAVE: Add 4 tablespoons steak sauce. (1) Prepare burgers as above. Coat both sides of each burger with 1 tablespoon steak sauce. (2) Cook 4 at a time, covered with waxed paper, on HIGH (100%) 2 1/2 minutes. Turn and cook 2 to 3 minutes longer. Proceed as above.

HAMBURGERS WITH AVOCADO AND CHEESE TOPPING

■ *Serves 4* ■

Prepare uncooked hamburgers as above, and continue as follows:

1 ripe avocado, peeled and sliced as thinly as possible
juice of 1 lime
4   uncooked hamburger patties
2   ounces Monterey Jack cheese, shredded
4   hamburger buns, toasted, grilled or broiled
1/2   iceberg lettuce, shredded

1 Coat avocado slices with lime juice to prevent discoloration.

2 Grill or broil hamburgers on one side 4 to 7 minutes, depending on desired doneness. Turn and cook 3 to 6 minutes longer.

3 Arrange avocado slices on top of each burger. Sprinkle with cheese. Broil 1 to 2 minutes to melt cheese. Serve on toasted, grilled or broiled buns and garnish with shredded lettuce.

MICROWAVE: Burgers may be microwaved with help of browning agent. (See hamburgers with sautéed onions, above.) Complete with topping using broiler as above.

HAMBURGERS WITH GOAT CHEESE AND SAUTÉED MUSHROOMS

■ *Serves 4* ■

Prepare uncooked hamburgers as on page 112 and continue as follows:

4   *uncooked hamburger patties*
1   *tablespoon butter or margarine*
1   *cup thinly sliced mushrooms*
salt and pepper
4   *tablespoons goat cheese, soft*
4   *hamburger buns, toasted, grilled or broiled, optional*

1 Grill or broil burgers on one side 4 to 7 minutes, depending on desired doneness. Turn and cook 3 to 6 minutes longer.

2 Melt butter or margarine in skillet and sauté mushrooms until liquid has evaporated. Season with salt and pepper. Top each burger with goat cheese and top cheese with mushrooms. Serve with or without buns.

MICROWAVE: Burgers may be microwaved with help of browning agent. (See hamburgers with sautéed onions, page 112.) Complete with topping as above.

HAMBURGERS WITH TOMATO, BASIL AND MOZZARELLA

■ *Serves 4* ■

Prepare uncooked hamburgers as on page 112, and continue as follows:

4   *uncooked hamburger patties*
4   *thick slices red, ripe tomato*
2   *tablespoons finely chopped basil or 1 teaspoon dried*
1/2 *cup bottled pizza sauce*
1/2 *cup grated mozzarella cheese*
4   *hamburger buns or bread slices, toasted, grilled or broiled*

1 Grill or broil burgers on one side 4 to 7 minutes, depending on desired doneness. Turn and cook 3 to 6 minutes longer.

2 Place slice of tomato on each burger. Sprinkle with basil. Top with 2 tablespoons sauce. Sprinkle cheese over sauce and broil 1 to 2 minutes to melt cheese. Serve on buns or bread slices.

MICROWAVE: Burgers may be microwaved with help of browning agent. (See hamburgers with sauteed onions, page 112.) Complete with topping using broiler as above.

HOT HUNGARIAN GOULASH

■ *Serves 6* ■

Stewed tomatoes come in several ways on supermarket shelves. Those used here have chopped green chilies; if these are not on your supermarket shelf, add 1/4 teaspoon red pepper flakes or a chopped fresh or dried chili pepper to plain stewed tomatoes. Goulash is usually served with broad egg noodles, but brown or white rice can be substituted.

  1   tablespoon vegetable oil
  2   pounds beef, fat trimmed, cut into 1-inch cubes
  1   tablespoon Hungarian paprika
  1   envelope (1.2 ounce) onion soup mix
  1   can (16 ounces) stewed tomatoes with green chilies (see above)
  2   tablespoons all purpose flour
  1   cup water
  6   cups cooked white or brown rice
1/4   cup chopped fresh parsley or scallions

1 Heat oil in large saucepan and brown beef. Combine paprika, soup mix and tomatoes in bowl and add to beef. Bring to boil, lower heat, cover and simmer 1 to 1 1/2 hours or until beef is 3/4 cooked.

2 Combine flour and water and stir into stew. Bring to boil, lower heat, and simmer stirring until sauce thickens. Continue cooking until beef is tender.

3 Serve piping hot in shallow dishes with cooked rice on the side. Sprinkle with parsley or scallions.

MICROWAVE: Omit oil. (1) Combine paprika, soup mix and tomatoes in 3-quart microwave-safe container. Cover and cook on HIGH (100%) 5 minutes. (2) Add beef, cover and cook on MEDIUM (50%) 60 minutes, stirring twice during cooking. (3) Combine flour and water and stir in. Cook on HIGH 10 minutes or until sauce thickens, stirring twice. Let stand 3 minutes.

PARTY MEAT LOAF

■ *Serves 4 to 6* ■

Make two for a larger group. Two slices of hearty grain bread in processor will make 1/2 cup crumbs.

  8   ounces each ground beef, veal and pork (1 1/2 pounds total)
  1   egg, beaten
1/2   cup fresh whole-grain breadcrumbs
1/2   cup sweet vermouth or red wine
  1   small onion, chopped
  2   garlic cloves, minced
  1   teaspoon instant chicken bouillon
  1   teaspoon spicy brown mustard
salt and pepper

Preheat oven to 375°F (190°C). Combine all ingredients and pat into 9 × 5-inch loaf pan. Bake about 1 hour or until cooked through.

MICROWAVE: (1) Combine ingredients and pat into microwave-safe 9 × 5-inch loaf pan. Cook on HIGH (100%) 15 minutes; if not on carousel, turn twice during cooking. Let stand 5 minutes before serving.

GRILLED MEAT LOAF BURGERS

■ *Makes 8 burgers* ■

*U*se crumbs made from stone-ground wheat bread, available in a number of brands in most supermarkets. I prefer breads made with molasses and honey, which add more flavor and nutrition. Three slices of bread will make about 1 1/2 cups fresh breadcrumbs. Use a food processor to make the crumbs, but do not overprocess.

2	*pounds ground chuck*
1 1/2	*cups soft breadcrumbs*
2	*eggs*
1/2	*cup water*
1/3	*cup chili sauce*
1	*envelope (0.9 ounce) mushroom soup mix*

1 Combine ground chuck and crumbs in large bowl.

2 Combine eggs, water, chili sauce and soup mix in another bowl and mix well. Add to meat and mix lightly with splayed fingers; do not overmix. Divide into 8 portions (about 4 ounces each) and shape lightly into patties.

3 Grill over charcoal fire, using oiled wire basket, or cook burgers in large oiled skillet, or broil.

MICROWAVE: Add 4 tablespoon steak sauce. (1) Prepare burgers as above. Coat both sides of each burger with 1 tablespoon steak sauce. (2) Cook 4 burgers at a time, covered with waxed paper, on HIGH (100%) for 2 1/2 minutes. Turn and cook 2 to 3 minutes longer.

CHILI MEATBALLS WITH RICE

■ *Serves 4* ■

1 1/4	*pounds ground chuck*
2	*eggs, beaten*
1/2	*cup fresh breadcrumbs*
2	*teaspoons chili powder*
salt and pepper	
2	*tablespoons vegetable oil*
1	*can (16 ounces) stewed tomatoes*
4	*scallions, white and green parts, thinly sliced*
1	*red bell pepper, cored, ribs and seeds removed, thinkly sliced into rings*
3/4	*cup raw instant rice*

1 Mix beef, eggs, breadcrumbs, chili powder, salt and pepper in bowl. Form into 2-inch meatballs. Heat oil in skillet and brown meatballs. Transfer to caserole.

2 Preheat oven to 375°F (190°C). Add all remaining ingredients to meatballs, cover and bake until meatballs and rice are cooked, about 30 minutes.

MICROWAVE: Omit oil. (1) Prepare meatballs as above and place in 2-quart casserole. Cook on HIGH (100%) 7 minutes, turning once. (2) Add remaining ingredients, cover and cook on HIGH 7 minutes. Let stand 3 minutes before serving.

LITTLE MEATBALLS FOR HORS D'OEUVRE

■ *Makes about 40* ■

*T*o shape, place the required amount of meat in the palm of one hand and gently roll two or three times with the palm of the other hand to form a little meatball.

1	*pound ground chuck*
3/4	*cup Italian-seasoned breadcrumbs*
1	*egg, lightly beaten*
1	*garlic clove, minced*
1/2	*cup water*
1/2	*cup grated onion*
1/4	*cup grated Parmesan cheese*
	salt and pepper
1/4	*cup olive oil*
1	*can (15 ounces) tomato sauce*
1/2	*cup red wine vinegar*
1/3	*cup brown sugar, packed*

1 Combine meat, 1/4 cup breadcrumbs, egg, garlic, water, onion and cheese in a bowl and blend well, but do not overmix. Shape into small meatballs, using about 1 teaspoon of mixture for each. Roll in remaining breadcrumbs.

2 Heat olive oil in skillet and brown meatballs. Drain on paper towels. Discard oil remaining in skillet. Return meatballs to skillet, add remaining ingredients and stir well. Cover and simmer slowly 15 to 20 minutes. Serve with picks or wooden skewers.

MICROWAVE: Omit olive oil. Prepare meatballs as above and place in 2-quart baking dish. Cook on HIGH (100%) 6 to 7 minutes; if not on carousel, turn dish once. Drain. Combine remaining ingredients in small bowl and pour over meatballs. Cover and cook on HIGH 4 minutes to bring sauce to boil. Reduce power to MEDIUM (50%) and cook 5 minutes longer.

HEALTHY HOMEMADE MEAT LOAF WITH PARMESAN AND SCALLIONS

■ *Serves 6* ■

*E*qually delicious hot or cold. This loaf is tasty and colorful with specks of red (tomatoes), green (scallions) and white (onion soup mix). Serve with garlicky green beans.

1 1/2	*pounds lean ground chuck*	1/2	*cup grated Parmesan cheese*
1	*cup soft breadcrumbs*	1/2	*cup finely chopped scallions*

1   envelope (1.25 ounces) onion soup
    recipe mix
2   egg whites, beaten
1   can (10 ounces) diced tomatoes with
    green chilies or plain stewed tomatoes
    (if using the latter, add 1 teaspoon
    finely chopped chilli or 1/4 teaspoon red
    pepper flakes)

Preheat oven to 375°F (190°C). Combine all ingredients in large bowl and mix with splayed fingers; do not overmix. Turn onto large shallow baking pan and shape into loaf about 10 inches long, 4 inches wide and 2 1/2 inches high. Bake until done, about 45 minutes. Let stand 5 minutes before slicing.

MICROWAVE: (1) Combine ingredients as above. (2) Shape into loaf in pie dish and cook on HIGH (100%) 15 minutes. If not on carousel, turn dish twice during cooking. (3) Carefully drain fat. Let stand 3 minutes before slicing.

BALSAMIC-GLAZED THREE-MEAT LOAF WITH WALNUTS

■ Serves 8 to 12 ■

Soda crackers, a classic supermarket item, work beautifully in this special meat loaf. Grind the crackers in a food processor—about 36 of them to make 1 cup. Use the processor to chop the fresh spinach leaves as well; they add a mosaic look to the loaf in addition to providing good nutrients.

1   pound each ground lean pork, skinned and
    boned chicken breast and finely chopped
    smoked baked ham
2   cups fresh spinach leaves, chopped
1   cup coarsely chopped walnuts
1   cup soda cracker crumbs
1   cup milk
2   eggs, beaten
black pepper
balsamic glaze, see below

1 Preheat oven to 375°F (190°)C. Combine all ingredients in large bowl and mix well but do not overmix. Shape into 12 × 5 × 2-inch loaf place on shallow baking pan.

2 Bake 1 hour and 10 minutes, brushing with 1/3 of the glaze after 30 minutes, another 1/3 after 45 minues and remaining 1/3 at 1 hour. Remove from oven and let stand 5 minutes before slicing.

BALSAMIC GLAZE:
1/3   cup balsamic vinegar
  1   cup dark brown sugar, packed
  2   tablespoons Dijon-style mustard

Combine all ingredients in heavy saucepan and mix well. Bring to boil, lower heat and simmer, uncovered, 15 minutes.

MICROWAVE: (1) Mix glaze ingredients in bowl, cover loosely with waxed paper and cook on HIGH (100%) 3 to 6 minutes until sugar is dissolved, stirring 2 or 3 times. (2) Combine meat loaf ingredients and cook on HIGH 15 to 20 minutes. Add half of glaze after cooking time is half over and remaining glaze 3 to 4 minutes before end of cooking. If not on carousel, turn loaf twice during cooking.

JALAPEÑO MEAT LOAF WITH MONTEREY JACK CHEESE

■ *Serves 8* ■

Here's how to use herbs, spices and soda crackers in a meat loaf. Serve with hot corn pudding and a fresh green salad accented with chopped cilantro. Or, instead of pudding, add 1 cup cooked frozen corn niblets to green salad and toss with an oil and vinegar dressing.

2   *pounds ground chuck*
1   *can (28 ounces) plum tomatoes, chopped and well drained*
2   *cups grated Monterey Jack cheese (8 ounces)*
3   *eggs, beaten*
2   *fresh jalapeño peppers, minced*
1   *large onion, finely chopped*
4   *garlic cloves, minced*
1   *red bell pepper, cored, ribs and seeds removed, cut into 1/4-inch cubes*
1   *cup crumbs made from soda crackers*
2   *tablespoons finely chopped fresh oregano or 2 teaspoons dried*
2   *tablespoons chili powder*

2   *teaspoons ground cumin*
1   *teaspoon salt*

Preheat oven to 375°F (190°C). Combine all ingredients in large bowl and mix well but do not overmix. Shape into 12 × 6 × 2 1/2-inch loaf on shallow baking pan. Bake 1 hour. Let stand 10 minutes, covered, before slicing and serving.

MICROWAVE: (1) Combine ingredients as above. (2) Cook on HIGH (100%) 15 minutes; if not on carousel, turn twice during cooking. Let stand 5 minutes before serving.

ROAST BEEF

■ *Serves 6* ■

Whether to use the high- or low-temperature method in roasting standing rib roasts is a question that has not been answered, but I've always preferred the high-temperature method because I think it seals in juices, browns better and saves time.

1   *3-rib roast, trimmed (about 7 pounds)*
salt
freshly ground pepper

1 Preheat oven to 450°F (230°C). Wipe roast all over with damp cloth or moistened paper towel. Salt all sides and liberally sprinkle with black pepper. If using thermometer, insert in thickest part of roast.

2 Place meat on rack in roasting pan and roast for 30 minutes. Reduce heat to 300°F (150°C) and continue to roast to desired doneness (see chart on page 119). Let roast rest 15 minutes before carving.

SUPERMARKET SAVVY

COOKING ROAST BEEF

There are two basic ways to cook standing rib roasts: the high-and low-temperature methods. Use this table as your guide.

	Thermometer reading	HIGH Temperature without thermometer	LOW Temperature without thermometer
RARE	140°F(60°C)	16 min. per lb	18 min. per lb
MEDIUM-RARE	150°F(65°C)	18 min. per lb.	20 min. per lb
MEDIUM	160°F(70°C)	20 min. per lb.	22 min. per lb
WELL DONE	170°F(75°C)	26 min. per lb.	28 min. per lb

HIGH-TEMPERATURE METHOD: Cook 30 minutes in preheated 450°F (230°C) oven. Reduce heat to 300°F (150°C) and follow thermometer reading or timing chart above.

LOW-TEMPERATURE METHOD: Cook in preheated 300°F (150°C) oven and follow thermometer reading or timing chart above.

BEEF SHORT RIBS BAKED IN BEER

■ Serves 4 ■

Beef eaters like short ribs and here's a good way to prepare them.

2 tablespoons vegetable oil
3 pounds beef ribs, cut into 3-inch pieces
1 onion, chopped
2 celery stalks, thinly sliced
2 garlic cloves, minced, or 1/2 teaspoon garlic salt
1 can (12 ounces) beer
salt and pepper

1 Heat oil in large skillet and brown beef ribs on all sides. Transfer ribs to flameproof casserole with cover. Sauté onion and celery in skillet until tender. Add garlic pieces or garlic salt and cook 1 minute longer.

2 Transfer vegetables to casserole. Cover with beer, season with salt and pepper (careful with salt if garlic salt was used), cover and cook slowly about 1 hour or until thoroughly cooked. Alternatively, bake in preheated 375°F (190°C) oven 1 1/2 hours.

MICROWAVE: (1) Combine all ingredients in 5-quart microwave-safe casserole and cook, covered, on HIGH (100%) 5 minutes, then on MEDIUM (50%) 20 to 25 minutes. Stir once and continue to cook on MEDIUM 30 minutes longer. Let stand 10 to 15 minutes before serving.

POT ROAST, AMERICAN STYLE

■ *Serves 6 to 8* ■

*T*his is not a quickie, but it is an easy-to-prepare classic.

> 2 tablespoons vegetable oil
> 1 boneless beef rump or chuck, 3 to 4 pounds
> 1 packet onion or onion-mushroom soup mix (0.9 ounce) or vegetable soup and recipe mix (1.4 ounces)
>
> 2 1/2 cups water

1 Heat oil in Dutch oven or enameled flameproof casserole and brown roast on all sides.

2 Combine soup mix with water and pour over beef. Cover and simmer until beef is cooked and tender, about 3 hours, turning meat 3 or 4 times during cooking.

MICROWAVE: Blend soup mix with water in 3-quart casserole. Cook on HIGH (100%) 5 minutes. Add beef and cook 10 minutes on HIGH, turning once. Cover and cook on DEFROST (30%) 1 hour, turning 3 times. Let stand, covered, 5 minutes before serving.

VARIATIONS:

ITALIAN STYLE: Put 1 can (16 ounces) tomatoes through food mill to remove seeds. Combine with soup mix, 3/4 cup water, 1/2 cup red wine and 2 tablespoons finely chopped fresh basil or 1 teaspoon dried. Pour over beef and proceed as above.

FRENCH STYLE: Combine soup mix with 1 1/2 cups red wine, 1 cup water and 1 tablespoon finely chopped fresh thyme or 1 teaspoon dried. Pour over beef and proceed as above.

GERMAN STYLE: Combine soup mix with 1 1/2 cups beer, 1 cup water, 1 tablespoon brown sugar and 1/2 teaspoon caraway seed. Pour over beef and proceed as above.

SUPERMARKET SAVVY

 ■
HAMS

1. Supermarkets sell a spiral-sliced, honey-basted, ready-to-eat type of baked ham. Look for it; it's delicious and a real timesaver.
2. If you want to roast your own, consider buying half a ham:
>   (a) the upper half, known as the butt or
>   (b) the lower end, known as the shank.

Each has its good points—the butt has more meat, the shank more flavor.

3. From the shoulders come the Boston and picnic butts. They are somewhat fatty, but many who prefer this cut say it has more flavor.
4. If the ham is bone-in, count on about 12 ounces per person.
5. Many companies make boneless hams or canned hams that have been reformed, but some people say that hams with the bone are tastier.
6. Leftover ham, wrapped properly, may be frozen for about two months.

SWEET AND SOUR PORK LOIN

■ *Serves 4* ■

*U*se a loin with or without bone. If it is bone-in, ask butcher to cut almost to bone in 1- or 1 1/2-inch slices—a 4-pound loin should make 4 or 5 portions.

1   *pork loin, about 4 pounds*
2   *large garlic cloves, peeled and halved*
pepper
8   *small new potatoes*
8   *small carrots*
1/4   *cup finely chopped scallions, white and green parts*
Sweet and Sour Sauce with Pimiento, see below

1 Preheat oven to 325°F (170°C). Wipe loin clean; score fat if needed. Rub generously with garlic and liberally sprinkle with pepper. Bake on rack in roasting pan 30 minutes per pound.

2 Meanwhile, prepare sauce. When meat is half-cooked, pour off any fat and pour sauce over. Add potatoes and carrots to pan and complete roasting, basting meat several times. Garnish with scallions.

PORK LOINS

Here are some other tips:
1. Wine and Garlic: Insert 3 or 4 cloves (cut in half) in fat on loin and baste frequently with red or white wine.
2. Use garlic as above, add a good bit of rosemary, and baste with orange juice.
3. Use garlic as above. Sprinkle fennel seed, black pepper and butter on all sides of pork. Baste with juices from meat and a bit more butter.

MICROWAVE: (1) Prepare loin as above and cook fat side down on HIGH (100%) 5 minutes. Then cook on MEDIUM-HIGH (70%) 20 minutes; if not on carousel, turn once. (2) Combine all ingredients in bowl and cook on HIGH 1 1/2 minutes, stirring once and turning once if not on carousel. (3) Pour sauce over meat, add vegetables, cover with waxed power and cook on MEDIUM-HIGH 15 minutes. Turn once if not on carousel. Let stand 5 to 10 minutes before serving. If using thermometer, insert before microwaving and follow cooking times given here. Thermometer should read 165°F (75°C) at end of cooking time, and 170°F (77°C) at end of standing time.

SWEET AND SOUR SAUCE WITH PIMIENTO

1   *jar (4 ounces) diced pimiento*
1/2   *cup dark brown sugar, packed*
1/3   *cup red or white wine vinegar*
3   *tablespoons butter or margarine*
1   *garlic clove, minced*
1   *teaspoon spicy brown mustard*
1   *tablespoon Worcestershire sauce*
1   *teaspoon hot pepper sauce*

Combine all ingredients in saucepan and cook over medium heat until sugar dissolves, about 5 minutes.

COUNTRY-STYLE SPARERIBS WITH GARLIC AND HONEY

■ *Serves 4 to 6* ■

*G*arlic, honey, teriyaki sauce and ginger are tastier than ever when brushed over pork spareribs.

3 to 4 pounds country-style spareribs
2/3 cup teriyaki sauce
2 large garlic cloves, minced
2 tablespoons honey
1-inch piece fresh ginger, peeled and minced,
*   or 2 tablespoons chopped candied ginger, or*
*   1 teaspoon ground ginger*

1 Preheat oven to 325°F (170°C). Place ribs in baking pan and roast about 1 hour. Pour off fat.

2 Combine remaining ingredients and brush on ribs, covering well. Return to oven and roast 30 minutes longer, basting frequently.

MICROWAVE: (1) Arrange ribs in baking dish, cover with plastic or waxed paper and cook on HIGH (100%) 15 minutes. If not using carousel, turn ribs at least once. Drain off fat. (2) Combine remaining ingredients and brush over ribs. Cover again and cook on HIGH 15 minutes. Turn ribs over, brush with sauce in dish, uncover and cook on HIGH 5 minutes longer.

ROAST PORK LOIN WITH PINEAPPLE, HONEY AND GINGER

■ *Serves 6* ■

*C*enter-cut pork loins don't cost much more than end cuts. Look for pork sales that include center-cut loins.

1/2   cup honey
1/4   cup white wine vinegar
*   2   tablespoons minced fresh ginger or 2*
*   teaspoons ground*
*   1   cup canned crushed pineapple*
1/2   cup light soy sauce
center-cut pork loin, 3 1/2 to 4 pounds

1 Combine first 5 ingredients to make marinade. Place pork in dish, pour in marinade and refrigerate 12 hours or overnight, turning meat several times. Remove loin from marinade and bring to room temperature before cooking.

2 Preheat oven to 350°F (180°C). Place loin on large sheet of heavy-duty foil and pour about 1 cup marinade over. Wrap loin completely and bake about 2 hours, opening foil and adding remaining marinade during last 30 minutes. Baste 3 or 4 times while cooking. Let stand about 15 minutes before slicing.

MICROWAVE: (1) Marinate as above. Remove pork and place marinade in microwave-safe bowl. Cook on HIGH (100%) 2 to 3 minutes. (2) Place loin in baking dish with half of marinade. Set thin strips of foil over top of each end of loin. Cook on HIGH 5 minutes, then on MEDIUM-HIGH (70%) 40 minutes, basting several times. Add remaining marinade halfway through cooking; if not on carousel, turn loin once. Let stand 10 minutes, loosely covered with foil.

Italian Sausage and Sauce in Open Sandwich with Fennel Seed

■ *Serves 4* ■

*E*asy-to-find supermarket ingredients make this great sandwich.

4 Italian-style sausage links, about 1 pound
1 jar (15 1/2 ounces) spaghetti sauce
1 loaf (at least 8 ounces) Italian or French bread, split lengthwise and cut in half to make 4 pieces
1 teaspoon fennel seed
1 cup shredded mozzarella cheese (4 ounces)

1 Brown sausage in skillet about 10 minutes. Drain fat. Add spaghetti sauce, bring to boil, lower heat and simmer, uncovered, 15 minutes.

2 Grill or broil bread on cut side. Spoon half of sauce over bread. Cut sausage links in half lengthwise and place on top of sauced bread. Add remaining sauce; sprinkle fennel seed and then cheese over the 4 sandwiches. Broil until cheese is melted and beginning to brown. Serve right away.

MICROWAVE: (1) Cook sausage on HIGH (100%) 3 minutes. Turn links and cook on HIGH 3 minutes more. Add sauce and cook on MEDIUM (50%) 15 minutes, stirring once. (2) Assemble sandwiches as above and place on microwave-safe individual plates. Cook two at a time on HIGH 2 minutes or until cheese melts. If only one plate fits, cook on HIGH 75 seconds.

HERBED LEG OF LAMB

■ *Serves 6* ■

Roast lamb makes a delicious meal. If you can possibly roast this leg with fresh herbs, do so, but the dried will suffice. Lamb can take more garlic and herbs than most other meats.

4- to 5-pound leg of lamb
4   garlic cloves, peeled and halved
1/4   cup olive oil
2   tablespoons butter
1   tablespoon each chopped fresh thyme, tarragon and rosemary, or 1 teaspoon each dried
salt and pepper

1 Preheat oven to 450°F (230°C). Remove excess fat from lamb. Cut slits in sides of leg and insert garlic pieces. Place in roasting pan.

2 Heat oil and butter in small saucepan. Add herbs, salt and pepper and bring to simmer. Brush all over lamb.

3 Roast 15 minutes. Reduce heat to 350°F (180°C) and roast 1 1/2 hours, basting every 20 minutes or so. Let rest 5 to 10 minutes before serving.

MICROWAVE: If using thermometer, internal temperature of meat should be 120°F (50°C) for rare, 135°F (57°C) for medium and 150°F (65°C) for well done. (1) Prepare lamb with garlic as above. (2) In microwave-safe bowl, combine oil, butter, herbs, salt and pepper and heat on HIGH (100%) 45 seconds. Brush all over lamb. Cook on HIGH 5 minutes with fat side down. (3) Cook on MEDIUM (50%) 11 minutes per pound for rare, 12 for medium and 14 for well done; turn leg at midpoint of cooking time. (4) Let stand 10 minutes, covered, before serving.

LAMB CHOPS WITH OREGANO

■ *Serves 4* ■

These are best grilled; don't overcook them.

4   1 1/2-inch-thick lamb rib chops
4   garlic cloves, peeled and halved
2   tablespoons finely chopped fresh oregano or 1 teaspoon dried
2   tablespoons butter, room temperature
salt and pepper

1 Rub both sides of each chop with garlic. Combine oregano and butter and mash with fork to mix well. Spread on all surfaces of chops.

2 Grill or broil chops about 5 minutes per side. Use sharp knife point to test doneness; chops should be pink inside. Let rest 2 to 3 minutes before serving.

MICROWAVE: (1) Perform step 1 above. Arrange chops in 10-inch square microwave-safe dish with meaty portions toward outside. Cover. (2) Cook on MEDIUM-HIGH (70%) 12 minutes. If not on carousel, turn dish and rearrange chops twice. Let stand 3 minutes before serving.

LAMB STEW WITH LIMA BEANS

■ *Serves 6* ■

*U*se lean meat from the shoulder or leg. A delicious stew for any occasion.

2   tablespoons olive oil
2   tablespoons butter
2   pounds boneless lamb, cut into 1- to
     1 1/2-inch pieces
1/4 cup all purpose flour
pepper
2 1/2 cups beef broth, heated
2   garlic cloves, minced
1   teaspoon dried thyme
1/2 teaspoon dried oregano
2   cups canned or fresh small potatoes
2   cups frozen or fresh carrot slices
1   package (10 ounces) frozen lima beans
juice of 1/2 lemon

Heat oil and butter in large skillet. Combine lamb pieces, flour and pepper in a plastic bag and toss to coat meat. Brown lamb in skillet and transfer to 3-quart flameproof casserole with cover. Add broth, garlic, thyme and oregano, cover and cook 1 1/4 hours. Add potatoes, carrots and limas, cover and cook until vegetables are tender, 15 to 20 minutes. Stir in lemon juice before serving.

MICROWAVE: (1) Add 1 teaspoon brown bouquet sauce. Combine oil, butter, lamb, flour, pepper, broth, garlic and herbs in 3-quart microwave-safe casserole, cover and cook on HIGH (100%) 10 minutes. (2) Reduce power to MEDIUM-HIGH (70%) and cook 35 minutes, stirring twice. (3) Add vegetables, cover and cook on MEDIUM-HIGH 20 minutes, stirring once. Let stand 5 minutes. Stir in lemon juice and serve.

VEAL SCALLOPS WITH SOUR CREAM

■ *Serves 4* ■

1   pound veal scallops, pounded thin
salt and pepper
1/2 cup all purpose flour
4   tablespoons butter or margarine
1/2 cup white wine
1 1/2 cups sour cream
2   tablespoons finely chopped fresh
     tarragon or 2 teaspoons dried
8   thin slices cantaloupe or honeydew
     melon, seeds and skin removed

1 Ask butcher to pound scallops thin. Salt and pepper veal and lightly flour each slice. If slices are too large, cut in two. Set aside.

2 Melt 2 tablespoons butter or margarine in large skillet and sauté veal slices in batches until browned; about 2 minutes per side. Transfer to warm plate.

3 Remove veal from skillet, add wine and deglaze pan over high heat. When wine has thickened slightly, add sour cream and half of tarragon. Stir constantly until heated through, but do not boil.

4 To serve, place veal on individual plates and spoon some sauce on side, overlapping a third of the veal. Arrange 2 melon slices alongside veal. Garnish with remaining tarragon.

VEAL CUBES IN PIMIENTO SOUR CREAM SAUCE

■ *Serves 4* ■

Veal is more costly than some other meats, but when purchased boned and cubed, there is no waste as there is no bone and little fat.

1/4   *cup all purpose flour*
2   *garlic cloves, minced*
1/2   *teaspoon pepper*
1 1/2   *pounds veal, cut into 1 1/2-inch cubes*
2   *tablespoons butter*
1   *tablespoon vegetable oil or olive oil*
1   *cup beef broth*
pinch of ground cloves
2   *jars (4 ounces each) diced pimientos*
1   *jar or can (16 ounces) small white onions*
1/2   *cup dry white wine*
1/3   *cup sour cream*

1 Combine flour, garlic and pepper in plastic bag and shake to mix. Add veal cubes and shake to coat well. Melt butter and oil in flameproof casserole with cover and brown veal. Add broth and cloves, cover and simmer 40 minutes or until veal is tender.

2 Add pimiento, onions and wine and cook 10 minutes to heat thoroughly. Remove from heat and stir in half of sour cream. Serve on individual plates with a dollop of sour cream on top.

MICROWAVE: (1) Prepare veal for cooking as above. In 3-quart microwave-safe casserole, combine veal and all remaining ingredients except sour cream. (2) Cook covered on MEDIUM-HIGH (70%) 40 minutes or until veal is tender. Blend in half of sour cream; spoon dollop of remaining sour cream on top of each serving.

VEAL CUBES BAKED IN A PIE

■ *Serves 6* ■

This is tasty with or without a crust, but the crust gives it a festive air. The veal and sauce are exceptionally delicious.

2   *pounds boneless veal shoulder, cut into 1 1/2-inch cubes*
2   *tablespoons all purpose flour*
salt and pepper
2   *tablespoons vegetable oil*
2   *tablespoons butter*
1   *cup chopped shallots*
1   *large garlic clove, minced*
2   *cups canned plum tomatoes, put through a food mill, or canned tomato sauce*
1   *cup beef broth*
1/2   *cup dry white wine*
1   *teaspoon dried thyme*
1   *deep-dish prepared pie shell*

1 Shake veal cubes with flour, salt and pepper in plastic bag. Heat oil and butter in skillet and brown veal cubes. Transfer browned pieces to baking dish with cover.

2 Preheat oven to 350°F (180°C). Add shallots, garlic and tomatoes to same skillet and cook 10 minutes. Transfer to dish with veal. Deglaze skillet with broth, wine, and thyme; pour into dish. Cover and bake 1 to 1 1/2 hours or until veal is tender.

3 Transfer mixture to baking dish 10 inches wide and about 2 inches deep. Cover with pie crust; prick several times. Increase heat to 375°F (190°C) and bake until crust is browned, about 30 minutes.

MICROWAVE: (1) Combine oil, butter and shallots in 3-quart casserole. Cover and cook on HIGH (100%) 4 to 5 minutes. (2) Mix flour and broth. Add with all remaining ingredients except pie shell and cook uncovered on MEDIUM-HIGH (70%) 40 minutes. (3) Transfer mixture to 10-inch round, 2-inch-deep baking dish and top with pastry; prick several times. Cook on MEDIUM-HIGH 7 to 12 minutes. If browner crust is desired, run under broiler.

CHICKEN TARRAGON IN CREAM WITH RED PEPPER CONFETTI

■ *Serves 4* ■

Onion soup mix can enliven many dishes.

- 2 tablespoons vegetable oil
- 2 tablespoons butter unsalted
- 2 1/2 to 3 pounds chicken, cut into serving pieces, fat and half of skin removed
- 1 envelope (1.25 ounces) onion soup mix
- 1 cup water
- 1/2 cup dry white wine
- 1 teaspoon finely chopped fresh tarragon or 1/2 teaspoon dried
- 1 red bell pepper, cored, ribs and seeds removed, cut into 1/2-inch cubes
- 1 tablespoon all purpose flour
- 1/2 cup heavy cream

1 Heat 1 tablespoon each oil and butter in large skillet and sauté chicken until brown on both sides.

2 Combine onion soup mix, water, wine and tarragon in bowl and pour into skillet. Bring to boil, lower heat, cover and simmer about 40 minutes or until chicken is cooked. Transfer chicken to serving plate.

3 While chicken is simmering, heat remaining oil and butter in another skillet and sauté pepper until crisp-tender.

4 Combine flour and cream and add to skillet in which chicken cooked. Bring to boil, lower heat and simmer until sauce thickens, 4 or 5 minutes. Transfer pepper to sauce with slotted spoon. Stir well and pour over chicken.

MICROWAVE: (1) Combine 1 tablespoon each oil and butter, onion soup mix, water and wine in 3-quart microwave-safe casserole. Add chicken pieces, cover and cook on MEDIUM-HIGH (70%) 24 to 29 minutes, rearranging chicken at midpoint of cooking time. If not on carousel, rearrange chicken 2 or 3 times. Remove chicken from liquid. (2) Combine remaining oil, butter and pepper in small bowl and cook on MEDIUM-HIGH 30 to 60 seconds. (3) Stir flour, tarragon and cream into casserole with onion soup mixture and cook on HIGH (100%) 5 minutes or until thickened, whisking once or twice during cooking. Place chicken and red pepper in casserole and cook on MEDIUM-HIGH 3 to 5 minutes to heat through.

BAKED CHICKEN WITH HONEY AND CURRY

■ *Serves 6* ■

*T*he flavors of honey and curry on chicken are exciting. You'll want to cook this more than once.

3 pounds chicken parts, your preference
1/2 cup honey
4 tablespoons butter or margarine, melted, or vegetable oil
1/4 cup prepared mustard
1 tablespoon curry powder
salt and pepper

1 Preheat oven to 375°F (190°C). Remove all fat and skin from chicken pieces. Rinse and dry well.

2 Combine remaining ingredients in shallow baking pan and mix well. Coat chicken pieces thoroughly. Arrange in single layer in same pan.

3 Bake 40 minutes, basting several times; if using boneless skinned breasts, reduce baking time by 10 minutes. If sauce is thin, remove chicken pieces and keep warm. Transfer sauce to saucepan and boil over high heat until thickened as desired.

MICROWAVE: (1) Complete steps 1 and 2 above, using microwave-safe dish. (2) Cook uncovered on HIGH (100%) 20 minutes. Remove chicken and cover with plastic. Return uncovered dish to microwave and reduce sauce on HIGH 10 minutes (or boil on top of stove as above). Pour sauce over chicken and serve.

THINLY SLICED CHICKEN BREAST IN CHILLED "TONNATO"

■ *Serves 6 as main dish, 12 as appetizer* ■

*T*his takeoff on a classic Italian veal dish, *Vitello Tonnato,* is quickly and easily made. The beauty of this dish is that it can be made ahead and kept in the refrigerator for up to a week.

1 1/2 pounds boned chicken breasts, skinned, fat trimmed
6 tablespoons butter or margarine
1 package (0.9 ounces) hollandaise sauce mix
3/4 cup chicken broth
1/2 cup milk

1/4 cup white wine
1/4 cup fresh lemon juice
1 can (6 1/2 ounces) tuna, drained
1 can (2 ounces) flat anchovy fillets
1 tablespoon drained capers
1/2 cup sour cream
chopped fresh parsley

1 Cut away fillets from chicken breasts. Cut chicken breasts and fillets in half lengthwise. Pound between waxed paper until thin. Melt 2 tablespoons butter in skillet and sauté chicken on both sides but do not brown (less than 2 minutes per side). Set aside.

2 Melt remaining butter in saucepan, and whisk in hollandaise mix. Add broth, milk and wine, bring to boil, lower heat and simmer 1 minute. Set aside.

3 Combine tuna, anchovies, 1 tablespoon capers and sour cream in processor. Add hollandaise and process with on/off turns until well combined.

4 Alternate layers of chicken and sauce in shallow glass dish, ending with sauce. Cover tightly with plastic and chill completely. To serve, place chicken on plate.

Add a tablespoon or more of sauce, sprinkle with a little chopped parsley and top with several whole capers.

MICROWAVE: (1) Arrange pounded chicken pieces in one layer in glass pie dish. Sprinkle with wine, cover with plastic and cook on HIGH (100%) 3 to 5 minutes. Repeat until all chicken is cooked. (2) In bowl, melt 4 tablespoons butter on HIGH 30 to 60 seconds. Whisk in hollandaise mix and gradually stir in chicken broth and milk. Cook on HIGH 5 to 6 minutes, stirring twice. Add lemon juice. (3) Continue with steps 3 and 4 above.

CRISPED OVEN-BAKED CHICKEN PIECES

■ *Serves 6* ■

*T*he trick here is using cornstarch instead of flour.

1   *box (7 ounces) corn flakes (about 7 cups), crushed into 2 cups crumbs*
1/2   *cup cornstarch*
1   *egg, lightly beaten*
1   *cup milk*
3   *tablespoons vegetable oil*
salt and pepper
3   *pounds chicken parts, some skin and all fat removed, rinsed and dried*

1 Place corn flake crumbs in shallow dish and set aside.

2 Preheat oven to 350°F (180°C). Grease rimmed baking sheet. Combine cornstarch, egg, milk, oil, salt and pepper in bowl and beat well until completely smooth. Dip dried chicken pieces first in batter and then in crumbs, coating both sides. Arrange on prepared baking sheet. Bake 1 hour or until done. To maximize crispness, do not cover or turn chicken.

MICROWAVE: (1) Prepare crumbs, batter and chicken as above. Place coated chicken on paper-lined microwave-safe round dish with meatier portions to outside. Cover loosely with waxed paper to prevent splatter. Cook at MEDIUM-HIGH (70%) for 25 minutes. If not using carousel, turn dish and rearrange chicken halfway through cooking time.

TACO-SEASONED CHICKEN WITH MUSHROOMS AND TOMATOES

■ *Serves 4 to 6* ■

*G*enerally, taco seasonings are made of ground chili peppers, onion, cumin, garlic, oregano and salt, and are added to beef. Try them with baked or microwaved chicken instead for a most satisfactory dish.

1   *package (1 1/4 ounces) taco seasoning
    mix*
1/3 *cup breadcrumbs*
3   *pounds chicken parts, rinsed and dried*
2   *cups sliced fresh mushrooms (about 6
    ounces)*
1   *can (14 1/2 or 16 ounces) stewed
    tomatoes with juice*
1/2 *cup dry white wine*
1   *teaspoon chopped fresh cilantro*

1 Preheat oven to 350°F (180°C). Combine taco mix and breadcrumbs in plastic bag. Shake chicken pieces in bag until well coated. Arrange skin side up on large rimmed baking sheet, leaving space between pieces. Bake 30 minutes.

2 Combine remaining ingredients in bowl and spoon into pan between chicken pieces. Bake 30 minutes longer.

MICROWAVE: (1) Prepare chicken as above and cook skin side up on HIGH (100%) 10 minutes. Rearrange chicken and add mushrooms, wine, tomatoes and cilantro between chicken pieces. Cover with waxed paper and cook at MEDIUM-HIGH (70%) 10 to 14 minutes.

ROAST CHICKEN PRIMAVERA

■ *Serves 4* ■

*O*ne chicken will serve four; two will be enough for eight. Cook them side by side and prepare each in the same way.

1   *whole frying chicken, 2 1/2 to 3 pounds*
salt and pepper
2   *carrots, each cut lengthwise into 4 strips*
2   *celery stalks, cut in half and cut lengthwise
    into 3 strips*
1   *tablespoon butter or margarine*
vegetable oil
4   *onions, peeled and halved*
6   *white boiling potatoes, peeled and cut into
    "thick fry" pieces (6 or 8 slices per potato)*
1   *bacon slice, halved*
1   *teaspoon chopped fresh oregano or 1/2
    teaspoon dried.*

1 Remove chicken liver, heart and gizzard and save for another use. Rinse chicken inside and out. Remove excess skin and fat from tail and neck ends. Dry well. Salt and pepper inside and out.

2 Steam carrots and celery in as little water as possible until half-cooked. Fill cavity of chicken with these vegetables, which should be about 1/3 exposed. Add butter to cavity. Rub a little oil over chicken with palms of hands. Place chicken in lightly oiled baking pan and crisscross pieces of bacon over breast.

3 Preheat oven to 375°F (190°C). Combine onions and potatoes in large bowl. Add 2 tablespoons oil, salt, pepper and oregano and toss. Arrange around chicken; if there's no room, roast in separate pan, turning vegetables two or three times to prevent sticking.

4 Bake chicken and vegetables 1 1/4 hours or until chicken juices run clear and potatoes pierce easily when stuck with fork or sharp paring knife.

MICROWAVE: Add 1 tablespoon bouquet sauce. (1) Combine butter, bouquet sauce and 1 tablespoon oil in small cup and cook on HIGH (100%) for 30 to 60 seconds. Place chicken in 3-quart dish, brush with bouquet mixture and cook on HIGH 3 minutes. Reduce to MEDIUM-HIGH (70%) and cook 24 to 29 minutes. (2) Combine carrots, celery, onions, potatoes and oregano in bowl. Add 2 tablespoons vegetable oil and toss. Add to chicken 15 minutes before end of cooking time. Crisscross bacon over breast 6 minutes before end of cooking time.

CHICKEN BREASTS WITH HONEY, CHUTNEY AND PEARS

■ *Serves 4 to 6* ■

Chicken cooks well with almost any fruit but it is especially good with pears. The honey and chutney add to the taste too; serve with more chutney if you wish.

1	*can (29 ounces) pear halves, drained*
	juice of 1 lemon
4	*tablespoons butter or margarine*
6	*chicken breast halves, boned, skinned, fat trimmed (about 2 pounds)*
1/4	*cup orange juice*
1/4	*cup honey*
1/4	*cup chutney*
1	*teaspoon curry powder*
salt, optional	

1 Combine pears and lemon juice. Toss.

2 Preheat oven to 350°F (180°C). Melt butter in skillet, add chicken and sauté on both sides. Transfer chicken to shallow glass baking dish. Combine remaining ingredients, mix well and pour over chicken. Place pears in same dish, adding all of lemon juice. Bake 30 minutes or until chicken is done.

MICROWAVE: (1) Combine 2 tablespoons butter, orange juice and chicken in microwave-safe dish and cook on MEDIUM-HIGH (70%) 9 to 12 minutes. Add pears. (2) Combine honey, chutney, curry powder, lemon juice and salt, stir well and spread over chicken. Cover and cook on MEDIUM-HIGH 5 to 7 minutes longer, stirring once or twice during cooking.

DEEP FRIED CHICKEN PIECES ON PICKS

■ *Serves 4, 8 as appetizer* ■

*T*hese are easy and so good as a wonderful hors d'oeuvre. Pass with a sauce, such as thin chutney mayonnaise (1/2 cup mayonnaise combined with 2 tablespoons chutney and 1 teaspoon fresh lemon juice, thinned with cream, sour cream, yogurt or milk). As a lunch entree, combine with lettuce pieces and toss lightly in a honey vinaigrette dressing.

2 *whole chicken breasts (4 halves), boned, skinned, fat trimmed*
1 *package (5 1/2 ounces) or 1 1/2 cups buttermilk pancake mix*
1 *cup water*
1 *teaspoon dried tarragon, crumbled*
salt and pepper
oil for deep frying

1 Rinse and dry chicken and cut into 1-inch squares.

2 Combine pancake mix, water, tarragon, salt and pepper in bowl and toss chicken pieces in mixture. Deep fry in oil preheated to 350°F (180°C) until golden. Remove pieces as they cook and drain on paper towels. Spear with 5- or 6-inch wooden skewers and serve.

MICROWAVE: (1) Coat chicken pieces as above. Lay on paper towels in microwave and cook on MEDIUM-HIGH (70%) 9 to 14 minutes.

CHICKEN CUTLETS FILLED WITH ITALIAN CHEESES

■ *Serves 4* ■

*A*sk the butcher, if there is one, to pound the chicken breasts to 1/4-inch thickness, or do it yourself at home. Then just lay the cutlets flat on a countertop to receive the filling.

4 *boneless chicken breast halves (5 to 6 ounces each), skinned, fat trimmed*
1/3 *cup ricotta cheese*
1/4 *cup grated Parmesan cheese*
2 *scallions, white and green parts, finely sliced*
1 *teaspoon dried thyme*
salt and pepper
1 *jar (15 1/2 ounces) spaghetti sauce*
1 *cup shredded mozzarella cheese*

1 Preheat oven to 375°F (190°C). Combine ricotta, Parmesan, scallions, thyme, salt and pepper in bowl. Spread on cutlets. Fold in sides and roll up, fastening with wooden picks or small skewers. Transfer rolls seam side down to 8- or 9-inch square baking dish.

2 Pour spaghetti sauce over chicken and bake 30 minutes or until chicken is tender. Five minutes before end of cooking time, top with mozzarella, return to oven and continue baking until cheese is melted.

MICROWAVE: (1) Prepare cutlets and filling; roll and secure as above. Arrange seam side down in baking dish and add spaghetti sauce. Cover loosely with waxed paper and cook on HIGH (100%) 11 to 15 minutes. If not using carousel, turn dish twice. (2) Top with mozzarella cheese and cook on MEDIUM (50%) 2 to 4 minutes. Let stand 1 to 2 minutes before serving.

CHICKEN MILANESE

■ *Serves 4* ■

Chicken breasts, pounded thin, are always a good and less expensive substitute for veal cutlets. If you like a thicker sauce, add 1 teaspoon cornstarch to the wine before adding it to the skillet with the lemon juice. A crisp salad and hot mashed potatoes are perfect accompaniments.

1/4	cup safflower oil
1	egg, beaten
1	teaspoon water
1	pound chicken breasts, boned, skinned, fat trimmed, pounded to 1/4-inch thickness
3/4	cup seasoned Italian-style breadcrumbs
1/2	cup white wine
3	tablespoons fresh lemon juice
fresh	parsley, basil or watercress for garnish
4	lemon wedges

1 Heat oil in large skillet. Beat egg with water in shallow bowl and dip chicken into mixture. Then dip chicken in breadcrumbs, coating both sides. When oil is hot, cook chicken about 3 minutes per side until nicely browned; do not overcook. Drain chicken on paper towels and wipe out skillet.

2 Add wine and lemon juice to same skillet, bring to boil and deglaze pan about 1 minute; sauce should thicken somewhat. Return chicken to skillet and heat 1 minute. Serve with freshly chopped parsley, basil or a watercress spray and a wedge of lemon for squeezing over cutlet.

MICROWAVE: (1) Prepare and coat chicken as above. Arrange on dish, cover loosely with waxed paper and cook two at a time on MEDIUM-HIGH (70%) 6 to 10 minutes. (2) Combine wine, 1 teaspoon cornstarch and lemon juice in small bowl and cook on HIGH (100%) 2 to 3 minutes until thickened. Pour over chicken.

DONNA HELLER'S NEW YORK CHICKEN SUPERB

■ *Serves 4* ■

1 *broiler chicken, cut up*
2 1/2 *tablespoons margarine*
1 *cup sliced mushrooms*
1 *tomato, peeled, seeded and chopped*
2/3 *cup white wine*
1/2 *cup chicken broth*
1 *tablespoon cognac*
1 *teaspoon salt*
1/2 *teaspoon paprika*
1 *garlic clove, minced*
1 *tablespoon minced fresh parsley*

1 Rinse chicken pieces under cold fresh running water. Pat dry with paper towels.

2 Melt margarine in large skillet and brown chicken pieces on both sides, about 10 minutes. Add mushrooms and tomato and cook 5 minutes. Stir in wine, broth, cognac, salt and paprika and cook until chicken is tender, about 15 minutes.

3 Transfer chicken to warm platter and skim off fat in skillet. Add garlic and parsley to skillet and reduce liquid over high heat, about 5 minutes. Pour over chicken and serve.

MICROWAVE: (1) Melt margarine in 2-quart dish on HIGH (100%) 1 minute. Arrange chicken pieces in dish with meatiest parts to outside and turn over so both sides are greased. Cook on HIGH 6 minutes. Spoon off fat and discard. Add mushrooms and tomatoes and cook on HIGH 3 minutes. (2) Add wine, broth, cognac, salt and paprika. Cover and cook on HIGH 10 minutes. Transfer chicken pieces to warm plate. Add garlic and parsley to dish, return to oven and cook uncovered on HIGH 4 minutes. (3) Complete as above.

CHICKEN LIVER PÂTÉ

■ *Serves 8* ■

The sherry in this recipe is optional; use it if you can for that extra bit of flavor. To serve the pâté, unmold it and pass with crackers.

14 *ounces chicken livers*
4 *tablespoons margarine or rendered chicken fat*
1 *cup finely chopped onion*
2 *garlic cloves, minced*
salt and pepper
3 *drops hot pepper sauce*
2 *hard-cooked eggs*
2 *tablespoons sweet sherry, optional*

1 Rinse chicken livers under cold water. Cut in half, trimming as necessary. Pat dry and salt lightly. Broil until cooked through, rinse and set aside.

2 Melt margarine in skillet, add onion and sauté 3 minutes. Add garlic and cook 1 minute longer. Transfer to food processor or blender. Add salt, pepper and hot pepper sauce and process 1 minute. Add eggs, sherry and livers and process until smooth.

3 Lightly grease a 2- to 2 1/2-cup mold with oil or melted chicken fat. Spoon pâté into mold, cover and refrigerate for several hours to firm and to allow flavors to blend.

CHICKEN THIGHS IN VELVET SAUCE WITH CREMINI MUSHROOMS

■ *Serves 6* ■

*T*highs are usually packed 4 or 6 in a package and also in larger family packs at less cost. If cremini mushrooms are not available in your supermarket, use ordinary whites, or shiitakes if affordable. Make this ahead, reheat, freeze or whatever—it's almost impossible to lose the good flavor.

2   *tablespoons vegetable oil*
8   *chicken thighs (about 2 1/2 pounds) most of skin removed, fat trimmed*
1   *Knorr or 2 Herb-Ox chicken bouillon cubes*
2   *cups water*
4   *white boiling potatoes, peeled and cut 1-inch cubes*
2   *carrots, cut into 1/2-inch diagonal slices*
2   *medium to large onions, chopped*
2   *tablespoons margarine*
2   *tablespoons all purpose flour*
8   *ounces mushrooms, sliced*
pepper
1/4   *cup chopped fresh parsley*

1 Rinse and dry chicken pieces. Heat oil in heavy saucepan with cover and brown chicken on both sides. Add bouillon cubes, water, potatoes, carrots and onions and bring to boil. Lower heat, cover and simmer until chicken and vegetables are done, 30 to 40 minutes. Transfer chicken and vegetables to bowl with slotted spoon.

2 Combine margarine and flour on small plate and mash with fork until blended. Add to sauce and whisk until velvety. Add mushrooms and pepper and cook 5 minutes longer; mushrooms should be crisp-tender. Return chicken and vegetables to pan and bring just to boil. Serve garnished with parsley.

MICROWAVE: (1) In 3-quart dish, combine all ingredients except margarine, flour, mushrooms and parsley. Cover loosely with waxed paper and cook on MEDIUM-HIGH (70%), stirring halfway through cooking time, for 24 to 29 minutes or until chicken is no longer pink at bone. (2) Remove chicken and vegetables. Add margarine, flour and mushrooms to dish, stir and cook on HIGH 3 to 5 minutes until sauce thickens somewhat. (3) Return chicken and vegetables and cook on HIGH 3 minutes to blend flavors. Serve garnished with parsley.

BONED CHICKEN TENDERS WITH MUSTARD AND THYME

■ *Serves 4* ■

Boned chicken tenders (the fillet of the breast) save time and are delicious prepared this way. Cut off the small bits of fat (scissors make it easy). Serve with rice to mop up the sauce.

1 *pound chicken tenders, boned, skinned, fat trimmed*
juice of 1/2 lemon
1/4 *cup thick teriyaki baste and glaze sauce*
2 *teaspoons Dijon-style mustard*
1 *tablespoon chopped fresh thyme or 1 teaspoon dried, crumbled*

1 Rinse and dry chicken pieces and arrange side by side in shallow glass dish. Pour lemon juice over, turning to coat both sides.

2 Combine teriyaki sauce, mustard and thyme in small bowl and blend well. Brush on to both sides of chicken. Let stand 10 to 15 minutes at room temperature.

3 Broil chicken 2 minutes or so per side, basting several times with sauce.

MICROWAVE: (1) Follow steps 1 and 2 above. Arrange tenders in baking dish, cover with plastic and cook on MEDIUM-HIGH (70%) 7 to 9 minutes. If not on carousel, rearrange chicken twice. Transfer to warm plate, cover and let stand 2 to 3 minutes. (2) Add 1/4 cup water or white wine to dish in which chicken was microwaved and cook on HIGH 2 minutes. Remove, stir and spoon over chicken before serving.

CHICKEN AND RICE WITH CELERY AND ONIONS

■ *Serves 6* ■

When I had this dish at Jerry Ann and Gene Woodfin's home, I thought they had spent all day preparing it. But they said it was superfast and supermarket. Use various uncooked long-grain rices, for example, curry rice.

1 *cup uncooked long-grain rice*
6 *chicken thighs and 6 drumsticks or 1 chicken (2 1/2 to 3 pounds), cut into serving pieces, skinned, fat trimmed, rinsed and dried*
1 *can (10 3/4 ounces) cream of celery soup*
1 *package (1.9 ounces) French onion soup and recipe mix*
2 *tablespoons chopped fresh parsley*

1 Preheat oven to 400°F (200°C). Butter 2-quart baking dish and cover bottom with rice. Arrange chicken pieces over rice.

2 Combine celery soup, onion soup mix and 2 soup cans of water in bowl and stir well. Pour over chicken and rice. Bake uncovered 30 minutes. Reduce heat to 350°F (180°C), cover dish with lid or foil and bake 20 minutes longer. Garnish with parsley and serve.

MICROWAVE: (1) Prepare as above. (2) Cook uncovered on HIGH (100%) 15 minutes. Cover with plastic and cook on HIGH 10 minutes longer. If not on carousel, turn twice during cooking. Garnish with parsley.

BAKED CHICKEN THIGHS WITH CARAWAY CRUSTS

■ *Serves 4 to 6* ■

One of the best supermarket buys, chicken thighs can be prepared in many interesting ways. Here's one.

8 to 10 chicken thighs, 2 1/2 to 3 pounds
juice of 1 lemon
1   cup seasoned dry breadcrumbs
1   tablespoon caraway seed
1   tablespoon finely chopped fresh tarragon
    or 1 teaspoon dried
1/2   envelope (.6 ounce) onion soup mix
1   egg
1/4   cup beer, wine or water
1/4   cup melted butter substitute

1 Remove fat and skin from thighs; rinse under cool water and dry. Place thighs in bowl, add lemon juice, toss and let stand 15 minutes.

2 Preheat oven to 375°F (190°C). Combine crumbs, caraway seed, tarragon and onion soup mix.

3 Beat egg with beer and butter substitute. Dip each thigh in egg mixture, then in crumb mixture. Arrange in shallow pan large enough to hold all the chicken. Bake 1 hour or until done; do not turn thighs while cooking.

MICROWAVE: (1) Follow steps 1, 2 and 3, except for baking. Arrange thighs on rack in microwave-safe dish or directly on carousel. Cook on HIGH (100%) 15 to 25 minutes. If not on carousel, turn twice during cooking.

CHICKEN SALAD FOR SANDWICHES

■ *Serves 4* ■

Some people prefer this well ground but I find it more interesting to give it some texture. Be careful of overprocessing.

2   *hard-cooked eggs*
1   *small onion, peeled and quartered*
1/2 *green bell pepper, cored, ribs and seeds removed, cut in chunks*
1 1/4 *cups cooked boned, skinned chicken*
1/3 *cup mayonnaise*
1   *tablespoon chili sauce*
1   *tablespoon sweet pickle relish*
1/2 *teaspoon Worcestershire sauce*

Combine eggs, onion, pepper and chicken in food processor and process using on/off turns until contents are chopped to 1/4-inch pieces. Add remaining ingredients and blend with a few more on/off turns.

CHICKEN SALAD WITH LEMON, GINGER AND BURNT ALMONDS

■ *Serves 4* ■

I love chicken salad. Here is one of my favorite versions. Serve it on red, ripe tomato slices or on a layer of sliced avocado, or simply put a large scoop in the center of a plate and encircle with thin slices of fresh cantaloupe.

3/4 *cup mayonnaise*
1/4 *cup sour cream*
1   *tablespoon minced lemon zest*
1   *tablespoon fresh lemon juice*
1   *tablespoon minced candied ginger*
1   *tablespoon sugar*
salt and pepper
2   *cups cooked chicken pieces, cut into 1-inch pieces*
1   *cup finely sliced celery hearts*
1/4 *cup almond slices, sautéed in a pat of butter until edges are browned*

1 Combine mayonnaise, sour cream, lemon zest and juice, ginger, sugar, salt and pepper in large bowl and mix well.

2 Add chicken, celery and almonds and toss lightly but well.

MICROWAVE: To cook chicken, remove as much fat and skin as you can. Place chicken in dish, add 1/4 cup chicken stock or water, cover with plastic and cook on MEDIUM-HIGH (70%) 7 to 12 minutes. Let cool, remove meat and cut into 1-inch pieces. If not on carousel, turn chicken once. Proceed as above.

CHICKEN AND MUSHROOMS VELOUTE

■ *Serves 4* ■

My favorite way to use classic cream of mushroom soup.

1 small onion, finely chopped
1/4 cup finely diced celery heart
2 tablespoons butter
2 tablespoons olive oil
4 boneless chicken breast halves, skinned, fat trimmed, cut into 1-inch strips
1 19-ounce can ready-to-eat cream of mushroom soup, or one 10-ounce can condensed cream of mushroom soup plus 1 can milk
1/4 cup white wine
4 cups cooked wild or white rice
pepper

Melt 1 tablespoon each butter and oil in skillet and sauté onion and celery 5 minutes. Remove from skillet with slotted spoon. Melt remaining butter and oil in same skillet and sauté chicken strips until browned, about 3 minutes. Add soup (and milk), wine and onion mixture and cook uncovered over low heat 15 minutes. Serve over cooked rice and sprinkle with pepper.

CORNISH HENS ADOBO

■ *Serves 2 to 4* ■

In the Philippines, pork adobo is considered a national dish; but they also prepare chicken and fish adobo. Here is an interpretation using frozen Cornish hens.

2 frozen Cornish hens, 1 pound each, thawed and split in half
1/4 cup soy or teriyaki sauce
2 garlic cloves, minced
2 tablespoons white wine vinegar
2 tablespoons sherry
1 tablespoon dark brown sugar, packed
pepper

1 Rinse and dry hen halves and place skin side down in large, shallow dish.

2 Combine all remaining ingredients and pour over hens, coating well. Cover tightly and marinate at least 6 hours, preferably overnight. Bring to room temperature before cooking.

3 Remove hens from marinade. Broil 4 to 6 inches from heat for 20 to 30 minutes or until juices run clear, turning and basting every 8 to 10 minutes.

MICROWAVE: (1) Remove from marinade and arrange hens skin side up in microwave-safe dish. Cover with waxed paper and cook on HIGH (100%) 8 minutes. Turn over and rearrange, cover again and cook 5 minutes longer. (2) Turn skin side up, cover with waxed paper and cook on HIGH 6 minutes. Let stand 3 minutes. Check for doneness; juices should run clear. Run under broiler, skin side up, 2 to 3 minutes to brown and crisp skin.

TURKEY BURGERS WITH MINTED YOGURT SAUCE

■ *Serves 4* ■

Burgers made with turkey are becoming popular. Here's a recipe for the diet-conscious person.

SAUCE

1	1 x 6-inch cucumber
1/2	cup low-fat yogurt
2	tablespoons finely chopped fresh mint or 1 teaspoon dried
2	scallions, sliced finely
1/4	teaspoon ground cumin
1/4	teaspoon cayenne pepper

1 With a parer, peel cucumber every half inch lengthwise. Halve, scoop out seeds if necessary and cut into small dice. Place in towel and wring to remove excess moisture.

2 Combine yogurt, mint, scallions, cumin and cayenne with cucumber. Mix well and refrigerate.

BURGERS

1	pound ground turkey
1	garlic clove, minced
1	scallion, white and green parts, finely sliced

1/2	cup fresh breadcrumbs
2	tablespoons finely chopped fresh mint or 1 teaspoon dried
1/2	teaspoon ground cumin

salt and pepper

1 Combine all ingredients and form 4 burgers. Cook in nonstick skillet about 5 minutes on each side. (Burgers may also be broiled or grilled.) When browned, transfer to plates and spoon some sauce over each.

MICROWAVE: (1) Prepare sauce as above. (2) Combine turkey ingredients and form into burgers. Arrange on rack and cover with waxed paper. Cook first side on HIGH (100%) 2 1/2 minutes. Turn over and cook other side on HIGH 2 to 3 minutes. Let stand 2 minutes, covered with waxed paper. For browner burgers, use browning dish, sprinkle with paprika or brush with melted butter.

SPICY TURKEY FRANKS

■ *Serves 6* ■

Turkey franks and cold cuts are in view more and more in supermarket refrigerated meat counters. Serve this over rice.

2	tablespoons margarine
1	pound turkey franks, cut into 1-inch pieces

2/3	cup sliced scallions
1/2	cup ketchup
2	tablespoons brown sugar

2   tablespoons Worcestershire sauce
1   tablespoon red wine vinegar
1   tablespoon prepared mustard
1   teaspoon chili powder

1 Melt margarine in large skillet and sauté franks and scallions until edges begin to brown, stirring frequently.

2 Add all remaining ingredients and bring to boil. Lower heat, cover and simmer until heated through, about 5 minutes.

MICROWAVE: (1) Melt margarine in large dish on HIGH (100%) for 1 minute. Add franks and scallions and cook on HIGH 4 minutes. (2) Add all remaining ingredients, cover with plastic and cook on HIGH 4 minutes. Serve as above.

TURKEY AND BACON BURGERS

■ *Serves 4* ■

*T*urkey, bacon and ground sage make a wonderful burger, especially if it's topped with zucchini and mushrooms. Serve with tomatoes vinaigrette.

BURGERS

1 1/4   pounds ground turkey
1   small onion, finely chopped
1/3   cup seasoned breadcrumbs
1/4   cup milk
1   egg, beaten
1   teaspoon dried sage, crumbled
salt and pepper
6   thin slices bacon, cooked until crisp, crumbled

1 Combine all ingredients and form into four 1-inch-thick burgers. Arrange in baking pan.

2 Broil on each side 5 minutes or until centers are cooked; test with fork. When done, place on individual warm plates and top with vegetables.

VEGETABLE TOPPING

2   tablespoons butter or margarine
1/2   cup thinly sliced mushrooms
1/2   cup zucchini cut into 1/4-inch cubes
1/4   cup seasoned breadcrumbs
salt and pepper

1 Using skillet in which bacon was cooked, melt butter and sauté mushrooms, zucchini and breadcrumbs, until crisp-tender, 4 to 5 minutes. Season with salt and pepper. Spoon over burgers.

MICROWAVE: (1) Cook bacon slices on HIGH (100%) 2 minutes or until crisp. Reserve fat; crumble bacon. (2) Combine turkey ingredients with bacon and form burgers. Arrange them in dish and set aside. (3) In 1-quart casserole, combine bacon fat, mushrooms and zucchini. Cook on HIGH 2 to 3 minutes. Stir in crumbs, salt and pepper. Spoon over burgers. (4) Cook burgers on HIGH (100%) 6 to 9 minutes.

BARBECUED TURKEY BREAST

■ *Serves 4* ■

Delicious tastes from a reasonably inexpensive cut of meat. If you can't find cutlets, use a 3-pound turkey breast half, skinned, boned and cut lengthwise into 4 or 5 slices.

1/4   *cup mayonnaise*
1/4   *cup soy sauce*
  1   *tablespoon fresh lemon juice*
  2   *garlic cloves, minced*
  3   *tablespoons olive oil*
  2   *tablespoons finely chopped fresh oregano*
      or 2 teaspoons dried pepper
  4   *turkey breast cutlets, about 1/4 inch thick*

1 Combine mayonnaise, soy sauce, garlic, oil, lemon juice, 2/3 of oregano and pepper and blend well.

2 Arrange cutlets in a shallow glass dish and pour sauce over, turning so both

sides are covered. Cover and marinate at least 2 hours or overnight. Grill over charcoal, 4 to 5 minutes per side, or broil 4 to 5 inches from heat source. Garnish with remaining oregano.

MICROWAVE: (1) Prepare cutlets and marinate as above. Place in dish two at a time, cover with waxed paper and cook on MEDIUM-HIGH (70%) 9 to 14 minutes. Brush 3 or 4 times with marinade and turn over once during cooking. Sprinkle with remaining oregano.

ROAST TURKEY WITH SAUSAGE STUFFING

■ *Serves 8 to 10* ■

You can stuff the turkey, or put the stuffing in a baking dish and cook it on the side, which is the way I do it; it's easier to carve the turkey and serve the stuffing this way. Also, the stuffing can be made while the turkey is roasting, as it cooks for only an hour or so.

1   *turkey, about 12 pounds, rinsed and dried*
salt and pepper
2   *celery stalks, cut into 3-inch pieces*
1   *orange, quartered*
2   *parsley sprigs*
4   *tablespoons butter or margarine*
sausage stuffing, see page 143

1 Season inside of turkey with salt and pepper. Add celery, orange pieces and parsley sprigs to cavity. Arrange large double thickness of cheesecloth over turkey to cover sides.

2 Preheat oven to 325°F (170°C). Melt butter and brush over cheesecloth and other exposed parts of turkey. Place turkey on rack in roasting pan. Roast about 4 hours, basting with drippings three or four times, until leg joint moves up and down or breaks easily and juices run clear from it when pierced with fork. Brown turkey by removing cheesecloth 40 to 50 minutes before end of roasting time. Let rest 15 minutes before carving.

MICROWAVE: (1) Season inside of turkey with salt and pepper. Place celery, orange and parsley inside cavity. (2) Set turkey breast side down on microwave-safe roasting rack. Brush with browning agent and some of butter. Cover with waxed paper and cook on HIGH (100%) 4 minutes per pound. (3) Turn breast side up. Pour off drippings. Brush bird with browning agent and remaining butter. Cook at MEDIUM (50%) 6 minutes per pound, or until juices run clear when leg joint is pierced with fork and thermometer inserted in breast reads 170°F (77°C). Cover turkey with foil and let stand 15 minutes before carving.

SAUSAGE STUFFING

■ Serves 8 to 10 ■

*T*urkey giblets may be sautéed in a little butter or margarine and added to the stuffing.

12	*ounces sausage meat*
2	*medium onions, chopped*
2	*celery stalks with leaves, chopped*
1	*cup (2 sticks) butter or margarine, melted*
2	*tablespoons poultry seasoning*
1/4	*cup chopped fresh parsley*
10	*cups stale bread cubes or cornbread crumbs*
3	*cups chicken broth*

1 Brown sausage meat in skillet. Transfer to large bowl with slotted spoon.

2 Sauté onion and celery in same skillet. Transfer to bowl using rubber spatula.

3 Add butter, seasoning, parsley and bread to bowl and toss until well combined. Add chicken broth and toss again. Stuff turkey, or transfer stuffing to baking dish and bake in preheated 325°F (170°C) oven 1 hour.

MICROWAVE: Prepare as above and cook covered on HIGH (100%) 20 minutes.

APRICOT/GLAZED TURKEY WITH DRESSING

■ *Serves 12 to 15* ■

The apricot glaze is a good touch here and the dressing uses only one egg.

1 whole turkey, 10 to 14 pounds
1 pound soda crackers
2 carrots, sliced
2 celery stalks, sliced
1 medium onion, sliced
1 egg
salt, pepper, paprika and garlic powder

For glaze:

1 cup apricot jelly
1 cup water

1 Rinse turkey under cold running water. Dry with paper towels.

2 To make dressing, soak crackers in water, drain and crush with fingers.

Combine carrots, celery, onion and egg in processor or blender and grind finely using on/off turns. Mix with crackers and add salt, pepper, paprika and garlic powder. Stuff turkey and salt and pepper outside.

3 Preheat oven to 325°F (170°C). Cover turkey with foil and roast 3 to 3 1/2 hours until juices run clear. Meanwhile, to prepare glaze, combine jelly and water in small saucepan and bring to boil. Simmer 5 minutes. About 1 hour before turkey is done, begin basting with glaze and pan juices; baste frequently until fully cooked. Cook and baste until done.

TURKEY SALAD FOR ALL SEASONS

■ *Serves 6* ■

Look for cooked turkey breast in the frozen foods section of the supermarket; it almost always there. Serve this salad on crisp lettuce leaves and garnish with a pimiento slice, or a cut olive, or a watercress spray.

2 cups cooked turkey breast, diced or
 julienned
2 hard-cooked eggs, coarsely chopped
2 celery stalks, thinly sliced
1 small onion, diced
1 carrot, grated
1 cup light mayonnaise
1 tablespoon dry mustard
white pepper

1 Combine turkey, eggs and vegetables in bowl and toss lightly.

2 Combine mayonnaise, dry mustard and pepper in small bowl and beat with fork until well combined. Fold into turkey mixture. Chill until serving time.

8

THE DELI RESOURCE AND CANNED, BOTTLED AND PACKAGED MEATS AND FISH

For some time now, consumer advocates have been campaigning to get food manufacturers to reformulate some of their most popular products. Prompted by health considerations and growing public concern, some companies are replacing highly saturated oils with less saturated fats. There is still a long way to go, but there seems to be a move in the right direction. When it comes to canned and packaged foods, it is especially important to check labels. A "no cholesterol" sign doesn't tell the full story—check the composition of foods on cans, bottles and packages and avoid those with excessive animal fats whenever possible. Actually, all of us should remember that the two biggest sources of saturated fat are meat (not just fresh, packaged too) and dairy products; this is where the cutting back should take place. Let's consider some guidelines for better supermarket shopping and improved eating habits.

1. Cut back on foods containing large quantities of saturated fat, but don't cut out fats altogether. Fats are necessary for a normal, healthy body. They are good for

the nervous system, skin and other essential body functions.

2. Try to keep your weight down. Do this by reducing calorie intake and not just by eliminating fats. For example, have some canned chili but just don't go overboard. Eat two inches of sausage instead of five. If you have chili or sausage, say no to heavy cream, butter and pastries for the remainder of the meal. Use polyunsaturated oils on your salad with chili or sausage.

3. Read food labels more carefully to recognize the origin of fat in the food (animal versus vegetable). The expression "hydrogenated vegetable fat" means that some of the fat in that food is saturated. Remember that saturated fats generally raise your blood cholesterol level while polyunsaturated fats tend to lower it.

With these points in mind, you should learn to take advantage of canned, packaged foods in the supermarket and the many items at the deli counter. In most of the following recipes, note that only one or two cans of meat or fish (6 1/2 ounces each) are used to serve six to eight people; for example, look at the Classic Tuna and Cannellini dish—and you can even use tuna packed in water, not oil.

EXPRESS CHECK-OUT

■ ■

CANNED/DELI

1 Combine a can of chopped or minced clams with a can of condensed vegetable soup and add 2/3 soup can of water for fast Manhattan clam chowder.

2 Combine a can of chopped or minced clams with a can of condensed cream of potato soup and add 2/3 cup milk for fast New England chowder.

3 Combine a can of chopped or minced clams with a can of condensed chicken gumbo and add 2/3 can of water for fast clam gumbo.

4 For hors d'oeuvre: buy thin slices of Genoa salami from the deli section, lay them on a baking sheet and sprinkle lightly with Parmesan cheese. Bake in a 325°F (170°C) oven until crisp, about 10 minutes. Serve hot.

5 Ask the deli attendant to thinly slice smoked salmon. At home, butter thin pumpernickel slices, lay salmon on top and cut into triangles. Add a sprinkle of black pepper and a dash of fresh lemon juice and pass.

6 Many canned foods are high in sodium. Use them but pay particular attention to menu planning. For example, serve a salad but omit salt—use herbs, lemon juice, and a little oil instead. Don't serve canned soup as a first course with a canned dish as a second course, and so on.

7 Packaged meats can be used to spike main courses instead of featuring as the main course. For example, slice only one link of kielbasa or other sausage and add to escarole or bean soup instead of serving one link per person as a main course. Use a little in omelets, or in rice dishes or salads. In other words, use these foods often as accents rather than centerpiece.

8 Do not leave food in cans in spite of packaging advances. Put any leftover canned meat, fish or vegetables in glass or plastic containers and refrigerate. Use clear glass or plastic so you can see what's inside.

9 Look for specials at the deli resource. Almost every week, salads, cheeses, barbecued chickens, ribs and/or cold cuts are on sale.

10 When making a sandwich with ham and cheese, sliced turkey or whatever, spread one of the bread slices with jalapeño jelly instead of butter, margarine or mayonnaise.

SMOKED MEAT CANAPES WITH HAZELNUT BUTTER

■ *Makes about 3 dozen* ■

"*C*old cuts" doesn't do justice to the many items offered at the deli section, which is a real resource. In this receipe, use thin slices of cured ham, smoked turkey or barbecued chicken.

1/2 cup hazelnuts
   6 tablespoons unsalted butter
pepper
10 to 12 thin square slices firm whole-grain
      or pumpernickel bread
   6 ounces thinly sliced smoked or cured
      chicken, turkey or ham
fresh parsley
pitted olive slices

1 Preheat oven to 300°F (150°C). Toast nuts in shallow pan 15 minutes. Transfer to coarse sieve and rub nuts around until skins come off. Cool.

2 Blend nuts and butter in food processor. Add pepper and refrigerate several hours or overnight.

3 Spread slices of bread generously with nut butter. Top with sliced meat. Trim edges and cut each slice in thirds. Garnish with parsley and sliced olives.

LYDIA'S QUICK MEAL

■ *Serves 2 or 3* ■

*L*ydia Moss, a fine cook, prepared this with smoked duck in place of the roast beef and it was delicious. It's an ideal fast supermarket dish.

   2 tablespoons peanut oil
   1 pound deli meat (roast beef or smoked
      turkey), coarsely chopped
1/2 cup bottled barbecue sauce
   1 can (15 or 16 ounces) baked beans
2 or 3 corn tortillas, warmed, optional
salad greens, optional

1 Heat oil in skillet. Add meat and cook briefly, about 2 minutes. Add barbecue sauce and mix well. Stir in beans and heat through.

2 Serve in bowls like chili with optional tortillas. Or, if you wish, arrange salad greens on individual plates and spoon some of the bean mixture over them.

MICROWAVE: (1) Combine oil and meat in glass dish and cook on HIGH (100%) 1 1/2 minutes. Stir. (2) Add barbecue sauce and beans, mix well and cook on HIGH 3 minutes. Serve as above.

RAINY DAY MADNESS

■ *Serves 8* ■

(BEANS, BEEF, MUSHROOMS, TOMATOES, AND HOT SPICE)

Don't let the list of ingredients keep you from this hearty dish. Most of the items are in the cupboard, and who knows—you may even have the ground beef in the refrigerator or freezer.

> 1   can (28 ounces) plum tomatoes, put through food mill, with juice
> 1   can (15 ounces) kidney beans, drained
> 1   can (8 ounces) mushrooms, drained
> 1   can (6 ounces) tomato paste
> 1 1/2   cups tomato juice
> 4   ounces sliced pepperoni, coarsely chopped
> 2   teaspoons Italian seasoning
> pinch of red pepper flakes
> 8   ounces lean ground beef
> 1   medium onion, coarsely chopped
> 1   bell pepper, cored, ribs and seeds removed, cut into 1/2-inch pieces
> 1   celery stalk, sliced
> 2   garlic cloves, minced

1 Combine first 8 ingredients in large saucepan with cover. Set aside.

2 Brown beef in skillet. When half cooked, stir in onion, bell pepper, celery and garlic and cook until beef is no longer pink. Transfer to saucepan with tomato mixture.

3 Bring to boil, lower heat, cover and simmer 1 hour. Test seasoning. If tomatoes are bitter, add 1 to 2 teaspoons sugar. Season with salt if you wish. If mixture is too thin, remove cover and cook down to desired consistency.

■ **CHOP BEEF AT HOME** ■

By chopping meat at home, you can control the proportion of fat to lean and you can choose the beef that is the best buy in terms of economy and flavor. I remember my grandmother chopping pieces of beef with a large, sharp knife, as she was readying ingredients for her homemade meatballs. I use the food processor and it's a snap. After trimming the meat, I cut it into 1- to 1-1/2-inch cubes and process a few pieces at a time by turning the machine on and off in quick spurts. Do not process on and off more than a few times or you'll end up with beef puree. Do NOT use a home food grinder.

MICROWAVE: (1) Combine beef, onion, bell pepper, celery and garlic in 3-quart microwave-safe casserole. Cover and cook on HIGH (100%) 6 minutes. Stir to break up meat; if not on carousel, turn twice. (2) Add all remaining ingredients, cover and cook on HIGH 20 minutes. If not on carousel, turn twice. (3) Uncover and cook on HIGH 12 minutes. Replace cover and let stand 5 minutes before serving.

MARINATED THREE-BEAN SALAD WITH SALAMI

■ *Serves 6* ■

Sliced cold cuts fit well in sandwiches but they also can be diced and added to a variety of foods, including soups, casseroles, omelets and so on. Here salami is added to a hearty and tasty bean salad.

1 can each (10 1/2 ounces each) red kidney beans, cannellini beans and chickpeas, all drained
4 ounces sliced salami, diced
1 celery stalk, thinly sliced
1 green bell pepper, cored, ribs and seeds removed, julienned
1 small carrot, diced
1 small onion, thinly sliced into rings
1/4 cup olive oil
1/4 cup red wine vinegar
3/4 teaspoon Italian seasoning
1 teaspoon sugar
salt and pepper
2 tablespoons grated Parmesan cheese

1 Combine beans, salami, celery, pepper, carrot and onion in large bowl and toss lightly.

2 Whisk remaining ingredients in another bowl and pour over beans. Refrigerate several hours or overnight to allow flavors to blend. Remove from refrigerator at least 30 minutes before serving. Toss again and serve.

SUPERMARKET SAVVY

SHERRY VINEGAR

Some of the largest supermarkets are offering sherry vinegar, aged 25 years in Jerez de la Frontera, Spain's famous sherry-producing area, near Cadiz. Only a small quantity of this vinegar is required to impart its exquisite flavor. It is always used in preparing gazpacho, Spain's favorite soup, which is now so popular in the United States. The bottle I have is numbered 44485; I'm lucky because only 47,600 bottles were made of it that year. In salad dressings, use about one half the amount of sherry vinegar that you would use of your usual red wine vinegar. In other recipes where vinegar is called for, consider substituting sherry vinegar if the color permits, but use less.

SMOKED TURKEY SALAD WITH SHERRY VINEGAR

■ *Serves 4* ■

If your supermarket has a deli section, they probably have smoked turkey breast. Instead of machine slicing, ask to have it sliced 1/4 inch thick.

1	cup mayonnaise
2	tablespoons dry vermouth
1	teaspoon sherry vinegar
1 1/2	pounds smoked turkey breast, cut into 1/2 × 2-inch julienne
4	scallions, finely chopped
1	cup frozen peas, blanched
4	large lettuce leaves

pepper

1 Combine mayonnaise, vermouth and vinegar and blend well.

2 Combine turkey, scallions and peas in large bowl. Add mayonnaise mixture and toss well but carefully. Refrigerate about 2 hours to allow flavors to develop (salad may be made one or two days ahead).

3 Arrange lettuce leaf on each of 4 plates and divide salad among them. Grind black pepper over.

SMOKED SALMON QUICHE WITH GRUYÈRE

■ *Serves 8* ■

Use milk instead of cream for a leaner dish.

5	eggs
1	cup half-and-half
1/2	cup heavy cream
1/4	teaspoon nutmeg

salt and pepper

1	tablespoon prepared mustard
1	baked 10-inch pie shell
8	ounces thinly sliced smoked salmon, cut into 1/2-inch strips
1 1/2	cups grated Gruyère cheese

1 Preheat oven to 350°F (180°C). Beat eggs in bowl. Mix in half-and-half, cream, nutmeg, salt and pepper.

2 Spread mustard on bottom of baked pie shell. Arrange half of salmon in shell. Sprinkle cheese over salmon. Pour in egg mixture and top with remaining half of salmon.

3 Carefully set filled pie shell on baking sheet. Bake about 45 minutes or until quiche is set. Let cool before serving.

MICROWAVE: (1) Prepare step 1 above and cook on MEDIUM (50%) 4 minutes or until lightly set. (2) Complete step 2 above and cook on MEDIUM 12 minutes. If not on carousel, turn three times during cooking. Let quiche stand 5 minutes, covered, before serving.

BACON, ONION AND PIMIENTO SPREAD

■ *Makes about 1 cup* ■

The ingredients can be blended in a food processor but the result will be a rather smooth spread. If you prefer something with more texture, mix the spread with a fork. This is tasty on toast pieces or almost any variety of cracker.

6	*thin slices bacon, cooked crisp and crumbled*
1/2	*cup light mayonnaise*
1	*jar (4 ounces) pimiento, drained well*
1/2	*small onion, minced*
pepper	

Mix all ingredients by hand or in food processor and place in bowl for serving with toast or crackers.

PEPPERONI SUCCOTASH

■ *Serves 8 to 12* ■

Those long pepperoni sausage sticks at the deli counters have many uses. The easiest is to slice them and use as hors d'oeuvre: ask the attendant to cut 4-inch pieces, and then slice lengthwise as thinly as possible.

1	*tablespoon vegetable oil*
6	*ounces pepperoni, thinly sliced crosswise, then cut into 1/2-inch squares*
1	*cup chopped onion*
1	*can (8 ounces) tomato sauce*
2	*tablespoons spicy brown mustard*
1	*package (10 ounces) frozen lima beans*
1	*package (10 ounces) frozen okra*
2	*packages (10 ounces each) frozen corn*
2	*tablespoons chopped fresh basil or 1 teaspoon dried pepper*
1/2	*cup soft breadcrumbs*
2	*tablespoons butter, melted*
2	*tablespoons finely chopped fresh parsley*

1 Preheat oven to 350°F (180°C). Heat oil in large flameproof casserole and sauté pepperoni and onion 4 minutes (onion should just begin to brown).

2 Stir in tomato sauce, mustard, vegetables, basil and pepper. Toss well and bring just to boil, then remove from heat.

3 Combine crumbs, butter and parsley and sprinkle over vegetables. Bake 30 minutes or until vegetables are tender.

MICROWAVE: (1) Combine oil, pepperoni and onion in microwave-safe shallow dish, cover and cook on HIGH (100%) 3 minutes. (2) Add vegetables, mustard, tomato sauce, basil and pepper. Cover again and cook on HIGH 8 minutes if vegetables are thawed or 12 minutes if frozen, stirring after 2 to 3 minutes. Combine crumbs, butter and parsley and sprinkle over vegetables. Run under broiler to brown crumbs.

TOPPINGS FOR HOT DOGS

Hot dogs may be grilled, broiled, pan fried or boiled, and they only take minutes to cook. To enjoy them fully, the roll should be toasted: smear butter or margarine on each side of the open frankfurter roll and run under the broiler. Fill each roll with a cooked hot dog and top with mustard, ketchup, chili, relish, piccalilli or one of these special toppings.

MAYONNAISE AND BARBECUE SAUCE

■ *Makes enough for 12 dogs* ■

1   cup light mayonnaise
6   tablespoons barbecue sauce

Combine in a bowl and mix well.

CHILI, CHILI SAUCE

■ *Makes enough for 8 dogs* ■

1   cup bottled chili sauce
1   can (4 ounces) chopped mild green chilies
1/4   cup finely chopped onion
1/4   cup finely chopped celery

Combine all ingredients and mix by hand; sauce should be chunky.

HOT DOG REMOULADE

■ *Makes enough for 24 dogs* ■

1 1/2   cups light mayonnaise
1   small onion, finely chopped
1/4   cup pickle relish
2   tablespoons ketchup
2   tablespoons fresh lemon juice
1   tablespoon chopped fresh parsley
1   tablespoon prepared mustard
1   tablespoon sugar

Combine all ingredients in bowl and mix by hand; sauce should be chunky. Thin with light cream if needed, but sauce should be consistency of lightly whipped cream.

HOT DOGS

Some say the hot dog was first made in Vienna, Austria (those people call them wieners); others say Frankfurt, Germany (they call them frankfurters). As far as the American hot dog is concerned, most will agree that it made its debut at Coney Island in 1871. It's almost as American as baseball, yet the term "hot dog" started at a football game at New York's Polo Grounds, where they were sold from a tank that kept them heated. The phrase was coined by Tad Dorgan, a sports cartoonist at the turn of the century who was reporting the game. Up against deadline, he realized he couldn't spell "dachshund sausage," as they were called then, so he titled his artwork "Hot Dog." In this country, about 12 billion hot dogs are sold each year—that's almost 100 per person.

HICKORY-SMOKED HAM STEAK

■ *Serves 4* ■

Packaged ham steaks, available in the supermarket's open meat coolers, can be cooked in a variety of ways: pan fried, grilled, broiled or microwaved. They are easy to handle, they cook quickly and, best of all, they invite special barbecue sauces and glazes. This ham dish goes well with canned black beans, drained, heated and served with a wedge of fresh lemon.

1/3 *cup maple syrup*
  1 *tablespoon ketchup*
  1 *tablespoon spicy brown mustard*
  1 *slice (about 1 pound) hickory-smoked ham steak*

1 Combine maple syrup, ketchup and mustard in small bowl and blend well.

2 Place ham in 9 × 14-inch oval glass dish. Brush or spoon glaze over both sides. Let marinate at room temperature about 30 minutes, or several hours or overnight in refrigerator.

3 Preheat broiler. Transfer ham to broiler pan, reserving excess glaze. Broil 3 to 4 inches from heat source about 3 minutes per side. Remove from broiler and brush with more glaze. Cut into 4 pieces or 1/2-inch strips and serve.

MICROWAVE: (1) Marinate as above. Place ham slice in large glass dish and cook on HIGH (100%) 5 minutes. Remove from oven. Brush on more glaze and serve as above.

BARBECUED COCKTAIL FRANKS

■ *Makes about 40 to 50* ■

Supermarket shelves are loaded with barbecue sauces and everyone finds a favorite. Here's another way to use it.

1 *small onion, grated*
2 *cups barbecue sauce*
1 *pound cocktail franks or sliced precooked smoked sausage*

Combine onion, barbecue sauce and franks in saucepan and heat through. Thin with a little water, if necessary. Serve hot.

MICROWAVE: (1) Combine ingredients in 1 1/2- or 2-quart microwave-safe dish. Cover with plastic and cook on MEDIUM-HIGH (70%) 4 minutes. If not using carousel, stir once or twice.

FIRST-COURSE CHICKEN CURRY WITH CHUTNEY

■ *Serves 8* ■

Chicken, curry and chutney are one of the world's best combinations of food. Use canned chicken, bottled chutney and a packaged curry sauce for this interesting and tasty dish. For a lunch entree, fill 8 scooped-out tomatoes, set on lettuce leaves, allowing some chicken mixture to run over.

1 package (1 1/4 ounces) curry sauce mix
1 cup sour cream
1/4 cup milk
1 tablespoon finely chopped fresh tarragon or mint or 1 teaspoon dried
sprinkle of cracked black pepper
2 cans (5 ounces each) chicken, drained and flaked
1/4 cup chutney
16 very thin ripe tomato slices

Garnish:

1/4 cup toasted coconut flakes
1/4 cup toasted slivered almonds
crackers or toast points

1 Combine curry sauce mix, sour cream, milk, tarragon and pepper in bowl and stir until well mixed. Fold in chicken and chutney.

2 Arrange one tomato slice on each of 8 plates and top with chicken mixture. Add another tomato slice. Sprinkle with coconut and almonds and arrange crackers on side of each plate.

SWEET SPAM POTATOES

■ *Serves 6* ■

Spam passes its physical in this dish. If only they had served it this way during the war.

2/3 can (12 ounces) SPAM, cut into cubes
1 can (29 ounces) sweet potatoes, drained and cut into 1-inch pieces
2 cups whole cranberries, picked over, rinsed and drained
1/4 cup brown sugar, well packed
pinch of nutmeg
salt and pepper

1 Preheat oven to 350°F (180°C). Mix all ingredients in bowl and toss lightly.

2 Liberally butter 10-inch glass pie dish and add sweet potato mixture. Bake 30 minutes or until heated through and bubbling.

MICROWAVE: (1) Prepare as above. Cover with plastic and cook on HIGH (100%) 9 minutes. Let stand 4 minutes before serving.

SPAM SANDWICH, UPDATED

■ *Serves 1* ■

You can vary the cheese and use the mustard of your choice. Add more or less sauerkraut, SPAM or cheese. Make two at a time in a 10- or 12-inch skillet.

  4 *thin slices SPAM*
butter or margarine
  2 *tablespoons prepared mustard*
  2 *slices light rye bread*
  2 *thin slices Swiss cheese*
1/3 *cup sauerkraut, drained*
  2 *tablespoons butter*

1 Saute SPAM slices in a little butter and set aside. Spread mustard on each slice of bread. Arrange 2 slices SPAM on one slice. Top with cheese. Put sauerkraut on top of cheese and close sandwich.

2 Melt 2 tablespoons butter in skillet and, when hot, carefully add sandwich. Sauté until browned. Turn with spatula and brown other side. Cover skillet, lower heat and cook 2 to 3 minutes, being careful not to burn bread. Transfer to plate and serve hot.

■

SPAM was one of the best-known symbols of World War II. If medals had been awarded to any food that had gone to battle, SPAM would have received the Purple Heart. After the war, SPAM went from one war-torn country to another. One would think that postwar America would have welcomed SPAM with open arms, but quite the opposite was the case: GIs referred to SPAM as "ham that didn't pass its physical," and millions thought the product was dead. But this contempt, probably bred by familiarity, didn't last long. Today, SPAM is in every supermarket. It has been packaged and repackaged and its appeal to newlyweds, older couples, those living alone and others continues to increase. It is without question one of the more popular luncheon *meats and it can serve as the basis for some appetizing, easy-to-prepare dishes.*

■

CHILI CHEDDAR CASSEROLE WITH HOMINY

■ *Serves 6 to 8* ■

Amazing results from canned goods. Gutsy peasant food, so tasty and easy to make.

2 cans (15 ounces each) chili without beans
2 cans (15 ounces each) whole hominy, drained and rinsed
1 1/2 cups grated cheddar cheese (6 ounces)
1/4 cup finely chopped cilantro
1 cup chopped onion

1 Preheat oven to 400°F (200°C). Grease 8-inch square baking pan or other 1 1/2- to 2-quart dish. Spread 1 can chili in bottom. Spoon 1 can hominy over the chili. Repeat with remaining cans of chili and hominy.

2 Sprinkle cheddar over hominy and top with cilantro. Bake 30 minutes or until heated through; cheese should be melted and casserole bubbling. Spoon raw onion over each serving.

MICROWAVE: (1) Prepare as above and cook in microwave-safe dish on HIGH (100%) 12 minutes. Sprinkle onion over each serving.

VARIATION: Chili Cheddar Casserole with Cornbread
In place of hominy, use one 6 1/2-ounce package cornbread mix (white, yellow, Mexican or whatever you wish, prepared according to package instructions). Add grated cheddar and cilantro to batter and pour over chili. Bake as above.

MICROWAVE: (1) Cook chili in microwave-safe dish on HIGH (100%) 4 minutes, stirring once after 2 minutes. (2) Mix cheese and cilantro into cornbread batter. Pour over chili and cook on MEDIUM-HIGH (70%) 6 minutes or until bread is level on top. To keep corners from overbrowning, cover each corner with foil during cooking. Remove foil corners and cook on HIGH 3 minutes or until center is almost dry. Let stand 10 minutes (it will continue to cook). Sprinkle raw onion over each serving.

HOMINY

Whole hominy, as called for in the chili cheddar casserole recipe, is corn which has had the hull and germ removed and has been ground to a rather coarse state. It looks a little like popped corn.

Hominy grits, on the other hand, are a coarse meal and look somewhat like cream of wheat or farina. Both whole hominy (sold in cans) and hominy grits (sold in paper sacks) are white.

PASTA WITH WHITE CLAM SAUCE

■ *Serves 3 to 4* ■

　2　tablespoons olive oil
　1　cup onions, coarsely chopped
1/2　carrot, cut into 1/4-inch cubes
　4　garlic cloves, minced, or 2 teaspoons
　　　bottled minced garlic in oil
1/2　cup white wine
　2　cans (10 ounces each) baby clams
cracked black pepper
juice of 1 lemon
　9　ounces angel hair pasta, cooked and
　　　drained

1 Heat oil in skillet and sauté onions with carrot 8 minutes or until onions have softened. Add garlic and cook 2 minutes longer.

2 Add wine and liquid from clams and bring to boil. Cook until liquid is reduced by half, about 20 minutes.

3 Add clams, pepper and lemon juice and heat through. Serve over pasta.

MICROWAVE: (1) Combine oil, onions, carrot and garlic in dish and cook on HIGH (100%) 3 minutes. Add wine and liquid from clams and cook on HIGH 5 minutes. (2) Add clams, pepper and lemon juice and cook on HIGH 2 minutes. Serve over pasta.

RED BELL PEPPER TAMALE PIE

■ *Serves 4 to 6* ■

　　2　tablespoons olive or vegetable oil
　　2　fresh red bell peppers, cut into 1/2-inch
　　　　cubes, or 2 jars (4 ounces each) roasted
　　　　peppers, drained and cut into 1/2-inch
　　　　cubes
　　2　cans (15 ounces each) chili without
　　　　beans
1 1/2　cups grated cheddar cheese (6 ounces)
　　1　package (6 1/2 ounces) cornbread mix
　3/4　cup water
　　1　egg, optional

1 Heat oil in skillet and sauté peppers until tender.

2 Preheat oven to 375°F (190°C). Spread chili in 9-inch pie plate or 8-inch square baking dish and sprinkle evenly with cheddar. Arrange peppers over cheese.

3 Combine cornbread mix, water and egg in bowl and whisk until blended. Pour evenly over ingredients in baking dish. Bake 30 minutes or until browned; if necessary, brown briefly under broiler.

MICROWAVE: (1) Heat oil in microwave-safe 9-inch round or 8-inch square dish on HIGH (100%) 45 seconds. Add peppers and cook on HIGH 2 minutes. Transfer to bowl. Add chili to dish in which peppers cooked and cook on HIGH 4 minutes. (2) Top with peppers and sprinkle evenly with cheese. (3) Mix cornbread mix, water and egg in bowl and pour into chili dish. Cover corners with foil and cook on MEDIUM-HIGH 6 minutes. Remove foil and cook on HIGH 3 minute

CRAB CAKES

■ *Makes 6 cakes* ■

Lump crabmeat in cans, on ice in the fish section, costs a little more but it is the best crabmeat. It makes delicious crab cakes.

    1   pound canned or fresh crabmeat
    1   cup fresh breadcrumbs
    1/4 cup light mayonnaise
    2   tablespoons butter or margarine, melted
    1   egg, beaten
    1   teaspoon dry mustard
    1/2 teaspoon paprika
    2   teaspoons Worcestershire sauce
salt and pepper
vegetable oil

1 Combine crabmeat and breadcrumbs in large bowl. Combine remaining ingredients except vegetable oil in smaller bowl. Add to crabmeat and crumbs, mix well and form into 6 cakes.

2 Heat oil in skillet and sauté crab cakes on each side about 3 minutes or until done.

MICROWAVE: Omit vegetable oil. (1) Combine all ingredients except Worcestershire sauce and form into 6 cakes. Lightly brush both sides with Worcestershire. Arrange on microwave-safe dish or directly on carousel and cook on HIGH (100%) 3 1/2 minutes each side. For crustier cakes, cook on browning dish.

SALMON DILL SALAD

■ *Serves 6* ■

Canned fish or meat can be greatly enhanced if combined with sparkling-fresh vegetables. Here is an example of how far a single can of salmon can go.

    1   can (15 ounces) salmon
    2   cups shredded lettuce
    2   cups chopped ripe tomatoes
    1/2 cup sliced pitted ripe olives
    2   cups thinly sliced cucumbers
    1   cup sliced red radishes

Dressing:

1 1/2 cups light mayonnaise
    1/4 cup milk
    2   scallions, thinly sliced
    1   tablespoon finely chopped fresh dill or
    1   teaspoon dried dillweed

1 Drain and flake salmon, checking carefully for any pieces of cartilage; these should be discarded. Set aside.

2 Spread lettuce shreds on large platter. Distribute tomatoes over lettuce. Sprinkle olives overall. Place cucumber slices on top, then salmon and radishes.

3 Mix dressing ingredients until well combined. Pour half of dressing on top of salad, letting some vegetables show through. Pass remaining dressing separately.

SALMON WITH NOODLES IN TOMATO CREAM SAUCE

■ *Serves 4* ■

*T*his is a delightful and easy-to-prepare dish that needs only a crisp green salad along with it. Perfect for lunch or a light supper at any time of year.

>   4   *tablespoons butter or margarine*
>   3   *tablespoons all purpose flour*
>   1/4   *cup finely chopped onion*
> 1 1/2   *cups milk*
> *salt and pepper*
> *pinch of nutmeg*
> *pinch of cayenne pepper*
>   2/3   *cup canned tomatoes, put through food mill*
>   2   *cans (7 ounces each) or 1 can (15 1/2 ounces) salmon, drained, picked over to remove bones, and flaked (about 2 cups)*
>   1/2   *cup heavy cream*
>   8   *ounces fresh noodles, cooked and drained*
> *chopped scallions for garnish*

1 Melt 2 tablespoons butter in small saucepan, add flour and whisk 2 minutes. Add onion and cook 2 minutes. Whisk in milk. Season with salt, pepper, nutmeg and cayenne and simmer until thickened, about 5 minutes. Add tomatoes and cook 3 minutes longer. Add cream and heat thoroughly but don't boil.

2 Melt 1 tablespoon butter in skillet, add salmon and heat through.

3 Add remaining 1 tablespoon butter to cooked noodles in warmed serving dish and toss to coat. Top with salmon and pour sauce over. Sprinkle with scallions and serve right away.

MICROWAVE: (1) Melt 2 tablespoons butter in deep dish on HIGH (100%) 45 seconds. Add flour, onion, milk, seasonings, tomatoes and heavy cream and stir well. Cover with plastic and cook on MEDIUM-HIGH (70%) 6 minutes or until thickened, stirring 1 or 2 times. (2) Melt 1 tablespoon butter in another dish 45 seconds. Add salmon and cook on HIGH 1 1/2 minutes. (3) Proceed as above.

■   ■
SMOKED SALMON

One of the world's great delicacies is now found in many supermarket deli counters. Serve it tissue thin on thin slices of dark pumpernickel with butter and freshly ground pepper. Or enjoy it with capers, horseradish sauce and sliced onions. I like it plain on buttered dark bread with a lemon wedge for a sprinkle of fresh lemon juice.

DEVILED SARDINES

■ *Serves 6* ■

Here's a different way with canned sardines. It makes an interesting and tasty appetizer or first course.

4   tablespoons butter or margarine, melted
4   thin slices white sandwich bread, each trimmed of crusts and cut into 3 strips (12 strips total)
12 boneless and skinless sardines
2   tablespoons mayonnaise
2   tablespoons prepared mustard
2   tablespoons white wine or dry vermouth
1/3 cup fresh breadcrumbs
6   lemon wedges

1 Preheat oven to 400°F (200°C). Using half the melted butter, brush one side of each bread strip with butter. Arrange on cookie sheet, butter side up. Toast in oven about 5 minutes or until lightly golden.

2 Place one sardine atop each piece of toast. Combine mayonnaise, mustard and wine in bowl and mix well. With a teaspoon, run a strip of the sauce over the length of each sardine. Sprinkle breadcrumbs and drizzle remaining melted butter overall. Run under broiler to crisp and brown crumbs. Serve 2 sardines per plate with a lemon wedge.

SUPERMARKET "BOUILLABAISSE"

■ *Serves 6* ■

To make a real bouillabaisse, certain fish would have to be flown in from France and you'd need to spend many hours in preparation.

3   tablespoons olive oil
4   garlic cloves, minced
2   bottles (8 ounces each) clam juice
1   tablespoon finely chopped orange zest
1   can (16 ounces) plum tomatoes, cut up, with liquid
2   cans (7 1/2 ounces each) chopped clams
1   pound medium shrimp, shelled and deveined
8   ounces white fish fillets, cut into 1-inch pieces
8   ounces swordfish, cut into 1-inch chunks
1/2 cup loosely packed chopped fresh parsley or 1 teaspoon dried
1/2 teaspoon pepper

1 Heat oil in large saucepan and sauté garlic until it begins to color; do not brown. Add clam juice, orange zest and tomatoes and bring to boil. Lower heat and simmer 5 minutes.

2 Add clams, shrimp, fish fillets, swordfish chunks and parsley and cook until shrimp turn pink and fish pieces are opaque, about 4 to 5 minutes. Add pepper and serve.

MICROWAVE: (1) Combine oil, garlic, clam juice, orange zest and tomatoes in 3-quart dish and cook on HIGH (100%) 4 minutes. (2) Add all fish and parsley, cover with plastic and cook on HIGH 4 minutes. Remove from oven and test for doneness; if fish doesn't flake, return for 1 to 2 minutes longer. Add pepper and serve.

COUNTRY-STYLE TUNA CHOWDER

■ *Serves 6* ■

*T*his recipe was developed for those who shop in supermarkets with no fresh fish counters; it uses canned tuna and abounds with flavor. But you can also make the chowder with fresh fish fillets (about 1 pound of flounder, sole, catfish and so on), or with fresh tuna (sliced 1/2 inch thick and broiled quickly, then cut into 3/4-inch cubes and added to chowder).

6	*thin slices bacon*
1	*cup chopped onion*
1	*package (5 1/2 ounces) au gratin scalloped potatoes*
2	*cups hot water*
1 1/2	*cups milk*
1	*cup defatted chicken broth*
1	*can (15 ounces) corn, drained*
2	*cans (6 1/2 ounces each) tuna, drained*
1/2	*cup fresh tomato cut into 1/2-inch cubes, or chopped canned plum tomatoes, drained*
1	*cup half and half*

chopped fresh parsley or scallions for garnish

1 Fry bacon until crisp in large skillet or saucepan. Drain on paper towels, leaving 2 to 3 tablespoons fat in pan.

2 Sauté onion in bacon fat until it begins to color. Add potato slices and seasoning envelope, water, milk, broth and corn. Bring to boil, lower heat and simmer 30 minutes or until potatoes are cooked, stirring 3 times.

3 Add tuna, tomato and half and half and heat through, stirring frequently. Crumble bacon over, garnish with parsley and serve hot.

MICROWAVE: (1) Lay 4 paper towels on bottom of oven and arrange bacon slices on them. Cover with 2 more paper towels. Cook on HIGH (100%) 6 minutes or until bacon is crisp. Let stand 5 minutes. (2) Squeeze about 2 tablespoons bacon fat from paper towels into large baking dish. Add onion and cook on HIGH 3 minutes. Add potato slices and seasoning envelope, water, milk, broth and corn. Cover with plastic and cook on MEDIUM-HIGH (70%) 20 minutes. (3) Add tuna, tomato pieces and half and half. Cover and cook on MEDIUM-HIGH 5 minutes. Let stand 5 minutes. Crumble bacon on top, sprinkle parsley and serve.

TUNA TOMATO SAUCE FOR PASTA

■ *Serves 4* ■

My grandmother used to make this, and I believe tuna packed in oil was the only canned food she used. She always had anchovies in a jar, but I'm suggesting anchovy paste because it's easier. We did not add grated cheese of any kind to this pasta.

1/3   *cup olive oil*
2   *garlic cloves, minced*
1   *teaspoon anchovy paste*
1/4   *teaspoon red pepper flakes*
2 1/2   *cups canned plum tomatoes with some liquid, put through food mill*
1   *can (6 1/2 ounces) tuna packed in oil*
1/3   *cup loosely packed chopped flat-leaf parsley*
8   *ounces regular or thin spaghetti, cooked*

1 Heat oil in saucepan and sauté garlic until it begins to color. Add anchovy paste, pepper flakes and tomatoes and bring to boil. Lower heat and simmer 10 minutes, stirring to be sure anchovy paste is dissolved.

2 Invert tuna onto small plate and break it up. Add to saucepan with half the parsley and cook just until heated through, about 5 minutes. Serve over pasta with remaining parsley as garnish.

MICROWAVE: (1) Combine oil and garlic in 1- or 2-quart dish and cook on HIGH (100%) 1 minute. Add anchovy paste, pepper flakes and tomatoes, cover with plastic and cook on HIGH 7 minutes. (2) Add tuna and half the parsley, cover and cook on HIGH 4 minutes. Serve over pasta with remaining parsley as garnish.

JARS OF SPAGHETTI SAUCES

There are many types of spaghetti sauces on supermarket shelves. I use those that have not been thickened with flour. Often, I will thin some sauces with a little water, chicken or beef stock.

CLASSIC TUNA AND CANNELLINI

■ *Serves 6 to 8* ■

*I*f I'm eating alone and don't want to bother shopping, this is what I prepare. I love it. I also like to make it ahead as a buffet item.

2 cans (6 1/2 ounces each) tuna packed in oil
2 cans (19 ounces each) cannellini (white kidney beans), drained well
1/2 cup finely chopped scallions, including some green part
2 large garlic cloves, minced
2 tablespoons finely chopped fresh parsley
1 tablespoon finely chopped fresh oregano or 1 teaspoon dried
1/2 cup olive oil
1/4 cup fresh lemon juice

pinch of red pepper flakes
salt and pepper

1 Combine tuna and oil, cannellini, scallions, garlic, parsley and oregano in large bowl.

2 Combine olive oil, lemon juice, red pepper flakes, salt and pepper in another bowl and mix well. Add to tuna mixture and toss lightly but well. Serve at room temperature.

SUPERMARKET SAVVY

■ ■

Tips for Cannellini Beans

Use 19-ounce can and vary as follows:
1. Drain beans; add 1/2 cup tomato sauce and a sprinkle of red pepper flakes. Heat thoroughly, stirring often.
2. Drain beans. Slice 2 onions and 1 bell pepper and sauté in 2 tablespoons oil until tender. Add beans and heat through. Season with salt and pepper to taste.
3. Drain beans. Combine with 1/2 cup vinaigrette dressing and toss well. Let stand at room temperature for 15 to 30 minutes before serving.

TUNA AND RICE FRITTERS

■ *Serves 4* ■

*T*here aren't many deep fried foods in this book, but this is a worthy exception. I fry the fritters in a skillet and turn them once to brown on both sides. These do not work in the microwave.

vegetable oil for deep frying
  1   can (6 1/2 ounces) chunk light tuna,
        drained and flaked
1/4   cup milk
  2   eggs, separated
  2   tablespoons all purpose flour
        generous pinch of pepper
2/3   cup rice, cooked

1 Preheat oil in deep fryer or skillet to 375°F (190°C).

2 Combine tuna, milk, egg yolks, flour and pepper in small bowl and mix well. Place cooked rice in larger bowl and stir in tuna mixture. Beat egg whites until stiff and fold into mixture.

3 Drop by heaping tablespoons into hot oil and fry until brown. Transfer to paper towels and serve right away.

PACKAGING

New designs in packaging continue to play an important role in attracting consumers to the various "self-service" luncheon meats available in the markets. Major features of the new packages are: (1) A high vacuum, it keeps the food fresh. (2) They're easy to open. (3) Most packages can be resealed to keep remaining contents fresh for a longer period. (4) Rewrapping in other material is unnecessary—a timesaving feature. One major food processor has introduced "Perma Fresh" packaging; it has a stronger seal to aid in maintaining freshness and flavor, and a reinforced plastic bubble and pull tab for easier opening. These clear, handy-size packages have proven to be remarkably successful. Luncheon meats have now assumed an important place on supermarket shelves.

TINY TUNA LOAVES

▪ *Serves 8* ▪

*T*his is a novel way of preparing tuna loaves, and they take less than 30 minutes to cook.

6	tablespoons butter or margarine
1	cup finely chopped onion
1	cup finely chopped celery
1/4	cup finely chopped fresh dill or 1 scant tablespoon dried dillweed
3	cans (6 1/2 ounces each) chunk light tuna, drained and flaked
2	eggs, beaten
1/2	cup frozen green peas, thawed
1	cup dry breadcrumbs
3/4	cup evaporated milk
3	tablespoons fresh lemon juice

salt and pepper

1 Melt 4 tablespoons butter in large skillet, add onion and celery and sauté until onion colors, about 5 minutes. Stir in dill. Transfer to large bowl.

2 Preheat oven to 350°F (180°C). Add tuna, eggs, peas, breadcrumbs, milk, lemon juice, salt and pepper and mix well. Shape mixture into 8 tiny loaves and arrange on lightly greased jelly roll pan.

3 Melt remaining 2 tablespoons butter and brush on loaves. Bake 25 minutes or until loaves are browned.

MICROWAVE: Add 2 tablespoons Worcestershire sauce to ingredients. (1) Combine 4 tablespoons butter or margarine, onion and celery in dish and cook on HIGH (100%) 3 minutes. Transfer to large mixing bowl. (2) Add dill, tuna, eggs, peas, breadcrumbs, milk, lemon juice, salt and pepper and mix well. Shape into 8 loaves and divide between two microwave-safe dishes. Melt remaining butter in small bowl with Worcestershire sauce on HIGH 45 seconds. Brush over loaves and cook 4 at a time on HIGH 6 minutes. Let stand 4 minutes before serving.

GORTON'S BONELESS COD

was already a household term in the 1890s. It was first packed in a wooden box and later in cans. Housewives had to freshen the product with overnight soaking. That's a far cry from today's convenient frozen seafood varieties.

9

HISPANIC AND ASIAN FOODS

Until recently it was difficult for most Americans to prepare ethnic foods, because ingredients were hard to come by. Even in New York, I usually made a subway trip to Chinatown for fresh Chinese vegetables, water chestnuts and canned Chinese sauces just to prepare the simplest Oriental food. For something Spanish, a trip to Casa Moneo on 14th Street was the only solution.

Now I live in Key West, Florida, and even the supermarkets there are well stocked with ethnic foods. But today this is true of most cities in America. And it is interesting to note how certain other foods (Italian, French and German, for example) have been integrated to the point that special sections are rarely seen except perhaps for dried and fresh pasta. There is no question in my mind that the availability of ethnic ingredients has been one of the main reasons for the food revolution in this country. Everyone from Vermont to New Mexico is cooking Tex-Mex and grilling Chinese-style ribs on the barbecue. With this in mind, here are some Spanish and Oriental recipes easily made with supermarket products.

EXPRESS CHECK-OUT

1 Make sauces ahead and refrigerate or freeze (most will last up to a week). Salsa, especially, can be added at the last minute to many chicken, rice, bean and egg dishes.

2 Bottled and canned salsas flood supermarket shelves; they are good and timesaving. Be sure to check the label for "hot" or "mild."

3 Don't be afraid of chilies; they are one of the finest natural digestives in the world.

4 The best meals should come in variations of texture, flavor and temperature, in an ordered succession. So serve separate courses and pause between them.

5 Soy and teriyaki sauces are high in sodium; buy brands offering lower-sodium products. Teriyaki sauce is a good browning agent for many meats to be microwaved, especially burgers and chicken.

6 Learn to use somen noodles, as they are versatile and easy to cook. They're usually spiked with other ingredients (see page 178) and can be served at room temperature, a helpful plus when you need an extra few minutes to stir-fry other menu items.

7 Avoid inexpensive cuts of pork in preparing Oriental dishes; they're too fatty and gristly. Most recipes don't ask for much pork, so you can afford the better grade.

REFRIED BEAN APPETIZER, HOT OR COLD

■ *Makes about 4 cups* ■

*T*ortilla chips are everywhere and here is a good way to serve them—scoop up this hot appetizer with the chips for a satisfying snack. You eat one, and you can't stop. Be inventive and serve this with chopped fresh cilantro, chopped jalapeño peppers, more sour cream and slices of grilled chorizo.

1 1/2 cups refried beans
1 cup sour cream
1 cup shredded cheddar cheese
1 cup chunky salsa, mild or hot
1/4 cup milk
1 package (.9 ounce) vegetable soup mix

Combine all ingredients in saucepan and heat slowly; be careful not to scorch. Transfer to warm bowl and serve with crisp tortilla chips.

MICROWAVE: (1) Combine all ingredients in microwave-safe bowl and cover with plastic. Cook on HIGH (100%) 2 minutes. Reduce power to MEDIUM-HIGH (70%) and cook 3 minutes. Stir and serve.

BEEF TACOS IN SOFT TORTILLAS

■ *Serves 4 to 6* ■

*S*oft flour tortillas can be used to make soft tacos or fajitas or can be eaten as you would fresh bread (as a sandwich with a savory spread or just plain). The tortillas can be filled and set out on a serving plate, but it is better still to set out the various items and have each person prepare his or her own.

1 pound lean ground beef
2 medium onions, finely chopped
1 package (1 1/4 ounces) taco seasoning mix
8 to 12 flour tortillas
2 cups finely shredded lettuce
2 ripe tomatoes, diced
2 cups shredded cheddar cheese
1 cup sour cream

1 Brown beef and half of onions in large skillet.

2 Combine taco seasoning mix with water. Add to beef and cook until most of liquid is absorbed.

3 Heat tortillas in ungreased skillet and place about 1/4 cup beef mixture across middle of each warm tortilla. Top with lettuce, tomato, onion and cheese and add a dollop of sour cream. Fold tortilla and place seam side down. Serve hot.

MICROWAVE: (1) Break up meat, combine with half of onions and spread in dish. Cook on HIGH (100%) 4 minutes, stirring twice. (2) Combine taco seasoning mix with water and add to beef, stirring well. Cover with plastic and cook on HIGH 3 minutes. (3) Proceed as above.

CILANTRO CHICKEN STRIPS WITH CORN ONION SALSA

■ *Serves 4* ■

This shows how simple it is to prepare a super meal from the supermarket. Selling chicken in parts has obviously been one of the wisest marketing decisions by supermarkets and their suppliers. Boneless chicken breasts, for example, though fairly expensive, are actually a good buy; there is virtually no waste, aside from the occasional lost piece of wishbone or cartilage. Always check sell dates to ensure freshness.

4   *large boneless chicken breast halves, skin and fat removed*
3   *tablespoons fresh lime juice*
2   *tablespoons finely chopped cilantro*
2   *tablespoons peanut oil*
2   *teaspoons chili oil*
1   *tablespoon sugar*
Corn Onion Salsa, see below

1 Check chicken breasts to be sure all bones have been removed. Dry well and slice in long, 1/4-inch-wide strips. Place in bowl, add lime juice and cilantro and toss well. Let stand at least 30 minutes or refrigerate for a longer time, but return to room temperature before cooking.

2 Heat both oils in large skillet or wok. Drain chicken pieces and sauté over high heat several minutes. Add sugar and sauté over high heat until chicken is lightly browned. Spread salsa on 4 warm plates, set chicken on top and serve.

MICROWAVE: (1) Prepare chicken and marinate as above. (2) Combine oils in dish, add drained chicken strips and toss well. Sprinkle with sugar. Cover with plastic and cook on HIGH (100%) 4 minutes. (3) Proceed as above.

CORN ONION SALSA

■ *Serves 4* ■

Unless fresh tomatoes are really red-ripe, do not use them in this recipe. Instead, use canned plum tomatoes, drained, seed and chopped. (Do not chop them in blender or food processor.)

2   *tablespoons olive oil*
1 1/2   *cups finely chopped red onion*
2   *cups fresh, canned or frozen corn*

2   *cups chopped fresh tomatoes or canned plum tomatoes, drained, seeded and chopped*

1 tablespoon finely chopped cilantro
juice of 1 lemon
salt and pepper

1 Heat olive oil in skillet or wok and sauté onion 3 to 4 minutes until translucent.

2 Add corn, tomatoes and cilantro and cook 5 minutes longer. Sprinkle with lemon juice; add salt and pepper. Serve hot.

MICROWAVE: (1) In a dish, heat oil on HIGH (100%) 1 minute. Add onion, stir and cook on HIGH 2 minutes. (2) Add remaining ingredients, cover with plastic and cook on HIGH 3 minutes.

CHILI CALABACITAS WITH CORN AND CHEDDAR

■ *Serves 4 to 6* ■

Yellow, green, red and orange make this side dish festive. Actually, there is enough here for a light lunch entree without fish or meat. Use small zucchini; they are crisper and less pulpy.

2 tablespoons corn, peanut or vegetable oil
1 red bell pepper, cored, ribs and seeds removed, cut into 1/2-inch cubes
1 medium onion, cut into 1/2-inch cubes
2 garlic cloves, minced
4 serrano chilies, chopped
2 small zucchini, sliced
1 cup fresh or frozen corn
1 teaspoon ground cumin
salt
1 cup shredded cheddar cheese

1 Heat oil in large skillet and sauté the bell pepper and onion until onion is soft. Add garlic and sauté 1 minute. Add remaining ingredients except cheese and cook until vegetables are crisp-tender and most liquid has evaporated, 15 minutes or longer.

2 Transfer to serving dish and sprinkle cheddar over all.

MICROWAVE: (1) Heat oil in dish on HIGH (100%) for 30 seconds. Add bell pepper and onion and cook on HIGH 2 minutes. (2) Add remaining ingredients except cheddar and cook on HIGH, covered, 7 minutes. Let stand 2 minutes. Uncover, sprinkle with cheese and serve.

POTATOES, ONIONS AND CHILI

■ *Serves 4* ■

A different way to prepare potatoes, and delicious with chicken or grilled meats.

2   tablespoons margarine
1/2 cup chopped onion
1   tablespoon chili powder
3   medium white boiling potatoes (about 1 1/2 pounds), boiled with skins on, cut into 1/2-inch cubes
salt

Preheat oven to 350°F (180°C). Melt margarine in skillet and sauté onion and chili powder until onion is soft. Add potatoes and salt and toss to combine. Transfer to baking dish. Heat thoroughly in oven, about 20 minutes.

MICROWAVE: (1) Prick each potato twice with fork and rub with 2 tablespoons vegetable oil. Place in microwave-safe 1 1/2-quart dish and cook on HIGH (100%) 16 minutes. (2) Heat margarine in shallow dish on HIGH 1 minute. Add onions and chili powder and cook 3 minutes on HIGH. Add cooked potatoes and cook on HIGH 3 minutes. Salt and serve.

SPANISH PUMPKIN OMELET

■ *Serves 2 or makes 8 to 10 appetizers* ■

If your supermarket has Latin American products, you may be able to get serrano ham. If so, use it; if not, opt for prosciutto or any other raw ham.

4   tablespoons olive oil
1   small onion, chopped
1/3 cup chopped serrano or other ham
3/4 cup pureed pumpkin
4   large eggs
2   tablespoons water
salt

1 Heat 2 tablespoons oil in large skillet and cook onion and ham until onion becomes translucent. Add pumpkin and heat through. Remove from heat and let cool to room temperature.

2 Beat eggs, water and salt in large bowl. Blend in pumpkin mixture and set aside.

3 Clean skillet or use a fresh one. Heat remaining oil in skillet, add pumpkin mixture and cook until bottom is set. If using iron skillet, run under broiler to set top. If using non-ovenproof skillet, cover handle with foil before broiling.

MICROWAVE: (1) Combine oil, onion and ham in glass pie dish, cover and cook on HIGH (100%) 2 minutes. Add pumpkin and cook uncovered 1 minute longer. (2) Combine eggs, water and salt in bowl and beat well. Add to plate, stir well and cook on MEDIUM-HIGH (70%) 2 minutes. Stir and cook 1 1/2 minutes longer.

HOMEMADE SALSA

■ *Makes 2 cups* ■

*T*his salsa is high in vitamin C and fiber but low in sodium. Be sure the tomatoes are red-ripe; if they aren't, it is better to use drained, seeded and chopped canned tomatoes. This is especially good with grilled meats.

4   red-ripe tomatoes, cored, peeled, seeded and chopped
4   green chilies, cored, seeded and chopped
2   jalapeños peppers, chopped
1   medium-size red onion, chopped
1   garlic clove, minced
2   tablespoons chopped cilantro
2   tablespoons corn or vegetable oil
2   tablespoons fresh lime juice

Combine all ingredients in bowl and mix well. Let stand at least 1 hour to allow flavors to combine.

TORTILLA FLATS WITH JAM AND CHEESE

■ *Serves 4* ■

*C*orn and flour tortillas, available in see-through packages, can provide the basis for tasty "sandwiches" for lunch or appetizers for other meals. Flour tortillas can make unusual breakfast treats.

8   flour tortillas, about 6 inches in diameter
8   tablespoons apple or other fruit butter, or strawberry or other jam
8   ounces cheese (American, ricotta, cream cheese or mozzarella, or use 1-ounce wedges of pasteurized process Gruyère)
1/2   cup chopped onion
2   tablespoons butter or margarine

1 Heat each tortilla 30 seconds per side in skillet over medium heat. Transfer to work surface.

2 Spread 1 tablespoon fruit butter or jam over each tortilla, then place 1 ounce cheese in center. Add a sprinkle of onion. Fold neatly to make an envelope (fold the edge nearest you over the cheese, fold in both sides, and then fold over farthest edge to complete the packet).

3 Preheat oven to 400°F (200°C). Butter baking pan with 1 tablespoon butter. Arrange tortillas in pan seam side down. Dot with remaining butter and bake 15 minutes or until cheese is melted. Serve hot.

VARIATION FOR LUNCH ENTREE: Substitute salsa for fruit butter or jam. Serve with green beans vinaigrette and several slices of pickled or hot buttered beets.

GRILLED BEEF SHORT RIBS WITH ORIENTAL SPICES

■ Serve 4 to 6 ■

*T*hese ribs are marinated, cooked on top of the stove and then finished off on the grill. Delicious.

1	can (8 ounces) tomato sauce
1/2	cup sugar
1/3	cup rice vinegar
1/4	cup black bean sauce
1/4	cup hoisin sauce
2	tablespoons soy sauce
2	tablespoons minced fresh ginger
1	teaspoon five-spice powder
4	pounds beef short ribs

1 Combine all ingredients except ribs in saucepan and bring to boil. Lower heat and simmer 10 minutes. Let cool a little.

2 Pour all but 1/3 of sauce over ribs in flameproof pan that can accommodate ribs in one layer. Marinate at least 1 hour or refrigerate as long as overnight. Bring ribs to room temperature. Simmer on top of stove 1 1/2 hours, then transfer to grill to crisp, basting frequently with reserved sauce.

MICROWAVE: (1) Combine all ingredients except ribs in bowl. Reserve 1/3 of sauce. (2) Place ribs in one layer in shallow dish and marinate as above. Bring to room temperature if necessary. Cover and cook on HIGH (100%) 30 minutes. (3) Finish off on grill, as above, or in broiler, basting with reserved sauce.

SOY SAUCE is naturally brewed from soybeans, wheat, salt and water. An ancient product (Kikkoman, for example, says it has been brewed this way since 1630) with a distinctive flavor and reddish brown color, it is fermented for as long as six months. It is so commonly used these days, the product is almost as American as Parmesan cheese.

TERIYAKI SAUCE is a blend of soy sauce with wine, brown sugar, herbs and spices. It can be used to coat meats, fowl or fish if they are stir-fried, broiled, braised, microwaved, sautéed, poached or grilled.

TERIYAKI GLAZE is thicker than teriyaki sauce; one brush will give most meats, fowl and fish a reddish-brown glaze. It is often used in place of tomato-based barbecue sauces.

BLACK BEAN SAUCE is sold in jars and cans in oriental food sections. Made from fermented soy and black beans, sugar, flour, water, cornstarch and caramel color, it adds rich flavor to many Asian pork, chicken, beef and fish dishes.

CHICKEN SOUP WITH ORIENTAL FLAVORS

■ *Serves 4* ■

An ideal supermarket soup but not out of a can. Easy to make, very fragrant and healthy, too.

1 *package (1.9 ounces) French onion soup and recipe mix*
4 *cups water*
3 *tablespoons dry sherry*
8 *ounces boned, skinned chicken breasts, cut into slivers*
1 *carrot, cut into 1/4 × 1 1/2-inch strips*
1/4 *cup sliced water chestnuts*
2 *ounces snow peas, cut diagonally into 1/4-inch strips*
1 1/2 *teaspoons sesame oil*

1 Combine soup mix, water and sherry in saucepan and whisk to blend. Add chicken and carrot and bring to boil. Lower heat and simmer 5 minutes, partially covered.

2 Add water chestnuts and snow peas and simmer 5 minutes, partially covered. Add sesame oil and remove from heat. Stir and serve.

MICROWAVE: (1) Combine soup mix, water, sherry, chicken and carrot in 2-quart dish. Cover and cook on HIGH (100%) 3 minutes. (2) Add water chestnuts and snow peas and cook on HIGH 2 minutes. Stir in sesame oil just before serving.

YOUNG CHICKEN WITH SESAME FLAVOR

■ *Serves 4* ■

Look for sesame oil on the supermarket shelf; its distinct fragrance makes it a pleasant departure from other oils.

1 *small fryer chicken, 1 1/2 to 2 pounds, cut into small pieces, or its equivalent in cut chicken pieces*
1/4 *cup sesame oil*
1-inch piece fresh ginger, peeled and minced
2 *tablespoons oyster sauce*
2 *tablespoons soy sauce*

1 Rinse and dry chicken. Remove excess fat and skin.

2 Heat oil in wok and stir-fry ginger. Add chicken and stir-fry until almost done. Add oyster and soy sauces and cook 2 minutes longer. Serve over cooked rice.

MICROWAVE: (1) Combine chicken pieces, ginger, oil and oyster and soy sauces in shallow dish. Coat chicken pieces and marinate several hours. (2) Transfer chicken to shallow dish, arranging thicker parts to outside of dish. Cover with waxed paper. Cook on MEDIUM-HIGH (70%) 21 minutes, rearranging chicken after half the cooking time.

MARINATED CHICKEN WINGS FOR APPETIZERS

■ *Serves 8 to 12* ■

These are delicious if crisped properly.

1/4   *cup dark brown sugar, packed*
1/4   *cup water*
1/4   *cup soy sauce*
  1   *tablespoon each fresh lemon juice*
  1   *tablespoon dry sherry*
  1   *tablespoon Worcestershire sauce*
  1   *teaspoon ground ginger*
1 1/2 *teaspoons cornstarch*
 12 *medium chicken wings, tips removed, cut in half at joint to make 24 pieces*

1 Combine all ingredients except cornstarch and chicken wings in shallow bowl. Add wings and marinate at least 8 hours, preferably overnight. Drain chicken, reserving marinade.

2 Preheat oven to 350°F (180°C). Bake wings on cookie sheet about 25 minutes or until crispy and done. Transfer to a serving dish and keep warm. Combine marinade and cornstarch in small saucepan, mix well and stir over medium heat until lightly thickened. Pass sauce with wings.

MICROWAVE: (1) Prepare wings as above. When ready to cook, arrange 12 on rack in 2-quart dish. Cook on HIGH (100%) 9 minutes. Repeat with remaining 12 wings. Run all wings under broiler to brown. (2) Combine cornstarch and marinade in a small bowl and cook on HIGH 1 to 2 minutes or until thickened. Pass sauce with wings.

SZECHUAN NOODLES WITH PEANUT SAUCE

■ *Serves 4* ■

It's fun working with these noodles. They are served at room temperature and are excellent with other Oriental dishes as well as with Western foods. For example, they make an interesting side dish with hamburgers.

  1   *package (10 ounces) somen noodles*
1/3   *cup hot water*
1/3   *cup chunky peanut butter*
  2   *teaspoons light soy sauce*
  2   *teaspoons rice vinegar*
  2   *teaspoons sesame oil*
  2   *scallions, finely chopped*
  2   *garlic cloves, minced*
  1   *teaspoon sugar*
several drops chili oil

1 Prepare noodles according to package directions. Drain and rinse in cool water. Transfer to serving plate.

2 Combine hot water and peanut butter in bowl. Add all remaining ingredients except 1 tablespoon chopped scallion.

3 Pour over noodles, toss well and sprinkle remaining scallions overall. Serve at room temperature.

HOISIN ROAST DUCK
■ *Serves 4* ■

- 1 *duck, 4 to 6 pounds*
- 1/2 *cup water*
- 1/2 *cup hoisin sauce*
- 1 *teaspoon sesame oil*
- 1/2 *teaspoon soy sauce*
- 1/2 *teaspoon salt*

1 Wash duck inside and out and remove any loose fat. Lightly prick skin all over with fork so duckling will self-baste. Dry well. Place duck in shallow glass dish.

2 Combine remaining ingredients and mix well. Rub mixture into duck skin. Let stand, uncovered, about 3 hours.

3 Preheat oven to 350°F (180°C). Place duck on rack in roasting pan, breast side up. Add about 1/2 inch water to bottom of pan. Roast in center of oven 30 minutes per pound.

MICROWAVE: Additional ingredient: 1 cup canned chicken stock. (1) Cut duck into small serving pieces; cut once again to make smaller pieces. Prick with fork 3 or 4 times. Remove any loose fat. (2) Arrange pieces in shallow dish in one layer. Add 1 cup chicken stock, cover loosely with paper towel and cook on HIGH (100%) 17 minutes. (3) Combine remaining ingredients. Drain duck pieces, dry and coat with hoisin sauce. Place in broiler pan and broil 6 to 8 minutes or until crisped and browned.

ROAST LOIN OF PORK, CHINESE STYLE
■ *Serves 6* ■

This cut of meat is still one of the best buys. For a few cents more, the center cut can be baked, grilled, rotisseried or microwaved.

- 4 *pounds pork loin roast, preferably center cut*
- 1/2 *cup soy sauce*
- 1/3 *cup honey*
- 1/3 *cup dry sherry*
- 2 *garlic cloves, minced*
- *1-inch piece fresh ginger, minced, or 1 teaspoon ground ginger*

1 Score any fat on pork with sharp knife. Place meat in glass baking dish.

2 Combine all remaining ingredients and pour over pork, coating on all sides. Cover and refrigerate at least 8 hours or overnight, turning pork several times. Remove from refrigerator 1 hour before roasting.

3 Preheat oven to 325°F (170°C). Pour off and reserve marinade. Cover pork with foil and roast 1 hour. Remove foil and roast 1 1/2 hours longer, basting meat frequently with marinade. Any leftover marinade may be heated with pan drippings and served with meat.

MICROWAVE: (1) Marinate as above. Cover ends of loin with about 1 inch of foil. Cook on HIGH (100%) 5 minutes, then at MEDIUM-HIGH (70%) 9 to 12 minutes per pound. Remove foil ends after half of cooking time. Cover pork with foil and let stand 5 minutes. Pour any remaining marinade into baking dish, cover and heat on HIGH 30 to 60 seconds. Serve with meat.

SUKIYAKI

■ *Serves 6 to 8* ■

*T*his sukiyaki has the special touch of pimiento adding to its color and taste. It is easy to prepare if you have all the vegetables ready in bowls to add to the wok or skillet. Vegetables in their raw state take a lot of room, so divide all ingredients in half and use two woks or skillets. Boneless sirloin may be used instead of filet mignon. Serve this with rice.

1	*pound filet mignon, sliced as thin as possible in 2-inch strips*
1/2	*cup red wine*
1/4	*cup soy sauce*
2	*tablespoons corn or peanut oil*
1/3	*cup diced scallions, white and green parts*
10	*small mushrooms, sliced*
8	*ounces fresh spinach, cut into thin strips*
1	*small Chinese cabbage, thinly sliced, about 3 cups*
1	*jar (4 ounces) pimiento, diced*
1	*cup bean sprouts*

1 Marinate meat in wine and soy sauce at least 30 minutes. Drain, reserving marinade.

2 Brown beef in corn or peanut oil in wok or large skillet over high heat. Add scallions, then remaining vegetables one at a time, tossing well and stirring most of the time. Add marinade and cook 5 minutes.

MICROWAVE: (1) Prepare meat and vegetables as above. (2) Heat browning dish 5 minutes. Add corn or peanut oil and meat. Cook on HIGH (100%) 1 minute. Stir meat and cook 1 minute more. Add scallions and cook on HIGH 30 seconds. Add remaining vegetables, stirring well. Cook on HIGH 2 minutes. Add marinade and toss vegetables to coat. Cook on HIGH 2 minutes.

■   ■

SOMEN NOODLES

Sold in see-through cellophane packages, somen may make you think at first of white wooden skewers. These Japanese noodles are made from unbleached wheat flour and sea salt. Cooking directions are usually on the package; in case they aren't, spread out 10 ounces somen noodles in 10 cups boiling water, return to boil and cook 2 to 3 minutes. Drain and rinse in cold water.

GRILLED TERIYAKI STEAK WITH PINEAPPLE CHUNKS

■ *Serves 6* ■

Use good sirloin steak; don't try an inexpensive cut of meat even though this marinates overnight. The result will be succulent.

2 *pounds boneless sirloin steak, fat removed, about 1 inch thick*
1/2 *cup soy sauce*
1/2 *cup dry sherry*
1/4 *cup peanut oil*
2 *scallions, finely sliced*
2 *garlic cloves, minced*
2 *tablespoons minced fresh ginger*
1 *small pineapple, skin and core removed, cut into 1 1/2-inch cubes*

1 Slice steaks into strips about 6 × 1 × 1/4 inch and place in shallow container.

2 Combine all other ingredients except pineapple in bowl and mix well. Pour over steak strips, tossing to coat. Cover and marinate overnight in refrigerator.

3 Remove meat from marinade and thread on skewers, alternating with pineapple chunks. Lay skewers in shallow baking pan and brush on more marinade. Grill or broil until browned, about 3 minutes per side.

SHRIMP TOAST

■ *Makes 24 or 36 appetizers* ■

A classic Chinese delicacy that can be realized from simple items on supermarket shelves and counters. Canned or frozen shrimp may be used.

8 *ounces shrimp, peeled and deveined, coarsely chopped*
1/3 *cup all purpose flour*
1 *egg*
1 *tablespoon soy sauce*
2 *teaspoons minced fresh ginger*
1 *teaspoon vegetable oil*
1/2 *teaspoon baking powder*
1/2 *teaspoon salt*
12 *slices very thin white bread, lightly toasted, crusts trimmed*
vegetable oil for frying

1 Combine first 8 ingredients in food processor and process using on/off turns until spreadable (or mince shrimp by hand and mix well with next 7 ingredients). Spread on toast, applying mixture firmly.

2 Heat oil in large skillet, using just enough to cover bottom lightly. When oil is hot, sauté 4 pieces of toast at a time, shrimp side down, 2 minutes. Turn toast and sauté other side for 1 to 2 minutes. Transfer to paper towels to drain. Cook remaining toast. Cut carefully in thirds or diagonally in half and serve hot.

TOFU IN GARLIC CHILI SAUCE

■ *Serves 4* ■

*T*his is a savory way to prepare tofu. Serve over plain boiled white rice or noodles.

1   *cup water*
1/4 *cup light soy sauce*
1   *tablespoon chili sauce with garlic*
2   *teaspoons sugar*
1   *teaspoon arrowroot*
3   *slices fresh ginger, minced*
1   *scallion, finely sliced*
1   *pound tofu, cut into 1/2-inch cubes*

1 Combine all ingredients except tofu in saucepan and bring to boil. Stir well and boil 1 minute.

2 Add tofu and cook 2 minutes, stirring carefully to avoid breaking up tofu. Serve over rice or noodles.

MICROWAVE: (1) Combine all ingredients in 2-quart dish, cover and cook on HIGH (100%) 1 1/2 minutes. (2) Add tofu, stir carefully, cover and cook on HIGH 2 minutes. Serve as above.

SUPERMARKET SAVVY

TOFU

Soybean curds, formed from soy milk as dairy curds are formed from cow's milk, are pressed to remove excess moisture (not too different in procedure from making cheese). The resultant product is fresh tofu. It is marketed as is, or may be pressed into firm tofu or deep fried into cutlets.

Tofu's protein is as complete as that of chicken, eggs and beef. It is low in calories and easy to digest. It is also low in saturated fats while rich in iron, calcium and other minerals, B vitamins and vitamin E. Last but not least, it is still one of the least expensive supermarket items and shoppers are learning to integrate it into their cooking.

FRAGRANT VEGETABLE STIR-FRY

■ *Serves 4 to 6* ■

*T*his colorful dish takes only minutes to cook. Prepare the vegetables and measure out the flavoring agents and it's easy. Serve the stir-fry over plain rice.

2   tablespoons minced fresh ginger
2   tablespoons white wine
1   tablespoon light soy sauce
3   tablespoons sesame oil
2   cups broccoli florets
1   red bell pepper, cored, ribs and seeds removed, diced
4   scallions, white and green parts, sliced
1   can (15 ounces) baby corn, drained and cut into diagonal pieces
1   can (8 ounces) whole water chestnuts, drained
2   garlic cloves, minced
2   tablespoons oyster sauce

1 Combine ginger, wine and soy sauce in bowl and set aside.

2 Heat sesame oil in wok or large skillet. Add broccoli, pepper, scallions, baby corn, water chestnuts and garlic and stir-fry just until tender, 5 to 8 minutes. Add ginger mixture and oyster sauce and heat through, stirring. Serve over plain boiled rice.

MICROWAVE: Decrease wine and oyster sauce to 1 tablespoon each. (1) Combine vegetables, ginger and garlic in shallow dish. (2) Combine sesame oil, wine, oyster sauce and soy sauce and mix well. Pour over vegetables. Cover tightly with plastic. Cook on HIGH (100%) 4 minutes. Stir, replace cover and let stand 2 minutes before serving.

WILTED JAPANESE SALAD

■ *Serves 4* ■

*I*t's best to use fresh spinach, but two 10-ounce packages of frozen spinach may be substituted.

1   pound fresh spinach, stemmed and washed
8   ounces fresh bean sprouts
2   tablespoons rice vinegar
1   tablespoon light soy sauce
1   tablespoon sugar
2   tablespoons toasted sesame seeds

1 Bring a large saucepan of water to boil and blanch fresh spinach and bean sprouts for 10 seconds. Drain immediately and squeeze dry. Transfer to platter. If using frozen spinach, cook per directions on package, drain and squeeze dry.

2 Combine remaining ingredients, pour over vegetables, toss well and serve.

MICROWAVE: (1) Combine fresh or thawed frozen spinach and bean sprouts in 2-quart dish. Cover with plastic and cook on HIGH (100%) 2 minutes. Toss vegetables, cover and cook on HIGH 1 minute longer. (2) Combine remaining ingredients, pour over vegetables, toss well and serve.

HOT SALAD OF CHINESE CABBAGE

■ *Serves 6 to 8* ■

Whether you cook this traditionally or in the microwave, I suggest that you divide all ingredients in half and cook in two woks or skillets. Cook twice, in two dishes, in the microwave.

2 tablespoons vegetable oil
2 garlic cloves, minced
2 teaspoons minced fresh ginger
2 celery stalks, thinly sliced
8 cups Chinese cabbage cut into 1-inch pieces
8 ounces mushrooms, thinly sliced
12 ounces fresh spinach, stemmed, washed and coarsely cut
2 tablespoons soy sauce

1 Heat oil in large skillet or wok and sauté garlic and ginger until garlic just begins to color. Add celery, toss and sauté 2 minutes.

2 Add cabbage and mushrooms and stir-fry 2 minutes. Add spinach and cook 2 minutes longer. Add soy sauce, toss well and serve.

MICROWAVE: (1) In 2- or 3-quart dish, combine oil, garlic, ginger and celery. Toss and cook on HIGH (100%) 1 minute. Add cabbage, mushrooms and spinach, cover and cook on HIGH 3 minutes. Add soy sauce, toss well and serve.

SUPERMARKET SAVVY

■ ■

1 To peel garlic more easily, lightly pound with side of fist to partially split open; then peel off skin.

2 Use vegetable peeler on outside of celery stalks to remove strings. Result: tenderer celery.

3 Wipe whole fresh mushrooms with a clean cosmetic brush to remove specks of dirt.

4 Freeze cabbage leaves, then thaw them, instead of blanching them to make them supple for stuffings.

10

VEGETABLES—FRESH, FROZEN AND CANNED

Vegetables contain all the essentials of good nutrition: proteins, carbohydrates, minerals, vitamins, fiber and yes, even a little fat. These vary in amount from one vegetable to the next, but in no other food group is there more complete nourishment. Vitamin C is needed for bones and teeth; vitamin A for eyesight and healthy skin; iron, one of the many minerals in vegetables, is particularly essential for women during childbearing years; and potassium guards against excess salt in the diet. Moreover, one of the best features of vegetables is their low calorie count. Another great feature is their versatility. We know they combine well with fish, meat, game, poultry, pasta and eggs. But how wonderfully they combine with each other—for example, bean sprouts, celery and green peppers on page 187, red onions with fennel on page 196, and zucchini, eggplant, tomatoes, onions and red bell peppers in the fabulous ratatouille on page 203.

For too many years, too many people have overcooked, underpresented and deemphasized vegetables. But this seems to be changing, because the advent of "nouvelle cuisine," the move towards the microwave and the growing interest in ethnic cuisines have helped put vegetables where they belong. People now realize the importance of cooking in the nutrients, not cooking them out. The emphasis is on bright, natural colors in vegetables; they are there to begin with, so why destroy them? The variety of vegetables is infinite and there are so many ways to cook them. Here are a few.

EXPRESS CHECK-OUT

VEGETABLES

1 Push several toothpicks into potatoes when microwaving them. As they stand up this way, they cook more evenly.

2 Corn in the husk can be cooked in a microwave. Cook on HIGH (100%) 3 minutes.

3 Cook cauliflower in milk to get a more delicate flavor; then use the milk in soup.

4 When cooking greens, count on 1 pound for two people. Wash several times; usually the water that clings to the leaves is enough to cook them.

5 Cook leeks in the microwave. Put them in glass baking dish with 2 tablespoons water and cook on HIGH (100%) 10 to 12 minutes. Serve with butter or a vinaigrette sauce, or puree them, adding butter or margarine, salt and pepper.

6 A few drops of fresh lemon juice will make almost any vegetable taste livelier.

7 Plunge freshly peeled sweet potatoes into salted water to prevent discoloration.

8 Fiddlehead ferns may be eaten in the springtime when their tightly curled fronds pop out of the soil. On occasion I see them in pint-size cartons in the supermarkets. Cook briefly in salted water and toss lightly with melted butter or olive oil, some minced garlic and a few drops of vinegar. You may find canned or frozen fiddlehead ferns in your supermarket.

BEANS, WATER CHESTNUTS AND BASIL

■ *Serves 4* ■

Fresh, frozen, canned or bottled green beans will work here. If frozen, use two packages (10 ounces each) and cook according to package directions. Then use as below.

1   *tablespoon vegetable oil*
1   *tablespoon butter or margarine*
1   *pound fresh green beans, strings removed, washed and cooked until crisp-tender, or 1 can (16 ounces) green beans, drained*
1   *can (8 ounces) sliced water chestnuts*
3   *tablespoons finely chopped fresh basil or 1 teaspoon dried*
1   *garlic clove, minced*
salt and pepper

Heat oil and butter in large skillet and add cooked beans, water chestnuts and basil. Toss well and sauté over high heat 2 minutes. Add garlic and sauté another 3 minutes. Add salt and pepper and serve.

MICROWAVE: Add 3 tablespoons water to ingredients. (1) Place fresh beans in dish. Add water, cover and cook on HIGH (100%) 9 minutes, turning once during cooking. (2) Add water chestnuts, basil, oil and garlic; dot with butter and season with salt and pepper. Cook on HIGH 2 minutes.

SUPERMARKET SAVVY

SOME BASIL IDEAS

1. When stems are removed, wash, dry and stack leaves. Snip with scissors into pasta sauces, soups or casseroles.
2. Use fresh or dried basil with sour cream, yogurt, butter or margarine as a topping for baked potatoes or add to a bowl of hot vegetable soup.
3. Combine basil and butter and spread it over thick slices of Italian or French bread before grilling or broiling.
4. Combine basil with melted butter or margarine and spread on freshly boiled or grilled corn.
5. Sprinkle on open-face grilled cheese and tomato sandwiches or combine with mayonnaise and spread on bread before layering cheese and tomatoes.

GARLICKY GREEN BEANS

■ *Serves 6* ■

*T*his is a simple, delicious way to prepare fresh green beans.

1 1/2   *pounds fresh green beans, ends and*
        strings removed
2   *tablespoons vegetable oil*
1   *tablespoon margarine*
4   *garlic cloves, peeled and halved*
        lengthwise
salt and pepper

1 Rinse beans in cool water. Place in saucepan and add water just to cover. Bring to boil, lower heat and cook until tender; do not overcook. Drain well.

2 Heat oil and margarine in large skillet and sauté garlic until it begins to color, then remove and discard. Add beans and sauté over high heat 3 to 4 minutes, shaking skillet frequently. Add salt and pepper and serve right away.

MICROWAVE: (1) Place beans in dish with 1/4 cup water. Cover and cook on HIGH (100%) 9 minutes. (2) Combine oil, margarine and garlic in bowl. Cover and cook on HIGH 2 minutes. Pour over beans, cover and cook on HIGH 1 minute. Discard garlic before serving.

BASIL

Known as the "herb of kings," basil has been used in Italy for generations. One of my earliest childhood recollections is of basil growing in window boxes in a New York third-floor brownstone apartment. When I went to the "country" (Naugatuck, Connecticut) at age 10, it was the central attraction in my cousin's vegetable garden; he planted the popular green-leaf and purple (opal) varieties. I was taught to pick only a few top leaves, always leaving some leaves on the stem to stimulate further growth. We stored fresh basil by washing and drying the leaves, layering them in a wide-mouthed jar (we now use plastic containers) and pouring olive oil over all. The jar, with a tight lid, was kept in the refrigerator. The fact that a few leaves would discolor never bothered us; we moved them aside or tossed them, and brought up for use a little of the brighter ones below. The oil picks up the basil's sweet, savory, somewhat spicy flavor and a tablespoon or two of it is marvelous in salads, on pasta or in soups.

My mother put up basil in that way until her 91st year. However, she also froze some by blanching it for a minute in boiling water, draining it, drying it well and packing it tightly in plastic containers. No oil was used. When she needed it, she just chipped away at the frozen block with a spoon, knife or fork. It lasted a long time—almost a year—but not at the rate at which she used it!

Today every supermarket offers dried basil and, although there is no substitute for fresh, I actually use the dried a lot. But I buy a small quantity, for once opened, the freshness fades in a matter of weeks.

BEAN SPROUTS, CELERY AND GREEN PEPPERS IN A WOK

■ *Serves 6*■

any recipes call for removing the "heads and tails" from bean sprouts, but that is foolish and a waste of time. Much of the nutritional value is in the tiny, nutlike textured hulls that are attached to the sprouts, so why remove them?

1/4 cup peanut oil
3   celery stalks, thinly sliced, to make 2 cups
3   small or 2 large green bell peppers, cored, ribs and seeds removed, cut into 1/2-inch cubes to make 2 cups
2   cups bean sprouts
1   large garlic clove, minced
2   tablespoons brandy, optional
1/4 cup soy sauce (if not using brandy, increase to 6 tablespoons)

pepper

1 Heat oil in wok until hot but not smoking. Add celery and peppers and sauté 3 minutes, stirring frequently.

2 Add bean sprouts and garlic and sauté over high heat 2 minutes. Add brandy, soy sauce and pepper to taste and toss frequently over high heat until heated through.

MICROWAVE: (1) In 2- or 3-quart dish, heat oil on HIGH (100%) 1 to 1 1/2 minutes. Add celery and peppers, cover and cook on HIGH 4 minutes, stirring once. (2) Add remaining ingredients, cover and cook on HIGH 2 to 4 minutes.

BEAN SPROUTS

I used to go to Chinatown to buy bean sprouts for two reasons: they were cheap and they were available. When they hit the uptown gourmet markets, they were available but expensive. Now the supermarkets feature them daily with other Chinese vegetables. They are either sold loose or in packages; they are usually offered at the salad bar, too.

Bean sprouts are tiny curved delicacies, usually the sprouts of mung beans and now sometimes soybeans. Every year, my friend Jean Ducas used to give me Christmas gifts of foil trays filled with sprout-your-own mung beans, accompanied by an endless list of environmental conditions I had to meet to produce the sprouts for the Chinese supper she inevitably expected me to serve no later than Chinese New Year. The routine was exasperating, to say the least, so I for one was happy to see the sprouts' appearance in supermarket produce sections. In memory of Jean, here is a favorite and tasty dish: Bean Sprouts, Celery and Green Peppers in a Wok.

BEET AND APPLE PUREE

■ *Serves 8* ■

This keeps refrigerated for a week or so. It's convenient to have it ready to serve with grilled or fried chicken, pork, sandwiches or burgers, or any barbecued meats.

1/2 cup (1 stick) butter
1 cup chopped onion
4 cups chopped apples (use 3 large Granny Smith or McIntosh)
2 tablespoons sugar
1/4 cup cider vinegar
4 cups cooked cubed beets or two 16-ounce cans or jars
salt

1 Melt butter in saucepan, add onion, cover and simmer 15 minutes. Add apples, sugar and vinegar and simmer uncovered 15 minutes longer. Stir in beets.

2 Puree in food processor in batches. Add salt to taste. Serve hot.

MICROWAVE: (1) Combine onion, apples, sugar and vinegar in dish and cook on HIGH (100%) 8 minutes. Add beets. (2) Cut butter into 8 pieces and melt on HIGH 45 to 60 seconds. (3) Puree beet mixture in processor in batches. Mix butter into puree, add salt and serve.

SUPERMARKET SAVVY

FRESH BEETS

To keep the red color in beets, cook them whole. Cut the greens above the roots, add water to cover and cook up to 2 hours, depending on size; they are done when easily pierced with a knife. Plunge cooked beets into cold water to ease removal of the skins, which will slip off easily. Cut out any bruises or dark spots. Serve beets in many ways: slice or cube them and simply add butter, salt and pepper, or add oil, vinegar, salt, pepper and basil. For an elegant dinner, scoop out the centers with a melon baller and fill with sour cream mixed with finely sliced scallions and a touch of salt and pepper, or whipped cottage cheese mixed with horseradish.

Strange, but in Roman times the sweet roots were not eaten; the greens were, however. Beets are rich in iron, sodium and vitamin A. If you make borscht or another dish that you want to tint red, cut up the beets before cooking.

An absolute favorite of mine is to grill beets. Wash and dry whole small beets, cut greens above the root and wrap the roots in aluminum foil with a little butter, salt and pepper. Roast in the coals as you would potatoes. They may be oven-baked in this way also. And beets cook beautifully in the microwave. A half pound of small beets in one layer on HIGH (100%) takes 8 minutes in a glass dish, covered; 6 large beets, each wrapped in plastic, take 25 to 30 minutes on HIGH.

FRESH BEETS VINAIGRETTE

■ *Serves 4* ■

Cooking beets in water seems to be traditional but you should try baking them whole, steaming or microwaving them. Fresh beets, simply dressed with oil and vinegar, are a good accompaniment to almost any meat or fish.

1   *pound beets, trimmed*
balsamic vinegar dressing, see page 266

Cook beets in water to cover until done, about 40 minutes depending on size. Peel and slice. Add about 1/4 cup dressing and toss well. Serve warm or cold.

MICROWAVE: (1) Place whole beets in 2-quart dish, cover and cook on HIGH (100%) 18 minutes. (2) Proceed as above.

ACORN SQUASH WITH SWEET-SOUR SAUCE

■ *Serves 4* ■

This sauce adapts easily to other vegetables; for example, one of the easiest and best things to do with it is to fill the cavities of room-temperature avocados for a really unusual first course. This acorn squash dish is meant as a side dish, but it could be a first course too.

2   *acorn squash, about 2 pounds each*
1/2   *cup chicken broth or water*
2   *tablespoons sugar*
2   *tablespoons fresh lemon juice*
2   *tablespoons vinegar*
2   *tablespoons ketchup*
1   *tablespoon soy sauce*
1   *tablespoon butter*
salt and pepper

1 Preheat oven to 400°F (200°C). Cut squashes in half and place in baking dish. Cover and bake 45 minutes or until tender.

2 Combine all remaining ingredients in small saucepan and bring to boil. Lower heat and simmer 3 minutes. Spoon sauce into center of each squash half and serve.

MICROWAVE: (1) Prick skin of squash and cook on HIGH (100%) 10 to 12 minutes. If not on carousel, turn squash once. Let stand 3 to 4 minutes. (2) Combine remaining ingredients in bowl and cook on HIGH 3 to 4 minutes, stirring at least once during cooking. Spoon sauce into center of squash and serve.

ACORN SQUASH WITH PEAR

■ *Serves 2*■

Acorn squash gets a special lift from pear. Add a sprinkle of cinnamon, allspice or nutmeg, too.

1 acorn squash, cut in half, seeds and strings removed
1 pear, peeled, seeded and coarsely chopped, or 2 canned pear halves, drained
2 tablespoons butter
cinnamon, allspice or nutmeg
salt and pepper

1 Slice squash into 1-inch strips, remove skin and cut into 1-inch pieces. Place in saucepan with water to cover. Cook until tender and drain.

2 If using fresh pear, cook in saucepan over low heat until tender. Combine with squash, butter and a sprinkle of selected spice. Mash by hand or puree in food processor. Add salt and pepper and serve hot.

MICROWAVE: (1) Place squash cut side down in glass pie dish. Prick skin every inch or so. Cook on HIGH (100%) 10 minutes. (2) Leave squash in microwave. Put fresh pear pieces in bowl, cover with plastic and place alongside squash in microwave; cook on HIGH 5 minutes. (3) Spoon out squash pulp and discard skin. Combine squash with pears, add butter, spice, salt and pepper and puree in food processor. Serve hot.

CARROT TARRAGON PUREE

■ *Serves 4*■

Experiment with different flavors. For example, try substituting 1/2 teaspoon dried thyme, or allspice, cinnamon or a dash of curry, for the tarragon.

1 pound carrots, peeled and cut into 1-inch pieces
salt
1 tablespoon finely chopped fresh tarragon or 1 teaspoon dried
4 tablespoons butter or margarine, room temperature

1 Bring 1 quart water to boil. Add carrots and salt and cook until tender, about 12 minutes. Drain well.

2 Puree carrots in processor, adding tarragon and butter. Serve hot.

MICROWAVE: Reduce water to 1/4 cup. (1) Combine carrot pieces, water and salt in microwave-safe dish, cover and cook on HIGH (100%) 7 minutes. Drain and puree as above.

CHEESE-COVERED CAULIFLOWER WITH VELOUTÉ SAUCE

■ *Serves 4* ■

The whole head of cauliflower makes a dramatic presentation. The only tricky part is removing it from the boiling water when cooked; try pouring it out into a colander, being careful not to break the head. This is very easy to cook in the microwave; if you have one, use that method.

1   *head fresh cauliflower, trimmed (about 2 pounds)*
4   *tablespoons butter or margarine, room temperature*
1   *cup hot chicken velouté sauce, page 266*
1/4   *cup grated Parmesan cheese*
sprinkle of chopped parsley

1 Cook whole fresh cauliflower in boiling water to cover until tender, about 10 to 15 minutes; do not overcook. Drain well in colander.

2 Place drained cauliflower stem side down in broilerproof dish. Smear with soft butter or margarine and pour velouté sauce over. Sprinkle cheese all over. Run under broiler to brown lightly. Garnish with chopped parsley.

MICROWAVE: (1) Put trimmed cauliflower in microwave-safe dish, cover with plastic and cook on HIGH (100%) 6 minutes. Let stand 2 minutes. (2) Remove plastic and complete as above.

COLE SLAW WITH CARROTS AND RAISINS

■ *Serves 6* ■

Buttermilk dressing and cabbage slaw are meant for each other. The addition of raisins and celery seed gives this additional texture and taste.

1/2   *cup mayonnaise*
1/2   *cup buttermilk*
2   *tablespoons minced onion*
1   *tablespoon fresh lemon juice*
1   *teaspoon dried dillweed*
salt and pepper
4   *cups thinly sliced cabbage*
1   *cup grated carrots*
1/2   *cup raisins*
2   *tablespoons celery seed*

1 Combine mayonnaise, buttermilk, onion, lemon juice, dillweed, salt and pepper and blend until smooth.

2 Combine cabbage, carrots, raisins and celery seed in large bowl. Pour in dressing and toss well. Cover and refrigerate at least 2 hours to allow flavors to blend.

BROCCOLI TIMBALES WITH LIME SILK SAUCE

■ *Serves 4* ■

An impressive first course. Note that some food companies offer packaged sauces that provide the option of using less butter or margarine in preparing them. If package directions give this option, use it.

1   *package (0.9 ounce) Hollandaise sauce mix*
1   *fresh lime*
1   *package (10 ounces) frozen chopped broccoli, thawed and drained*
1   *egg*
salt
nutmeg

1 Prepare sauce mix according to package directions, adding 2 teaspoons grated or finely chopped lime zest and 2 tablespoons lime juice.

2 Preheat oven to 350°F (180°C). Combine broccoli, 1/2 cup prepared sauce (reserve remainder), egg, salt and nutmeg in food processor or blender and process lightly; mixture should have texture. Grease 4 timbales or custard cups and divide broccoli mixture among them. Place cups in larger dish and add water to a depth of 1 1/2 inches.

3 Bake 30 to 40 minutes or until knife inserted in timbales comes out clean. To serve, reheat remaining sauce. Invert timbales onto individual plates. Spoon sauce around and on top of timbales, allowing it to run down sides.

MICROWAVE: (1) Prepare timbales as above. Cook in water bath on HIGH (100%) 12 minutes. If not using carousel, turn dish 3 times. (2) Prepare sauce in microwave according to package directions, adding lime zest and juice. Serve as above.

NO COOK CUCUMBER CHUTNEY WITH YOGURT

■ *Serves 6* ■

Fresh and tasty with chicken, fish, burgers and sandwiches.

1   *cucumber, seeded and cut into small cubes to make about 1 1/2 cups*
1   *apple (preferably Granny Smith), peeled, cored and cut into small cubes*
1   *cup plain yogurt*
1/2   *cup golden raisins*
1/2   *cup finely sliced scallions*
1/2   *red bell pepper, cored, ribs and seeds removed, diced to make 1/2 cup*

1   *tablespoon sugar*
juice of 1/2 lime
1/4   *teaspoon ground cumin*

Combine all ingredients in bowl and toss well. Cover and refrigerate at least 1 hour or overnight to develop flavor.

CORN WITH GINGER AND GREEN PEPPERS

■ *Serves 4* ■

Corn and peppers fare well together, and they get a special lift by the addition of some candied ginger.

1   tablespoon butter or margarine
1   tablespoon peanut or vegetable oil
1   whole green bell pepper, cored, ribs and seeds removed, cut into 1/2-inch cubes
2   tablespoons minced candied ginger
1   can (17 ounces) corn, drained, or its equivalent in frozen corn (or use kernels scraped from cooked fresh or frozen ears of corn)
salt and pepper

1 Heat butter and oil in saucepan and sauté green pepper 4 to 5 minutes. Add ginger and sauté 1 minute.

2 Add corn, cover and heat through, about 5 minutes.

MICROWAVE: (1) Combine butter, oil and green pepper in dish. Cover and cook on HIGH (100%) 4 minutes. (2) Add corn and ginger, cover and cook on HIGH 3 to 4 minutes, stirring once.

GRILLED HERBED CORN

■ *Serves 4* ■

There's nothing like grilled fresh corn. Add fresh lemon juice in place of cheese if you wish, and bake instead of grilling. To bake, follow all the steps below but bake in a preheated 350°F (180°C) oven for about 25 minutes. This corn is also great microwaved; see below.

4   ears corn, husked and washed free of silk
4   tablespoons butter or margarine, room temperature
2   tablespoons finely chopped fresh basil or 1/2 teaspoon dried
1   tablespoon finely chopped fresh oregano or 1/2 teaspoon dried
1   garlic clove, minced
salt and pepper
1/2   cup grated Romano or Parmesan cheese

1 Set each ear of corn on sheet of foil.

2 Whisk butter with basil, oregano, garlic, salt and pepper and spread over each ear of corn. Wrap foil around corn and grill 15 to 20 minutes, turning several times to cook each side.

3 Remove foil and sprinkle cheese over corn. Serve at once.

MICROWAVE: (1) Prepare corn as above but wrap in plastic instead of foil. Cook on HIGH (100%) 12 to 16 minutes. If not on carousel, rearrange after 3 and 6 minutes of cooking. Let stand, covered, for 5 minutes. Complete as above. (2) If using frozen corn, cook on HIGH 10 to 12 minutes. Let stand, covered, 3 minutes.

CRANBERRY ASPIC WITH HORSERADISH

∎ *Serves 6* ∎

*T*his ruby red berry, native to the U.S., has long been taken for granted, especially in jelly or relish form on holiday tables. But there are other exciting uses for this tart and delicious fruit; here it is combined with juice, beets and red horseradish. Sort through the berries and keep the plump, shiny and firm ones; discard the dark or soft ones. They keep for up to one month in the refrigerator and freeze beautifully for up to a year. There is no reason not to use cranberries all year round.

2 *cups bottled cranberry juice*
2 *cups water*
1 *cup fresh or frozen cranberries*
1/2 *cup sugar*
2 *envelopes (.25 ounce each) unflavored gelatin*
1 *cup diced canned or cooked fresh beets*
2/3 *cup bottled red horseradish, drained*
1 *tablespoon red wine vinegar*
shredded lettuce leaves

1 Combine juice, water, cranberries and sugar in large nonaluminum saucepan and bring to boil. Lower heat and simmer 10 minutes. Strain, reserving berries.

2 Place 1/4 cup water in small bowl and sprinkle in gelatin. Let stand until softened, about 5 minutes. Add to saucepan in which berries cooked, also adding strained liquid. Stir over low heat to completely dissolve gelatin. Transfer to bowl and refrigerate, stirring occasionally, until slightly thickened.

3 Add berries, beets, horseradish and vinegar to gelatin mixture. Transfer to lightly oiled 6-cup mold and refrigerate 4 hours or until set. Unmold and garnish with shredded lettuce leaves.

MICROWAVE: In step 1, cook on HIGH (100%) 4 minutes. Proceed as above.

COUNTRY SKILLET EGGPLANT AND TOMATOES

■ *Serves 6* ■

A fast and tasty way to bring together this classic combination of vegetables, and an excellent way to use prepared spaghetti sauce other than on pasta.

1/4 *cup olive oil*
1 *medium onion, sliced*
1 *large garlic clove, minced*
1 *jar (15 1/2 ounces) spaghetti sauce, about 1 3/4 cups*
1 *small eggplant, ends removed, cut into 1-inch cubes to make 3 to 4 cups*
1 *red bell pepper, cored, ribs and seeds removed, cut into 1-inch squares to make about 1 cup*
2 *small zucchini, sliced to make about 1 cup*

1 Heat oil in large skillet and cook onion until soft. Add garlic and cook 1 minute. Add all remaining ingredients.

2 Reduce heat to low and simmer until vegetables are tender, about 20 minutes, stirring occasionally.

MICROWAVE: (1) In 2-quart round dish, combine all ingredients except sauce. Cover and cook on HIGH (100%) 10 minutes, stirring once during cooking. If not on carousel, turn once. (2) Add sauce, stir well, cover and cook on HIGH 3 minutes. Let stand 4 minutes before serving.

SUPERMARKET SAVVY

■ ■

GARLIC

1. Garlic can be bought in many forms—powdered, minced, chopped, sliced, pureed.
2. Dehydrated garlic is used in the processed food industry in soups, mayonnaise, mustard, ketchup, salad dressings, pickles, sausages—an almost endless list.
3. It is also an important ingredient in canned dog foods. In their kennel feed-testing programs, dog food manufacturers have proven that dogs adore garlic.
4. It has become American custom to add garlic to buttered or oiled bread, to insert it in legs of lamb, to rub it into salad bowls and to demand it in barbecue sauces.

CURLY ENDIVE SALAD WITH TOASTED PINE NUTS

■ *Serves 4* ■

It's easy to toast the nuts—just melt 1/2 teaspoon butter or margarine in a small skillet, add pine nuts, and shake and stir over low heat until they just begin to color. Remove from heat and cool a little before adding to salad. Dress this salad into the sour cream dressing below.

1	head curly endive, trimmed, washed, dried and cut into pieces
2	navel oranges, peeled, sectioned and cut into 1-inch pieces
1/2	cup halved seedless red grapes
4	very thin slices Bermuda onion, separated
1/2	cup pine toasted nuts

Sour Cream Dressing

Combine all ingredients in bowl and toss with dressing.

SOUR CREAM DRESSING

2/3	cup sour cream
1/4	cup white wine vinegar
1	teaspoon Dijon-style mustard
1	teaspoon finely chopped fresh tarragon or 1/2 teaspoon dried salt and pepper

Combine all ingredients until well mixed.

RED ONION SALAD WITH FENNEL

■ *Serves 6* ■

Crisp slices of red onion in a fennel-flavored vinaigrette may be served with sliced cold meats or grilled flavorful sausages and new potatoes.

1 1/4	pounds red onions, thinly sliced to make about 5 cups
1	tablespoon salt
2/3	cup olive or vegetable oil
3	tablespoons red wine vinegar
2	tablespoons finely chopped fresh chives
1	tablespoon sugar
1/2	teaspoon fennel seed

pepper

1 Place onions in large bowl and sprinkle with salt. Toss and cover with ice cubes. Let stand 20 minutes.

2 Combine remaining ingredients in small bowl and whisk until well blended. Drain onions and dry well on paper towels. Place in serving bowl, add dressing and toss. Let marinate 20 to 30 minutes at room temperature before serving.

ROMAINE LETTUCE WITH HONEY LEMON DRESSING

■ Serves 6 ■

One of the easiest and freshest of salads.

juice of 2 lemons
  3   tablespoons honey
1/2   cup olive oil
salt and pepper
  1   head romaine lettuce, washed, dried and
       cut into small pieces

Combine first 4 ingredients and pour over lettuce. Toss well and serve right away.

SUPERMARKET SAVVY

■ ■

LEMONS

I can still picture my grandmother preparing her *gremolata* (finely chopped lemon peel or zest, garlic and parsley) and carefully strewing it over her osso buco (veal shanks cooked slowly in wine, tomatoes and other vegetables); I believe I remember that introduction to lemons before my first lemonade. My mother often substituted orange peel or zest for the lemon. I keep lemons and oranges in the refrigerator at all times because I don't think I can cook without them: in salads, marinades, as an alternative to salt, on fish, with fruit, with vegetables, with butter, in mayonnaise, in pie fillings, with lamb and other meats, on smoked salmon and with, on and in everything else.

Lemons are rich in vitamin C or ascorbic acid as everyone knows; in cooking, this acid is most useful in preventing the discoloration of artichokes, apples, pears, peaches and bananas. Lemon juice is an important marinade ingredient, tenderizing and flavoring many foods. It actually "cooks" some fish if they are marinated in it for a long enough period of time.

More flavor comes from the colored part of the peel—the zest—than the juice. To take off the zest, use a vegetable peeler and cut away the outer rind without the white pith. When peeled properly, the zest is almost transparent. Mince it as finely as you can by hand or in a small food processor (the larger ones do not handle this task adequately, and it's aggravating to see strips of lemon peel dodging the steel blade as if it were a red cape in a bull ring). Buy lemons with a slight greenish cast and with thin skins. Pick them up; the heavier ones are juicier. You'll get a lot more juice if you put lemons in boiling water for 2 or 3 minutes before squeezing. But if you do this, don't try to peel lemon zest afterward.

I don't use bottled lemon juice. The taste is never quite right. A display of fresh lemons is hard to beat, as is their taste.

FRESH FENNEL, BUTTERED AND CRUMBED

■ *Serves 6* ■

This is a superb accompaniment to roast poultry of all kinds.

3 *bulbs fresh fennel*
1/2 *cup (1 stick) butter, room temperature*
2 *cups chicken broth*
1 *garlic clove, minced*
1 *teaspoon fennel seed*
pepper
1 *cup fresh breadcrumbs*
salt, optional

1 Prepare fennel bulbs for cooking by cutting away stem end and any bruised spots. Wash and slice into 1/2-inch-thick rounds.

2 Arrange rounds in large skillet with 2 tablespoons butter and chicken broth. Bring to boil, lower heat and simmer 15 minutes. Transfer to buttered baking dish with slotted spoon. Empty skillet, add 2 tablespoons butter and crumbs and sauté for several minutes. Set aside.

3 Preheat oven to 350°F (180°C). Dot fennel with remaining butter and add garlic, fennel seed, pepper and crumbs. Add some salt if you wish. Bake 30 minutes or until tender.

MICROWAVE: Decrease broth from 2 cups to 1/2 cup. (1) Place fennel slices in dish with 1/2 cup chicken broth and 2 tablespoons butter, cover with plastic and cook on HIGH (100%) 5 minutes. (2) Dot fennel with remaining butter. Sprinkle with garlic, fennel seed, pepper and breadcrumbs. Cook uncovered on HIGH 5 minutes.

STUFFED MUSHROOMS WITH CREAMY ITALIAN DRESSING

■ *Serves 4 as appetizer or side dish* ■

Here is a foolproof combination of supermarket items.

8 *large stuffing mushrooms, wiped clean,*
   stems removed (reserve stems)
3 *ounces cream cheese, room temperature*
bottled creamy Italian dressing
1/4 *cup chopped fresh chives*

1 Preheat oven to 350°F (180°C). Bake mushrooms 5 minutes.

2 Clean mushroom stems. Combine with cream cheese, 1/4 cup dressing and chives in processor and blend. Increase oven temperature to 375°F (190°C). Stuff mushrooms with mixture and bake again for 3 to 5 minutes to heat stuffing. Run under broiler to brown lightly. Serve with a little extra creamy Italian dressing on top, if you like.

MICROWAVE: (1) Wipe mushrooms clean and remove stems. Cook caps on HIGH (100%) 2 minutes. (2) Prepare stuffing as above. Stuff mushroom caps and cook on HIGH 2 minutes longer. Serve as above.

GRILLED OYSTER MUSHROOMS

■ *Serves 4* ■

Use large mushrooms and grill them in a wire basket as you would hamburgers. Or skewer them before grilling and serve one skewer per person.

1/3   *cup peanut oil*
1   *pound oyster mushrooms, stems trimmed*
salt and pepper
grated Parmesan cheese

1 Place peanut oil in bowl, add mushrooms and toss until they are coated with oil.

2 Thread mushrooms on skewers or arrange in narrow hinged wire basket. When coals are gray, grill mushrooms about 3 minutes per side. Remove from grill and add salt, pepper and a sprinkle of grated cheese.

SUPERMARKET SAVVY

OYSTER MUSHROOMS

A most amazing sight in many supermarkets is the oyster mushroom—an item that was, until recently, found only in fancy greengrocers. In England it is known as the shellfish of the woods, probably because it looks like an oyster but tastes like a mushroom—usually a mild-flavored mushroom.

I prefer buying the loose variety, that is, not packaged, so I can see and feel them better. The convex caps should be firm, moist and almost without a mushroom smell. They can vary in color from white to beige to silver. They're versatile and I've included a favorite of mine, grilled oyster mushrooms, but I also like them sautéed in small pieces. Melt 2 tablespoons butter (for 8 ounces mushrooms, cut into pieces) and sauté 2 to 3 thinly sliced scallions for a minute or so. Add about 1/2 cup chicken broth and bring to boil. Add the mushroom pieces and cook over high heat until the liquid disappears. Season with salt and pepper, sprinkle with a pinch of red pepper flakes if you wish, and add a touch of snipped fresh parsley. These mushrooms are rich in iron and the B vitamins.

FRESH MUSHROOMS IN SHERRIED YOGURT SAUCE

■ *Serves 4* ■

Supermarkets feature fresh white mushrooms sold by the pound, but invariably they are side by side with cellophane-wrapped 10- or 12-ounce packages. Markets learned some time ago that the public wants vegetables fresh and unpackaged, especially not shrink-wrapped. Mushrooms seem to be an exception, however, and I will admit that although there are better-tasting mushrooms (these are now being offered more and more in the supermarkets), the packaged ones are better than I used to think they were.

2   tablespoons vegetable oil
2   tablespoons butter or margarine
8   ounces white mushrooms, wiped clean, stems trimmed, thinly sliced
4   scallions, finely sliced
1/4 cup plain yogurt
1   cup chicken broth
1/4 cup dry sherry
2   tablespoons all purpose flour
1   teaspoon minced fresh thyme or 1/2 teaspoon dried
4   slices buttered toast, halved diagonally, or 1 package (about 8 ounces) biscuits, baked (according to package directions), split open and buttered

1 Heat oil and butter in large skillet. Add mushrooms and scallions and sauté 6 minutes. Remove mushrooms and onions with slotted spoon.

2 Combine yogurt, chicken broth, sherry, flour and thyme in bowl and whisk until well combined. Add to skillet and bring to boil. Lower heat and simmer for several minutes until sauce is thickened. Return mushrooms and onions to sauce and heat through. Place 2 pieces of toast on each plate, spoon mushrooms over center and serve immediately.

MICROWAVE: (1) Combine oil, butter, mushrooms and scallions in dish and cook on HIGH (100%) 2 minutes, stirring once. (2) Stir in yogurt, broth, sherry, flour and thyme and cook on MEDIUM-HIGH (70%) until thickened, 3 to 5 minutes, stirring every minute. Serve as above.

SUPERMARKET SAVVY

MUSHROOMS

Since the early 1900s the mushroom industry has grown so fast that cultivated mushrooms can be found in supermarkets at any time of the year. Since they're so available, let's talk about them.

1. Don't wash them. They absorb water like a sponge and when cooked will throw off water unlike unwashed ones which will retain most of their natural moisture.

2. Don't peel them. You will lose considerable flavor and texture. If the mushrooms are discolored, don't buy them. Baskets of fresh, white mushrooms are readily available, so there's no excuse for buying inferior ones.

3. Learn to tell mushroom age by looking at the space between the bottom of the cap and the stem. In a young mushroom there will be no space there. As it matures, the cap opens as moisture evaporates. Buy young ones.

4. Remember that size of cap has nothing to do with quality. The U.S. Department of Agriculture grades mushrooms and only then classifies them small to extra large; therefore, cap size is of little consequence unless you want to stuff them.

5. The length of a mushroom stem *is* important; look for short ones and avoid tougher, more fibrous longer ones.

6. The creative cook will find many uses for mushrooms. They may be stuffed with anything from the simplest cream cheese mixture accented with herbs to chopped raw filet mignon dotted with caviar. Remember that raw mushrooms in salads are simplicity itself. I slice them as thinly as possible and dress them with olive oil, vinegar and fresh herbs. If you cook them, do it quickly; if sliced no longer than 4 or 5 minutes, if whole no longer than 10. Mushrooms should be added to casseroles and stews when the dish is almost cooked.

7. Supermarkets now offer fresh shiitakes, cèpes, chanterelles, creminis, morels and others. If affordable, use them. However, I stay clear of jarred and canned wild mushroom varieties—I just don't like the taste of them. What I really enjoy are the dried varieties, which are worth the price. They lack some texture but are rich in flavor. Unlike fresh mushrooms, they can be cooked for long periods of time. Also consider frozen mushrooms—they really are rather remarkable, with good color and consistency. I prefer fresh ones, but frozen can be a satisfactory substitute.

RUTH'S PASSOVER POTATO CARROT KUGEL

■ *Serves 8* ■

Not all supermarkets are likely to carry rendered chicken fat, so you can substitute peanut or vegetable oil. It will taste almost as good.

3   *large white boiling potatoes, finely grated*
6   *carrots, grated*
2   *medium onions, grated*
1/4   *cup rendered chicken fat or peanut or vegetable oil*
6   *eggs, beaten*
3/4   *cup matzo meal*

1 Combine potatoes, carrots and onions in large bowl. Add chicken fat or oil and toss. Add eggs and mix well. Blend in matzo meal.

2 Preheat oven to 350°F (180°C). Grease 3-quart casserole and pour in kugel mixture. Bake 1 hour. Serve hot.

MICROWAVE: (1) Follow step 1 above. (2) Place mixture in greased 3-quart dish, cover with plastic or lid and cook on HIGH (100%) 20 minutes.

RED RADISHES WITH CHIVE BUTTER

■ *Serves 4* ■

To save time, buy red radishes with stems removed; they come in plastic packages. But remember that these will still need some sorting and paring.

1   *pound red radishes, ends and blemishes cut off, washed and halved*
4   *tablespoons butter, cut into small pieces*
2   *teaspoons sherry vinegar*
1/4   *cup finely chopped fresh chives or scallions*
1   *tablespoon sugar, optional*
salt and pepper

Cook radishes with butter and vinegar in tightly covered skillet or saucepan until tender, about 8 to 10 minutes. Add chives, sugar, salt and pepper and toss well. Heat 1 minute longer, uncovered, over high heat.

MICROWAVE: (1) Combine radishes and vinegar in 2 1/2-quart dish. Cover with plastic and cook on HIGH (100%) 6 minutes. Remove from oven, puncture plastic to release steam and uncover. (2) Add chives, butter, sugar, salt and pepper. Cook uncovered on HIGH 1 minute. Toss and serve.

RED PEPPER RATATOUILLE

■ *Serves 8* ■

This combination of flavorful vegetables produces a wonderful-tasting ragout. Make a lot—it makes a good cold appetizer if any is left over, or it can be rewarmed as a side dish.

1/4 cup plus 2 tablespoons vegetable or olive oil

3 small zucchini, washed, ends removed, peeled in 1/2-inch-wide lengthwise strips, sliced 1/3 inch thick

1 eggplant (about 1 pound), washed, ends removed, peeled in 1-inch-wide lengthwise strips and cut into 1-inch cubes

2 red bell peppers, cored, ribs and seeds removed, cut into 1-inch squares

2 large garlic cloves, minced

1 can (16 ounces) peeled plum tomatoes with juice, coarsely chopped

1 cup water

1 package (1.9 ounces) French onion soup and recipe mix

2 tablespoons finely chopped fresh basil or 1 teaspoon dried

2 tablespoons finely chopped fresh oregano or 1 teaspoon dried

dash of hot pepper sauce or a sprinkle of red pepper flakes

1 Heat 1/4 cup oil in large skillet and sauté zucchini, eggplant and pepper together for 15 minutes, adding more oil if needed. Transfer cooked pieces to large saucepan with cover. Add garlic 1 minute before all vegetables are cooked, then transfer all to saucepan.

2 Combine tomatoes and juice, water, soup mix, basil, oregano and hot pepper in bowl and mix well. Pour into saucepan. Bring to boil, lower heat and simmer, stirring several times, 30 minutes or until vegetables are tender.

MICROWAVE: (1) In casserole, combine oil, zucchini, eggplant, pepper, garlic and 1/2 cup water. Cover and cook on HIGH (100%) 6 minutes, stirring twice. (2) In bowl, combine tomatoes and juice, remaining 1/2 cup water and remaining ingredients. Add to vegetable dish. Cover and cook on HIGH 12 minutes, stirring 3 times. Let stand 2 to 3 minutes before serving.

RADICCHIO WITH WATERCRESS AND JAPANESE MUSHROOMS

■ *Serves 4* ■

3   *tablespoons butter or margarine*
1   *tablespoon olive or vegetable oil*
1   *packet enoki mushrooms, or 6 large*
    shiitake mushrooms, thinly sliced
1   *head radicchio, leaves separated,*
    washed, dried and cut into 1-inch pieces
1   *bunch watercress, heavy stems removed,*
    washed and dried, cut in half to make
    smaller pieces.
salt and pepper
pinch of red pepper flakes

Heat butter and oil in wok or large skillet. Add mushrooms and sauté over high heat 2 minutes. Add remaining ingredients and sauté 4 minutes; do not burn.

MICROWAVE: (1) In a dish, combine butter, oil and mushrooms and cook on HIGH (100%) 2 minutes, stirring once. (2) Add remaining ingredients and cook on HIGH 2 minutes.

SUPERMARKET SAVVY
■ ■ ■ ■ ■ ■ ■ ■ ■ ■ ■ ■ ■ ■ ■ ■ ■ ■ ■

RADICCHIO

I see radicchio, broccoli rape and Belgian endive in every supermarket I've entered recently; five years ago, such vegetables were found only in ethnic markets in New York, Chicago and San Francisco. Radicchio (say ra-DICK-e-o) is rich in vitamins A and C. It looks like a very small red cabbage and can have curly or flat leaves. Radicchio leaves make excellent containers for other foods and it is delicious itself. To prepare, simply remove the core, separate the leaves, run under cold water and dry in a salad spinner or with paper towels. Radicchio is delicious grilled. Core a head, cut it in half, brush with olive or vegetable oil, place on grill and grill both sides. Add salt and pepper and serve hot.

SAUTÉED SUGAR SNAP PEAS

■ *Serves 4* ■

8   *ounces fresh sugar snap peas*
1   *tablespoon butter or margarine*
generous sprinkle of mushroom powder (if not available, use a seasoned salt, pepper or herb combination)

1 Remove ends from peas and cut away any blemishes. Rinse and pat dry.

2 Melt butter in skillet, add peas and sauté over high heat. Sprinkle with mushroom powder or seasoned salt and toss again. Cooking should take less than 5 minutes.

MICROWAVE: Combine peas in dish with 2 tablespoons water. Cover and cook on HIGH (100%) 3 minutes. Add mushroom powder or seasoned salt and toss well. Cover and cook on HIGH 1 minute longer.

CARAMELIZED SHALLOTS

■ *Serves 6* ■

*T*here are uses for shallots apart from chopping and adding them to other foods. They are especially delicious when prepared as a vegetable on their own.

36   *shallots, about 1-inch size, peeled*
milk to cover shallots in saucepan
  3   *tablespoons butter*
  1   *tablespoon sugar*
salt and pepper

1 Combine shallots and milk in saucepan and bring to boil. Reduce heat and simmer 5 minutes; do not overcook. Drain and set aside.

2 In skillet large enough to hold shallots in one layer, heat butter and sugar with salt and pepper. Add shallots and turn to coat with butter mixture. Cook over low heat until caramelized on outside and tender on inside.

MICROWAVE: Increase sugar to 2 tablespoons. (1) Combine shallots and milk in shallow dish, cover with plastic and cook on HIGH (100%) 3 minutes. Drain. Discard milk or use in cream soup. (2) In same dish, combine butter, sugar, salt and pepper and cook on HIGH 1 minute. Add shallots and toss well. Cover with plastic and cook on HIGH 3 minutes, stirring once.

SUPERMARKET SAVVY

SHALLOTS

Shallots are sold loose or in packages (usually 8 or 16 ounces). Peel shallot with a sharp paring knife, leaving root end intact. Make thin slices up to but not through root end. Turn peeled shallot on its side and, holding the root end with one hand, cut into small dice. Some markets sell shallots cleaned, diced and frozen, ready for use.

MASHED POTATOES WITH GARLIC, CREAM AND CHEESE

■ *Serves 8* ■

1 1/2   *cups heavy cream*
  6   *tablespoons butter or margarine*
  2   *garlic cloves, minced*
  8   *servings instant mashed potatoes, prepared according to package directions and kept hot*
  1/4   *cup grated Parmesan cheese*
Salt and white pepper

1 Combine cream, butter and garlic in saucepan and heat but do not boil. Add to potatoes in large bowl. Fold in cheese, salt and pepper.

2 Transfer to shallow baking dish and spread with rubber spatula. Run under broiler 1 to 2 minutes or until top is golden.

LITTLE RED POTATOES WITH TARRAGON CREAM

■ *Serves 6* ■

2 pounds new red potatoes, cooked and
  quartered
1 cup frozen green peas, thawed
4 scallions, finely sliced
1 package (0.9 ounce) Béarnaise sauce mix
3/4 cup water
2 tablespoons tarragon vinegar (or white
  wine vinegar plus 1/2 teaspoon dried
  tarragon flakes, crumbled)
salt and pepper
1/2 cup half and half

1 Combine vegetables in large bowl and
set aside.

2 Combine sauce mix, water, vinegar,
salt and pepper in small saucepan and
bring to boil, stirring constantly. Lower heat
and cook 1 minute, stirring. Stir in half and
half and cook for 3 minutes. Add to vegetables and toss well.

MICROWAVE: (1) Combine 1 pound quartered
raw potatoes in dish with 1/4 cup water and
a sprinkle of salt and cook on HIGH (100%)
9 minutes. Rearrange after 5 minutes if not
on carousel. Let stand 3 minutes. Repeat
with remaining pound of potatoes. Prepare
other vegetables as above, place in bowl and
set aside. (2) In another bowl or in 4-cup
glass measure, whisk together sauce mix,
water, vinegar, salt and pepper. Cook on
HIGH (100%) 2 minutes or until boiling. Stir
in cream and cook on HIGH 1 minute longer.
Pour over vegetables and toss well.

SUPERMARKET STUFFED ZUCCHINI

■ *Serves 6* ■

1 package (for 6 servings)
  chicken-flavored stuffing mix
4 tablespoons butter or margarine, cut
  into small pieces
1 1/2 cups hot chicken stock
1/4 cup grated Parmesan or Romano cheese
3 small zucchini

1 Combine contents of stuffing seasoning packet pieces and butter pieces in
bowl. Add hot chicken stock and stir just to
blend and partially melt butter. Add stuffing
crumbs and cheese and set aside.

2 Trim ends from zucchini. Cut zucchini
in half lengthwise and scoop out seeds
with melon baller or teaspoon. Drop zucchini
halves into boiling water and cook about 4
minutes or until barely tender. Drain and let
stand until cool enough to handle.

3 Preheat oven to 400°F (200°C). Stuff
zucchini with crumb mixture and bake
20 minutes.

MICROWAVE: (1) Bring chicken stock to boil in
microwave and make stuffing as above. (2)
Prepare zucchini for cooking as above. Place
in dish with 1/4 cup water, cover with plastic
and cook on HIGH (100%) 3 minutes. Remove and let stand until cool enough to
handle. Stuff with crumbs mixture. Cover
and cook on HIGH 10 minutes.

CLASSIC TOMATO ASPIC

■ *Serves 10* ■

*T*his is easy; the only cooking required is to bring some tomato juice to a boil. People always think of aspic as a summertime dish, but I serve it all year long. It helps round out a buffet and makes a change-of-pace salad if sliced and put on a lettuce leaf with a sprig or two of watercress and a little prepared salad dressing. Fill the center of the aspic mold with fruit, tuna (or other fish) or chicken salad and a full meal is at hand.

4 1/2   *cups tomato juice*
    3   *envelopes unflavored gelatin*
  1/3   *cup fresh lemon juice*
    2   *teaspoons Worcestershire sauce*
  1/3   *teaspoon hot pepper sauce*

1 Pour half of tomato juice into nonaluminum saucepan and bring to boil. Remove from heat. Pour remaining juice into large bowl, sprinkle with gelatin and let stand several minutes. Add hot tomato juice and stir until gelatin dissolves.

2 Add remaining ingredients and pour into 6-cup ring mold. Refrigerate until set.

MICROWAVE: (1) Heat half of tomato juice in covered bowl on HIGH (100%) 2 minutes. Proceed as above.

VEGETABLES AU GRATIN

■ *Serves 6* ■

*T*his can be prepared in the oven or in the microwave. It's another example of enhancing a packaged product (scalloped potatoes) with another package (frozen vegetables) and enriching it into a gourmet dish.

    1   *box (5.25 ounces) scalloped potatoes*
1 1/2   *cups half-and-half*
1 1/2   *cups water*
    2   *tablespoons butter or margarine*
    1   *tablespoon chopped fresh tarragon or 1 teaspoon dried*
    1   *package (10 ounces) frozen mixed vegetables, such as Italian mix, thawed*

1 Preheat oven to 400°F (200°C). Combine potatoes and potato sauce mix in ungreased 2-quart casserole. Add half-and-half, water, butter and tarragon.

2 Bake 20 minutes. Add thawed vegetables and cook 15 minutes longer.

MICROWAVE: Use 1 3/4 cups half-and-half and 1 cup hot water. (1) Combine potatoes, water, 1 cup half and half, butter and tarragon in dish. Cover with waxed paper and cook on HIGH (100%) 10 minutes. (2) Stir in potato sauce mix, thawed vegetables and remaining 3/4 cup half and half. Cover and cook on HIGH 6 minutes. Let stand 5 minutes before serving.

VEGETABLE BAKE, SUPERMARKET STYLE

■ *Serves 4* ■

Packages of frozen mixed vegetables come in surprising combinations. For this dish almost any will work; consider broccoli, corn and red peppers or broccoli, cauliflower and carrots.

> 2 cups canned plum tomatoes, drained and coarsely chopped
> 1 package (16 ounces) frozen vegetable mix, thawed
> 1/4 cup white wine
> 1 teaspoon dried basil
> pepper
> 1/2 cup grated Parmesan or Romano cheese

1 Preheat oven to 400°F (200°C). Coat 8-inch square or 9-inch round glass baking dish with vegetable cooking spray and arrange 1 cup tomatoes on bottom. Add vegetable mix on top. Sprinkle with wine, basil, pepper and half of cheese. Top with remaining tomatoes and add remaining cheese on top.

2 Bake 20 minutes or until bubbling and heated through.

MICROWAVE: (1) Assemble as above in microwave-safe dish. Cover with plastic and cook on HIGH (100%) 14 minutes. Let stand 3 minutes before serving.

LOW-FAT VEGETABLES IN A SKILLET

■ *Serves 4* ■

The amazing thing about this recipe is that each serving has only 30 calories and 1 gram of fat. It's very tasty; serve it often. Add herbs if you like, during or after cooking.

> 1 teaspoon margarine
> 1/2 cup thinly sliced fresh mushrooms
> 1 cup thinly sliced zucchini
> 1 cup 1-inch broccoli florets
> 1 cup thinly sliced yellow summer squash
> 1/2 cup water
> salt and pepper
> 1/2 teaspoon grated or minced lemon zest

Melt margarine in nonstick skillet and sauté mushrooms until browned. Add remaining ingredients except lemon zest, cover and simmer 10 minutes or until vegetables are tender. Drain. Sprinkle lemon zest over all and serve.

MICROWAVE: (1) Place margarine in dish and cook on HIGH (100%) 30 seconds. Add mushrooms and cook on HIGH 2 minutes. (2) Add remaining ingredients except lemon zest, cover with plastic and cook on HIGH 7 minutes. Let stand 2 minutes. Drain, add lemon zest and serve.

WARM VEGETABLE SALAD WITH WALNUTS

■ *Serves 6* ■

*T*his is a versatile preparation that can be served as a salad, as a lunch dish for four or as a first course. Don't overcook the vegetables.

2   cups sliced or French green beans, cooked
     and drained
2   cups sliced carrots, cooked and drained
2   cups broccoli florets, cooked and drained
1   tablespoon finely chopped fresh basil or 1
     teaspoon dried
salt and pepper
1   cup bottled Italian dressing, heated
lettuce cups
1   tablespoon butter or margarine
1   cup coarsely chopped walnuts

1 Combine vegetables in large bowl. Add basil, salt, pepper and dressing and toss lightly but well.

2 Divide warm vegetables among lettuce cups.

3 Melt butter in skillet, add walnuts and toss several minutes to toast them, seasoning with salt and pepper. Add to top of vegetables. Serve warm.

MICROWAVE: Vegetables may be cooked as follows: (1) Cook green beans in bowl with 1 tablespoon water, covered, on HIGH (100%) 3 to 4 minutes. (2) Cook carrots in bowl, covered, on HIGH 4 to 5 minutes. (3) Cook broccoli florets in bowl, covered, on HIGH 2 to 3 minutes. Heat dressing in bowl, covered, on HIGH 1 minute. Prepare walnuts in skillet on stovetop. Proceed as above.

WATER CHESTNUT AND BACON CRUNCH

■ *Makes about 24 appetizers* ■

1   can (8 ounces) whole water chestnuts
      (about 24), drained and patted dry
1/4 cup light soy sauce
6   bacon slices, chilled

1 Marinate water chestnuts in soy sauce for about 1 hour. Drain.

2 Cut bacon slices in half lengthwise and then in half again crosswise; use scissors to do this easily. Wrap a small bacon piece around each marinated chestnut and spear with pick if you wish.

3 Broil 4 to 6 inches from heat source, turning once, until bacon is done. Drain on paper towels and serve hot.

MICROWAVE: (1) Prepare chestnuts and bacon as above. Arrange on outer rim of carousel and cook on HIGH 6 minutes. If not using carousel, set on outer surface of shallow dish and turn once or twice during cooking.

STIR-FRIED WATER CHESTNUTS, SNOW PEAS AND RED PEPPERS WITH GINGER

■ *Serves 6* ■

3	tablespoons peanut oil
1	tablespoon finely chopped fresh ginger
1/2	teaspoon salt
1	can (8 ounces) sliced water chestnuts, drained
1	can (8 ounces) bamboo shoots, drained
2	cups fresh or frozen snow peas (if fresh, strings removed and cut diagonally; if frozen, thawed and patted dry)
1 1/2	cups diced red bell pepper
2	tablespoons soy sauce

pepper

1 Heat wok or large skillet 30 seconds, add oil and heat. Add ginger and salt.

2 Add water chestnuts and stir-fry 30 seconds. Add bamboo shoots and stir-fry 30 seconds more. Add snow peas and fry another 30 seconds.

3 Add bell pepper and soy sauce and stir-fry 3 minutes. Season with pepper and serve right away.

MICROWAVE: (1) Heat oil in microwave-safe bowl on HIGH (100%) 45 seconds. Add ginger, salt and water chestnuts and cook on HIGH 1 minute. Stir in bamboo shoots and bell pepper and cook on HIGH 1 minute. Stir in snow peas, soy sauce and pepper and cook on HIGH 1 minute.

SUPERMARKET SAVVY

WATER CHESTNUTS

Low in sodium, with a small amount of B vitamins yet a substantial amount of potassium, this versatile vegetable is now a canned classic on supermarket shelves. Water chestnuts are really low in calories—only 35 per cup, cooked. They are appearing more frequently fresh; if you find them, cook in boiling water for about 5 minutes if you plan to add them to other dishes to be cooked further. Peel them after boiling and remove any dark spots before adding to other foods. If you want to use them in salads, cook in boiling water for 10 minutes, peel them and slice or add them whole to salads, rice or other already-cooked dishes. I remember childhood visits to New York's Chinatown, where water chestnuts were sold as a popular street snack—chilled in ice water and skewered on a stick just like a lollipop.

ZUCCHINI AND TOMATOES WITH SHOESTRING POTATOES

■ *Serves 6* ■

An easy lunch dish. Serve with cheddar cheese corn muffins.

3   tablespoons bacon fat or olive or vegetable
    oil
1   large onion, cut into 1/2-inch cubes
2   large garlic cloves, minced
1   can (14 ounces) stewed tomatoes
8   small zucchini, ends removed, peeled in
    1/2-inch lengthwise strips and cut into
    1/2-inch slices
5   ounces frozen shoestring potatoes
2   tablespoons chopped fresh basil or 1
    teaspoon dried
pinch of red pepper flakes
salt and pepper

1 Heat bacon fat or oil in large saucepan with cover and sauté onion 3 to 4 minutes; do not brown. Add garlic and cook 1 minute. Add tomatoes and simmer 5 minutes.

2 Add zucchini, potatoes, basil, red pepper flakes, salt and pepper. Stir and bring to boil, then lower heat, cover and simmer about 30 minutes or until zucchini are tender but not overcooked.

MICROWAVE: (1) Heat fat in 3-quart dish on HIGH (100%) for 30 seconds. Add onion and cook on HIGH 2 minutes. (2) Add remaining ingredients, stir well, cover with plastic and cook on HIGH 14 minutes. Let stand 2 minutes before serving.

BRUSCHETTA

■ *Serves 4* ■

A marvelous first course or side dish but be sure the tomatoes are really ripe; it just doesn't work with starchy, pink, tasteless tomatoes.

6   large red-ripe tomatoes, peeled, seeded and
    coarsely chopped
8   garlic cloves, peeled, 6 of which should be
    bruised (lightly pounded by bottom of fist
    to slightly open clove)
2   tablespoons finely chopped fresh basil plus
    4 whole leaves
salt and pepper
1/2   cup extra virgin olive oil
4   thick slices sourdough or wholewheat
    Italian bread

1 Put tomatoes in bowl with 6 bruised garlic cloves, basil, salt and pepper. Pour olive oil over all and marinate at least 1 hour.

2 Grill or broil bread slices. While hot, rub on all sides with remaining 2 garlic cloves. Place bread on 4 plates and spoon generous amounts of tomatoes on top, omitting garlic but being sure to add some oil. Garnish each with basil leaf and serve right away.

ZUCCHINI AND CAULIFLOWER SALAD WITH RED ONIONS AND BLACK OLIVES

■ *Serves 4 to 6* ■

So easy to pull together by steaming or microwaving the key vegetables. This can be a meal in itself, especially if served with a good cheese on the side. It also makes a terrific vegetable side dish, or double the recipe and serve on large platter for buffet parties.

1/2   *cauliflower, cut into florets*
2   *small zucchini, thinly sliced*
1/2   *red onion, thinly sliced*
1/2   *cup sliced pitted black olives*
1/3   *cup olive oil*
3   *tablespoons balsamic or red wine vinegar*
3   *tablespoons finely chopped fresh basil or 1 teaspoon dried*
salt and pepper

1 Steam cauliflower and zucchini separately until crisp-tender. Rinse each under cool water to stop cooking. Drain and pat dry. Transfer to bowl and add onion and olives.

2 Combine oil, vinegar, basil, salt and pepper in another bowl and pour over vegetables. Toss well and serve.

MICROWAVE: (1) Place cauliflower in dish with 1/2 cup water, cover and cook on HIGH (100%) 8 minutes. Drain, rinse under cool water and pat dry. Place in large mixing bowl. Cook zucchini in 1/4 cup water, covered, on HIGH 4 minutes. Drain, rinse under cool water and dry. (2) Proceed as above.

SWEET CORN AND STEWED TOMATOES

■ *Serves 4 to 6* ■

As with combining cans of soups, combining canned or frozen vegetables can make a delightful difference.

1   *can (16 ounces) stewed tomatoes*
1   *can (16 ounces) corn, drained*
2   *tablespoons sugar*

Place tomatoes and juice in saucepan. Add drained corn and sugar and bring to boil. Lower heat and simmer about 10 minutes; some of the liquid will cook away. Serve hot; no salt or pepper is needed.

11

FRUIT—FRESH, FROZEN AND CANNED

If I had to choose one family of food to live with for the rest of my life, I would have to seriously consider fruit. The variety is infinite—there are so many fruits and so many ways to prepare them. Moreover, I can't think of more beautiful things to look at. What can compare with the shape of a pear, the beauty of a well-formed, properly ripened strawberry; a bunch of grapes looking like a chandelier dripping with glistening crystals; a cut melon, with succulent flesh of the palest green and softest cantaloupe coloring. Think of the deep, sensual purple streaks in a ready-to-bite fresh fig. The shape, color and texture of sun-ripened mango or a shiny Delicious apple. Is there anything more regal than a pineapple? Who could improve on the design of a full bunch of bananas? How much we take for granted. All there, in the fresh fruit sections of our supermarkets.

Use fresh fruit whenever you can, but we all know that this is not always possible. I make use of the salad bars—they're called salad bars, but they might as well be called fruit bars. I see watermelon, cantaloupe, honeydew, strawberries, blueberries, kiwi slices and others, cut fresh, perched on ice, along with other "salad" ingredients. Some frozen fruit is better than others; a lot has to do with its state of ripeness at the time of picking and freezing. Although I don't make it a daily habit, I have had success with many cans and bottles of fruit. I especially like canned mandarin oranges, canned pear halves, bottled whole figs and peach halves. Look for mirabelles in jars—they're there. The fruit world is filled with opportunities for good eating.

EXPRESS CHECK-OUT

1 Use tart **apples** for cooking—on the East Coast use Greenings or Granny Smiths. Elsewhere, shop for Pippins in the spring and Gravensteins in the fall.

2 **Apricots** may not always be as ripe as they should be. If this is the case, use dried apricots—reconstitute them by soaking in water. Or use canned apricots.

3 For **orange** juice, use Spanish or Valencia type; for eating or slicing, use Temples; for slicing or sectioning and for general cooking, use navel oranges.

4 Most **pears** (Bartlett, Williams, Seckel, Anjou, Bosc, Comice, etc.) are good for poaching and baking. If baking, don't peel them—just cut in halves, core and bake them with brown sugar and a couple of cloves in a 325°F (170°C) oven for about 1 hour. Most pears in the supermarkets are underripe and hard. Buy them only when they are soft and ripe to the touch, or let them ripen at home.

5 Use an apple corer to core pears. Be sure to dip the cut fresh pear in lemon juice (or water mixed with lemon juice) to prevent discoloration.

6 **Pineapples** are available in supermarkets all year long because they come from Hawaii, Honduras, Costa Rica, the Dominican Republic and Mexico. Test for ripeness by pulling out a center frond; if it comes out easily, the fruit is ripe. Lift the fruit and judge if it's heavy with juice, and press the bottom for softness—also signs of ripeness.

7 To chop **raisins,** freeze them first. Oil the processor bowl and blade and chop.

8 Use chopped **dried apricots** or **prunes** in place of raisins.

9 Put granulated sugar in bottom of dish and put out-of-season **strawberries** on top. Cover and leave overnight, and berries will taste better.

10 To make **banana** snack food: slice ripe bananas, arrange on cookie sheet and freeze solid. When frozen, remove from tray and store in plastic bag in the freezer. Eat while still frozen.

APPLES AND APRICOTS WITH CHOCOLATE

■ *Serves 4* ■

4 *large Golden Delicious apples*
1/2 *cup (1 stick) butter*
3/4 *cup water*
1/2 *cup hot chocolate sauce, store-bought or homemade, or 8 ounces semisweet chocolate chips, melted*
1 *can (16 ounces) apricot halves*
2 *tablespoons butter*
1 *pint vanilla or butterscotch ice cream*
4 *fresh mint sprigs*

1 Preheat oven to 350°F (180°C). Cut 1/2-inch slice off top of each apple and core to within 1/2 inch of bottom. Place 1 tablespoon butter into hollows of each apple. Arrange in buttered 8-inch square baking dish and add a little water to bottom of dish. Bake uncovered 30 to 40 minutes.

2 Heat apricots in remaining 2 tablespoons butter in skillet.

3 To serve, place one cooked apple on each of 4 warm plates. Arrange apricot halves around apples. Top with ice cream and drizzle hot chocolate sauce over all. Garnish with mint sprig.

MICROWAVE: (1) Prepare apples as above except do not add water. Cook on HIGH (100%) 5 minutes. If not on carousel, rearrange apples once. Transfer to individual plates. (2) In same dish, cook apricots and butter on HIGH 2 minutes. Proceed as above.

SUPERMARKET SAVVY

COBBLERS

It's no surprise that Webster defines cobbler as a "deep dish fruit pie"—simply put, one of America's favorite foods, as the love affair with cobblers dates back to Revolutionary times. Over the years, bakers have learned ways to make them better. Here are some ideas:
1. For better browning, use non-shiny metal pans, casserole dishes and glass bakeware.
2. Check volume of baking container by filling pan with measured cups of water. Use inside dimensions to measure pan.
3. Handle the pastry gently to get a flakier, tenderer crust. Do not overwork the dough; just mix until dry ingredients are moistened.
4. Grease the pan before filling it; it'll be a lot easier to clean.
5. If frozen fruit is substituted for fresh, use one that's unsweetened. It is not necessary to thaw it. The blueberry cobbler presented here is versatile; other fruit can be substituted. If using frozen fruit, here's a conversion guide.

Fruit	Fresh	Frozen
Blueberries	2 cups	12 ounces
Peaches	7 cups (sliced)	3 pounds
Blackberries	6 cups	2 pounds

SUPERMARKET BLUEBERRY COBBLER

■ *Serves 6 to 8* ■

It's wonderful to see hundreds of fresh blueberries piled high in pint cartons, with a special price sign stuck in the middle of the pile. Can anyone walk past without adding one or more cartons to the basket?

1 *cup self-rising flour, see Note*
3/4 *cup sugar*
3/4 *cup milk*
1/2 *cup (1 stick) butter or margarine*
2 *cups fresh blueberries*
1/2 *cup water*
1/4 *cup dark brown sugar, well packed*

1 Mix flour, 1/4 cup sugar and milk in bowl.

2 Preheat oven to 350°F (180°C). Melt butter by cutting into thin pats, placing them in shallow 1 1/2-quart baking dish and setting it in oven.

3 Combine blueberries, remaining 1/2 cup sugar and water.

4 Pour batter over melted butter or margarine in baking pan. Sprinkle batter with brown sugar. Spoon berries over; do not stir. Bake 45 minutes.

Note: If using all purpose flour, sift with 1 1/2 teaspoons baking powder and 1/2 teaspoon salt.

MICROWAVE: (1) Assemble as above in microwave-safe dish. Cook on HIGH (100%) 9 minutes.

SWEET BLUEBERRIES WITH ORANGE LIQUEUR

■ *Serves 4 to 6* ■

This is a good topping for ice cream—or put several tablespoons of heavy cream in each glass and spoon these berries on top.

1 *pint fresh blueberries or 2 packages (10 ounces each) frozen*
1/3 *cup confectioner's sugar (use 2 1/2 tablespoons if using frozen berries)*
1/4 *cup orange liqueur*
juice of 1 lemon

Combine all ingredients in bowl and toss well. Serve in champagne glasses.

BLUEBERRY SAUCE

■ *Serves 6 to 8* ■

*T*his is delicious over plain cakes, puddings and ice cream.

4   cups fresh blueberries, rinsed and drained
1   cup sugar
2   tablespoons fresh lemon juice
2   teaspoons cornstarch
2   tablespoons water
2   tablespoons fruit liqueur—kirsch,
    framboise, etc.

1 Puree blueberries in food processor. Combine puree in saucepan with sugar and lemon juice and simmer 5 minutes.

2 Combine cornstarch and water and add to blueberry mixture. Cook until thickened, about 3 minutes, stirring constantly. Strain to remove skins, if you wish. Stir in liqueur and remove from heat. Serve hot or cold.

MICROWAVE: (1) Puree berries as in step 1 and place in dish with sugar and lemon juice. Cover and cook on HIGH (100%) 3 minutes. (2) Combine cornstarch and water and add to berry mixture. Cook on HIGH 1 1/2 minutes. Strain to remove skins, if you wish. Add liqueur, stir and serve hot or cold.

LIQUEURS

At one time, before supermarkets, liqueurs were drunk only for medicinal and digestive reasons. This has generally changed, for today they are sipped as cordials and used to flavor soups, meats, fowls, creams, and cakes. In the blueberry sauce on this page, kirsch or framboise is suggested, but actually orange, cherry, pear, or other fruit and nut liqueurs would work well.

SUPERFAST CHERRY COBBLER

■ *Serves 4 to 6* ■

*I*t's not necessary to add a dollop of whipped cream or some soft ice cream, but it's awfully good.

1   can (21 ounces) cherry pie filling
1   package (5 1/2 ounces) or 1 1/4 cups
    biscuit mix
1   tablespoon sugar
1/4   cup milk
6   tablespoons butter or margarine, melted
cinnamon

1 Preheat oven to 400°F (200°C). Grease 2-quart shallow baking dish and pour in pie filling.

2 Combine biscuit mix, sugar, milk and butter in bowl and stir just to form soft dough. Drop dough onto filling in 6 spoonfuls. Sprinkle with cinnamon. Cover with foil.

3 Bake 20 minutes. Remove foil and bake 15 minutes longer.

MICROWAVE: (1) Prepare as in steps 1 and 2 above, but do not cover with foil. Cook on HIGH (100%) 9 minutes.

SEMIFROZEN MELON BALLS WITH BRANDY AND MINT

■ *Serves 4* ■

1   melon (honeydew, cantaloupe or
     muskmelon)
1/2 cup brandy
4   fresh mint sprigs

1 Scoop out seeds from melon. With a melon baller, make as many balls as you can. Place in plastic bag and freeze.

2 Just before dinner, divide among champagne or other glasses. Drizzle 2 tablespoons brandy over each and add mint sprig. Serve for dessert; melon balls should be about half-frozen at serving time.

SUPERMARKET SAVVY

MELONS

To test for ripeness, smell the stem end—it should smell sweet and musky. But also lightly press at the point where the stem was attached—it should give a little. Ripe cantaloupes should not be green under their netting; honeydews should be white or cream-colored, with smooth skins. To ripen further, keep the honeydew at room temperature; do not refrigerate. Cantaloupes, on the other hand, should ripen in the refrigerator.

Melons are low in calories, high in vitamins A and C and rich in potassium. They also provide beta carotene, phosphorus and calcium. There is no need to salt any melon; each pound of flesh (the edible portion of a 2-pound cantaloupe) contains 54 mg of sodium.

MANGO PIE

■ *Serves 6 to 8* ■

2   packages (14 ounces each) frozen mango,
     thawed, or enough fresh mangoes to make
     2 cups puree
1   tablespoon fresh lime juice
1   cup sugar
1/4 cup sifted all purpose flour
1/4 cup evaporated milk
pinch each of salt and nutmeg
2   eggs separated
1   prepared 10-inch graham cracker crust
whipped cream for garnish

1 Preheat oven to 350°F (180°C). Heat mango puree and lime juice in saucepan. Add sugar, flour, milk, salt and nutmeg and cook 3 minutes. Remove from heat.

2 Beat egg yolks and fold in. Beat egg whites to soft peaks and fold into mango mixture. Spread in pie shell and bake 40 minutes or until filling is set. Let cool before serving.

FRUIT SALAD TROPICANA

■ *Serves 4* ■

Make this ahead and be sure to chill thoroughly before serving. Present it on lettuce leaves and garnish with a slice of fresh strawberry, a mint sprig or whatever is easy and colorful for you to add.

3/4   cup mayonnaise
1/4   cup sugar
1/4   cup fresh orange juice
salt and white pepper
paprika
 1   large banana, peeled and sliced
 1   cup fresh pineapple chunks
 2   medium mangoes, peeled, seeded and
     cubed
 1   medium avocado, peeled, seeded and cubed
 1   large apple, cored and cubed
1/2   cup pecan halves
1/2   cup grated coconut

1 Combine mayonnaise, sugar, orange juice and seasonings in bowl and set aside.

2 Combine remaining ingredients in larger bowl. Add sauce and toss to coat. Cover with plastic wrap and chill thoroughly.

MANGO SEASON IN JAMAICA

June to August is mango season in Jamaica, a time that everyone looks forward to. Most of the mango groves are found in the parishes of St. Elizabeth, Portland and Clarendon. The ripe fruit's golden yellow color makes the groves very pleasing to the eye. The most prestigious mangoes are the East Indians, Robbins and Julians. Other varieties include common mangoes, Green Skin, No. 11, Bombay and so on. (Common mangoes are so named because they are found in most parishes and are the cheapest of all.) A mature one should weigh about 1 1/2 to 2 pounds.

People drive their cars, vans and trucks, and some even go on donkeys to the large mango groves. Here one can eat to his heart's content and pay a few dollars for a load of mangoes to take home. The fruit can be made into chutney, nectar, jams and jellies, compotes and pies. Mangoes are also packaged and frozen in small-block form.

Miriam Barnes, Educator, Jamaica, BWI

HONEYDEW MELON SORBET

■ Serves 6 to 8 ■

2 quarts ripe melon cubes, seeds and skin
    removed
2 cups chablis
2 cups water
1 1/4 cups sugar
3 egg whites
sliced strawberries, mint sprigs or whole
    blueberries for garnish

1 Puree melon in food processor. Add wine, water and sugar. Taste and add more sugar if needed.

2 Add egg whites and process for 60 seconds. Transfer to 2 × 8 × 12-inch pan and freeze. Spoon out with ice cream scoop and decorate with strawberries, mint sprigs or blueberries.

MANDARIN ORANGE FRUIT SALAD

■ Serves 4 ■

Mandarin orange slices in cans are surprisingly good. They are real timesavers: nothing more than draining them is usually necessary. With other fruits, coconut flakes and yogurt, they make this appetizing salad.

1 can (11 ounces) mandarin orange
    segments, drained
1 cup sliced ripe banana
1 cup sliced fresh strawberries
1 cup canned or fresh pineapple chunks
1 cup seedless white or red grapes
1/2 cup flaked coconut
1 cup yogurt or sour cream
2 tablespoons finely chopped fresh mint or 1
    teaspoon dried

Combine all ingredients except 4 strawberries and 4 orange segments. Toss well and divide among 4 plates. Accent top of fruit with a strawberry slice and an orange segment.

FRESH ORANGE, WALNUT AND RADICCHIO SALAD CUPS

■ *Serves 4* ■

This is a colorful, tasty salad. Don't substitute for the radicchio. It's now available in most major supermarkets; if you really can't find this lovely purple-streaked-with-white lettuce, use curly endive hearts.

4 oranges, peeled and sliced, seeds removed
2 heads radicchio, one very thinly shredded
  and the other with leaves separated,
  washed and dried
1/2 cup coarsely chopped walnuts
2 scallions, thinly sliced
1/4 cup olive oil
3 tablespoons fresh lemon juice
salt and pepper

1 Combine oranges and shredded radicchio in large bowl. Add walnuts and scallions.

2 Mix oil, lemon juice, salt and pepper in small bowl. Add to salad and toss well.

3 Arrange radicchio leaves in cup shapes on 4 salad plates. Divide salad into cups and serve.

SWEET AND SPICY PEACH COBBLER

■ *Serves 4 to 6* ■

Canned pie fillings can be useful in certain preparations. Here they make a very good cobbler with a minimum of time and effort.

1 can (21 ounces) peach pie filling
1/2 cup chopped walnuts
1 1/4 cups biscuit mix
2 tablespoons brown sugar
1/4 cup milk
4 tablespoons butter or margarine, melted
1 teaspoon almond extract
1 tablespoon sugar
1 teaspoon nutmeg

1 Preheat oven to 400°F (200°C). Grease 1- to 2-quart shallow baking dish and spread pie pilling in it. Sprinkle with walnuts.

2 Combine biscuit mix, brown sugar, milk, butter and almond extract in bowl and mix well. Drop onto pie filling in 6 large spoonfuls.

3 Combine sugar and nutmeg and sprinkle over dough. Bake 20 minutes.

MICROWAVE: (1) Assemble as above, using microwave-safe dish. Cook on HIGH (100%) 9 minutes or until biscuits are almost dry. If not on carousel, turn 2 or 3 times. Let stand 2 minutes before serving.

PUREE OF PEACH AND PLUM WITH WHIPPED CREAM

■ *Serves 4 to 6* ■

This is a dessert served in a soup bowl, easy to prepare and a conversation piece.

>   2   packages (10 ounces each) frozen peaches
>   1   pound ripe fresh plums (any kind), peeled
>   and cut up, or 2 cups canned plums
>   without pits, drained
>   1   cup water
>   1   cup plus 2 tablespoons white wine
>   3-inch cinnamon stick
>   juice of 1/2 lemon
>   1   tablespoon cornstarch
>   1/2 cup sugar, or less as needed
>   1   cup heavy cream
>   1/4 cup peach brandy or liqueur

1 Combine peaches, plums, water, 1 cup wine, cinnamon stick and lemon juice in saucepan with cover and bring to boil. Lower heat, cover and simmer 15 minutes. Remove from heat and discard cinnamon stick. Puree fruit in processor. Return fruit to saucepan.

2 Blend cornstarch with remaining 2 tablespoons wine and add to puree. Test puree for sweetness; if needed, add up to 1/2 cup sugar. Bring to boil, stirring constantly with wooden spoon or wire whisk until puree thickens. Remove from heat.

3 Add 1/2 cup cream and brandy. Cover and refrigerate until very cold. When ready to serve, ladle puree into soup bowls. Beat remaining cream and add a spoonful on top.

MICROWAVE: (1) Combine peaches, plums, water, 1 cup wine, cinnamon stick and lemon juice in microwave-safe dish. Cover with plastic and cook on HIGH (100%) 9 minutes. Remove from oven, discard cinnamon stick and puree fruit. (2) Return puree to dish. Mix cornstarch with remaining wine and add to puree. Taste for sweetness and, if needed, add up to 1/2 cup sugar. Cover with plastic and cook on HIGH 2 minutes or until mixture thickens. (3) Remove from oven and complete step 3 above.

PEACHES WITH RUM SAUCE AND NUTMEG

■ *Serves 6* ■

*T*his is a never-fail dessert. One added touch is to cut a flattened prepared pie crust into 6 or 8 wedges and bake them until crisp. Add a wedge to a plate; top with peaches, sauce and whipped cream.

1/2   cup dark rum
1/2   cup dark brown sugar, well packed
* 1   package (20 ounces) frozen sliced peaches, thawed*
juice of 1 lemon
1/2   cup heavy cream, whipped
nutmeg

1 Combine rum and sugar in small sauce pan and bring to boil. Lower heat and simmer 3 minutes or until sugar is dissolved.

2 Place peach slices in bowl and top with lemon juice. Pour rum sauce over and toss well. Serve on individual plates (with wedge of pie crust if you wish) or in wine or champagne glasses. Top with a dollop of whipped cream and a sprinkle of nutmeg.

PEACHES AND PINE NUTS AFLAME

■ *Serves 6* ■

* 6   ripe fresh peaches or 2 packages (10 ounces each) frozen, thawed*
juice of 1 lemon
1/2   cup raspberry or strawberry jelly
1/2   cup pine nuts, browned in 1 small pat butter
1/3   cup brandy, rum, cognac or bourbon

1 If using fresh peaches, blanch for 30 seconds, plunge into cold water and remove skin and pit. Slice and place in shallow ovenproof dish. Toss with lemon juice. If frozen, drain and place in ovenproof dish with lemon juice.

2 Preheat oven to 350°F (180°C). Melt jelly in saucepan and brush or pour over peaches. Sprinkle with toasted pine nuts. Bake 15 minutes.

3 Heat brandy just to boiling point. Pour over warm peaches and immediately light with match. Serve as soon as flames subside.

MICROWAVE: (1) Prepare as in steps 1 and 2, using microwave-safe dish. Cover with plastic wrap and cook on HIGH (100%) 4 minutes. If not on carousel, turn once. (2) Remove plastic and proceed with step 3.

POACHED WHOLE PEARS IN PEAR BRANDY

■ *Serves 4* ■

Poached whole pears look and taste beautiful and always seem to say that you went to considerable trouble to prepare dinner, although they're quite easy to make. Serve with plain cake, cookies or whipped cream, or just as they are.

2   *cups water*
1   *cup sugar*
1/2   *cup pear brandy*
1   *tablespoon finely chopped preserved ginger*
4   *whole pears, peeled*
nutmeg

1 Combine water, sugar, brandy and ginger in saucepan that will just hold pears and liquid. Bring to boil, then lower heat and simmer until sugar has dissolved. Place pears carefully in saucepan and return to boil. Lower heat and simmer 20 to 30 minutes or until pears are tender. Remove from heat and let pears cool in liquid.

2 When ready to serve, spoon some sauce onto each of 4 dessert plates. Sprinkle with nutmeg. Carefully place a whole pear, stem up, on each plate.

MICROWAVE: (1) Cook water, sugar, brandy and ginger in a dish that will just hold pears on HIGH (100%) for 1 minute. Add pears, cover with plastic and cook on HIGH 15 minutes. (2) Proceed as above.

PEAR BALLS WITH MINT IN CHARDONNAY

■ *Serves 4 to 6* ■

1/2   *cup Chardonnay*
3/4   *cup sugar*
1/4   *cup fresh mint leaves or 1 teaspoon dried*
6   *fresh pears*
juice of 1 lemon
whipped cream or softened vanilla ice cream
fresh mint leaves or nutmeg for garnish

1 Combine wine, sugar and mint in saucepan and bring to boil over high heat. Lower heat, cover and simmer 20

minutes. Remove fresh mint with slotted spoon; if using dried mint, strain syrup through 2 layers of cheesecloth. Return sauce to cleaned pan.

2 Meanwhile, peel pears and cut flesh into balls with melon baller, making as many as you can. Add lemon juice and toss.

3 Simmer half of pear balls in syrup just until tender; do not overcook. Transfer fruit to clean bowl and repeat with remaining pear balls. Pour all syrup over pears and refrigerate at least 3 hours or overnight.

4 To serve, place a dollop of whipped cream or vanilla ice cream on each plate and add some pears alongside. If fresh mint is available, add one mint leaf to the arrangement; otherwise add a light sprinkling of nutmeg.

MICROWAVE: (1) Cook wine, sugar and mint on HIGH (100%) 6 minutes. Remove fresh mint with slotted spoon or dried mint by straining as above. (2) Make pear balls, toss in lemon juice and cook on stovetop. Proceed as above. Refrigerate 3 hours or overnight and serve as above.

PEAR HALVES STUFFED WITH WALNUTS

■ *Serves 4* ■

Ripe, fresh pears work best here, but canned pear halves give good results and take half the cooking time.

1/4　cup chopped walnuts
1/4　cup golden raisins
juice of 1/2 lemon
　3　tablespoons brown sugar
　4　fresh pears or 8 canned pear halves
1/2　cup light corn syrup

1 Combine walnuts, raisins, lemon juice and sugar in small bowl.

2 Preheat oven to 350°F (180°C). If using fresh pears, cut in half; peel if you wish. Hollow out centers of pears and fill with walnut stuffing. Arrange in shallow baking pan just large enough to hold them. Pour syrup over pears. Bake about 30 minutes if using fresh pears, about 15 minutes for canned.

MICROWAVE: (1) Perform steps 1 and 2 above but cook on HIGH (100%) 12 minutes for fresh pears, 5 for canned.

SUPERMARKET SAVVY

COOKING DRIED FRUITS IN MICROWAVE

To 1 cup dried fruit add water as below and cook on HIGH (100%). Stir and let stand 2 minutes.

Fruit	Water	Microwave Time
Apple chunks	1 cup	4 minutes
Apricots	1 cup	2 minutes
Figs	1/2 cup	2 minutes
Mixed fruit	1 cup	3 minutes
Peaches	1 cup	4 minutes
Prunes	1/2 cup	3 minutes

SUPERMARKET PEAR CRISP

■ *Serves 6* ■

*T*his can work with canned peaches also. It's good and easy.

  2 cans (16 ounces each) pear halves,
     drained
juice of 1 small lemon
1/4 *cup honey*
  1 *teaspoon nutmeg*
  2 *tablespoons butter or margarine*
  2 *tablespoons sugar*
  2 *tablespoons all purpose flour*
1 1/2 *cups wholewheat and/or bran cereal*

1 Preheat oven to 375°F (190°C). Combine pears, lemon juice, honey and nutmeg in bowl. Transfer to shallow round glass baking dish (about 1 1/2 quarts) or 8-inch pie dish.

2 Cream butter with sugar and flour until light and fluffy. Fold in cereal. Sprinkle over pears. Cover with foil and bake 15 minutes. Uncover and bake 15 minutes longer.

MICROWAVE: (1) Perform step 1 above. (2) Follow step 2 but cook in microwave on HIGH, uncovered, 12 minutes.

THREE-SPICE PUMPKIN PIE

■ *Serves 6 to 8* ■

*T*his pie requires no baking, although some stovetop cooking is required. It has a creamy texture and I think the spice is just right.

  1 *envelope unflavored gelatin*
1/2 *teaspoon each nutmeg, cinnamon, ginger*
     and salt
  1 *can (14 ounces) sweetened condensed*
     milk
  2 *eggs, beaten*
  1 *can (16 ounces) pumpkin*
  1 *ready-to-fill graham cracker pie crust*
whipped cream for garnish

1 Combine gelatin, spices, salt, milk and eggs in heavy saucepan and let stand for a couple of minutes.

2 Cook mixture, stirring frequently, until thickened, about 8 minutes. Remove from heat. Fold in pumpkin. Fill pie crust and refrigerate at least 8 hours or overnight. Add a dollop of whipped cream and a sprinkle of nutmeg to each serving.

MICROWAVE: (1) Combine gelatin, spices, salt, milk and eggs in microwave-safe bowl. Cook on MEDIUM (50%) 6 minutes or until thick. (2) Fold in pumpkin, mixing well. Fill pie crust. Refrigerate until set, 8 hours or overnight. Serve as above.

PUMPKIN CRÈME BRÛLÉE

■ *Serves 8* ■

Be sure to cover tightly with plastic wrap during refrigeration to preserve this dessert's soft, creamy texture.

3   cups heavy cream
1/2   cup sugar
6   egg yolks
2/3   cup canned pumpkin
pinch each of cinnamon, cloves and ginger
2   tablespoons dark rum
1/4   cup light brown sugar, well packed

1 Cook cream and sugar in top of double boiler, stirring constantly, until sugar dissolves.

2 Preheat oven to 325°F (170°C). Whip egg yolks until light and fluffy. Whisk in pumpkin, spices, cream mixture and rum until well blended. Transfer to 6-cup soufflé dish. Set in roasting pan; add several inches of hot water to pan. Bake about 1 1/2 hours or until knife inserted in center comes out clean.

3 Remove from water bath and cool on rack about 30 minutes. Cover with plastic and refrigerate at least 6 hours or overnight.

4 Preheat broiler for 15 minutes. Sprinkle brown sugar as evenly as possible over soufflé (pressing it through sieve is helpful here). Place dish on cookie sheet and broil 3 inches from heat source just until sugar is melted; do not burn. Serve right away.

RASPBERRY TRIFLE

■ *Serves 8* ■

This is a versatile recipe: for example, use angel food or pound cake, vanilla wafers or sponge cake in place of ladyfingers. Or substitute strawberries, apricots, peaches or plums for raspberries.

1/4   cup sugar
1   envelope (.25 ounce) unflavored gelatin
1/2   cup boiling water
2   cups pureed frozen raspberries
1/4   cup fresh lemon juice
6   cups ladyfingers cut into 1-inch pieces
1   cup heavy cream, whipped

1 Combine sugar and gelatin in large bowl. Add boiling water and stir until clear.

2 Stir in fruit and lemon juice. Refrigerate, stirring 2 or 3 times, until mixture mounds slightly when dropped from a spoon.

3 Fold in cake pieces and cream. Transfer to 8-cup glass serving bowl and refrigerate until set.

RHUBARB FRAMBOISE

■ *Makes about 1 quart* ■

*T*his is delicious by itself but can also be used as a sauce over plain cake or ice cream. Rhubarb is tart; you may want more sugar. If you prefer to use a sugar substitute, consider that 10 packets equal 6 tablespoons.

4 *cups frozen or fresh rhubarb*
1 *cup water*
6 *tablespoons sugar*
pinch of salt
2 *cups sliced fresh or frozen strawberries*
2 *tablespoons framboise liqueur*

1 Combine rhubarb, water, sugar (or sugar substitute) and salt in saucepan, cover and bring to boil. Lower heat and cook, stirring frequently, until rhubarb is soft, about 15 minutes.

2 Add strawberries and cook 5 minutes longer. Stir in liqueur. Serve warm or cold.

MICROWAVE: (1) Cook rhubarb, water, sugar and salt (if using substitute, do not add now) on HIGH (100%) 6 to 8 minutes or until rhubarb is tender. (2) Add strawberries and cook on HIGH 2 minutes. Stir in sugar substitute, if using, and liqueur. Serve warm or cold.

FRESH STRAWBERRY AND CHOCOLATE TART

■ *Serves 6 to 8* ■

*F*rozen, uncooked pie shells can be turned into tart shells by thawing until dough is pliable and then fitting them into tart pans of about the same size as the pie shell. Follow directions on package for baking. Here's the filling recipe.

1 *prepared frozen pie shell, thawed*
2/3 *cup semisweet chocolate chips*
2 *quarts fresh whole strawberries, stem ends sliced off*
1/2 *cup strawberry jam*
1 to 2 *tablespoons kirsch, optional*
1/2 *cup heavy cream, whipped*

1 Fit pie shell into tart pan and bake according to package directions. Cool. Melt chocolate over simmering water and spread over bottom of shell.

2 While chocolate is still warm, arrange whole strawberries upside down in tart shell side by side, filling tart completely.

3 Melt jam over low heat; if too thick, thin with 1 to 2 tablespoons water or kirsch. Brush berries with warm jam. Serve with a dollop of whipped cream.

MICROWAVE: (1) This tart is not baked, but chocolate can be melted at MEDIUM (50%) 2 minutes. Proceed as above.

STRAWBERRIES AND MINTED SOUR CREAM

■ Serves 6 ■

Most any variety of fruit may be used, but I particularly like strawberries and bananas with this sauce. Try fresh pineapple chunks, chunks or slices of ripe peaches, sliced nectarines, apricots and so on.

2   pints fresh strawberries, hulled, washed and drained
2   bananas, peeled and cut into 3/4-inch slices
3/4   cup honey
1/4   cup rum or orange juice
juice of 1 lemon
1   cup sour cream
3   tablespoons chopped fresh mint or 1 tablespoon dried

1 Place fruit in shallow dish.

2 Combine 1/2 cup honey, rum and lemon juice and pour over fruit. Toss well. Marinate about 2 hours.

3 Combine sour cream, 1/4 cup honey and mint and mix well. Chill.

4 To serve, put some fruit on plate with a little marinade. Add 1 to 2 tablespoons sour cream sauce at side.

LUSCIOUS STRAWBERRY PIE

■ Serves 6 to 8 ■

Strawberries are a favorite of mine. They're versatile and make a wonderful pie with homemade strawberry glaze spooned over the fresh fruit. Use a prepared crust from the supermarket, make your own, or consider the low-cholesterol pie crust on page 245.

3   pints fresh strawberries, hulled
1/2   cup sugar
3   tablespoons cornstarch
1/2   cup cool water
2   tablespoons kirsch, optional
1   baked 9-inch pie crust
softened vanilla ice cream or whipped cream, optional garnish

1 Choose 2 cups of the best berries; slice and set aside. Slice remaining berries and place in saucepan with sugar. Dissolve cornstarch in water and add to berries. Cook, stirring constantly, 5 minutes or until mixture bubbles and thickens. Remove from heat and stir in kirsch if you wish. Let cool.

2 Arrange reserved berry slices in bottom of prepared crust. Spoon berry glaze over fresh berries in shell and refrigerate pie at least 1 hour before serving. Serve with soft ice cream, with whipped cream or just as is.

MICROWAVE: (1) Cook glaze on HIGH (100%) 3 minutes or until thick and bubbling. Add kirsch if you wish. Proceed as above.

STRAWBERRY SHERBET IN AN ORANGE BOWL

■ *Serves 4* ■

This is what I call a "lovin' hand" dessert. It's a bit cute but the colors are gorgeous, it tastes delicious and it shows that you fussed over something.

4   *perfect navel oranges*
1 1/2   *pints strawberry sherbet, softened slightly*
1/4   *cup kirsch, optional*
orange juice, optional
4   *large fresh strawberries*

1 Wash and dry oranges. Cut a thin slice from bottom of each orange so it can stand upright. Cut about 1 inch from top of each. Use a curved grapefruit knife to scoop out inside of each orange.

2 Fill each hollow orange with sherbet, lacing it, as you go, with 1/2 to 1 teaspoon kirsch, if you wish. Mound sherbet in center. Freeze until 10 minutes before serving.

3 Puree reserved orange pulp in processor. Thin with orange juice if necessary. Place 3 tablespoons orange puree on each of 4 dessert plates. Place filled orange in center. Slice each strawberry 3 or 4 times but keep intact at stem end. Slightly fan out strawberry alongside filled orange and serve.

DRIED FRUIT COMPOTE WITH LEMON AND HONEY

■ *Serves 4 to 6* ■

Serve this as is or use it as a sauce over ice cream or plain cake. For extra-special flavor, add 1/4 cup light or dark rum along with the honey.

1   *package (11 ounces) or 2 cups dried mixed fruit*
2   *cups water*
1   *cinnamon stick*
3   *lemon slices*
2   *tablespoons fresh lemon juice*
1/3   *cup honey*
1/4   *cup light or dark rum, optional*

Combine all ingredients in saucepan except honey and rum. Bring to boil, lower heat and simmer 15 minutes. Add honey and rum and simmer 5 minutes longer. Cool. Remove cinnamon stick before serving.

MICROWAVE: (1) Combine all ingredients except honey and rum in dish. Cover with plastic and cook on HIGH (100%) 7 minutes. (2) Add honey and rum. Cover and cook on HIGH 3 minutes. Let stand 2 minutes before serving. Remove cinnamon stick.

APPLE TART WITH STREUSEL TOPPING

■ *Serves 8* ■

1   *package (6 ounces) dried apple chunks,*
    chopped
1   *cup apple juice*
1   *egg, beaten*
1   *cup sour cream*
1/2 *cup sugar*
2   *tablespoons all purpose flour*
1   *teaspoon grated orange zest*
1   *unbaked 9-inch pie shell*
streusel topping, see below

1 Combine apples and juice in saucepan and bring to boil. Lower heat and simmer until liquid is absorbed. Cool.

2 Preheat oven to 450°F (230°C). Combine egg, sour cream, sugar, flour and orange zest in bowl and mix well. Add apples. Transfer to pie shell and top with streusel. Bake 10 minutes. Lower oven heat to 350°F (180°C) and bake 30 minutes or until browned.

Streusel topping:
1/2 *cup all purpose flour*
1/3 *cup brown sugar, well packed*
1/2 *teaspoon cinnamon*
1/4 *cup butter or margarine, room*
    temperature
1/3 *cup chopped walnuts*

Combine all ingredients and blend well.

MICROWAVE: (1) Combine apple chunks and juice in dish and cook on HIGH (100%) 3 minutes or until liquid is absorbed. Add to remaining filling ingredients and transfer to pie. Add topping. (2) Cook tart on HIGH 12 minutes.

SUPERMARKET SAVVY

DRIED FRUIT

Apple chunks:
How to cook: Combine 1 cup apple chunks and 1 1/2 cups water and bring to boil. Cook uncovered over medium heat 15 to 20 minutes or until soft. Microwave: Combine 1 cup apple chunks with 1 cup water. Cover and cook on HIGH (100%) 4 minutes. Stir and let stand 2 minutes.

Mixed Fruit:
How to cook: Combine 1 cup dried fruit and 1 1/4 cups water and bring to boil. Cook uncovered over medium heat 15 to 20 minutes or until soft. Microwave: Combine 1 cup dried fruit with 1 cup water. Cover and cook on HIGH (100%) 2 minutes. Stir and let stand 2 minutes.

Dried prunes:
How to cook: Combine 1 cup prunes and 1 cup water and bring to boil. Cook covered over medium heat 7 to 10 minutes or until prunes are soft. Microwave: Combine 1 cup prunes with 1/2 cup water. Cover and cook on HIGH (100%) 3 minutes. Stir and let stand 2 minutes.

How to chop dried fruit: Coat chopping knife or scissors lightly with vegetable oil to prevent sticking. Repeat oiling as necessary. If prunes have pits, cook them first, remove pits and then chop.

RICH RICE PUDDING WITH DRIED FRUIT

■ *Serves 6* ■

3   eggs
2   cups half-and-half
1/2   cup sugar
1/2   teaspoon nutmeg
1/2   teaspoon vanilla
1 1/2   cups cooked white rice
1   cup chopped dried fruit

1 Preheat oven to 350°F (180°C). Beat eggs with half-and-half, sugar, nutmeg and vanilla. Fold in rice and fruit. Transfer to a buttered 1 1/2-quart baking dish. Set dish in a larger pan half-filled with hot water.

2 Bake 1 hour or until pudding is set. Serve warm or cold.

MICROWAVE: Beat eggs with half-and-half, sugar, nutmeg and vanilla. Fold in rice and fruit. Transfer to buttered microwave-safe 1 1/2-quart dish and cook on MEDIUM (50%) 20 minutes.

GOURMET PRUNE WHIP

■ *Serves 6* ■

I like eating pitted prunes right out of the can, but if I'm a little ambitious I'll eat them this way.

1   cup chopped, cooked and drained pitted prunes
1/2   cup brown sugar, well packed
3   egg whites, room temperature
pinch of salt
1   tablespoon fresh lemon juice
custard sauce, see below

Preheat over to 325°F (170°C). Combine prunes, sugar, egg whites and salt and beat until peaks form. Transfer to 1-quart shallow baking dish and place in water bath. Bake 40 minutes or until whip puffs and forms a crust. Cool and serve with sauce.

CUSTARD SAUCE

■ *Makes 1 1/2 cups* ■

1 1/4   cups milk
2   tablespoons sugar
1   teaspoon cornstarch
pinch of salt
3   egg yolks, room temperature, beaten
1/2   teaspoon vanilla

Combine milk, sugar, cornstarch and salt in saucepan and bring to boil, stirring constantly. Add to beaten eggs a little at a time, then return to low heat. Cook 1 minute longer, stirring; do not boil. Remove from heat, add vanilla and serve warm or cold.

CAKE MIXES, PIE SHELLS, COOKIES, CHOCOLATE AND OTHER DESSERTS

For me, the best desserts are the ones that don't take all day to prepare. Using many of the prepared foods in supermarkets (ready-made crusts and so on) does not mean sacrificing flavor, lightness or freshness. Nor does it mean serving a dull dessert, as you'll see in the following pages. Check the previous chapter, too, for many interesting fruit desserts.

There are so many ways to spruce up ordinary desserts. There's nothing wrong with a simple scoop of ice cream, but why not try serving it in different ways—for example, see Hot Buttered Rum Sauce over a Square of Ice Cream on page 251. Puddings are perfect candidates for new treatments, and a good pudding is never out of style; see the Chilled Vanilla Almond and Chocolate Ice Cream Puddings on pages 249 and 250.

Don't overlook ready-made desserts in jars. One of my favorites is babas, which come in 8- and 16-ounce jars. I suggest soaking them in rum and serving them with sautéed bananas.

EXPRESS CHECK-OUT

1 To make pie crust flakier and less greasy, add a teaspoon of vinegar to the water that is added to the dough.

2 Shake raisins and nuts in a tiny amount of flour to coat them before adding them to flour, muffin or cake doughs; this way they won't sink to the bottom.

3 Eliminate white spots on the sides and bottoms of chocolate cakes by dusting the baking pan with cocoa instead of flour.

4 Use a vegetable peeler to shave hard chocolate.

5 Use ice-cold cider in place of water when making crust for apple pie.

6 Use corn syrup instead of butter to brush over pie crusts and other pastry—Danish, for example—to glaze.

7 Don't waste cutouts from doughnut centers. Fill muffin cups with 3 centers, bake and sprinkle with powdered sugar.

8 Store brown sugar, before and after opening the package, in refrigerator to keep it moist.

9 Toast wheat germ and use it in place of ground nuts for cakes, ice cream toppings and other items.

10 If cake is crumbly and difficult to ice, try spreading with a very thin layer of very soft butter or margarine, then chilling cake in the freezer. Spread icing over hardened butter.

SUPERMARKET SAVVY

USE AND CARE OF NONSTICK PANS

As a rule, no conditioning of a nonstick pan is necessary except washing it before using. Wash in hot, soapy water with a cloth, sponge, plastic mesh pad or scrubber recommended for nonstick finishes; steel wool or abrasive cleaners will harm nonstick coatings. Rinse and then towel dry thoroughly. They are usually not recommended for dishwasher cleaning.

For best results, grease and flour the pan according to the recipe or package directions, especially when preparing baked goods like cupcakes, muffins, brownies, bar cookies, butter cakes and so on. Greasing these pans may not be necessary when preparing other foods—yeast breads, biscuits, pies, turnovers, meat loaves, roast chicken, lasagna and casseroles. Some of the manufacturers of these pans advise against using vegetable cooking sprays.

To lengthen the life of nonstick pans: (1) do not use metal tools or sharp knives for cutting in the pan; (2) do not use the pans as storage containers in freezer or refrigerator; (3) do not use them on top of the stove to make sauces or gravies; and (4) use them for baking only.

SUPER-MOIST BROWNIE FUDGE CAKE

■ *Serves 12* ■

*F*antastic richness. Serve with fresh raspberries and 2 tablespoons heavy cream spread on the plate. If you freeze this, first allow to cool and wrap in freezer foil. Thaw at least 1 hour at room temperature. This is one of the best recipes in this book.

1 *package (21 1/2 ounces) fudge brownie mix*
1/3 *cup canned ground sweet chocolate or rich cocoa powder*
2 *eggs*
1/2 *cup water*
1/4 *cup vegetable oil*
1 *cup coarsely chopped walnuts*

1 Butter 13 × 9-inch baking pan. Preheat oven to 350°F (180°C), or 325°F (170°C) if using glass pan. Combine brownie mix and ground chocolate and sift into large bowl.

2 Combine eggs, water and oil in another bowl and beat until well mixed. Add to brownie mixture and stir with wooden spoon about 50 strokes or until well combined. Fold in walnuts.

3 Transfer to prepared pan and bake 25 minutes; do not overcook. (Cake will be set but center will be slightly soft.) Let cool before cutting.

UPSIDE-DOWN COFFEE CAKE

■ *Serves 6 to 8* ■

Pineapple slices and only three other ingredients make this version of the traditional upside-down dessert much less work.

1 can (8 1/2 ounces) sliced pineapple, well drained, liquid reserved
8 maraschino cherries
1/2 cup dark brown sugar, well packed
1 tube (7.5 ounces) refrigerated buttermilk biscuits

1 Cut pineapple slices in half and arrange in buttered 8- or 9-inch cake pan. Set cherries into spaces between pineapple slices. Combine brown sugar with 2 tablespoons reserved fruit juice in saucepan and bring to boil, stirring constantly. Remove from heat.

2 Preheat oven to 375°F (190°C). Separate biscuits and arrange over pineapple. Pour brown sugar mixture over. Bake 17 to 25 minutes or until golden. Cool in pan 10 minutes, then invert onto plate. Serve warm or at room temperature.

SUPERMARKET SAVVY

CHOCOLATE

I sometimes think that living in the U.S. is like swimming in a pool of melted chocolate—it is with us everywhere and our appetite for it grows (as does the sale of it) in spite of diets and higher levels of health consciousness. As I said in the introduction to this book, we want to have our cake and eat it too. Some points about chocolate:

1. Melt chocolate in the top pan of a double boiler over simmering water. Stir all the time and don't ever let it boil. If it gets stiff, stir in 1 tablespoon vegetable shortening for each 6 ounces chocolate. Chocolate to be melted must be absolutely dry or it may get gummy. Once melted properly, any amount of liquid may be added.
   To melt chocolate in the microwave, cut or break into small pieces (1/2 to 1 ounce), place on microwave-safe plate and heat on HIGH (100%), tightly covered, 45 seconds for 1 ounce, 2 minutes for 4 ounces and 3 1/2 minutes for 8 ounces.

2. One ounce of unsweetened chocolate mixed with 1 tablespoon sugar equals 1 ounce semisweet chocolate. Three ounces of unsweetened plus 3 tablespoons sugar are the equivalent of 4 ounces semisweet.

3. It is best to allow most chocolate desserts to come to room temperature before serving. There is no question that chilled chocolate loses a lot of flavor. I let chocolate ice cream stand about 10 minutes or so at room temperature before serving; I think it's more flavorful that way.

BOONSTRA RUM CAKE

■ *Serves 12* ■

*J*ohanna Boonstra is a watercolor teacher who could also be a pastry instructor.

1 *package (18 1/2 ounces) golden or yellow cake mix*
1 *package (3 ounces) instant vanilla pudding and pie mix*
4 *eggs*
1/2 *cup water*
1/2 *cup vegetable oil*
1 *cup pecans*
Rum glaze
1/2 *cup (1 stick) butter or margarine*
1 *cup sugar*
1/4 *cup water*
1/2 *cup dark rum*

1 Preheat oven to 325°F (170°C). Combine cake and pudding mixes in large bowl. Blend eggs, water and oil in another bowl and add to mixes.

2 Grease 10-inch tube pan and arrange pecans on bottom. Pour in batter and bake 1 hour or until tester inserted in center comes out clean. Cool 10 minutes, then turn out on rack.

3 Melt butter in saucepan. Add sugar and water and bring to simmer. Cook 5 minutes or until slightly thickened and sugar is dissolved. Remove from heat and add rum.

4 Prick cake with wooden skewer. Spoon glaze carefully and slowly over cake. Let cool completely.

SHERRY VANILLA BUNDT CAKE

■ *Serves 8 to 12* ■

*T*his has a mellow flavor, just like cream sherry. Delicious served with coffee, or at a special breakfast or tea. It pairs beautifully with fruit served separately in a champagne glass or pretty glass bowl.

1 *package (1 pound 2 1/2 ounces) yellow cake mix*
1 *package (3 5/8 ounces) instant vanilla pudding mix*
1/2 *teaspoon allspice*
4 *large eggs*
3/4 *cup cream sherry*
3/4 *cup vegetable oil*
confectioner's sugar

1 Preheat oven to 350°F (180°C). Combine all ingredients in large bowl of electric mixer. Mix at low speed 1 minute, then 3 minutes at medium speed. If you want to mix by hand, beat about 5 minutes.

2 Transfer to greased and floured 10-inch Bundt pan. Bake 45 minutes or until springy to touch. Cool about 20 minutes, then turn out onto rack and cool completely. Sift confectioner's sugar over cake before serving.

SISTER MARY'S EASY CHOCOLATE ALMOND CAKE

■ *Serves 8 to 12* ■

Serve this in one-layer slices with scoop of ice cream or on several tablespoons of strawberry sauce (use pureed frozen strawberries flavored with a few drops of almond extract). Then put a tablespoon of cocoa powder in a small strainer and sift over the cake.

4	tablespoons unsalted butter, room temperature
1/4	cup peanut oil
2	cups sugar
1 1/2	teaspoons almond extract
2	eggs
1 3/4	cups all purpose flour
1	cup cocoa powder
1	teaspoon baking powder
1/2	teaspoon baking soda
1 3/4	cups milk

1 Preheat oven to 350°F (180°C). Combine butter, peanut oil, sugar and almond extract and beat or whisk until light and fluffy. Blend in eggs.

2 Combine flour, cocoa, baking powder and soda. Add to butter mixture alternately with milk.

3 Liberally grease two 9-inch round pans and dust with cocoa. Divide batter between them and bake 30 minutes or until tester inserted in center comes out clean. Cool on racks 10 minutes, then remove from pans. Serve as above.

PECAN FUDGE

■ *Makes sixteen 2-inch squares* ■

4	tablespoons plus 1 teaspoon unsalted butter
2/3	cup half-and-half
1/3	cup light corn syrup
2	cups sugar
2	ounces unsweetened chocolate
1	teaspoon vanilla
1/2	cup chopped pecans

1 Use 1 teaspoon butter to coat 8 x 8-inch pan. Set aside.

2 Blend half-and-half, corn syrup and sugar in saucepan. Add chocolate and stir over low heat until chocolate melts and sugar dissolves.

3 Bring mixture to boil. Add candy thermometer to pan and slowly let temperature reach 238°F (114°C); do not stir. Remove from heat and add 4 tablespoons butter. When temperature reaches 150°F (66°C), remove thermometer.

4 Add vanilla and beat 2 minutes with wooden spoon; mixture will lose some sheen.

5 Add pecans and beat another 10 strokes. Pour into buttered pan and quickly spread with rubber spatula. Cut into 16 squares with sharp knife and let cool.

CHOCOLATE COCOA TRUFFLES

■ *Makes 36* ■

You can make these for yourself, but they are also ideal Christmas presents. Put 36 into a doily-lined box, tie a pretty Christmas ribbon around it and you'll make someone happy.

1   *cup canned chocolate frosting*
1   *cup flaked coconut*
1   *package (6 ounces) dried fruit bits*
36   *walnut or pecan halves*
1   *cup cocoa*

Blend frosting, coconut and fruit bits in bowl. Chill until thick and workable. Form into 1-inch balls with walnut or pecan in center. Roll in cocoa powder. Refrigerate until ready to box or serve.

CHOCOLATE TRUFFLES À L'ORANGE

■ *Makes about 2 1/2 dozen* ■

Chocolate has a little iron and protein, and choline—which some say causes a short high. Though chocolate is not considered good food because of its high fat and caffeine content, who can say no to it? Pass these on one plate and orange slices with chopped fresh mint on another.

10   *ounces semisweet chocolate, coarsely chopped*
1/4   *cup heavy cream*
6   *tablespoons unsalted butter, room temperature*
1   *tablespoon orange liqueur*
1/4   *cup cocoa powder*

1 Melt chocolate in heatproof bowl over boiling water, stirring until smooth.

2 Add cream, butter and liqueur and mix well. Refrigerate until chilled but still malleable.

3 Sift cocoa onto waxed paper. Shape rounded teaspoon of chocolate mixture into a ball between palms of hands. Roll in cocoa and arrange on doily or plate. Store truffles between layers of waxed paper in container with tight-fitting lid.

MICROWAVE: (1) Melt chocolate in microwave-safe bowl on HIGH (100%) 2 minutes. Stir until smooth. Proceed as above.

HELEN SCHANBACK SCHWARTZ'S

PASSOVER CHEESECAKE

■ *Serves 6 to 8* ■

Helen is the home economist at Friendship Food Products and is the daughter of the company founder.

6   matzos
6   tablespoons butter
1   container (16 ounces) cottage cheese
3   eggs, beaten
1/2   cup sugar
1/4   teaspoon salt
juice of 1 lemon

1 Dip matzos in water and drain. Grease 8 × 8-inch baking dish with 4 tablespoons melted butter. Line bottom and sides of dish with matzos, trimming to fit as necessary.

2 Preheat oven to 350°F (180°C). Mix cheese, eggs, sugar, salt and lemon juice. Spread half of mixture over matzo "crust." Repeat with another layer of matzos, then with remaining cheese filling. Brush top with remaining 2 tablespoons melted butter.

3 Bake about 1 hour or until golden brown. Sprinkle with powdered sugar and cut into squares to serve.

NO-BAKE CHEESECAKE WITH STRAWBERRIES

■ *Serves 6 to 8* ■

Extremely easy to make. Be sure the cream cheese is soft and the whipped topping is thawed.

1   package (8 ounces) cream cheese, room
     temperature
1/3   cup sugar
1   cup sour cream
2   teaspoons vanilla
4   cups (8 ounces) frozen whipped topping,
     thawed
1   prepared graham cracker pie crust
1   package (10 ounces) frozen sliced
     strawberries, thawed

1 Beat cheese until smooth and light. Beat in sugar a tablespoon at a time. Fold in sour cream, vanilla and whipped topping.

2 Spread mixture in pie shell and refrigerate at least 4 hours. Serve with strawberries.

VANILLA CHEESECAKES WITH CHOCOLATE CRUMBS

■ *Serves 4* ■

Here's an elegant dessert you'll want to make often. Although chocolate crumbs are specified, you may prefer crumbs made from gingersnaps, lemon cookies or whatever else seems appropriate.

2 packages (3 ounces each) cream cheese, room temperature
1/4 cup sugar
3 tablespoons sour cream
1 egg
1/2 teaspoon vanilla
4 chocolate wafers, crushed to crumbs
whipped cream for garnish

1 Preheat oven to 350°F (180°C). Blend cream cheese and sugar in bowl of electric mixer. Add sour cream, egg and vanilla and beat until smooth.

2 Divide among 2 buttered 3/4-cup glass bowls and bake 30 minutes or until set. Cool, then chill.

3 Remove from refrigerator 10 minutes before serving. Unmold carefully on individual plates and sprinkle crumbs over cheesecakes. Add dollop of whipped cream to side of cake.

MICROWAVE: (1) Blend cream cheese and sugar in bowl of electric mixer. Add sour cream, egg and vanilla and whip until smooth. (2) Divide among 4 buttered 3/4-cup glass bowls and cook on LOW (20%) 10 minutes or until set. Cool, then chill. (3) Remove from refrigerator 10 minutes before serving. Unmold carefully on individual plates. Sprinkle each with chocolate crumbs. Add dollop of whipped cream to side of cake.

SUPERMARKET SAVVY

Ideas for Brownies

1. Top brownie with a scoop of frozen vanilla yogurt and cover with hot fudge sauce. Garnish with several raspberries.
2. Split brownies on individual dessert plates. Spread soft ice cream or frozen yogurt on bottom slice and cover with other half.

3. Cut regular-size brownies into two or three small pieces. Roll in confectioners' sugar and serve on individual plates, or stack on larger plate and pass.
4. Enrich packaged brownie mixes semisweet chocolate chips; add about 1 cup to the batter made by an 18-ounce package.

CHOCOLATE DATE BROWNIES

■ *Makes sixteen 2-inch squares* ■

*T*here is always temptation in the dried fruit section of the supermarket—temptation to open a box of dried apricots, prunes, raisins or dates to munch on while shopping the aisles. Save some dates for this easy, delicious brownie.

3/4   cup all purpose flour
  1   teaspoon baking powder
pinch of salt
  4   ounces unsweetened chocolate, coarsely
      chopped
1/3   cup vegetable oil
  2   eggs
  1   cup sugar
  1   cup chopped dates

1 Preheat oven to 350°F (180°C). Sift flour, baking powder and salt into bowl. Set aside.

2 Melt chocolate with oil in heatproof bowl over simmering water. Remove from heat and blend in eggs and sugar.

3 Combine flour and chocolate mixtures. Fold in dates. Spread batter in greased 8-inch square pan. Bake about 35 minutes or until done. (Cake will be set but center will be slightly soft.)

HAZELNUT AND DATE SQUARES

■ *Makes thirty-five 2-inch squares* ■

2 1/2   cups hazelnuts, toasted, skinned and
        chopped
    2   cups chopped pitted dates
    2   cups sifted all purpose flour
    2   teaspoons baking powder
  1/2   teaspoon ginger
  1/2   teaspoon allspice
pinch of salt, optional
    4   eggs
  1/2   cup (1 stick) unsalted butter or
        margarine, melted
    2   cups light brown sugar, well packed

1 Preheat oven to 300°F (150°C). Liberally grease and flour 15 × 11 × 1-inch jelly roll pan.

2 Place nuts and dates in large bowl. Sift in flour, baking powder, ginger, allspice and salt.

3 Beat eggs, butter and sugar in small bowl, add to nut mixture and mix well. Spread into prepared pan. Bake 40 minutes. Cool, then cut 4 times lengthwise and 6 times crosswise to make 35 squares.

LEMON SUGAR SCONES WITH APRICOT BUTTER

■ *Makes 12* ■

Scones:

1 3/4	cups all purpose flour
1/4	cup sugar
1	tablespoon baking powder
2	teaspoons grated lemon zest
1/2	cup (1 stick) plus 2 tablespoons butter or margarine
2	eggs, each lightly beaten in separate bowls
1/4	cup half-and-half
1/2	cup walnuts

Apricot butter:

1/2	cup (1 stick) butter or margarine
2	tablespoons apricot jam

1 Combine flour, sugar, baking powder and lemon zest in bowl. Cut in butter or margarine until mixture resembles bread-crumbs. Add 1 egg and half-and-half and mix until dough is reasonably dry, yet moist enough to roll out (if needed, add another tablespoon of half-and-half).

2 Preheat oven to 400°F (200°C). Turn dough out onto floured surface and knead a dozen times; do not overwork.

3 Roll dough into 9- or 10-inch circle and press in walnuts. Cut into 12 wedges. Transfer to baking sheet and brush with remaining egg. Bake until browned, about 10 minutes. Serve with apricot butter.

4 To make apricot butter, combine butter or margarine and jam in small saucepan and heat, stirring, until jam is melted. Transfer to small bowl and refrigerate to solidify. Serve with scones.

BUTTER COOKIES

■ *Makes 6 dozen* ■

Packages of pecans are easy to keep on hand in the freezer. Here's a classic cookie sparked with these sweet nuts.

1	cup (2 sticks) butter or margarine, room temperature
1	cup sugar
2	eggs
1	teaspoon vanilla
3	cups all purpose flour
72	pecan halves

1 Cream butter and sugar until light and fluffy. Blend in eggs and vanilla. Stir in flour. Cover and refrigerate at least 1 hour.

2 Preheat oven to 350°F (180°C). Roll out dough on lightly floured surface to 1/8-inch thickness. Using a 2 1/2-inch cookie cutter, cut out and arrange on ungreased cookie sheets. Press pecan half into center of each cookie. Bake 10 minutes or until golden. Transfer to racks to cool.

PRUNE MERINGUE KISSES

■ *Makes 36* ■

*U*se any plain cereal of the flake type, such as plain corn flakes. This makes a lot for the money and tastes good.

2   egg whites
1   cup sugar
1/2   teaspoon vanilla
pinch of salt
2   cups cereal flakes
1   cup flaked coconut
3/4   cup chopped pitted prunes

1 Preheat oven to 350°F (180°C). Whip egg whites until stiff but not dry, gradually adding sugar. Blend in vanilla and salt. Fold in cereal, coconut and prunes with rubber spatula.

2 Liberally butter baking sheets. Drop heaping teaspoons of meringue on prepared sheets and bake 12 minutes or until lightly browned. Cool on wire racks.

16 PEANUT BUTTER SQUARES

■ *Makes 16* ■

*T*he combination of peanut butter and shredded coconut is special here. Make ahead and have them handy to serve with fruit ices or ice cream on the back porch, or wrap and take them on picnics.

1/3   cup vegetable oil
1/2   cup smooth peanut butter
1   cup sugar
2   eggs
1   teaspoon vanilla
1   cup sifted self-rising flour (see Note)
1   cup shredded coconut
confectioner's sugar

1 Preheat oven to 350°F (180°C). Blend oil, peanut butter, sugar, eggs and vanilla. Stir in flour and coconut.

2 Grease 8-inch square pan and spread batter in it. Bake 30 minutes. Remove from oven and let rest 5 to 10 minutes, then cut into 16 squares. Roll each in confectioner's sugar.

NOTE: If using all purpose flour, add a sprinkle of salt and 1 teaspoon baking powder.

NO-CHOLESTEROL PIE CRUST

■ *Makes two 9- or 10-inch shells* ■

1 1/2 cups all purpose flour
1 teaspoon baking powder
1/4 teaspoon salt
1/2 cup (1 stick) corn oil margarine, frozen
3 to 4 tablespoons ice-cold water

1 Sift flour, baking powder and salt into processor or electric mixer bowl. Quickly cut margarine into 16 pieces and process with dry ingredients to cornmeal consistency. With machine running, add water a little at a time until dough is formed. Remove, wrap in plastic and refrigerate 1 hour or overnight.

2 Preheat oven to 400°F (200°C). Cut dough in half and roll out to diameter 1 inch larger than pie plate. Fit into plate and cover with waxed paper. Fill with rice or dried beans and bake 5 minutes. Cool slightly and remove rice and paper. Reduce oven heat to 300°F (150°C) and bake another 5 minutes; do not brown.

MICROWAVE: (1) Fit pastry into pie dish but do not stretch or it will shrink. Prick bottom and sides of crust with fork. Do not fill with rice or beans. Cook on HIGH (100%) until crust appears dry and opaque through bottom of plate, about 6 minutes. If not on carousel, turn once.

SUPERMARKET SAVVY

 ■

FROZEN PIE CRUSTS

Since they are usually brittle, enough thawing time must be allowed to prevent cracking, especially when separating one frozen crust from another—defrosting can take about 15 minutes. Even with this precaution, cracks will appear but they are easy to fix: simply moisten edges of split and press them together. If a top pie crust is to be used, first flatten the thawed edge of the bottom crust and moisten it with water. Arrange top crust over pie filling and fold flat bottom edge over top. Seal well and flute as you wish.

Baked pie shells to be filled later should be pricked before baking; pierce with the tines of a fork every 1/2 inch all over the crust. Set another pie plate into the crust and bake about 10 minutes. Then remove top pie plate and continue baking until crust is barely golden. Pricking prevents puffing, so if needed, prick again after removing top plate.

It is best to use a cookie sheet or tray under pie plate when baking fruit or custard pies.

GINGER COOKIE APPLE CRISP

■ *Serves 6* ■

*T*hese ingredients are almost always on hand, so if you need a simple dessert on a rainy day, here it is.

2 *cups gingersnap crumbs*
4 *tablespoons butter or margarine, melted*
1 *jar (16 ounces) applesauce*
1/3 *cup brown sugar, well packed*
1/2 *cup heavy cream, whipped, or 1 cup softened vanilla ice cream*

1 Preheat oven to 350°F (180°C). Combine crumbs and butter in bowl and toss well.

2 Press half of crumb mixture into well-greased 8-inch square baking dish.

Distribute applesauce over crumbs. Sprinkle remaining crumbs on top of applesauce.

3 Sprinkle brown sugar overall. Bake 30 minutes or until crisp bubbles and caramelizes; run under broiler for a few seconds to brown top if needed.

4 Serve warm or cool with whipped cream or soft ice cream.

MICROWAVE: (1) Prepare crisp as above and cook on HIGH (100%) 12 minutes. Run under broiler to brown top. Serve as above.

SISTER LOUISE'S OLD TIME RUM BUTTERSCOTCH PIE

■ *Serves 6 to 8* ■

*T*his pie will make a hit whenever it is served. To save time, use a frozen crust. You can use margarine instead of butter but the butter is so good with the rum.

1 *cup brown sugar, well packed*
1/3 *cup all purpose flour*
salt
3 *eggs, separated*
2 *cups milk*
1/4 *cup dark rum*
4 *tablespoons unsalted butter, room temperature*
6 *tablespoons granulated sugar*
1 *baked 9- or 10-inch pie shell*

1 Combine 1/4 cup brown sugar, flour and a pinch of salt in large saucepan and mix well. Add egg yolks, milk and rum

and mix well. Cook over low heat, stirring constantly, until thickened.

2 Add butter and stir over low heat until melted. Pour filling into baked shell.

3 Preheat oven to 350°F (180°C). Whip egg whites until frothy, adding granulated sugar a little at a time. Add a pinch of salt and whip until stiff. Swirl meringue onto top of pie with rubber spatula and seal to edges of crust. Bake 15 minutes. Cool before serving.

NO COOK CREAM LIME PIE

■ *Serves 8* ■

There is no question that this is an express check-out dessert. It is supermarket cooking at its best, provided you are willing to squeeze fresh limes.

1 can (14 ounces) sweetened condensed milk
1/2 cup lime juice (use fresh or if not possible, use concentrate)
1 cup heavy cream, whipped
1 graham cracker pie crust

1 Combine milk and lime juice in bowl and blend well. Gently fold in whipped cream. Transfer filling to pie crust.

2 Refrigerate until pie is set, about 3 hours.

LEMON CHOCOLATE CHIFFON PIE

■ *Serves 8* ■

Lemon and chocolate are a great combination—as this dessert testifies.

1 teaspoon unflavored gelatin
1/4 cup cool water
3 eggs, separated
1 cup sugar
juice of 2 lemons (about 1/2 cup)
1 tablespoon grated lemon zest
1 cup (2 ounces) frozen whipped topping, thawed
2 ounces semisweet chocolate, shaved
1 baked 9-inch pastry shell or unbaked graham cracker crust

1 Sprinkle gelatin over water and let stand until softened, about 5 minutes.

2 Combine egg yolks, 1/2 cup sugar and lemon juice in double boiler and cook over simmering water until mixture coats a spoon. Remove top pan from bottom, add lemon zest and gelatin and mix well. Let cool until slightly thickened.

3 Add half of chocolate shavings to pie shell.

4 Whip egg whites to soft peaks, gradually adding remaining sugar. Fold into lemon mixture, then fold in cream. Transfer to pie shell. Refrigerate at least 2 1/2 hours. Before serving, sprinkle remaining chocolate shavings over top of pie.

CHOCOLATE BOURBON MOUSSE PIE

■ *Serves 6 to 8* ■

*T*ry this to believe it. No eggs. One teaspoon of vanilla or almond extract may be used in place of the bourbon if you prefer not to use spirits.

1 1/2   *cups milk*
   1   *envelope (.25 ounce) unflavored gelatin*
   1   *package (6 ounces) semisweet chocolate chips*
   2   *tablespoons bourbon*
   2   *cups (4 ounces) frozen whipped topping, thawed*
   1   *graham cracker pie crust*

1 Pour milk into saucepan. Sprinkle gelatin over milk and let stand 5 minutes.

Stir over low heat until gelatin is completely dissolved, about 4 to 5 minutes.

2 Add chocolate and bourbon and cook, stirring constantly, until all chocolate is melted. Cool about 1 hour or until mixture mounds when dropped from spoon.

3 Gently fold in whipped topping. Transfer to pie crust and refrigerate until set, about 3 to 4 hours.

CHOCOLATE BROWNIE PIE

■ *Serves 6 to 8* ■

*T*his is a rich dessert but easy to prepare. It is here for chocoholics, or anyone who enjoys an occasional live-it-up dessert. To make it more sinful, serve with whipped cream or soft vanilla or chocolate ice cream.

1/2   *cup (1 stick) butter or margarine*
  2   *ounces unsweetened chocolate*
  1   *cup sugar*
  2   *eggs*
3/4   *cup self-rising flour*
  1   *teaspoon vanilla*
3/4   *cup chopped pecans*

1 Preheat oven to 325°F (170°C). Melt butter with chocolate in saucepan over low heat. Blend in sugar, then eggs, flour, vanilla and pecans. Transfer to greased 10-inch glass pie plate.

2 Bake 25 to 30 minutes. Cool at least 15 minutes before serving.

MICROWAVE: (1) Combine butter and chocolate in microwave-safe bowl. Melt at MEDIUM (50%) 2 to 3 minutes. Add remaining ingredients and transfer to greased 10-inch microwave-safe dish. (2) Cook at MEDIUM-HIGH (70%) 3 to 5 minutes. If not on carousel, rotate 1/4 turn every 2 minutes. (3) Finish cooking at HIGH (100%) 2 to 4 minutes or until center is almost done. Let stand 10 minutes, then cool 10 more minutes before serving.

WALNUT CARAMEL PIE CRUST

■ *Makes one 9-inch crust* ■

This crust is delicious filled with ice cream.

1   *stick pie crust mix*
2   *tablespoons brown sugar*
1/2 *cup finely chopped walnuts*
1   *egg yolk, lightly beaten*
1   *teaspoon vanilla*

Preheat oven to 375°F (190°C). Combine pie crust mix and sugar with fork. Add walnuts,

egg yolk and vanilla and mix well. Butter and flour 9-inch glass pie plate. Press dough into it. Bake 10 minutes or until lightly browned.

MICROWAVE: (1) Prepare pie crust as above and cook on HIGH (100%) 4 minutes. Let stand 2 minutes.

CHILLED VANILLA ALMOND PUDDING

■ *Serves 4* ■

Everyone loves a dessert that is made ahead, refrigerated and not to worry about until serving time. This is one of those, and it is a lot more sophisticated than just plain packaged vanilla pudding.

1   *package (3 1/4 ounces) vanilla pudding*
     mix
1 2/3 *cups milk*
1/3 *cup sour cream*
1/2 *teaspoon almond extract*
1/2 *cup sliced toasted almonds*
1/2 *cup heavy cream*

1 Combine pudding mix with milk in saucepan and stir over medium heat until mixture comes to boil. Simmer 1 minute, stirring. Remove from heat—it will thicken more as it cools. Cool 10 to 15 minutes.

2 Fold in sour cream, almond extract and all but 12 of almond slices. Pour mixture into 4 dessert glasses, cover each with plastic wrap and chill 2 hours.

3 When ready to serve, whip cream. Spread cream over entire surface of each glass with rubber spatula. Arrange 3 almond slices on top in form of a clover.

BUTTERSCOTCH CRÈME BRÛLÉE

■ *Serves 4* ■

*T*his is not a diet dish. You can substitute whole milk for the half-and-half if you wish. Consider this dessert after a light entree.

    1   package (3 1/2 ounces) butterscotch
        pudding mix
1 1/2   cups half-and-half
  1/4   cup dark rum
    4   tablespoons dark brown sugar

1 Combine pudding mix, half-and-half and rum in saucepan and stir over medium heat until mixture comes to boil. Simmer, stirring, 30 seconds; it will thicken as it cools.

2 Divide among 4 broilerproof ramekins and refrigerate 2 hours.

3 Before serving, preheat broiler. Sprinkle 1 tablespoon brown sugar evenly over entire surface of each ramekin. Broil about 3 inches from the heat source until sugar melts and a crust forms, about 1 to 2 minutes. Serve right away.

CHOCOLATE ICE CREAM PUDDING

■ *Serves 4 to 6* ■

*T*his can be served warm or cold. The recipe given is for warm; if you want it cold, cover the filled glasses with plastic and chill about 2 hours. Just before serving, spread ice cream over cooled mixture. Warm or cold, garnish by adding a couple of whole nuts or by sprinkling some additional ground chocolate or cocoa over the ice cream.

    1   package (3 5/8 ounces) chocolate pudding
        mix
  1/3   cup ground chocolate or cocoa powder
    2   cups milk
    1   teaspoon vanilla
    1   tablespoon light corn syrup
    1   pint chocolate ice cream (with or without
        nuts), softened

1 Combine pudding mix, ground chocolate, milk and vanilla in saucepan and bring to boil, stirring frequently. Simmer exactly 1 minute, then remove from heat.

2 Add corn syrup and cool a few minutes. Pour into 4 to 6 dessert or champagne glasses, ramekins or other appropriate dishes. Spoon soft ice cream into glasses and spread with rubber spatula to cover pudding mixture. Serve right away.

HOT APRICOT RUM SAUCE OVER A SQUARE OF ICE CREAM

■ *Serves 6* ■

*T*his is one of my favorite desserts. Brick ice cream in half-gallon containers is plentiful and a pleasant change from the scoop. If the blocks are cut into 1/2-inch slices, the ice cream softens more quickly than scoops do, and so is more flavorful.

1/2   cup dark rum
  2   tablespoons butter or margarine
  2   tablespoons apricot jam
juice of 1 lemon
  6   thick slices ice cream, about 3 1/2 × 3 1/2 × 1/2 inch
walnut halves

1 Heat rum and butter in small saucepan. Add jam and stir until completely dissolved. Simmer 4 to 5 minutes. Remove from heat and add lemon juice.

2 Place an ice cream square on each of 6 plates. Spoon some sauce over ice cream and dot with 1 or 2 walnut halves.

MICROWAVE: (1) Combine rum, butter and jam in bowl. Cover with plastic and cook on HIGH (100%) 3 minutes, stirring every minute. If not on carousel, turn and stir every minute. (2) Add lemon juice and serve as above.

CHERRY BLINTZES WITH MARMALADE/CURRANT SAUCE

■ *Serves 4 to 6* ■

1/4   cup orange or lemon marmalade
1/4   cup red currant jelly
  2   tablespoons water
  2   tablespoons cognac or orange liqueur
  1   can (17 ounces) pitted black cherries to make 1 cup drained
  2   packages frozen cherry blintzes, 5 to 6 per package

1 Combine marmalade, jelly and water in sauce pan and heat, stirring, until melted. Add cognac and cherries and heat through.

2 Heat blintzes according to package directions. Place 2 hot blintzes on each plate and spoon sauce over (about 4 tablespoons per plate). Serve right away.

MICROWAVE: (1) Combine marmalade, jelly and water in microwave-safe bowl. Stir, cover and cook on HIGH (100%) 30 seconds. Stir, cover and cook on HIGH 30 seconds. If not melted and combined, cook 30 seconds longer. (2) Add cognac and cherries, cover and cook on HIGH 1 minute. (3) Microwave blintzes per package directions. Place 2 on each plate, spoon sauce over and serve.

RUM BABAS WITH SAUTÉED BANANAS

■ *Serves 4* ■

Babas in a jar are rarely a disappointment. Sauté bananas in butter or margarine and serve with heated rum sauce and whipped cream. A very good dessert.

1   *jar (16 ounces) babas in rum sauce*
2   *tablespoons butter or margarine*
2   *bananas, halved crosswise*
2   *tablespoons dark rum*
3/4   *cup heavy cream, whipped*
sprinkle of nutmeg

1 Place babas and their sauce in saucepan and heat gently; do not cook.

2 Melt butter in skillet and sauté banana pieces on all sides for several minutes, being careful not to break them. Add rum and heat through. Remove from heat.

3 Place one banana piece on each of 4 warmed plates. Distribute babas and sauce among plates. Add dollop of whipped cream. Sprinkle with nutmeg and serve right away.

13

SAUCES

*T*he supermarket spares us long hours of from-scratch saucemaking, for its shelves are overflowing with every imaginable type of packaged and canned sauce. To assist in your purchases, it would be helpful to know some of the basic sauce groupings.

"Espagnole" or brown sauce is considered a "mother sauce," for other sauces are made from it—*poivrade, périgourdine, bordelaise* and *madeira*. Some plain brown sauces you buy may be used as a base for fancier ones.

White sauces made from a butter-and-flour mixture called roux, cooked just long enough to eliminate its raw flour taste. If the liquid used is white chicken, veal or fish stock, the sauce is known as *velouté*. If milk is used, it becomes a *bechamel*. If cream is added, it's *sauce suprème*.

Tomato sauces can be based on meat stocks or made without meat. These days, fresh, uncooked tomato sauces seem to be the rage, a most welcome trend.

Yolk and butter sauces, also known as emulsified sauces, include the ubiquitous mayonnaise, hollandaise, béarnaise and beurre blanc.

Dessert sauces comprise a vast variety among which are vanilla and chocolate sauces, cream sauces of all kinds and a vast array of fruit mixtures.

EXPRESS CHECK-OUT

■ ●

SAUCES

1 After adding flour to heated butter in making a sauce, allow it to cook for at least 2 minutes without browning to eliminate raw flour taste.

2 To thicken sauce after other ingredients have cooked, combine flour and water in a small jar with a lid, shake well and add to sauce.

3 What the French call *beurre manié* is simply a combination of flour and butter (a tablespoon of each, for example), worked together with a fork. When they are well combined, they are added to a sauce to thicken it.

4 When cooking delicate egg-based sauces in a double boiler, have water in bottom pan simmering or very hot—not boiling.

5 If mayonnaise or similar sauces separate, add a tablespoon of warm water or a dash of prepared mustard and whip again to smooth out sauce. If this doesn't work, you may have to start over.

6 Remember that a bit of lemon juice will make almost any sauce sparkle.

7 Sometimes a little half-and-half or a tablespoon or two of heavy cream will work in place of rich custards (especially those made with many yolks). For example, spoon some half-and-half on a plate before adding berries, or place berries on half the plate and cream on the other, and sprinkle some cocoa or nutmeg lightly over the cream.

8 It's not necessary to cook tomato sauces for hours. See index for lighter and quicker sauces.

9 When grilling, don't baste too soon with tomato- or sugar-based marinades; they will blacken before food is cooked. Baste liberally in the last 5 minutes or so of grill time.

SUPERMARKET SAVVY

CHIVES

What a joy! Low in calories but high in vitamin C, they add a special flavor to almost everything. Just about everyone I know has a pot of chives on a windowsill or in the garden. I freeze three or four containers of them each season. Rinse them in cool water first, shake out well (use a salad spinner) and put into several plastic bags or containers with lids. Keep one in the refrigerator for current use and freeze the others, either whole or chopped. Either way, they last for months.

Chives have many uses. Add them to butter or margarine as a dressing for fresh corn on the cob, or mince them and add to steamed or sautéed carrots. Throw some minced chives into the center of a cooked half squash. They are always good in yogurt dressings or mixed with butter, margarine, cream cheese and cottage cheese for use as spreads.

MICROWAVED CHIVE BUTTER

1/2   cup (1 stick) butter or margarine
6   tablespoons finely chopped fresh chives
6   tablespoons white wine

(1) Cut butter into small pieces and place in microwave-safe bowl. Melt on HIGH (100%) 45 to 60 seconds. Add chives and wine and stir well. Use hot over vegetables or let cool and use as a spread for breads, vegetables such as corn on the cob, etc.

FISH

DILL AND CHIVE BUTTER WITH WHITE WINE

■ *Serves 6* ■

Here's an easy sauce that's delicious with fish and excellent over carrots, squash and other vegetables.

1/2   cup (1 stick) butter or margarine
1/4   cup finely chopped fresh chives or 1 tablespoon dried
2   teaspoons finely chopped fresh dill or 1 scant teaspoon dried dillweed
1/3   cup white wine

Slice butter into 8 to 10 pieces and melt in small saucepan over low heat. Add remaining ingredients, bring to simmer and cook 2 to 3 minutes. Serve over broiled, grilled, baked or sautéed fish.

MICROWAVE: (1) Place butter in dish and cook on HIGH (100%) 1 minute. (2) Add remaining ingredients and cook on HIGH 1 minute longer. Spoon over cooked fish.

FISH

GREEN CHILI TOMATO SAUCE

■ *Makes 2 1/2 cups* ■

This is an excellent sauce for frozen, prepared fish, such as the fish sticks and fillets that come with a variety of coatings: breadcrumb, crisp potato, or egg batter.

2 tablespoons vegetable oil
2 tablespoons finely chopped onion
1 garlic clove, minced
1 can (16 ounces) whole tomatoes
1 can (4 ounces) chopped mild green chilies, drained
1 tablespoon finely chopped oregano or 1 teaspoon dried salt

Heat oil in 2-quart saucepan and sauté onion until soft. Add garlic and cook 1 minute. Snip tomatoes in can with scissors to cut them up and add to pan with remaining ingredients. Bring to boil, lower heat and simmer uncovered 10 minutes. Serve warm.

MICROWAVE: (1) Place oil in 2-quart dish and cook on HIGH (100%) 30 seconds. Add onion and garlic and cook 1 minute. (2) Add remaining ingredients (be sure to chop tomatoes), cover with plastic and cook on HIGH 5 minutes.

FISH

HORSERADISH CREAM SAUCE

■ *Makes 1 generous cup* ■

This goes especially well with cold fish, such as sliced lobster tail or crabmeat.

3/4 cup plain low-fat yogurt
1/4 cup low-calorie mayonnaise
3 tablespoons prepared horseradish
1 tablespoon prepared mustard
1 tablespoon soy sauce
1 1/2 teaspoons Worcestershire sauce
4 teaspoons sugar or 2 packets sugar substitute

Combine all ingredients and mix well. Refrigerate until needed.

FISH

SAUCE IMPERIALE

■ *Makes about 1 1/4 cups* ■

This is a basic sauce for shrimp cocktail and other seafood, but my family enjoys it as a dip for raw vegetables, too. We always add the hot pepper sauce.

1/2   cup mayonnaise
1/2   cup chili sauce
1/4   cup honey
  2   tablespoons fresh lemon juice
  1   tablespoon prepared horseradish
  2   teaspoons Worcestershire sauce
2 or 3 drops hot pepper sauce, optional

Combine all ingredients and mix well. Cover and refrigerate until needed.

FISH

SOUR CREAM AND MUSTARD SAUCE FOR PACKAGED FISH

■ *Makes 1 cup* ■

To brown fish sticks or fillets more evenly, turn them once while baking. Here's a good sauce for them.

  1   cup sour cream
1 1/2   tablespoons prepared mustard
2 or 3 drops hot pepper sauce
salt and pepper

Combine all ingredients and mix well. Refrigerate at least 1 hour.

FISH

SPICY COCKTAIL SAUCE FOR FROZEN FISH

■ *Makes 1 cup* ■

When cooking packaged fish, be sure to preheat oven to get desired crunchiness. Use this with fillets or fish sticks.

1   cup ketchup
2   tablespoons prepared horseradish
2   tablespoons finely chopped onion
1   tablespoon Worcestershire sauce
2 or 3 drops hot pepper sauce

juice of 1 lemon
salt

Combine all ingredients and mix well. Refrigerate at least 1 hour.

MEAT

CRANBERRY MAPLE SAUCE

■ *Serves 10* ■

Tart cranberries join with sweet maple syrup to give just the right touch to roasted, grilled or baked chicken, turkey and other fowl.

1 bag (12 ounces) fresh cranberries, picked over and washed
1 cup maple syrup
1 cup cranberry/raspberry juice
grated zest of 1 orange or lemon
1 cup walnut pieces

1 Combine all ingredients except walnuts in saucepan and bring to boil. Lower heat and simmer uncovered until berries pop, about 10 minutes. Skim off any foam on surface.

2 Add walnuts, remove from heat and let cool. Refrigerate until needed.

MICROWAVE: (1) Combine all ingredients except walnuts in dish, cover and microwave on HIGH (100%) 4 minutes. Add walnuts, cool and refrigerate.

MEAT

SPICED FIG CHUTNEY

■ *Makes 1 1/2 cups* ■

Most meats can take a condiment with character, and dried figs prepared as a chutney with a variety of spices are just that.

1 cup finely chopped dried figs
1 can (8 ounces) crushed pineapple with liquid
1/3 cup cider vinegar
1/4 cup brown sugar, well packed
1 garlic clove, minced
1/2 onion, minced
1 teaspoon finely chopped candied or fresh ginger
pinch each of cayenne pepper, cinnamon and cloves

Combine all ingredients in saucepan and bring to boil. Lower heat and simmer, uncovered, 30 minutes or until chutney thickens, stirring frequently. Let cool a little, cover and refrigerate overnight to allow flavor to develop.

MICROWAVE: (1) Combine all ingredients in dish and cook on HIGH (100%) 12 minutes or until thick, stirring several times. Refrigerate overnight before serving.

MEAT

ROASTED GARLIC MAYONNAISE

■ *Makes 2 cups* ■

An excellent way to add a new taste dimension to bottled mayonnaise. This is very tasty with grilled or baked chicken or pork, and in many salads. It may be used as a sandwich spread also. The garlic completely changes from sharp to sweet upon baking.

6   *large garlic cloves, unpeeled*
2   *cups mayonnaise*
juice of 1/2 lemon
pinch of cayenne pepper

1 Preheat oven to 500°F (260°C). Cut one end off each garlic clove. Wrap all cloves in single piece of foil and bake 30 minutes. Remove and let stand until cool enough to handle. Squeeze garlic pulp into small bowl. Mash well and add mayonnaise.

2 Add lemon juice and cayenne pepper and mix well. Store in refrigerator.

MICROWAVE: (1) Cut one end off each garlic clove and wrap in plastic. Cook on HIGH (100%) 12 minutes. Remove and let stand until cool enough to handle. Squeeze garlic pulp into small bowl and mash well. Proceed as above.

MEAT

MUSTARD SAUCE FOR HAM

■ *Makes 1 1/2 cups* ■

Cider may be used in place of apple juice.

1 1/2   *cups apple juice*
3   *tablespoons Dijon-style mustard*
2   *tablespoons brown sugar*
1 1/2   *tablespoons cornstarch*
1   *teaspoon finely chopped fresh tarragon*
or 1/2 teaspoon dried

Combine all ingredients in saucepan and cook over medium heat until sauce thickens. If too thick, thin with more apple juice. Serve warm.

MICROWAVE: (1) Combine all ingredients in 2-cup glass measure or bowl. Cover with plastic and cook on HIGH (100%) 3 minutes, stirring 2 or 3 times.

MEAT

GINGER/RAISIN SAUCE FOR HAM

■ *Makes 1 1/4 cups* ■

This is especially good with packaged ham slices and canned ham.

1   cup water
1   tablespoon cornstarch
3/4   cup raisins
1/4   cup brown sugar, well packed
1   teaspoon minced fresh ginger or finely
     chopped candied ginger, or 1/4 teaspoon
     ground ginger
1/2   teaspoon cinnamon
salt and pepper
1   tablespoon butter or margarine

Combine water and cornstarch in saucepan. Add all remaining ingredients except butter and bring to boil. Lower heat and stir until mixture thickens. Remove from heat and add butter. Serve warm.

MICROWAVE: Follow procedure above except cook in dish on HIGH (100%) 2 minutes. Add butter and stir well.

■   ■

GINGER

Ginger has been known in many civilizations. Its tuber resembles an iris root, with a paper-thin, light brown skin that can be peeled off with a parer. It freezes well, grates well, and slivers well. Probably its most popular use is in ginger cookies or gingerbread. Ginger is one of the most exciting flavors and its use is no longer limited to Oriental cooking. American supermarkets now sell it as a staple. It will keep in the refrigerator for a week or so, but it's easier to freeze it (it keeps frozen for months) and use it as you need it. Frozen, it grates easily.

MEAT

SPICY MUSTARD SAUCE

■ *Makes 1/2 cup* ■

A tasty dip for chicken nuggets, fish sticks and many other items found in frozen meat and fish sections of the supermarket.

1/2   cup light mayonnaise
1/4   cup prepared spicy brown mustard
1/2   teaspoon sugar
juice of 1/2 lemon

Combine all ingredients and whisk until well blended. Chill for at least 1 hour.

MEAT

PIMIENTO CHEESE SAUCE

■ *Makes about 1 cup* ■

Little jars of diced pimiento are found in most supermarkets. They're versatile—here they play an important role in a smooth and satiny cheese sauce, which is very good spooned over grilled burgers and many other meats, as well as vegetables.

1 cup shredded cheddar cheese
1 jar (4 ounces) diced pimiento
1/4 cup half-and-half or evaporated milk
1 teaspoon Worcestershire sauce

Combine all ingredients in saucepan and stir over low heat until cheese melts and sauce is smooth.

MICROWAVE: (1) Combine all ingredients in bowl and cook on MEDIUM (50%) 2 minutes. Stir; if not on carousel, turn bowl. (2) Cook on HIGH (100%) 30 seconds or until sauce is smooth and all cheese is melted.

MEAT

SALSA VERDE

■ *Makes about 1 cup* ■

Tomatillos are appearing in more and more markets. They're small green spheres with a slightly pointed end and a papery skin. They make a tasty Mexican-style sauce when combined with jalapeños, garlic and cilantro.

1 small jalapeño pepper, cored, seeded and coarsely chopped
4 garlic cloves, peeled
1/2 onion, coarsely chopped
6 tomatillos
leaves from several sprigs of fresh cilantro (about 2 tablespoons)
salt, optional

Combine jalapeño, garlic and onion in food processor and chop finely. Add tomatillos and cilantro and chop coarsely. Check seasoning; add a pinch of salt only if needed. Refrigerate until ready to use. Will keep about 1 week, refrigerated.

BARBECUE

HONEY/APPLE BARBECUE SAUCE

■ *Makes 1 cup* ■

A simple barbecue sauce but filled with flavor. It's especially good with ham and other pork products. Boil 2 lemons for 2 minutes and they will render considerably more juice.

1/2 cup applesauce
1/4 cup honey
1/4 cup fresh lemon juice
1/2 teaspoon cinnamon

pinch of cloves, ginger or nutmeg
pinch of salt

Combine all ingredients in bowl and mix well. Serve with roast pork, grilled pork chops or sautéed ham slices.

BARBECUE

ORANGE AND HONEY BARBECUE SAUCE

■ *Makes 3/4 cup* ■

Here orange juice, orange zest and honey ignite most store-bought barbecue sauces. This is good on hamburgers, ribs and chicken.

2/3 cup store-bought barbecue sauce (your favorite brand)
3 tablespoons honey
juice of 1/2 orange
1 tablespoon grated or minced orange zest

Combine all ingredients in bowl and use to baste grilled food; baste only during last 5 to 10 minutes of grilling time. If roasting meat in oven, coat meat with sauce from beginning. For grilled effect, broil baked meats for several minutes to brown.

BARBECUE

GOURMET PRUNE BASTE

■ *Makes 3/4 cup* ■

Don't overlook prune juice as a good ingredient for barbecuing. This is a versatile sauce and may be used with pork, chicken, beef and lamb. If not grilling, use as a baste with broiled meats.

1/2 cup prune juice
3 tablespoons ketchup
1 tablespoon soy sauce
1 tablespoon red wine vinegar

1 teaspoon prepared mustard
1 garlic clove, minced

Combine all ingredients in bowl and mix well. Use as baste or as marinade.

BARBECUE

TOMATO/SHERRY BARBECUE SAUCE

■ *Makes 2 cups* ■

*T*his is a good way to use cans or jars of spaghetti sauce, adding sherry, oil and garlic for a marinade with character. Use it when grilling or broiling burgers, steaks and spare ribs.

1   *tablespoon olive or vegetable oil*
1   *large garlic clove, minced*
1   *jar (15 1/2 ounces or 1 3/4 cups)*
      spaghetti sauce
1/2 *cup dry sherry*

Heat oil in saucepan and sauté garlic 1 minute. Add remaining ingredients and bring to boil. Lower heat and simmer uncovered 10 minutes, stirring occasionally.

MICROWAVE: (1) Place oil in 1- to 2-quart dish and heat on HIGH (100%) 45 seconds. Add garlic and cook on HIGH 30 seconds. (2) Add remaining ingredients, cover with plastic and cook on HIGH 5 minutes, stirring once or twice.

ALL PURPOSE

"FROM SCRATCH" HOLLANDAISE SAUCE

■ *Makes 1 cup plus* ■

*I*f you don't want to use store-bought hollandaise, here is a recipe that takes a little time—but you can say that it is from scratch.

1 *cup (2 sticks) butter, melted*
2 *egg yolks*
3 *tablespoons boiling water*
2 *tablespoons fresh lemon juice*
salt

1 Melt butter and keep it hot.

2 Place yolks in blender, add hot water and blend for 3 to 4 seconds. With machine running, add melted butter drop by

drop, then add lemon juice and salt. If too thick, thin with another spoonful of hot water.

MICROWAVE: (1) Blend yolks, water, lemon juice and salt in small bowl; set aside. (2) Cut butter into pats and place in another bowl. Heat on HIGH (100%) 45 seconds. (3) Blend yolk mixture into butter with whisk. Cook on MEDIUM (50%) until thickened, 1 to 2 minutes, whisking every 30 seconds.

ALL PURPOSE

APRICOT SHERRY SAUCE

■ *Makes 1 scant cup* ■

This is a succulent dip for fish sticks, fried chicken and other prepared frozen foods.

3/4 cup apricot jam
1/4 cup cream sherry
3 tablespoons ketchup
1 1/2 tablespoons light soy sauce
juice of 1 lemon
1/2 teaspoon ground ginger

MICROWAVE: (1) Combine all ingredients in small bowl, cover with plastic and cook on HIGH (100%) 4 minutes, stirring twice.

Combine all ingredients in small saucepan and cook over medium heat, stirring constantly, until jam melts and sauce is heated through. Serve warm.

ALL PURPOSE

MAYONNAISE SAUCE WITH TARRAGON AND PARSLEY

■ *Makes 1 1/4 cups* ■

This snappy sauce is fragrant with herbs. It's good with fish and all kinds of meat; use it as a sandwich spread, too.

1/2 cup white wine
1/2 cup finely chopped fresh parsley
1/4 cup white wine vinegar
1 small onion, quartered
2 large garlic cloves
1 tablespoon dried tarragon
1 cup mayonnaise

1 Combine all ingredients except mayonnaise in blender or small processor and process until finely ground.

2 Transfer to small saucepan and stir over medium heat until reduced to 1/3 cup. Strain. Return liquid to saucepan. Fold in mayonnaise and heat slowly until warm, stirring; do not boil.

ALL PURPOSE

LEMON MAYONNAISE SAUCE

■ *Makes 1 1/2 cups* ■

*T*his is an easy sauce but don't boil it or you'll ruin it. It's very good with most seafood, especially if grilled or broiled; with broccoli, boiled potatoes and other vegetables. It's delicious with poached eggs served on grilled crusty bread.

1	cup light mayonnaise
2	eggs
1/4	cup fresh lemon juice
1	teaspoon dry mustard
pinch of salt	

Combine all ingredients in small saucepan and whisk until smooth. Cook over low heat, stirring constantly, until sauce thickens; do not boil.

ALL PURPOSE

STILTON CHEESE SAUCE

■ *Makes 1 generous cup* ■

*T*his is easy to make and half-and-half may be substituted for the heavy cream. It is an excellent sauce for cold fish, chicken or meat. I also serve it on the side with club and hamburger sandwiches.

2	ounces Stilton or other blue-veined cheese
1	cup heavy cream
1	teaspoon fresh lemon juice
pinch of cayenne pepper	

Mash cheese to paste with fork. Work in heavy cream. (Alternatively, use small food processor to blend cheese and cream.) Add lemon juice and cayenne.

SUPERMARKET SAVVY

STILTON CHEESE

No one seems to be sure of the exact origin of Stilton cheese, but there is evidence that it was available in the early 18th century. Experts disagree over whether it is the oldest of the English blue-veined cheeses but most agree that it is the best.

It is made in the summer with the richest milk; sometimes cream is added. It is not pressed like cheddar (known as a hard cheese) so it is a so-called "semi-hard" type.

A Stilton is ripe after about six months and should be eaten within three months of ripening. Some people add port wine to the cheese to keep it moist. Buy smaller wheels or pieces to prevent drying out and, of course, cover it well between uses.

ALL PURPOSE

CHICKEN OR FISH VELOUTÉ

■ *Makes 2 cups* ■

A smooth, silky sauce of many uses. Try the chicken version over steamed broccoli or between layers of homemade lasagna. It's also good for enriching plain, low-fat foods.

2 tablespoons butter
2 1/2 tablespoons all purpose flour
1 cup chicken or fish broth
1/2 cup heavy cream
1 tablespoon fresh lemon juice

Heat butter and flour in saucepan and cook over low heat 3 minutes; do not brown. Add broth and cream and cook 10 to 15 minutes or until thickened enough to coat a spoon, stirring constantly. Stir in lemon juice.

MICROWAVE: (1) In microwave-safe 4-cup glass measure, heat butter on HIGH (100%) 1 minute. Mix in flour and cook on HIGH 1 minute longer. (2) Add broth and cream and cook on HIGH 3 1/2 minutes, stirring twice. Blend in lemon juice.

SALAD AND VEGETABLE

BALSAMIC VINEGAR DRESSING

■ *Makes about 1 cup* ■

Here's an updated, upscale, versatile sauce and dressing. Of course, it's wonderful on a salad of mixed lettuces (be sure lettuce leaves are washed and dried well), but try this also on sliced hot or cold potatoes, grilled, baked or sautéed leeks, hot or cold asparagus spears or a thickly sliced tomato and onion salad.

3 tablespoons balsamic vinegar
1 scant teaspoon Dijon-style mustard
1 egg white
1/4 teaspoon each dried basil, parsley, tarragon and thyme
salt and pepper
2/3 cup olive oil

Combine all ingredients except oil in bowl and whisk until well blended. Slowly whisk in oil until incorporated.

SALAD AND VEGETABLE

LEMON HONEY SALAD DRESSING

■ *Makes 1 cup* ■

*T*his dressing is especially good with slices of fresh fruit and chunks of cheese set in a nest of lettuce leaves. Serve with hot buttered biscuits.

3/4 cup mayonnaise
1/3 cup honey
  1 tablespoon grated lemon zest
  1 tablespoon fresh lemon juice
  1 teaspoon finely chopped candied ginger

Combine all ingredients in nonaluminum bowl and mix well. Refrigerate to chill a little; this dressing should not be ice cold.

SALAD AND VEGETABLE

LEMON SOY SALAD DRESSING

■ *Makes 1 cup* ■

*U*se on crisp salad greens or on cooked, cooled green beans, bean sprouts, broccoli, cucumbers, endive and so on. Boil the lemons for a minute or two and you'll be surprised how much more juice they render.

1/2 cup fresh lemon juice
1/2 cup vegetable oil
  2 tablespoons light soy sauce
  2 teaspoons sugar
  1 teaspoon grated lemon zest
  1 garlic clove, pressed or minced

Combine all ingredients and let stand about 1 hour.

ZEST OF LEMON OR ORANGE

The zest (seen so often in recipes) is the colored part of the rind, with almost no pith (the white, bitter layer under the fruit skin). Special zest peelers are available and work well, but I always use a vegetable parer—ordinary ones sold in most supermarkets—without cutting deeply into the pith. Use the zest as fresh as can be—that is, as soon as it is peeled away and minced. But dried zest will work well, too, as its flavor lasts a long time. The zest in the lemon soy salad dressing is an important ingredient.

SALAD AND VEGETABLE

TAPENADE DIP FOR VEGETABLES

■ *Makes 1 1/2 cups* ■

This is appetizing any time. It's healthy and tasty, too. Serve as a dip for fresh vegetables, such as mushrooms, snow peas, slices of small zucchini, broccoli spears, carrot spears, cauliflower florets, partially cooked green beans and especially fresh fennel and celery sticks.

1	egg, room temperature
2	tablespoons fresh lemon juice
1	tablespoon white wine vinegar
1	teaspoon Dijon-style mustard
1	cup vegetable, olive or safflower oil
6	flat anchovy fillets, mashed
2	large garlic cloves, minced
3	tablespoons capers, drained
3	tablespoons chopped fresh parsley
1	tablespoon minced lemon zest

1 Combine egg, lemon juice, vinegar and mustard in processor and blend 4 seconds. With machine running, add oil drop by drop until all is blended. Transfer to glass bowl.

2 Add remaining ingredients and blend well.

DESSERT

CHOCOLATE NUT SAUCE

■ *Makes about 1 cup* ■

Everyone knows how to use this sauce and with what. It's easy to make in the microwave because it doesn't require standing over and watching.

1/4	cup heavy cream
4	ounces semisweet chocolate pieces
1	tablespoon vanilla
1/4	cup chopped walnuts, pecans, almonds, macadamias, etc.

MICROWAVE: (1) In a microwave-safe 2-cup glass measure, combine cream and chocolate. Cook on HIGH (100%) 3 minutes, stirring every minute. (2) Add vanilla and nuts and mix well.

Combine cream and chocolate in small saucepan and cook over low heat, stirring constantly, until chocolate is melted. Remove from heat and stir in vanilla and nuts.

DESSERT

MAPLE AND BOURBON SAUCE

■ *Makes 1 1/2 cups* ■

*T*his sauce is delicious and very versatile. It can be poured over a scoop of ice cream, laced over vanilla puddings, trickled over lemon or white cakes or spooned into dessert soufflés at serving time.

1 cup half-and-half
1 tablespoon sugar
3 egg yolks, room temperature
1/4 cup pure maple syrup
1/4 cup bourbon

1 Heat half-and-half and sugar in small saucepan over low heat, stirring constantly, until sugar dissolves. Remove from heat.

2 Beat eggs in bowl. Add cream mixture a little at a time until all is incorporated. Return mixture to saucepan and simmer over low heat until thick, about 2 minutes, stirring constantly; do not boil.

3 Quickly transfer to bowl, stir in maple syrup and bourbon, cover with plastic and cool.

DESSERT

PINEAPPLE RUM SAUCE FOR ICE CREAM

■ *Makes 1 1/2 cups* ■

*L*ook for arrowroot near the cornstarch on your supermarket shelf. Some people prefer it to cornstarch; they say it makes the sauce shinier.

2 cups fresh pineapple chunks
1 cup pineapple juice
1/4 cup sugar or 6 packets sugar substitute, such as EQUAL
4 tablespoons rum
1 1/2 teaspoons arrowroot

1 Combine pineapple, 1/2 cup pineapple juice, sugar if using it, and 1 tablespoon rum in saucepan. Cover and simmer 15 minutes. Transfer pineapple pieces to bowl with slotted spoon.

2 Add remaining juice and 1 tablespoon rum to saucepan. Add arrowroot and whisk over high heat until thickened, about 4 minutes. Remove from heat. Add EQUAL, if using it, and remaining rum. Transfer to processor, add cooked pineapple chunks and blend with on/off turns to textured puree. Serve warm.

DESSERT

STRAWBERRY RHUBARB SAUCE

■ *Makes 3 cups* ■

Delicious topping for ice cream or rice or bread pudding. Also delicious with pancakes, waffles or crepes. Or spoon some sauce on a plate and turn out a vanilla custard mold onto it.

2 1/2 *cups frozen unsweetened or sliced fresh rhubarb*
   1 *cup water*
   1 *cup sugar*
   2 *tablespoons grated lemon zest*
 1/4 *teaspoon salt*
   1 *cup sliced fresh or frozen strawberries*
 1/4 *cup fresh lemon juice*
   3 *tablespoons brandy*
 1/4 *teaspoon cinnamon*

Combine rhubarb, water, sugar, lemon zest and salt in medium saucepan and bring to boil over high heat. Lower heat and simmer uncovered 5 minutes. Add strawberries, lemon juice, brandy and cinnamon and simmer 10 more minutes or until rhubarb is soft. Serve warm or cold.

MICROWAVE: (1) Combine rhubarb, 1/4 cup water, sugar, lemon zest and salt in dish and cook on HIGH (100%) 5 minutes. (2) Add strawberries, lemon juice, brandy and cinnamon. Cover with plastic and cook on HIGH 3 minutes. Let stand 2 minutes.

DESSERT

WHOLE BERRY CRANBERRY SAUCE

■ *Makes 3 cups* ■

This is good hot or cold.

1 1/2 *cups water*
   2 *cups sugar*
zest of 1 orange (large pieces)
1 pound whole cranberries, picked over, rinsed and drained

1 Combine water and sugar in a saucepan and cook until granules dissolve, 3 or 4 minutes.

2 Add orange zest, bring to a boil, lower heat and cook 5 minutes.

3 Add cranberries and cook 5 minutes longer. Remove zest pieces and serve hot or cold.

14

HEALTH FOODS AND SPECIAL DRINKS

Recipes in this section do away with most fat, fatty meats, butter and cream. Herbs replace salt, yogurt replaces cheese and cream, and vegetables and fruit play key roles.

There is still considerable concern over the uses of pesticides but the news is encouraging. A number of companies now in the food-testing business evaluate produce sent to supermarkets for the presence of up to 200 pesticides. If any are found, the supermarkets are advised right away and produce shipments can be returned. Lists of farmers whose produce shows residues are sent to the supermarkets regularly.

In California, Iowa, New York and New Jersey, to mention a few states, significant strides are being made in the creation of organic farms. Organically grown fruits and vegetables usually cost more, but many supermarkets from Maine to California are beginning to show that consumers needn't have to pay more for produce with little or no pesticide residue.

Even with pesticide-free produce, consumers must practice other eating habits, too. With this in mind, consider the basic Four Food Groups on page 273—and then enjoy the recipes here for healthier eating.

EXPRESS CHECK-OUT

1 Substituting honey for sugar in favorite baking recipes is quite simple. Just use the same amount of honey as sugar and reduce the liquid by 1/4 cup for each cup of honey used. Then lower the baking temperature by 25°F (10°C).

2 Do not refrigerate honey; it does not spoil. If crystals form, place the jar in a pan of hot water and they will disappear.

3 If you make your own stock, be sure to remove fat by chilling. Fat will solidify on top and is easy to remove.

4 For one-course pasta meals, use broccoli, spinach and other greens instead of meat and cream sauces.

5 Cut back on salt when preparing vegetables; season instead with chopped fresh herbs and a finely chopped scallion.

6 Combine vegetables for greater visual impact: snow peas with water chestnuts, carrots with onions, different lettuces in the same salad, cold endive with beets in vinaigrette, and so on.

7 Don't be afraid of cooking plain kale, mustard greens and broccoli rape, especially in the microwave. Just add fresh lemon juice and a drop or two of olive oil.

8 Use fruit for dessert as often as you can. One trick is to serve one fresh fruit (hulled strawberries, for example) on top of another fruit coulis (raspberries, for example, pureed with an optional tablespoon of liqueur).

9 Consider slicing fresh ripe peaches and mixing with fresh lemon juice and a little sour cream or vanilla yogurt.

10 Excellent frozen yogurts are now available in supermarkets. Use them in place of ice cream.

MINIATURE VEGETABLE QUICHES

■ Makes 12 small quiches ■

*T*hese are good to serve at lunch or dinner, on buffets and even at teatime. Use a nonstick miniature muffin pan or microwave-safe custard cups. When cooked, let rest about 5 to 10 minutes; then loosen with a knife and turn out. Each petite quiche has approximately 25 calories.

1/2	cup skim milk
1	whole egg plus 1 egg white
1/4	teaspoon dried dillweed
1/4	teaspoon each pepper and nutmeg
3/4	cup minced mushrooms
1	small tomato, finely chopped
1/2	small onion, finely chopped
1	garlic clove, minced
2	tablespoons finely chopped fresh parsley
1/3	cup finely grated Gruyère cheese

1 Combine milk, eggs and seasonings in bowl. Set aside.

2 Sauté all remaining ingredients except cheese in skillet until all liquid has evaporated.

3 Preheat oven to 350°F (180°C). Oil muffin pan. Distribute vegetable mixture among muffin cups. Do the same with cheese, then with egg mixture.

4 Bake about 20 minutes or until set and golden.

MICROWAVE: (1) In shallow microwave-safe dish, combine mushrooms, tomato, onion, garlic and parsley. Cover and cook on HIGH (100%) 3 minutes. (2) Mix milk, egg, egg white, nutmeg and pepper in bowl and set aside. (3) Oil custard cups. Distribute vegetable mixture into each. Do the same with cheese and then with egg mixture. (3) Cook 6 cups at a time on HIGH 1 1/2 to 2 minutes or until set. Let rest 2 to 3 minutes before turning out.

BASIC FOUR FOOD GROUPS FOR GOOD HEALTH

1. Breads, cereals, pasta and rice—eat 4 servings a day. Weight gain will not follow unless fat is added to these foods. For extra fiber, consider whole-grain breads, cereals and brown rice.

2. Fruits and vegetables—eat 4 or more servings a day. This category provides vitamins A and C and fiber. Choose deep green and yellow-orange vegetables. Vitamin C is plentiful in fruits and tomatoes.

3. Fish, fowl, meats and beans—eat 2 servings a day for protein. Beans also contain fiber. When using beef, pork, lamb and veal, make it lean. Do not exceed 3 egg yolks a week in any form.

4. Milk products—2 servings for adults, 3 for children and 4 for teenagers. Use low-fat or skim-milk products as good sources of calcium. Most cheeses, except for cottage, pot and farmer, are high in saturated fat.

DILLED SALMON SPREAD ON CUCUMBER SLICES

■ *Makes 2 cups spread* ■

Use cucumbers with few seeds; that means buying smaller ones. To prepare cucumbers, slice off ends. Use a vegetable peeler to strip off skin every 1/2 inch or so. Slice and keep in bowl with water, ice and a pinch of salt. When ready to use, drain and dry. Each slice will receive a level tablespoon of salmon spread.

1   *can (15 1/2 ounces) water-packed salmon, drained, bones removed, flaked*
4   *ounces low-calorie cream cheese, softened*
2   *tablespoons finely chopped fresh dill or 1 teaspoon dried dillweed*
1   *tablespoon finely chopped fresh parsley*
juice of 1/2 lemon
2   *teaspoons sugar or 1 packet Equal*
pinch each of salt and white pepper
32   *cucumber slices*

Combine all ingredients except cucumber slices and stir lightly but thoroughly to blend. Chill before spreading on cucumber slices.

SUPERMARKET SAVVY

WHAT ABOUT EQUAL?

Equal is a low-calorie tabletop sweetener which contains NutraSweet brand sweetener with no fat, cholesterol or sodium. NutraSweet is the NutraSweet Company's brand name for aspartame, a sweetening ingredient made of two amino acids. All the components of NutraSweet are identical to substances found naturally in foods and are used by the body in the same way as when they are obtained from everyday foods.

While Equal adds sweetness to a recipe, it does not provide the bulk, tenderness or browning properties of sugar and thus cannot be used as a replacement for sugar in all cooking applications. Equal is not recommended for recipes that require prolonged exposure to heat, due to possible loss of sweetness. It is usually added after the recipe has been removed from the heat, and this particular sweetener seems to work well with microwave recipes because they cook at high heat for a short period of time.

DIET SEAFOOD SAUCE

■ *Makes about 2 cups* ■

Serve with cooked and chilled shrimp, lobster or crabmeat.

1 1/2 cups unsalted ketchup
1/4 cup prepared horseradish, drained
juice of 1 small lemon
2 tablespoons finely chopped fresh parsley
2 tablespoons finely chopped celery leaves
1 tablespoon finely chopped chives or 1 teaspoon dried

Combine all ingredients in bowl, cover tightly with plastic and chill at least 1 hour.

DIET BARBECUE SAUCE

■ *Makes about 1 cup* ■

1/4 cup finely chopped onion
1 teaspoon dry mustard
1/4 cup red wine vinegar
1 cup sauterne
1 can (12 ounces) unsalted tomato puree
1 tablespoon liquid smoke
1 teaspoon dried tarragon

1 Combine onion, mustard and vinegar in small saucepan and heat until liquid is absorbed. Remove from heat.

2 Grind onion mixture with all remaining ingredients in food processor until smooth. Transfer to skillet or saucepan and cook until sauce is thick enough to spread.

MICROWAVE: (1) Combine all ingredients in large microwave-safe bowl and cook on HIGH (100%) 6 minutes, stirring twice.

GAZPACHO

■ *Serves 4* ■

This soup should have some texture; don't overprocess it.

1 small cucumber, peeled and chopped
2 ripe tomatoes, peeled and chopped
1/4 cup chopped onion
1 green bell pepper, cored, ribs and seeds removed, chopped
1 celery stalk, chopped
1 garlic clove, minced
1 cup unsalted tomato juice
1/4 cup red wine vinegar
1 tablespoon safflower oil
3 drops hot pepper sauce

Combine all ingredients in food processor and chop using on/off turns. Chill or serve at room temperature.

FETTUCCINE WITH SCALLOPS

■ *Serves 4* ■

*T*his lovely dish does not need butter or oil; the lemon juice, scallops, white wine and herbs result in a beautiful bouquet of flavors.

8   ounces fresh or frozen scallops
juice of 1 lemon
2   tablespoons white wine
1   large onion, finely chopped
1   garlic clove, minced
4   cups chopped red-ripe fresh or unsalted
    canned tomatoes, put through food mill
pepper
2   tablespoons finely chopped fresh basil or 1
    teaspoon dried
8   ounces fettuccine, cooked

1 Combine scallops and half of lemon juice in small saucepan and add water just to cover. Bring to boil, lower heat and cook 2 to 3 minutes. Drain.

2 Heat wine and remaining lemon juice in nonstick skillet, add onion and garlic and cook 3 to 4 minutes. Add tomatoes and pepper and bring to boil. Lower heat and simmer 20 minutes.

3 Add basil and scallops. If skillet is large enough, add drained pasta, toss and cook for about 2 minutes to bring everything together. If skillet won't handle pasta, heat sauce and scallops and dress pasta in bowl.

MICROWAVE: (1) Combine scallops and half of lemon juice in shallow dish, cover and cook on HIGH (100%) 3 minutes. (2) In another bowl, combine wine, onion, garlic, tomatoes and pepper. Cover and cook on HIGH 6 minutes. (3) Add scallops and toss. Sauce pasta and garnish with basil.

TART BEET SLICES

■ *Serves 4* ■

*O*ne of the few vegetables that is equally good canned or fresh. If you buy fresh, be sure they're small and firm with the tops still on. In this recipe, use canned beet slices; they are tart and tasty prepared this way.

1 can (16 ounces) unsalted beets, sliced
1 small red onion, thinly sliced
1 cup apple juice
1/4 cup red wine vinegar
2 teaspoons sugar or 1 packet Equal
1/4 teaspoon cinnamon
1/4 teaspoon ground cloves
pepper

Combine all ingredients and marinate in refrigerator for several hours, tossing several times. Serve cold or reheat.

HEALTH SALAD

■ *Serves 3 to 4* ■

Skim milk, low-fat milk, yogurt and cheese are high in calcium. Think of this: a cup of yogurt or milk plus 2 ounces of cheese supplies approximately 3/4 of your total calcium needs for the day. Surely the remaining 1/4 can come from a leafy, dark green vegetable.

2   cups low-fat cottage cheese
1   cup carrots cut into small cubes
3/4   cup green, red or yellow bell pepper, cored, ribs and seeds removed, cut into small cubes
3/4   cup chopped tomato
1/2   cup minced fresh parsley
1/4   cup thinly sliced scallions, white and green parts
1/4   cup plain low-fat yogurt
2   tablespoons chopped fresh dill or 1 teaspoon dried dillweed
3 to 4 large or 6 to 8 small lettuce leaves

Combine all ingredients except lettuce leaves in bowl and refrigerate. When ready to serve, arrange a lettuce leaf or two on individual plates and divide cottage cheese mixture among them.

YOGURT CHILI DRESSING

■ *Makes 1 cup* ■

This may be used on salads, but it's also good as a sandwich spread or with cold meats and grilled chicken.

1 1/3   cups plain low-fat yogurt
1/2   cup light mayonnaise
1/3   cup spicy tomato juice
2   tablespoons finely chopped scallions or chives or 2 teaspoons dried
1   tablespoon fresh lemon juice
2   tablespoons sugar or 3 packets Equal
1/2   teaspoon chili powder

LIGHT MAYONNAISE *has half the calories of regular—50 vs. 100 per quart. Ninety-nine per cent of the calories in regular mayo are derived from fat vs. 91% in light. Cholesterol amounts are the same in both types: 5 mgs per quart.*

Combine all ingredients and mix well. Use right away or keep in refrigerator for up to 1 week.

HERBED TOMATO DRESSING

■ *Makes about 1 1/2 cups* ■

Good on any lettuce, sliced cucumbers, sliced tomatoes and cooked vegetables—only 2 to 3 calories per tablespoon.

1   cup unsalted tomato juice
1/4 cup red or white wine vinegar
3   scallions, thinly sliced
1   tablespoon finely chopped celery leaves
1   tablespoon each finely chopped fresh basil, oregano and tarragon, or 1 teaspoon each dried
pepper

Combine all ingredients and mix well. Store in refrigerator.

BAKED CHICKEN BREASTS WITH HERBED TOMATOES

■ *Serves 4* ■

I like to add a pinch of red pepper flakes to the tomato sauce. If that's too spicy for you, add some black pepper.

4   chicken breast halves (4 ounces each), all skin and fat removed
1/2 cup white wine
1/2 medium onion, chopped
1/2 green bell pepper, cored, ribs and seeds removed, chopped
2   garlic cloves, minced
2   cups canned plum tomatoes, put through food mill, or 4 fresh tomatoes, cored, peeled, seeded and chopped
1/4 cup tomato puree
1/2 teaspoon each dried basil, fennel seed and oregano
pepper

1 Preheat oven to 500°F (260°C). Rinse and dry chicken and place in baking dish. Bake uncovered 10 minutes. Discard juices. Reduce oven heat to 350°F (180°C).

2 Heat wine in nonstick skillet. Add onion, pepper and garlic and cook until tender. Add remaining ingredients and bring to boil. Lower heat and simmer 5 minutes. Pour over chicken, cover and bake 20 minutes.

MICROWAVE: Decrease wine to 1/4 cup; drain tomatoes before putting through food mill. If using fresh tomatoes, squeeze dry. (1) Place chicken in 2-quart microwave-safe dish, cover tightly with plastic and cook on HIGH (100%) 5 minutes. (2) Mix and add all other ingredients and cook covered on HIGH 5 minutes.

TURKEY TOSTADA

■ *Makes 4* ■

*T*his is as lean as a tostada can be. Serve with a salsa.

12	ounces ground turkey
1/2	small onion, finely chopped
1	teaspoon chili powder
1	teaspoon cumin
pepper	
4	corn tortillas, warmed
1 1/2	cups shredded lettuce
1	cup chopped fresh tomato
2	scallions, thinly sliced
2	ounces cheddar cheese, grated

1 Brown meat in nonstick skillet and drain off fat and liquid. Add onion, chili, cumin and pepper and cook 1 minute longer.

2 Distribute mixture among 4 tortillas. Top with lettuce, tomato and scallions. Sprinkle cheese on top and run under broiler to melt cheese.

TENDERLOIN IN SHERRY YOGURT SAUCE

■ *Serves 4* ■

*T*he calorie count for this dish is between 150 and 200, including the sauce. Serve with Red Onion Salad and Fennel, or Low-Fat Vegetables in a Skillet.

1	pound beef tenderloin, cut into 4 pieces to make 4 small steaks, trimmed of fat
1	garlic clove, minced
2	tablespoons dry sherry
2	tablespoons unsalted beef bouillon
1/2	cup thinly sliced mushrooms
2	tablespoons tomato paste
1	teaspoon dry mustard
2	scallions, chopped
2	tablespoon plain low-fat yogurt
pepper	

1 Coat nonstick skillet with no-stick vegetable spray and brown tenderloin pieces on each side. Remove and keep warm.

2 Sauté garlic in same skillet until it begins to color. Quickly add sherry and deglaze pan. Add remaining ingredients except yogurt and cook over low heat until sauce coats a spoon. Stir in yogurt and heat through. Spoon some sauce on plate with tenderloin; season liberally with pepper.

VEAL LIMONE

■ *Serves 4* ■

A tasty dish. The way to keep the calorie count down is not to sauté in butter or oil. Serve this with Tart Beet Slices.

4 *thin veal scallops, about 4 ounces each*
1 *garlic clove, minced*
8 *ounces mushrooms, thinly sliced*
juice of 1 small lemon
1/2 *cup white wine*
pepper
2 *scallions, chopped*

1 Coat large nonstick skillet with no-stick vegetable spray and sauté veal 30 seconds on each side. Transfer to warm plate.

2 Add garlic and mushrooms to skillet and brown lightly. Add lemon juice and toss well. Transfer to plate with veal.

3 Deglaze pan with wine and boil until reduced by almost half. Return veal and mushrooms to pan, season liberally with pepper and heat through. Serve veal with some sauce and a sprinkle of scallions.

ON A CLEAR DAY FRUIT GEL SQUARES

■ *Serves 4 to 6* ■

V arious fruit squares may be made by combining gelatin with an appropriate fruit. For example, use two packages orange gelatin with 1/2 cup canned, drained mandarin oranges; lime gelatin with 1/2 cup canned, drained crushed pineapple; or banana gelatin with 1/2 cup diced ripe bananas.

2 *small packages fruit-flavored sugar-free gelatin*
2 *envelopes unflavored gelatin*
2 *cups boiling water*
1/2 *cup fruit*

1 Mix both types of gelatin and boiling water in bowl and stir until gelatin is dissolved. Cool to lukewarm. Add fruit and pour into 8-inch square dish. Chill 2 hours or until firm enough to cut.

2 To serve, cut into 1 1/2- or 2-inch squares and turn out onto serving platter.

CHOCOLATE MOUSSE ELITE

■ *Serves 8* ■

Reduced-calorie cocoa mix and skim milk combine into an acceptable mousse, obviously not as rich as the classic one.

1 envelope (.25 ounce) unflavored gelatin
1/4 cup cold water
2 cups skim milk
9 envelopes reduced-calorie hot cocoa mix
1 3/4 cups evaporated skim milk

1 Sprinkle gelatin over water in small bowl and let stand 5 minutes. Bring skim milk to boil in saucepan. Add cocoa mix and stir until smooth. Add softened gelatin and stir until dissolved. Pour into large bowl, cool and then chill, stirring 2 or 3 times, 1 hour or until almost set.

2 Pour evaporated milk into bowl and freeze 30 minutes or until slushy. Whip until stiff peaks form. Fold in half of chocolate mixture, then fold in remaining half. Transfer to serving bowl and chill until set.

MICROWAVE: (1) Perform step 1 above except heat milk in large microwave-safe bowl, covered with plastic, on HIGH (100%) 3 minutes. Complete recipe as above.

FRESH STRAWBERRY YOGURT

■ *Serves 4* ■

This takes a few hours to freeze but the effort is worth it; only about 50 calories per serving.

1 teaspoon unflavored gelatin
2 tablespoons warm water
1 cup plain low-fat yogurt
1 cup thawed frozen or sliced fresh strawberries
4 teaspoons sugar or 2 packets Equal
3 drops strawberry extract, optional

1 Sprinkle gelatin over warm water and let stand 5 minutes. Combine this and all remaining ingredients in blender and blend until frothy. Transfer to 2-inch-deep dish and place in freezer. Freeze until partially frozen, about 2 hours.

2 Transfer mixture to blender and whip again. Return to dish and freeze until set.

POACHED PEARS WITH GINGER AND CUSTARD SAUCE

■ *Serves 6* ■

The custard sauce is made with skim milk and sugar-free vanilla pudding mix. This is a marvelous "lite" dessert.

6   *firm-ripe pears, about 2 1/2 pounds*
1   *can (12 ounces) sugar-free ginger ale*
2   *tablespoons fresh lemon juice*
2   *tablespoons chopped candied ginger*
2   *cups cold skim milk*
1   *small package sugar-free vanilla pudding mix*
1   *kiwi, thinly sliced*

1 Keeping stems intact, peel pears and remove bottom core.

2 Combine ginger ale, lemon juice and ginger in nonaluminum saucepan and bring to boil. Add pears, cover and simmer 15 minutes or until tender. Cool and remove pears. Strain liquid to make 1 cup. Combine liquid with skim milk and pudding mix in bowl and whisk until smooth. Let stand 5 minutes.

3 To serve, spread 1/2 cup sauce on each plate. Place pear in center and garnish with kiwi.

MICROWAVE: Decrease ginger ale to 1 cup. (1) Peel pears and remove bottom core. Wrap each in plastic. Arrange on glass pie plate with bottom ends toward outside of plate. Cook on HIGH (100%) 8 minutes. (2) In 4-cup measure, combine 1 cup ginger ale, lemon juice and ginger. Cover with plastic and cook on HIGH 1 1/2 minutes. Combine with milk, add pudding mix and whisk until smooth. Let stand 5 minutes. (3) Serve as above.

GINNY SCARPA'S DIET "WHIPPED CREAM"

■ *Makes 1 1/2 cups* ■

The milk and the bowl must be absolutely chilled; put both in the freezer until the milk begins to form crystals and the bowl is ice cold.

2   *cups ice cold skim milk*
4   *teaspoons sugar or 2 packets sugar substitute*
1   *teaspoon vanilla*

Beat milk with sugar substitute in ice cold bowl of electric mixer until soft peaks form. When whipped, add vanilla and serve. This will not keep for long; prepare within 30 minutes of serving.

ALMOND SHAKE

■ *Serves 1* ■

This will make a 12-ounce serving and must be drunk right away.

1/2 cup milk
3 ice cubes
2 tablespoons sugar or 3 packets Equal
1 teaspoon vanilla

Combine all ingredients in blender and mix at high speed until smooth.

BANANA SHAKE

■ *Serves 4* ■

This is a wonderful and high-calcium recipe. Make it every day, but enjoy it especially for a Sunday or holiday breakfast. It will impress weekend guests, too.

2 cups yogurt, plain low-fat
1 cup low-fat or skim milk
1/4 cup honey
2 cups sliced ripe bananas
4 fresh strawberries with hulls, washed and dried

Combine all of ingredients except strawberries in blender or processor until smooth. Transfer to chilled glasses and top each with strawberry.

BLUEBERRY BANANA COOLERS

■ *Serves 4* ■

Use other fruit yogurts if blueberry is not available—for example, strawberry, pineapple or raspberry.

2 ripe bananas, sliced
2 cups skim milk
2 cups blueberry yogurt
nutmeg

Combine bananas, milk and yogurt in food processor or blender and blend until smooth.

Chill. When ready to serve, pour into 4 wineglasses and sprinkle lightly with nutmeg.

HONEY COCOA SHAKE

■ *Serves 2* ■

This will satisfy anyone—children, teenagers and grandparents too.

2 *cups milk*
2 *tablespoons cocoa powder*
1/4 *cup honey*
2 *large scoops vanilla or chocolate ice cream*

Combine milk, cocoa and honey in blender and mix at high speed 20 seconds. Pour into large glasses and add a scoop of ice cream to each.

YOGURT AND FRUIT SMOOTHIE

■ *Serves 1* ■

Consider this for breakfast, on or off a diet. It also makes a good midafternoon snack.

1/2 *cup cold prune juice*
1/4 *cup cold plain low-fat yogurt*
1/2 *banana, sliced*
1 *teaspoon honey*
skim milk

Combine all ingredients except milk and blend or process until smooth. Thin with cold skim milk if you wish.

■   ■

FAT IS FAT

Q: *Are vegetable fats lower in calories than animal fats?*
A: *No. All fat, animal or vegetable, saturated or unsaturated, has the same calorie count.*
Q: *What's the difference between fat and oil?*
A: *As a rule, we use the word fat for solid form, oil for liquid.*
Q: *What about body fat?*
A: *Our bodies make fat from any source of calories—not just from foods with fat in them. Like dietary fat, body fat isn't all bad. A certain amount of it is needed to keep healthy and for energy reserve.*

SWISS MOCHA CREAM

■ *Serves 2* ■

*T*his is an old-fashioned drink but made in a modern way. It makes a wonderful item for a special breakfast; just double or triple the recipe if needed.

2 packets (1 ounce each) or 6 heaping teaspoons hot cocoa mix
1 1/4 to 1 1/2 cups fresh, hot coffee
1/2 cup heavy cream, whipped
2 fresh strawberries with hulls, washed and dried

1 Divide cocoa between 2 mugs. Pour in coffee and stir well.

2 Top each drink with whipped cream. Place mug on saucer and set a strawberry on the side. Serve right away.

CECILE COVELL'S HOT RUM TEA

■ *Serves 1* ■

*T*his helps relieve cold symptoms but it also refreshes an afternoon.

3/4 cup hot brewed tea
2 teaspoons rum
sugar
1 cinnamon stick

Combine hot tea, rum and sugar to taste. Stir with cinnamon stick and serve.

VODKA CRUSH

■ *Serves 2* ■

*T*his will fill two 8-ounce glasses. It's a great summertime treat for back-porch or lawn get-togethers. One serving suggestion: make enough to fill a punchbowl and float many lemon slices and some chopped mint on top.

3 ounces vodka
1 1/2 cups brewed tea
4 teaspoons sugar
crushed ice
2 thin lemon slices

Combine vodka, tea and sugar in pitcher and stir with wooden spoon. Pour into 2 glasses. Fill with crushed ice and add a lemon slice.

SPIKED CRANBERRY COCKTAIL

■ *Serves 2* ■

*T*his is very tasty before dinner.

1/2 cup cranberry juice cocktail
1 ounce rum
1 tablespoon fresh lemon juice
4 teaspoons sugar
lemon wedge

Combine all ingredients in 4-cup measure, add a few ice cubes and stir until liquid is cool. Run cut edge of lemon around rims of glasses. Strain into 2 glasses.

CRANBERRY JUICE

For a nonalcoholic drink, combine equal amounts of chilled cranberry juice with canned or fresh grapefruit juice.

Or, to serve 4, combine 2 cups water and 1 pint cranberries. Cook until soft. Strain and add 1/4 cup sugar to the liquid. Boil until granules dissolve, about 3 minutes. Cool and add 1/3 cup orange juice and the juice from 1/2 lemon. Be sure to chill.

SUPERMARKET SAVVY

COFFEE

Supermarket shoppers are looking more for gourmet-type coffees and teas—not just beverages, but enjoyable experiences. Although coffee drinking has declined in the U.S. from 3.1 cups in 1962 to 1.7 a day in 1988, sales of specialty coffees and teas have grown about 20 percent a year. More and more supermarkets are stocking whole coffee beans, a greater variety of decaffeinated coffees and herbal teas. Here are some tips on how to make a better cup of coffee:

1. Clean the coffeepot thoroughly before using it.
2. Use fresh, cold water, never warm or hot.
3. If grinding your own beans, grind them just before brewing.
4. Bitter coffee is the result of using too much coffee or too fine a grind.
5. Remove the grounds quickly after brewing. This prevents some bitterness.
6. Stir the coffee before serving if using the drip method.
7. Drink the coffee right after brewing.

MENU SUGGESTIONS

SUNDAY BREAKFASTS

#1
Orange or Grapefruit Juice
Poached Eggs on Ranch-Style
    Potatoes
Country Style Corn Bread

#2
Spiked Cranberry Cocktail
Eggs and Cream in Ramekins
Potato Tarragon Biscuits

#3
Spanish Pumpkin Omelet
Corn Onion Salsa
Cheddar Cheese Corn Muffins

SPECIAL BRUNCHES

#1
Shirred Eggs with Ricotta Cheese and
    Orange Zest
Wild Rice Bread with Pecans
Peaches with Rum Sauce and Nutmeg

#2
Dilled Salmon Spread on Cucumber
    Slices
Fruit Salad Tropicana
Parsley and Parmesan Cheese Muffins

#3
Vodka Crush
Eggs and Cream in Ramekins
Oat Bread with Apricots and Walnuts
Honey Butter Spread
    OR Sweet Vanilla Diet Spread

LUNCHEON PARTIES

#1
Cottage Cheese and Spinach Quiche
Fresh Green Salad with Balsamic Vine-
    gar Dressing
Chocolate Bourbon Mousse Pie

#2
Chilled Carrot and Leek Soup
Goat Cheese Pizza with Salami Slivers
Puree of Peach and Plum with Whipped
    Cream

#3
Pasta with Pecans and Gorgonzola
Romaine Lettuce with Honey Lemon
    Dressing
Prune Meringue Kisses

EASY SUPPERS

#1
Bruschetta
Low-Fat Fish Rolls with Herbs
Garlicky Green Beans
No Bake Cheesecake with
    Strawberries

#2
Tomato Soup with Lemon
Baked Chicken with Honey and Curry
Acorn Squash with Pear
Boston Lettuce with Lemon Soy Salad
    Dressing

#3
Hot Dogs with Mayonnaise and
    Barbecue Sauce
Baked Beans Teriyaki
Health Salad

ENTERTAINING DINNERS

#1
Carrot Soup with Ginger, Curry and
    Mint
Thin Spaghetti with Shrimp and Dill
Lettuces with Balsamic Vinegar
    Dressing
Gorgonzola with Brandy (with Dry Toast
    or Crackers)

Boonstra Rum Cake
#2
Cream of Scallion Soup with Watercress
  Swirl
Poached and Chilled Salmon Steaks with
  Pink Mayonnaise
Country Skillet Eggplant and
  Tomatoes
Super-Moist Brownie Fudge Cake
#3
Fresh Fennel, Buttered and Crumbed
Shell Steaks with Blue Cheese
Curly Endive Salad with Toasted Pine
  Nuts
Sister Louise's Old Time Rum
  Butterscotch Pie

HOLIDAY MEALS

NEW YEAR'S DAY
Spiked Cranberry Cocktail
Fresh Mushrooms in Sherried Yogurt
  Sauce
Silk Snapper Fillets in Lobster and
  Tomato Sauce
Sautéed Sugar Snap Peas
  OR Black Eyed Peas prepared your
  way
Ginger Muffins
Sister Mary's Easy Chocolate Almond
  Cake
  OR Chocolate Ice Cream Pudding
VALENTINE'S DAY
Warm Vegetable Salad with Walnuts
Poached and Chilled Salmon Steaks with
  Pink Mayonnaise
Radicchio with Watercress and Japanese
  Mushrooms
Classic Tomato Aspic (on Lettuce
  Leaves)
  with Roquefort Dressing
Chocolate Cocoa Truffles
  OR Fresh Strawberry and Chocolate
  Tart
EASTER SUNDAY
Light Vegetable Soup Aromatic
Herbed Leg of Lamb

with Roasted Garlic Mayonnaise
  OR Baked Ham with Ginger/Raisin
  Sauce
Beet and Apple Puree
Grilled Oyster Mushrooms
Curly Endive Salad with Toasted Pine
  Nuts
Hot Apricot Rum Sauce Over a Square
  of Ice Cream
FOURTH OF JULY
Chilled Cucumber Soup with Sour
  Cream
Jalapeño Meat Loaf with Monterey Jack
  Cheese
  OR Burgers
Sliced Fresh Tomatoes with Balsamic
  Vinegar Dressing
Glazed Pinto Beans
16 Peanut Butter Squares
LABOR DAY
Steve Widdup's Pickapeppa Cream
  Cheese
Bruschetta
Grilled Beef Short Ribs with Oriental
  Spices
Garlicky Green Beans
Superfast Cherry Cobbler
  OR Supermarket Blueberry Cobbler
THANKSGIVING
Water Chestnut and Bacon Crunch
Cream of Pumpkin Soup
  OR Old-Fashioned Wild Rice Soup
Roast Turkey with Sausage Stuffing
  and Cranberry Maple Sauce
Baked Southern Cheese Grits
Corn with Ginger and Green Peppers
Lettuces with Roquefort Dressing
Sister Louise's Old Time Rum
  Butterscotch Pie
  OR Three-Spice Pumpkin Pie (if
  not using pumpkin soup)
CHRISTMAS DAY
Velvet Clam Chowder with Sherry
  OR Vichyssoise à la Supermarché
Roast Beef
  with Spiced Fig Chutney

Caramelized Shallots
Sautéed Sugar Snap Peas
Baked or Mashed Potatoes
Lettuces with Balsamic Vinegar
    Dressing
Brie Amandine
Poached Whole Pears in Pear Brandy
    and
Boonstra Rum Cake (with whipped
    cream)

PARTY BUFFETS

#1
Party Meat Loaf
Hot and Sweet Ginger Shrimp
Farfalle and Fennel Salad
Susan's Two-Cheese and Onion Tart
Zucchini, Tomato and Ricotta
    Casserole
    OR Red Pepper Ratatouille
Pilaf of Bulgar
    OR Garlicky Brown Rice
Fontina Cheese Bread with Bacon and
    Olives
Fresh Strawberry and Chocolate Tart
#2
Veal Cubes Baked in a Pie
Salmon Potato Pie with Dill
Corn Pudding with Cheshire Cheese
Country Style Corn Bread
    OR Grilled French or Italian Bread
Fragrant Vegetable Stir Fry
Curly Endive Salad with Toasted Pine
    Nuts
Luscious Strawberry Pie

OUTDOOR
GET TOGETHERS

#1
Marinated Chicken Wings for
    Appetizers
Grilled Sea Bass with Sesame and Soy
Szechuan Noodles with Peanut Sauce
Fresh Pineapple Chunks on wooden
    spears

#2
Rice Chowder with Tomatoes and
    Corn
Lamb Chops with Oregano
Lettuce and Cucumber Salad with
    Balsamic Vinegar Dressing
Strawberries and Minted Sour Cream
#3
Sour Cream and Tuna Dip
Grilled Burgers
New Orleans Lentils with Red
    Peppers
    OR Potatoes, Onions and Chili
Rhubarb Framboise

AFTERNOON TEAS

#1
Chicken Salad for Sandwiches
Apple Tart with Streusel Topping
#2
Sherry Vanilla Bundt Cake
Butter Cookies
    OR Lemon Sugar Scones with Apricot
    Butter
#3
Boonstra Rum Cake
(with whipped cream—when 1 cup
heavy cream is almost whipped, add 2
tablespoons rum and complete whip-
ping).

COCKTAIL PARTIES

#1
Yogurt and Avocado Dip
Goat Cheese Pizza with Salami Slivers
Bacon, Onion and Pimiento Spread
Little Meatballs for Hors D'oeuvre
#2
Steve Widdup's Pickapeppa Cream
    Cheese
Port du Salut Cheese Loaf
Marinated Chicken Wings for
    Appetizers
Shrimp Toast

MEASUREMENTS & EQUIVALENTS

TABLE OF FRUIT PREPARATION EQUIVALENTS

FRUIT	AMOUNT AS PURCHASED	PREPARATION EQUIVALENTS
Apples	4 medium (1 pound)	3 cups sliced
Bananas	3 to 4 medium (1 pound)	2 1/2 cups sliced; 2 cups mashed
Berries	1 pint	2 cups
Cantaloupes	1 medium	3 cups cubed
Cranberries	12 ounces	3 cups
Dates	12 medium (1 pound)	3 cups sliced
Grapefruits	1 medium	2 cups sectioned
Kiwifruit	5 medium	2 1/3 cups sliced
Lemons	1 medium	2 to 3 tablespooons juice; 1 tablespoon grated rind (peel)
Limes	1 medium	1 1/2 tablespoons juice; 2 teaspoons grated rind
Oranges	1 medium	6 tablespoons juice; 2 to 3 tablespoons grated rind
Peaches, Pears, Plums	4 medium (1 pound)	2 cups sliced
Pineapples	1 medium	5 cups cubed
Pumpkin	1 pound	1 cup pureed
Rhubarb	1 pound	3 1/2 cups sliced
Raisins	6 ounces	1 cup
Strawberries	2 cups (1 pint)	3 cups sliced
Tangerines	2 medium	1 cup sectioned

From Nutra Sweet Consumer Products, Inc

CONVERSION TABLES

SOLID MEASURES

For cools measuring items by weight, here are approximate equivalents, in both Imperial and metric. So as to avoid awkward measurements, some conversions are not exact.

	U.S. CUSTOMARY	METRIC	IMPERIAL
Butter	1 cup	225 g	8 oz
	1/2 cup	115 g	4 oz
	1/4 cup	60 g	2 oz
	1 Tbsp	15 g	1/2 oz
Cheese (grated)	1 cup	115 g	4 oz
Fruit (chopped fresh)	1 cup	225 g	8 oz
Herbs (chopped fresh)	1/4 cup	7 g	1/4 oz
Meats/Chicken (chopped, cooked)	1 cup	175 g	6 oz
Mushrooms (chopped, fresh)	1 cup	70 g	2 1/2 oz
Nuts (chopped)	1 cup	115 g	4 oz
Raisin (and other dried chopped fruits)	1 cup	175 g	6 oz
Rice (uncooked)	1 cup	225 g	8 oz
(cooked)	3 cups	225 g	8 oz
Vegetables (chopped, raw)	1 cup	115 g	4 oz

LIQUID MEASURES

The Imperial pint is larger than the U.S. pint: therefore, note the following when measuring liquid ingredients.

U.S.	IMPERIAL
1 cup = 8 fluid ounces	1 cup = 10 fluid ounces
1/2 cup = 4 fluid ounces	1/2 cup = 5 fluid ounces
1 tablespoon = 3/4 fluid ounce	1 tablespoon = 1 fluid ounce

U.S. MEASURE	METRIC APPROXIMATE	IMPERIAL APPROXIMATE
1 quart (4 cups)	950 mL	1 1/2 pints + 4 Tbsp
1 pint (2 cups)	450 mL	3/4 pint
1 cup	236 mL	1/4 pint + 6 Tbsp
1 Tbsp	15 mL	1 + Tbsp
1 tsp	5 mL	1 tsp

DRY MEASURES

Outside the United States, the following items are measured by weight. Use the following table, but bear in mind that measurements will vary, depending on the variety of flour and moisture. Cup measurements are loosely packed: flour is measured directly from package (presifted).

	U.S. CUSTOMARY	METRIC	IMPERIAL
Flour (all purpose)	1 cup	150 g	5 oz
Cornmeal	1 cup	175 g	6 oz
Sugar (granulated)	1 cup	190 g	6 1/2 oz
(confectioners)	1 cup	80 g	2 2/3 oz
(brown)	1 cup	160 g	5 1/3 oz

OVEN TEMPERATURES

Fahrenheit	225	300	350	400	450
Celsius	110	150	180	200	230
Gas Mark	1/4	2	4	6	8

LOW-CALORIE RECIPE INGREDIENT ALTERNATIVES

"TRADITIONAL"	LOW-CALORIE
Whole milk (1 cup = 155 calories)	Skim milk (1 cup = 86 calories)
Whole egg (1 medium = 79 calories)	Egg white (1 medium = 16 calories)
Butter (1/2 cup = 810 calories)	"Diet" margarine (1/2 cup = 400 calories)
Vegetable oil (1 tablespoon = 120 calories)	Non-stick vegetable spray (0 calories)
Mayonnaise (1/2 cup = 788 calories)	"Diet" mayonnaise (1/2 cup = 400 calories)
Sour cream (1/2 cup = 246 calories)	Plain, low-fat yogurt (1/2 cup = 72 calories)
Cream cheese (4 ounces = 396 calories)	Neufchatel cheese (4 ounces = 296 calories) "Light" (low-calorie) cream cheese (1/2 cup = 240 calories)
Whole milk ricotta cheese (1/2 cup = 216 calories)	Part-skim ricotta cheese (1/2 cup = 171 calories)
Flavored gelatin (2-cup mold = 315 calories)	Unflavored gelatin (2-cup mold = 23 calories)
Strawberries, frozen sweetened (4 ounces = 89 calories)	Strawberries, frozen unsweetened (4 ounces = 40 calories)
Pineapple canned in syrup (4 ounces = 89 calories)	Pineapple canned in juice (4 ounces = 37 calories)

EMERGENCY SUBSTITUTIONS

IF YOU DON'T HAVE	SUBSTITUTE
1 cup cake flour	1 cup minus 2 tablespoons all-purpose flour
1 tablespoon cornstarch (for thickening)	2 tablespoons all-purpose flour
1 teaspoon baking powder	1/4 teapoon baking soda plus 1/2 cup buttermilk or sour milk (to replace 1/2 cup of the liquid called for in the recipe)
1 package active dry yeast	1 cake compressed yeast
1 cup granulated sugar	1 cup packed brown sugar or 2 cups sifted powdered sugar
1 cup honey	1 1/4 cups granulated sugar plus 1/2 cup water
1 square (1 ounce) unsweetened chocolate	3 tablespoons unsweetened cocoa powder plus 1 tablespoon margarine or butter
1 cup buttermilk	1 tablespoon lemon juice or vinegar plus whole milk to make 1 cup. Let stand 5 minutes before using
1 cup whole milk	1/2 cup evaporated milk plus 1/2 cup water or 1 cup reconstituted nonfat dry milk plus 2 1/2 teaspoons margarine or butter
1 cup half-and-half	1 cup minus 2 tablespoons whole milk plus 2 tablespoons margarine or butter
2 cups tomato sauce	3/4 cup tomato paste plus 1 cup water
1 clove garlic	1/8 teaspoon garlic powder or minced dried garlic
1 small onion	1 teaspoon onion powder or 1 tablespoon minced dried onion, rehydrated
1 teaspoon dry mustard	1 tablespoon prepared mustard
1 teaspoon finely grated lemon peel	1/2 teaspoon lemon extract

NOTES ON FOOD STORAGE

FREEZER STORAGE

	RECOMMENDED STORAGE TIME	HANDLING SUGGESTIONS
DAIRY PRODUCTS		
Butter	6 to 9 months	Double-wrap or repackage all dairy products in moisture-vaporproof wrap or containers.
Margarine	12 months	
Ice cream, ice milk, sherbet	2 to 4 months	
Hard cheeses (brick, edam, cheddar, gouda, Swiss)	4 to 6 months	Cheese will become crumbly in thawing. Plan to use them for cooking.
FRUITS AND VEGETABLES		
Fresh or frozen	8 to 12 months	Freeze in moisture-vaporproof plastic bags or containers. Do not freeze cabbage, greens, green onions or radishes
MEAT, POULTRY AND FISH		
Beef	6 to 9 months	Remove fresh meat, poultry or fish from store package; wipe dry, if necessary and repackage in moisture-vaporproof wrap
Pork	3 to 6 months	
Variety meats	1 to 2 months	
Ground meats	2 to 3 months	
Fresh pork sausage	1 to 3 months	
Chicken, pieces	6 to 9 months	
Chicken, whole	12 months	
Turkey	6 months	
Lean fish (bass, cod, halibut, sole, swordfish)	6 months	Store purchased frozen fish in original wrap up to 2 weeks. For longer periods, double-wrap or repackage in moisture-vaporproof wrap.
Fat fish (catfish, mackerel, salmon, trout, tuna)	2 to 3 months	
PREPARED FOODS		
Meat casseroles	3 to 6 months	Be sure all foods are packaged in moisture-vaporproof wrap. Label packages with the type of food, number of servings and date.
Meat loaves	1 to 2 monthes	
Meat roasts with gravy	1 to 3 months	
Breads	2 to 3 months	
Yeast bread dough	1 month	
Soups	4 to 6 months	

INDEX